Rwandan Genocide

Rwandan Genocide

THE ESSENTIAL REFERENCE GUIDE

Alexis Herr, Editor

 ABC-CLIO™

An Imprint of ABC-CLIO, LLC
Santa Barbara, California • Denver, Colorado

Library of Congress Cataloging-in-Publication Data

Names: Herr, Alexis, editor.
Title: Rwandan genocide : the essential reference guide / Alexis Herr, editor.
Description: Santa Barbara, California : ABC-CLIO, LLC, 2018. | Includes bibliographical
    references and index.
Identifiers: LCCN 2017052499 (print) | LCCN 2017052929 (ebook) | ISBN 9781440855610
    (ebook) | ISBN 9781440855603 (hardcopy : alk. paper)
Subjects: LCSH: Genocide—Rwanda—History—20th century—Encyclopedias. |
    Rwanda—History—Civil War, 1994—Encyclopedias. | Rwanda—Ethnic relations—
    History—20th century—Encyclopedias.
Classification: LCC DT450.435 (ebook) | LCC DT450.435 .R93 2018 (print) |
    DDC 967.57104/31—dc23
LC record available at https://lccn.loc.gov/2017052499

ISBN: 978-1-4408-5560-3 (print)
       978-1-4408-5561-0 (ebook)

22 21 20 19 18   1 2 3 4 5

This book is also available as an eBook.

ABC-CLIO
An Imprint of ABC-CLIO, LLC

ABC-CLIO, LLC
130 Cremona Drive, P.O. Box 1911
Santa Barbara, California 93116-1911
www.abc-clio.com

This book is printed on acid-free paper ∞

Manufactured in the United States of America

In honor of the victims and survivors of the Rwandan Genocide
and all those who have helped rebuild Rwanda.

Contents

List of Entries

List of Primary Documents

1. Arusha Peace Accords
2. Chapter VI and VII of United Nations Charter for Peace Keeping Operations
3. Convention on the Prevention and Punishment of the Crime of Genocide
4. Death of Rwandan and Burundian Presidents in Plane Crash Outside Kigali
5. Excerpt from the Defense Attaché in Kigali, October 24, 1990
6. First Lady Hillary Rodham Clinton Radio Address to the People of Rwanda on March 25, 1997
7. Gaspard Gahigi RTLM Broadcast of May 17–18, 1994
8. The Genocide Fax and the United Nations' Reply
9. Hutu Ten Commandments
10. UN Report of the Independent Inquiry into the Actions of the United Nations During the 1994 Genocide in Rwanda
11. Journalist Kantano Habimana, RTLM Broadcast of May 28, 1994
12. Judgement of Judge Mohamed Shahabuddeen on Ferdinand Nahimana, Jean-Bosco Barayagwiza, and Hassan Ngeze in the Appeals Chamber of the International Criminal Tribunal for Rwanda, 28 November 2007
13. Pre-Meeting Briefing Notes for President Clinton in Anticipation of a Meeting with Rwandan vice president Paul Kagame, 1996
14. President Juvénal Habyarimana to Visit France, 1990
15. Resolution 925 Adopted by the United Nations Security Council
16. Statement by Alison Des Forges Before Congress, 1998
17. Statement by President Barack Obama on the Twentieth Commemoration of the Genocide in Rwanda, April 6, 2014
18. United Nations Security Council Resolution 918 (1994): Operation Turquoise
19. U.S. Ambassador to Rwanda Warns of Outbreak of Violence, April 1, 1994
20. USAID Input into Operation Support Hope Transition

Preface

Twenty-five years have passed since the Rwandan Genocide, yet visiting genocide memorials in Rwanda today can make the past feel like the present. Fearful that the international community would neglect, deny, or even forget about the Rwandan Genocide, many Rwandans chose to display the victims' human remains after the genocide to make certain the world could not forsake the past. While the gates of the Auschwitz concentration camp have become the hallmark image of the Holocaust, rows of skulls stand as the stark and now iconic visual reminder of the Rwandan Genocide.

When I first learned about the Rwandan Genocide while pursuing a doctoral degree in Holocaust Studies at Clark University, the images of skulls lined up inside churches—the sites where many of the most violent massacres occurred—shocked me. Holocaust museum curators and historians often debate whether it is appropriate to display the bodily remains of Jewish victims, and there is no general consensus on the issue. Some argue that it is insensitive, inappropriate, and unethical to display Jewish remains rather than bury them, in accordance to Jewish tradition. Others insist that using a victim's physical remains better communicates to visitors the immensity and horror of the genocide. It is for this reason that in the United States Holocaust Memorial Museum in Washington, D.C., visitors confront a large room of the victims' shoes—an example of material remains—while in the Auschwitz-Birkenau Memorial and Museum in Poland, in addition to exhibits of Jewish possessions, there is a room on display full of the victims' hair—an example of physical remains—that was shorn upon entry to the camp. Both memorial museums face the impossible challenge of trying to communicate the immensity of lives lost and the dehumanization the victims faced while simultaneously honoring the memory and souls of the slain. Each museum has answered the following question differently: Is it ethical to display a victim's bodily remains in order to memorialize the victims and teach about the tragedy? For Rwandans, the decision to display bones involved this and additional considerations.

It is now widely acknowledged that while Hutu hardliners (the perpetrators of the genocide) murdered 800,000 Tutsis and moderate Hutus over approximately 100 days between April and July 1994, the international community failed to take decisive actions to save countless lives. Although the United Nations (UN) had troops on the ground in Rwanda since 1993, when the genocide began in 1994, the UN Security Council withdrew the majority of its troops. Survivors of the genocide must have thought,

"If the international community turned a blind eye to the genocide, won't they continue to ignore the genocide once the killing is finally over?" The bold decision to use the bones, bloody clothes, and murder weapons in Rwandan memorials throughout the country made the world take notice. During the genocide, leading European, Asian, and American nations reasoned that Africans killing Africans on another continent did not concern them directly and thus abandoned the victims. After the genocide, photographers, journalists, and television programs spread images from Rwanda across the globe, and the aging white bones on display in ad hoc memorials throughout the country cut across ethnic, racial, and geographic divisions. Simply put, bones are not foreign to anyone.

While editing and writing entries for this reference guide, I kept asking myself, what does it mean to take notice of the genocide today, more than two decades since the killings began? What should be remembered and what can be learned? There are many insights one can gain from this reference guide, and a few stand out for me in particular.

First, the Rwandan Genocide is a reminder of the atrocities humanity is capable of committing. Overviews of the perpetrators, massacres, and bystanders included in this reference guide demonstrate that humans are able and willing to murder their neighbors for the sake of an ideal. This phenomenon is not unique to Rwanda and is a visible trend in genocide studies. For this reason, it is important to be vigilant against racial stereotyping. An offhanded comment can quickly be transformed into a powerful rallying call to kill.

Second, the history of the Rwandan atrocity demonstrates what happens when the international community forsakes people in need of assistance. The world knew what was happening and yet still chose inaction over action. Rwandans paid the price for the world's silence.

Third, several articles in this book elucidate the inspiring stories of Hutus and foreign nationals those who risked, and in some cases lost, their lives to save others. The entries on rescuers and resistors reveal that not everyone supported the mass slaughter of Tutsis. Compliance or silence were not the only options.

Finally, this reference guide demonstrates that although we have failed each other in the past, that does not mean we cannot do better in the future. For example, the landmark court cases held by the International Criminal Tribunal for Rwanda (ICTR) led by the UN—as well as Rwanda's own endeavor to pursue reconciliation and justice in its Gacaca Courts—illuminate the legal and societal advances that have occurred since the genocide. Furthermore, the treatment of rape as a crime of genocide during the ICTR forever changed the landscape of genocide studies and law by confirming what we already knew: rape constitutes a crime of genocide. In order to improve prevention, intervention, and post-atrocity justice and rebuilding, for now and in the years to come, it is essential to learn from the mistakes made in Rwanda.

While some genocide memorials in Rwanda still use human remains to ensure that the past does not seem abstract or unimportant to the present, this reference guide presents the history of the victims, perpetrators, bystanders, witnesses, and resistors in order to encourage readers to understand what has happened and what can still happen if we fail to take notice and learn from the past.

I am grateful to ABC-CLIO for pursing educational projects such as this one that are centered on human rights. Particular praise is warranted for Padraic (Pat) Carin, Managing Editor at ABC-CLIO, for suggesting this project in the first place. I have been fortunate enough to work with him on other ABC-CLIO projects and feel lucky to have done so. This project has benefited from the excellent guidance of both Carin and Steve Catalano, Senior Editor at ABC-CLIO. And I would be remiss if I did not thank Professor Robert Melson for first teaching me about the Rwandan Genocide more than a decade ago and my husband Shayle Kann for his continued support of me and my work.

Introductory Essays

Overview

The 1994 Rwandan Genocide, which followed a civil war between the Hutu (approximately 85 percent of the population) and Tutsi (14 percent) ethnics groups, resulted in the deaths of hundreds of thousands of Tutsis. Rwanda's small size of 10,169 square miles—slightly smaller than the state of Massachusetts belies the enormity of the bloodletting it suffered during one of the largest genocides of the 20th century.

Beginning in early April 1994, and continuing relentlessly over the next 100 days, an estimated 650,000 Tutsi civilians were killed at the hands of Hutu militia and government troops directed by politicians, local leaders, clergy members, prominent business figures, and other Hutu extremists. To these must be added tens of thousands of Hutu victims, commonly referred to as moderate Hutus, mostly from the southern parts of the country that opposed or appeared to oppose Hutu extremism. Assessing the causes and individual responsibilities for the killings is no easy task. Few other comparable dramas have generated as much discord and controversy among local actors and outside observers.

The geographical constraints, social structure, and basic facts of its history have had a profound impact on the destinies of Rwandans. Landlocked, overpopulated and overwhelmingly dependent on agriculture, Rwanda stood as one of the poorest countries in Africa in the decades leading up to the genocide. With one of the highest population densities in the continent, the shortage of cultivable land was and has remained a major source of social tension in the countryside. A population explosion starting in the 1960s has continued to exacerbate conflicts over resources. Since 1960, Rwanda has grown from a population of 2.5 million to approximately 12 million in 2017.

The arrival of European colonists in the late 19th century had an indisputable impact on Rwandan society. A former German colony later entrusted to Belgium—first as a Mandate under the League of Nations, and then as a Trust Territory under the United Nations (UN)—Rwanda's colonial era stood a classic example of "indirect rule." While the king (*mwami*) and his chiefs served as the legitimate instruments of colonial domination, the Tutsi saw their privileges substantially enhanced at the detriment of the Hutu. European colonists elevated Tutsis to a superior status by providing them with greater access to Western education and leadership posts. The rise of a Hutu revolutionary movement in the mid-1950s attempted to shift the balance of power.

As national tensions rose in Rwanda, the Belgians were pressured by the United Nations to end their colonial rule. After World War II (1939–1945), European powers withdrew from their colonial holdings and the United Nations pressured Belgium to follow suit. The postwar years saw a major shift in Belgian policies, owing in part to the rising influence of Christian Democracy among the missionary community, and UN pressures for hastening the pace of democratization. The publication in 1956 of the mildly reformist pro-Hutu Bahutu Manifesto must be seen as the first significant challenge to Tutsi hegemony, culminating in 1959 with the outbreak of widespread anti-Tutsi violence. Acting hand in hand with the Catholic clergy and with Belgian guidance, the newly created Party for Hutu Emancipation (French: Parti de l'émancipation du peuple Hutu, or Parmehutu) served as a vehicle for the defense of the Hutu masses against the elitist claims of the so-called feudal-hamitic monarchists (those supportive of the Tutsi monarchy). In response, Tutsi politicians sought to mobilize support through the Rwandese National Union (French: Union Nationale Rwandaise, or UNAR) a left-leaning monarchical party formally headed by a Hutu.

The Hutu uprisings that broke out in November 1959 eventually morphed into a full-fledged revolution, actively supported and encouraged by the Belgian authorities. While Rwanda crossed the threshold of independence on July 1, 1962, as a Hutu-dominated republic, some 200,000 Tutsi had been forced into exile, mostly in neighboring Uganda, Burundi, and Zaire (now known as the Democratic Republic of the Congo). Not until 32 years and a million deaths later would the country's destinies be once again entrusted to the Tutsi.

On October 1, 1990, some 6,000 refugee warriors of predominantly Tutsi origins who had fled Hutu-led violence in the 1950s and 1960s marched across the border from Uganda into Rwanda and proceeded to fight their way to the capital, Kigali. Most of them belonged to the Rwandan Patriotic Front (RPF), a politico-military organization created in 1979 by Tutsi exiles. Thus began a 30-month civil war accompanied by untold atrocities by both sides.

The intervention of UN forces in 1993 helped calm the civil war for a time. In August of 1993 representatives of the Rwandan government and RPF signed the Arusha Peace Accords in Arusha, Tanzania. The Arusha Accords sought to provide greater opportunities for Tutsi in governmental positions, the integration of RPF fighters into the military, and the establishment of a broad-based transitional government. For its part, the United Nations agreed to help facilitate the disarmament or rebel factions via the creation of the UN Assistance Mission for Rwanda (UNAMIR). All the hopes of a peaceful transition evaporated, however, with the pivotal event that triggered the genocide: the shooting down of Rwandan president Juvénal Habyarimana's plane on April 6, 1994, on a return flight from Dar es Salaam, Tanzania.

The killings began moments after the crash. The first to be targeted were Hutu officials identified with opposition parties and therefore of pro-RPF sympathies. Opposition leaders, Hutu and Tutsi, were disposed of in a matter of hours. Doing away with hundreds of thousands of Tutsi civilians proved a more difficult undertaking, especially in the southern region, where mixed marriages were more frequent. Nonetheless, the scale and swiftness of the massacre leaves no doubt about the determination of the machete-wielding militias. After setting up roadblocks and checkpoints, the death squads sprang into action. An estimated 20,000 people were killed in Kigali and its environs in the three weeks following the crash.

For weeks and months, hundreds and thousands of Tutsi civilians (and Hutu who looked like Tutsis) were shot, speared, clubbed, or hacked to pieces in their homes, church compounds, and courtyards. That carnage of this magnitude went on day after day, week after week, without interference from the international community speaks volumes for its lack of resolve in dealing with such massive human rights violations.

After weeks of vicious fighting in and around Kigali on July 4, the RPF effectively took control of the capital. The RPF victory and the new government were promptly recognized by the international community. On July 19, Pasteur Bizimungu, a Hutu member of the RPF, was proclaimed president of the republic for a five-year mandate, and Faustin Twagiramungu, also a Hutu, prime minister of a national unity government.

René Lemarchand

Further Reading

Barnett, Michael. *Eyewitness to a Genocide: The United Nations and Rwanda*. Ithaca, NY: Cornell University Press, 2002.

Dallaire, Roméo. *Shake Hands with the Devil: The Failure of Humanity in Rwanda*. Toronto: Random House, Canada, 2004.

Melvern, Linda. *Conspiracy to Murder: The Rwanda Genocide*. Rev. ed. London: Verso, 2006.

Prunier, Gérard. *The Rwanda Crisis, 1959–1994: History of a Genocide*. Kampala: Fountain Publishers, 1995.

Rittner, Carol, John K. Roth, and Wendy Whitworth, eds. *Genocide in Rwanda: Complicity of the Churches*. St. Paul, MN: Paragon House, 2004.

Straus, Scott. *The Order of Genocide: Race, Power, and War in Rwanda*. Ithaca, NY: Cornell University Press, 2008.

Causes

No particular event or set of circumstances can be singled out as the cause of the Rwandan Genocide. A multiplicity of underlying factors influenced the tragic outcome. That there are proximate and remote causes is not at issue. Where disagreements arise is on the question of responsibility in the chain of events leading to the genocide. This entry will examine some of the key events and influences that help to explain how, why, and when the genocide occurred.

While there is broad consensus about the determining impact of the crash of Rwandan president Juvénal Habyarimana's plane on subsequent events, there are basic differences of opinion as to who was responsible for shooting the SA-6 missiles (of Ugandan provenance) that brought the plane down on the evening of April 6, 1994. Some scholars—among them Philip Gourevitch, Jean-Pierre Chrétien, and Gérard Prunier—insist that the "dastardly deed" was the work of Hutu extremists associated with the presidential entourage, the so-called Akazu in Kinyarwanda, or "little hut." Scholars in this camp argue that the Akazu took issue with Habyarimana's decision to negotiate with the Rwandan Patriotic Front (RPF), a political and military movement formed by exiled Tutsis, and thus planned to eliminate the president to put the country back on the right path. Such is also the official version endorsed currently by the Rwandan authorities.

Others take a radically different view, pinning full responsibility on current Rwandan president Paul Kagame, who at that time was a leading member of the RPF. They claim that the Akazu would not have shot down the plane, because the crash of the presidential aircraft also took the lives of some of its key members. Additionally, they draw attention to the massive body of circumstantial evidence available from the testimonies of ex-RPF defectors, including the devastating accusations made by Lieutenant Abdul Joshua Ruzibiza in his *Rwanda: L'histoire secrète* (2005). They argue that only the RPF could have had access to SA-6 missiles from a Ugandan arsenal. Members in this camp also think that Kagame acted to kill Habyarimana in 1994 in order to prevent presidential elections three years later as had been agreed upon at the Arusha Accords between the RPF and Rwandan government in 1993. Given the long-standing ethnic tension between Hutu and Tutsi, they argue, Kagame did not think he could win a majority vote in a country whose majority was Hutu. This, by-and-large, is the position endorsed by several experts on Rwanda, most notably Filip Reyntjens and André Guichaoua.

Regardless of who shot down the plane, most of the Hutu leadership at the time blamed the crash on the RPF. This fact alone played a critical role in mobilizing the militias. Thus, in combination with the manipulative power of propaganda, Hutu extremists used the president's death to transform long-standing Hutu distrust of Tutsi into a contagiously persuasive motivation for murder.

While Hutu extremists parlayed the plane crash into a justification for genocide, the context in which it happened—namely a civil war—is no less significant. The civil war between the RPF and the Rwandan government lasted three years. From the beginning of the RPF invasion into Rwanda on October 1, 1990, the Hutus and Tutsis lived in a climate of extreme fear and uncertainty.

The country was awash in anti-Tutsi propaganda, which included rumors about the infiltration of Tutsi spies within the government and opposition parties. While the civil war exacted a mounting toll among civilians, anti-Tutsi sentiment gathered momentum. The assassination of several moderate Hutu politicians further raised intense fears within and outside the Hutu community. In such a highly charged political climate, it is easy to see how Hutu hardliners managed to channel anti-Tutsi feelings into mass killings. What is involved here has little to do with what some refer to as Rwanda's "culture of obedience"; the critical factor must be found in the capacity of Hutu extremists to manipulate ethnic fears to their advantage.

Though tempting it is to dismiss the importance of history as a predisposing factor, to do so is to make unduly short shrift of the broader context in which genocide occurred. The first point to stress is that the seeds of the RPF invasion were sown during the 1959–1962 Hutu revolution. The first and second generation of Tutsi refugees living in Uganda shared intense longings to return to their beloved homeland, a sentiment reinforced by the growing economic and political constraints they faced in their host country. The same applies to most exiles living in Zaire (now known as the Democratic Republic of the Congo, or DRC) and Burundi: they needed little prodding to join the RPF crusade. As for the million or so Tutsi living in Rwanda, they were generally considered as potential allies. Few had forgotten the anti-Tutsi *pogroms* (organized massacres) unleashed in Rwanda in December 1963, under the presidency of Grégoire Kayibanda, when, in the wake of an aborted raid by refugees coming from Burundi, thousands were killed. Kayibanda's overthrow by a northern army man, Juvénal Habyari-mana, in July 1975, resulted in a major power shift among Hutu politicians. As northern Hutu elements—a culturally distinct sub-group also known as the Kiga—became more influential, their anti-Tutsi disposi-tions, rooted in history and culture, came into sharper focus.

The regional context played a major role, too. While there is reason to believe that there would have been no genocide in the absence of the RPF invasion, the invasion would have never succeeded without the full support—military, logistical, and political—of Ugan-da's president, Yoweri Museveni. This is not to minimize Kagame's impressive military skills, but to stress the importance of external safe havens in facilitating the recruitment of RPF combatants. If support from Uganda proved critical for the RPF, political events in Burundi were equally important in sharpen-ing the edge of ethnic conflict in Rwanda. The assassination on October 21, 1993, of the first popularly elected Hutu president, Mel-chior Ndadaye, by a group of hardcore Tutsi elements within the Burundi army, meant that for the foreseeable future, the Tutsi-dominated military would reign supreme, allowing the free passage of Rwandan refu-gees to join the ranks of the RPF. In Rwanda, furthermore, the news of Ndadaye's death was received with consternation and anger; Hutu suspicions that "you just cannot trust the Tutsi" seemed amply confirmed. When five months later came the announcement that the newly appointed president of Burundi, Cyprien Ntaramyira, was among those on board when Habyarimana's plane exploded in mid-air, suspicion became cer-tainty. By then, few Hutu could ignore, let alone forgive the fact, that in five months three Hutu presidents had been killed (alleg-edly) at the hands of Tutsi elements.

To emphasize the significance of contex-tual factors is not to deny the contribution of environmental forces, of which the most obvious is population pressure on the land. This dimension has been ably analyzed by Jared Diamond in his chapter on Rwanda in his best-selling book, *Collapse: How Socie-ties Choose to Fail or Succeed* (2005). There is no question that Rwanda's increasing population cannot be left out of the account-ing in any attempt to explain not just Hutu-Tutsi hostility but intra-Hutu violence as well. Land hunger, and more generally the desire of perpetrators to acquire the prop-erty belonging to their victims, is indeed an important element in the background of the genocide. Equally plain, however, is that a tragedy of this magnitude is not reducible to exponential population growth.

René Lemarchand

Further Reading

Barnett, Michael. *Eyewitness to a Genocide: The United Nations and Rwanda*. Ithaca, NY: Cornell University Press, 2002.

Dallaire, Roméo. *Shake Hands with the Devil: The Failure of Humanity in Rwanda*. Toronto: Random House, Canada, 2004.

Diamond, Jared. *Collapse: How Societies Choose to Fail or Succeed*. New York: Pen-guin, 2005.

Consequences

The leadership that came to power in the wake of the genocide transformed nearly every sector of Rwandan society. While the country's rate of economic growth had sur-passed all expectations, the degree of coercion exercised by the new regime in suppressing the opposition raises serious questions about the state of democracy in Rwanda.

The process of political consolidation orchestrated by Paul Kagame began immediately after the Rwandan Patriotic Front (RPF) seized control of the capital. Approximately half of the newly appointed cabinet ministers were of Hutu origin, including the prime minister from the National Revolutionary Movement for Development party (French: the Révolutionnaire National pour le Développement, or MRND), Faustin Twagiramungu. Along with power-sharing at the top, however, every effort was made to remove most of the local officials appointed by the previous regime. Many simply disappeared. Meanwhile, the revenge killings as reported by Alison Des Forges in her definitive inquest into the genocide, *Leave None to Tell the Story* (1999), went on unabated, and resulted in the deaths of tens of thousands of Hutus.

The arrests of genuine and alleged *génocidaires* (French for those who commit genocide) that took place in the countryside soon took on dramatic proportions. From 30,000 in November 1994, the number of Hutu suspected of participating in the genocide jumped to 80,000 a year later, eventually reaching twice that number in the late 1990s. Simultaneously, the RPF was killing Hutus along the Congo-Rwanda boarder. One of the most famous massacres occurred in an internally displaced persons (IDPs) camp near Kibeho in south-west Rwanda. It is estimated that on April 22, 1995, RPF soldiers killed 4,000 to 5,000 IDPs, most of whom were Hutus. Another major crisis erupted in early 2000, when three high-ranking officials (two of them Hutu) resigned from their positions as speaker of the National Assembly (Joseph Sebarenzi), prime minister (Pierre-Célestin Rwigema), and president of the republic (Pasteur Bizimungu). On April 17, 2000, General Paul Kagame was formally elected president of the republic in a joint session of the government and the national assembly.

The trend towards dictatorial control was made clear during the 2003 presidential and legislative elections, the first held since the regime change. In view of newly adopted constitutional provisions giving the government a blank check to sanction anyone or any organization suspected of encouraging "divisionism"—a move clearly intended to eventually disqualify Hutu parties and candidates from running for office—it is no surprise that Kagame ran virtually unopposed in the 2003 presidential elections, winning 95 percent of the vote. The RPF, meanwhile, gained unfettered control of both houses. Much of the same scenario unfolded during the 2008 elections, when Kagame was re-elected with 98 percent of the vote. Both in 2003 and 2008, Hutu candidates were systematically discouraged or prevented from campaigning or running for the presidency. In April 2003, the MRND, until then the only significant opposition party, was dissolved on the grounds of being "divisionist." The same fate befell the leading human rights organization, *Ligue pour la promotion des droits de l'homme au Rwanda* (LIPRODHOR) and a similar accusation was used to discredit and arrest independent journalists, notably those associated with the newspapers *Le Partisan* and *Umuseso*. The most celebrated case of a candidate to the presidency disqualified and then arrested and brought to trial on the grounds of "divisionism" is that of Victoire Ingabire, president of the United Democratic Forces-Inkingi (UDF-Inkingi). On October 30, 2012, she was found guilty by Rwanda's Supreme Court on six counts, including genocide ideology and divisionism, and sentenced to eight years in jail.

With the banning of all references to Hutu and Tutsi, ethnic identities have been drastically reshaped. Starting from the premise that ethnicity was the root cause of the genocide, the regime chose to banish the use of such labels to best guarantee social harmony. Since Hutu and Tutsi have been legislated out of existence, Rwanda has officially become the land of the *Banyarwanda* ("the people of Rwanda"). Such drastic alteration of the country's ethnic map required drastic means. Only through a constitutional amendment, accompanied by extensive legal sanctions, could "divisionism" become an effective political tool to disqualify, harass, arrest, or expel Hutu opposition candidates.

Profound as the consequences have been domestically, the fallout from the genocide went far beyond Rwanda's borders. Beginning in July 1994, widespread fear of an impending counter-genocide caused a huge outflow of Hutu refugees into the Democratic Republic of the Congo (DRC). Over two million Rwandans, including civilians, members of the army, politicians, and civil servants sought asylum in eastern DRC. Soon countless cross-border raids were launched against Rwanda by remnants of the Rwandan Armed Forces (*Forces Armées Rwandaises*, or FAR) and other *génocidaires*. In November 1996, in response to mounting threats to the country's security, Kagame sent units of the Rwandan Patriotic Army (RPA) into eastern DRC with instructions to destroy every refugee camp along the border of Rwanda and Burundi. In a matter of days, some 20 camps were reduced to rubble. Countless refugees perished and over a million ran for their lives. Except for the half a million or so who went back to Rwanda, thousands died of exhaustion, disease, and hunger. A considerable number of those reported missing were killed by the Rwandan

army. Having made the DRC borderland safe for Rwanda, Kagame now proceeded to make sure his control would extend to the entire country.

Rwandan and Ugandan support of a rebel group in Congo seeking to overthrown the government complicated matters even further and ultimately contributed to the First Congo War (1996-1997). The Alliance of Democratic Forces for the Liberation of the Congo (French: Alliance des Fores Démocratiques pour la Libération du Congo-Zaïre, or AFDL), led by Laurent Kabila, received much of the credit for its victorious march on Kinshasa, however, the Rwandan army is no acknowledged to have done the heavy lifting. In May 1997, Mobutu Sese Seko was overthrown and replaced by Laurent Kabila as the new "king" of the Congo, but the Rwandan kingmakers continued to yield considerable influence in the affairs of the state. So much so that in August 1998, Kabila felt he had no choice but to get rid of his Rwandan advisers, a move that turned his former allies into bitter enemies and led straight to the catastrophic Second Congo War (1998–2003).

With the world's attention fixated on regime change in Kinshasa, little attention was paid to the 1996–1997 wholesale massacre of Hutu refugees in eastern DRC at the hands of Rwandan soldiers assisted by elements of AFDL. Although hints of the atrocities committed by Kagame's army had transpired in Western media long before, not until July 2010, with the publication of the *UN Mapping Report*, was the magnitude of the carnage disclosed to the outside world. As many as 300,000 Hutu civilians may have lost their lives between November 1996 and July 1997. Just how many *génocidaires* were able to survive the extensive "search and destroy" operations conducted jointly by the

RPA and the AFDL is unknown; what is beyond doubt is that among them are many of the Hutu extremists responsible for the violence now sweeping across eastern DRC.

René Lemarchand

Further Reading

Prunier, Gérard. *The Rwanda Crisis, 1959–1994: History of a Genocide.* Kampala: Fountain Publishers, 1995.

Perpetrators

The vast majority of perpetrators were ordinary citizens, mostly young men, many with a secondary education; they were fathers and husbands, schoolteachers, and farmers with no record of previous involvement in violence. Women hunted down, murdered, and supported and at times participated in raping victims.

As Scott Straus has convincingly demonstrated in his book *The Order of Genocide* (2006), far fewer were involved than suggested by the Paul Kagame government: between 175,000 and 210,000 is the overall figure cited by Straus, representing 7 percent to 8 percent of the active adult Hutu population. Approximately 50 percent of the killers were between the ages of 15 and 29; 70 percent were farmers; many belonged to party youths, with the National Revolutionary Movement for Development (French: Mouvement Révolutionnaire National pour le Développement, or MRND) youth wing, the so-called Interahamwe, playing a central role. Given that the MRND recruited the bulk of its members from the north, it is hardly surprising that the militias of northern origins were at the forefront of the anti-Tutsi violence. Every party had a youth wing, including opposition parties. Where the Interahamwe stood out, as a particularly

dangerous organization, is that their members were militarily trained and consistently egged on by radical elements to take a leading role in the genocide.

The perpetrators belonged to various social groups. At the core of the genocide stood the hardliners who ran the killing machine, drawn from the Akazu (an informal organization of Hutu extremists), the army, high-ranking members of the MNRD, and a handful of Hutus in the media. They were the orchestrators of the violence carried out in by the lower echelons, the prefectures, and the communes. Here a rough division of labor emerged between two distinctive groups. One group was composed of the prefectoral and communal elites, including prefects, communal councilors, communal secretaries and burgomasters, heads of nonprofit governmental organizations, and in some instances, local Church officials. The second group included the other grassroot "thugs" who formed the bulk of the militias—i.e., unemployed youths, delinquents, demobilized soldiers, and police officers. They are perhaps best described as the foot soldiers of the killing machine.

Although this pattern applies broadly to the country as a whole, the dynamics of violence were by no means the same everywhere. Depending on the personalities holding office, and the geographical context, the perpetrators met significant resistance in some places, such as in the Butare commune, where the incumbent prefect (and his administrators) courageously stood his ground against Hutu militias for three weeks after the start of the killings in Kigali.

For many perpetrators, the killings became a strategy for gaining power. But such calculations cannot be imputed to all perpetrators. Nor can the killings be reduced to a premise of blind obedience built into Rwanda's cultural matrix, or simply to greed, even though this may well have been the case sometimes. Although there is little question about the core group's visceral hatred of the Tutsi as an ethnic group, it is equally true that many of those who killed did so because they feared retribution if they did not. Many felt that their only option was to kill or be killed. Even when confronted with the choice of killing their Tutsi wives and relatives or being killed, many chose to save themself.

As tempting as it is to invoke the legacy of a strong state—the hallmark of the political system since pre-colonial times—as the normative framework for explaining compliance with orders from above, this argument has many flaws. As we now realize, as the killings got under way, bitter disagreements emerged among representatives of the state. In his most recent book, *Rwanda: De la Guerre au Génocide* (2010), André Guichaoua shows how the genocide, so far from resulting from a long-standing state-sponsored master plan, came about as the consequence of a bitter fight for supremacy between the moderates associated with the interim government headed by Prime Minister Jean Kambanda, and the three notorious hardliners who orchestrated the killings— Colonel Théoneste Bagosora, Joseph Nzirorera, and Mathieu Ngirumpatse, respectively adviser to the minister of defence, secretary-general, and chair of the MRND. In addition to having access to substantial financial resources, all three enjoyed wide-ranging connections within and outside the government. They stood out among the biggest of the big men (*bagaragu*) surrounding the presidency, and as such could reshape and reactivate the strategic patron-client ties that have always formed the axis around which much of Rwandan politics revolved.

In conclusion, the perpetrators of the Rwandan Genocide include a diverse cast of characters that includes men and women from every social class. Fear, greed, hatred, and racism are among the motivating factors that drove Rwandans to kill.

René Lemarchand

Further Reading

Brown, Sara E. "Female Perpetrators of the Rwandan Genocide," *International Feminist Journal of Politics*, Volume 16 (2014), Issue 3, 448–469.

Dallaire, Roméo. *Shake Hands with the Devil: The Failure of Humanity in Rwanda*. Toronto: Random House, Canada, 2004.

Victims

It is impossible to state with complete accuracy the number of victims who perished at the hands of the perpetrators during the Rwandan Genocide. The most plausible figure of Tutsi victims is 650,000. In addition to this number are the Hutu victims murdered because of their affiliation to opposition parties, or because they tried to protect their Tutsi friends and relatives. Furthermore, many died in the years leading up to the genocide and in its aftermath.

Beyond the challenges of conducting a macabre accounting of the victims of genocide, it is important to note that ethnically motivated killings preceded the 1994 genocide. Indeed, the murder of Tutsi civilians by the Rwandan Armed Forces (French: Forces Armées Rwandaises, or FAR) and other militias predated the genocide. Scores if not hundreds of Bagogwe—a Tutsi-related minority living in the northeast—were massacred by FAR soldiers in the wake of the January 23, 1991, surprise attack on the northern town of Ruhengeri by the Rwandan Patriotic Front (RPF). In March 1992, in the Bugesera region, east of Kigali, for the first time the authorities called upon groups of Interahamwe to kill Tutsi as part of their communal work, which in Kinyarwanda is called *umuganda*. The authorities failed to intervene in the killings, arguing that they could not control outbursts of popular anger. This became a standard argument in the arsenal of those officials who denied responsibility in the massacre.

In addition to the killings that predated the genocide, there were many deaths afterwards. Tens of thousands of Hutu civilians died at the hands of RPF troops during and following its invasion into Rwanda as well as the wholesale murder of Hutu refugees in the eastern areas of the Democratic Republic of the Congo (DRC) in 1996 and 1997. The scope and motivation of this violence has become a hotly debated topic among human rights practitioners and scholars. Some view the murder of Hutu civilians during the genocide by RPF troops as tantamount to war crimes or genocide, while others consider this violence a natural part of war.

During the genocide, the first to die at the hands of the perpetrators were those in positions of power who posed a threat (real or perceived) to the government. All cabinet ministers belonging to opposition parties, irrespective of ethnic identities, were killed after Habyarimana's assassination. This was essentially the work of the Presidential Guard. Their primary targets were moderate Hutus affiliated with the Democratic Republican Movement (French: Mouvement Démocratique Républicain, or MDR) the Social Democratic Party (French: Parti Social Democrate, or PSD) and the Liberal Party (French: Parti Liberal), which included its president, Lando Ndasingwa. Forty hours after the airplane crash that killed President Habyarimana on April 6,

1994, the Interahamwe set up roadblocks throughout the capital. The carnage then began to spread to rural areas and provincial towns, causing thousands of panic-stricken Tutsi civilians to flee their homes. While some were sheltered by Hutu neighbors, others tried to flee to RPF-controlled areas, and still others sought refuge in churches or went into hiding in neighboring swamps. The worst massacres took place in churches and mission compounds, as in Nyamata, Musha, and Karubamba. Throughout the genocide, the media, including Radio-Télévision Libre des Mille Collines, played a major role in inciting anti-Tutsi hatred. Through caricatures and semi-historical narratives, newspapers such as *Kangura* and *La Médaille-Nyiramacibiri* never missed an opportunity to remind their readers of the "evil-mindedness" of the Tutsi. When doubts arose about the victims' ethnicity, a look at their identity cards was enough to spell the difference between life and death. There are also cases of Hutu who looked like Tutsi being killed for supposedly looking like the enemy.

The methods employed by the *génocidaires* have now been described with clinical precision. According to reports and research conducted by Human Rights Watch and Physicians for Human Rights, the perpetrators' weapons of choice included machetes, massues (clubs studded with nails), axes, knives, and fragmentation grenades. Many victims were beaten to death while others were amputated and left to bleed to death or die from exposure. The perpetrators also drowned their victims or buried them alive. Women were routinely raped before being killed, while others were systematically and repeated raped and abandoned to die from their wounds. The use of firearms became increasingly frequent when soldiers and

The Rwandan government created six so-called reconciliation villages after the genocide with the aim of alleviating overcrowding in prisons and encouraging reconciliation between victims and perpetrators. This photo shows residents of Mbyo, one of the reconciliation villages, on March 12, 2014, taking part in Rwanda's monthly day of service called *umuganda*. (Phil Moore/Stringer/Getty Images)

militias joined hands in their cleansing operations. The perpetrators often used coded language, such as, calling killings "collective work" (*umuganda*), the cutting of limbs as "bush clearing," and the murdering of women and children as "pulling out the roots of the bad weeds."

It bears repeating that not all victims were Tutsi; nor were the perpetrators unilaterally Hutu. It is now widely believed that many of the moderate Hutu killed before and after the crash were dispatched by RPF elements, as a strategy designed to deepen the rifts between extremists and moderates. Again, there is now substantial evidence available from impartial observers to suggest that many horrendous crimes were committed by the

RPF in the course of its campaign. Nor is there any doubt that a large number of Tutsi could have been saved if, instead of making a run for the capital city, the RPF had attended to the urgency of saving endangered lives. Capturing power was all that mattered, even if it meant turning a blind eye to scenes of mayhem in the countryside.

René Lemarchand

Further Reading

Des Forges, Alison. *Leave None to Tell the Story: Genocide in Rwanda*. New York: Human Rights Watch, 1999.

Straus, Scott. *The Order of Genocide: Race, Power, and War in Rwanda*. Ithaca, NY: Cornell University Press, 2008.

Bystanders

Bystanders to genocide can take many forms, and the Rwandan Genocide is no exception. While many scholars have proposed their own definition of the bystander category, the common consensus is that a bystander—unlike a victim or perpetrator—is an individual who was not targeted for annihilation, not a direct perpetrator or planner of genocide, and either by choice or out of ignorance did nothing to stop and/or intervene in the genocide. Some have argued that inaction or passivity during genocide becomes a form of agency as it works to encourage the perpetrators to go on killing without giving it a second thought. By some accounts, bystanders are on the ground witnesses to genocide. In short, the definition of a bystander has many facets and its application is not always clear. Thus, true to form, when considering bystanders during the Rwandan Genocide, it is not always easy to determine who was a bystander.

Rwandan Hutu civilians who neither participated in the genocide nor acted as rescuers may be considered bystanders to the genocide. It is worth noting, however, that during the genocide, an individual could easily move from category to category and in the span of the 100 days of genocide, it is not implausible that an individual was at times a bystander and at others a rescuer or perpetrator.

In many ways, one could easily assert that the mandate for the United Nations Assistance Mission for Rwanda (UNAMIR) forced United Nations (UN) troops into the role of witness and bystander to genocide. UNAMIR was deployed to Rwanda in 1993 by the UN Security Council to help facilitate the Arusha Peace Accords. The Arusha Accords brought a tenuous end to a three-year-long Rwandan Civil War between the Hutu-led Rwandan government and the Rwandan Patriotic Front (RPF), a rebel group composed predominately of Rwandan Tutsi exiles. When UNAMIR was deployed in 1993, it was under a Chapter XI peacekeeping mandate that prohibited UN troops from using force except for instances of self-defense. When the genocide began on April 6, 1994, the UN chose to keep the original mandate until the genocide had all but ended. As a result, for the duration of the genocide, UNAMIR could not use military force to stop the perpetrators nor save victims. It is for this reason that some have criticized the UN for turning its soldiers into bystanders. It is also important to note, however, that despite the restrictions of their mandate, UN troops did everything within the bounds of their mandate to help civilians. For this reason, a person could also argue that the UN troops were witnesses and resistors, not passive bystanders.

General Roméo Dallaire, who headed UNAMIR prior to and during the genocide, has reflected upon his role as a witness in his book *Shake Hands with the Devil: The Failure of Humanity in Rwanda*. Describing how he felt as he watched Belgian nationals leave Rwanda when the genocide began, Dallaire explains, ". . . I had been left here with a ragtag force to witness a crime against humanity that the Belgians had unwittingly laid the spadework for" (Dallaire 2003, 318). Here Dallaire is commenting on the role Belgian colonizers had played in setting the conditions that helped spark the genocide. The failure of the UN to authorize Dallaire to use force and send more troops left Dallaire and his troops vulnerable and ill-equipped to handle the genocide. Despite these obstacles, however, Dallaire did everything within his power to save victims.

Dallaire's sense of abandonment as he watched Belgian and other foreign nationals leave Rwanda when the genocide began raises the question of whether international governing bodies, such as the UN, and foreign leaders, like President Bill Clinton of the United States, can or should be considered bystanders to the Rwandan Genocide. Again, the answer to this question depends on the definition of bystander being used. If a bystander is an on-the-ground witness to genocide then in this case the answer would be no. But if a bystander is a witness in a broader sense—either as a direct witness (present) or aware of events through official intel (in other words, a witness from afar)—than one could successfully claim that the United Nations, France, Belgium, and other nations and foreign leaders were bystanders to the Rwandan Genocide.

Alexis Herr

Further Reading

Barnett, Victoria J. *Bystanders: Conscience and Complicity During the Holocaust.* Westport, CT: Greenwood Press, 1999.

Dallaire, Roméo. *Shake Hands with the Devil: The Failure of Humanity in Rwanda.* Toronto: Random House, Canada, 2004.

Herr, Alexis. *The Holocaust and Compensated Compliance: Fossoli di Carpi, 1942–1952.* New York: Palgrave Macmillan, 2016.

Hilberg, Raul. *Perpetrator Victims Bystanders: The Jewish Catastrophe, 1933–1945.* New York: Aaron Asher Brooks, 1992.

International Reactions

The international community could have done more to upend the Rwandan Genocide when the killing began. Its active disengagement with the bloodshedding is elucidated by the April 21, 1994 United Nations (UN) vote to reduce the United Nations Assistance Mission for Rwanda (UNAMIR) to 270 men, which amounted to a 90 percent reduction in troops. The pullout of UNAMIR troops, precisely when the killing frenzy reached a new pitch of intensity, had disastrous consequences. Besides being readily interpreted as a sign of weakness by the Hutu extremists, it sent the wrong message to the foreign nations that had contributed UN troops to serve in Rwanda. By the time the UN Security Council adopted a new resolution providing for a 5,500-man deployment force operating under a Chapter VII mandate of the UN Charter—which allowed the potential use of force when the circumstances required—the crisis had already spun out of control.

The early withdrawal of UN troops at the start of the genocide illuminates the sense of confusion and impotence displayed by the permanent members of the UN Security Council after the killing of 10 Belgian soldiers by the Rwandan Armed Forces (French: Forces Armées Rwandaises, or FAR) on April 7, 1994. Some have argued that Belgium was too traumatized by the death of its Blue Helmets and the negative press at home that followed to react constructively to the crisis. The United States, still smarting from the backlash of its disastrous intervention in Somalia in 1992, showed little inclination to get involved in another messy situation in a country where it had no vital interests at stake. France, on the other hand, under rising domestic pressure, launched Operation Turquoise, a French-led military detachment under a UN mandate designed to provide protection and humanitarian assistance. Thus, beginning on June 23, immediately after the Security Council gave France the green light to intervene under a Chapter VII mandate, some 2,500 men, accompanied by impressive fire power and equipment, fanned out of Goma, Zaire (now known as the Democratic

Republic of the Congo) into eastern Rwanda, where they carved out a "safe zone."

Gérard Prunier, who was closely associated with the planning of the operation, openly admits in his book *The Rwanda Crisis* (1995) that the French intervention delivered far less than it promised. While it may have saved hundreds of Tutsi lives, it failed to prevent the massacre of thousands of others, while at the same time giving ammunition to critics who blamed the French for allowing the *génocidaires* to evade capture. A more devastating criticism points to the early failure of the French to rein in the murderous activities of the Rwandan Defence Forces (French: Forces Rwandaises de Défense, or RDF) whom they had provided military training in the years prior to the genocide.

In addition to the international community's failure to take decisive actions to stop the killings, it took far too long for foreign nations to call the atrocity actual genocide. While the French finally recognized the existence of genocide in May 1994, the representative of the U.S. State Department consistently refused to use the "g-word," instead referring to the events as "acts of genocide." By refusing to label the ongoing massacre as genocide, the United States felt it was under no obligation to intervene. Not until 1998 would President Bill Clinton express regrets, but conspicuously avoided taking personal responsibility.

The sense of shame and embarrassment felt by Western nations for their inaction goes far in explaining the vast quantities of financial and economic assistance to the new authorities after the genocide. Aid flows steadily increased over the years, growing by over 45 percent between 2006 and 2009 (reaching $711 million in official development ment assistance [ODA] in 2007). But as recent research by An Ansom and Donatelle Rostagno shows, Rwanda still has a long way to go. Inequality remains a major problem, as so does the rising levels of poverty: between 2000 and 2005, the absolute number of poor individuals increased by 560,000, while the number of those living in extreme poverty rose to 190,000. Nor did development aid from the West prevent the Paul Kagame government from intervening in the domestic politics in neighboring DRC. Only in 2012, after a UN report disclosed the military support given by Kigali to insurgents in eastern DRC, did donors, including the United States, finally agree to suspend their economic and/ or military assistance. Hence the paradox noted by humanitarian and scholar Eugenia Zorbas: while the sense of guilt shared by the West translates into high levels of aid dependence, the government of Rwanda remains blissfully indifferent to Western proddings in terms of its policy options. That this situation is becoming highly counterproductive in terms of U.S. interests in Central Africa is all too clear; how long it may endure is anybody's guess.

René Lemarchand

Further Reading

Kuperman, Alan. *The Limits of Humanitarian Intervention: Genocide in Rwanda*. New York: Brookings Institution Press, 2001.

Zorba, Eugenia, "Aid Dependence and Policy Independence: Explaining the Rwandan Paradox," in *Remaking Rwanda: State Building and Human Rights After Mass Violence*, Straus, Scott and Lars Waldorf, eds. Madison, WI: The University of Wisconsin Press, 2011: 103–117.

A

African Crisis Response Initiative/African Contingency Operations Training and Assistance Program

The U.S. government established the African Crisis Response Initiative (ACRI) in 1997 to improve the ability of the African armed forces to conduct humanitarian and peacekeeping missions in Africa. The immediate catalyst for the ACRI was the 1994 Rwandan Genocide, in which some 800,000 Rwandans were systematically killed in the span of three months. In 2004, the ACRI was renamed the African Contingency Operations Training and Assistance Program (ACOTA).

The ACRI and its successor agency were intended to offer training to African national armies so that they could be rapidly mobilized to provide humanitarian relief operations in response to natural and human-made disasters and to mount peacekeeping missions in the event of war or civil unrest. The training period for each army is 70 days and is conducted by 70 to 100 U.S. military specialists. Thereafter, the U.S. training team pays a follow-up visit every six months. The program is supervised, managed, and funded by the U.S. State Department. In its infancy, the ACRI began peacekeeping training programs in 4 African countries and has since then expanded to 21. According to 2008 statistics, the ACOTA trains around 20 battalions per year and tailors its services to meet the individual needs of each country (Council on Foreign Relations, 2008).

Initially, some members of Congress were concerned that Rwandan troops who had participated in the genocide were receiving American training, but that has not proven to be a significant problem. Several African leaders worried that the ACRI was an attempt on the part of the Americans to disengage from Africa, while others viewed it as a veiled attempt to advance U.S. interests there. The ACRI and ACOTA have worked closely with the United Nations Department of Peacekeeping Operations, as well as the Organization of African Unity and other African-based groups to ensure that the training is properly utilized.

Paul G. Pierpaoli Jr.

See also: International Reactions; Rwandan Genocide, U.S. Response to the

Further Reading

"Fact Sheet on Africa Contingency Operations Training and Assistance (ACOTA)," Council on Foreign Relations (June 2010), accessed February 2017, www.cfr.org.

Kamukama, Dixon. *Rwanda Conflict: Its Roots and Regional Implications*. 2nd ed. Kampala, Uganda: Fountain Publishers, 1998.

Akayesu, Jean-Paul

Jean-Paul Akayesu was the first person to be convicted of the crime of genocide by an international tribunal. Born in 1953 in the Taba commune in Rwanda, he had been a schoolteacher, an active member of the local football team, and later, a school district inspector. A member of the Democratic Republican Movement (French: Mouvement Démocratique Républicain, or MDR), a Hutu political party he joined in 1991, he soon rose through the party ranks and eventually became the local branch president. In April 1993, Akayesu was elected *bourgmestre*, or mayor, of Taba. He served as mayor until he fled from Rwanda in June 1994.

In his capacity as mayor of Taba, Akayesu had formal control of the communal police, and was responsible for the maintenance of order, subject only to the district prefect. His authority, however, extended beyond these formal limits. In Rwanda, a considerable degree of informal dominion fell upon the role of the mayor, who acted as a kind of "father figure" within the commune. As a communal leader, he was respected, widely considered to be a man of high morals, intelligence, and integrity. A family man, he was the father of five children.

Initially, Akayesu managed to spare Taba the mass genocidal killing that began on April 6, 1994. He refused to let the Interahamwe militia operate there, and struggled with them to protect the local Tutsi population. On April 18, however, after a meeting of *bourgmestres* and leaders of Rwanda's interim government, a fundamental change occurred—both in Taba and Akayesu himself. Conscious that his political and social future depended on joining those carrying out the genocide, Akayesu began collaborating directly with the extremists, and from this point on started to incite his citizens to join in the killing.

During the genocide, it has been estimated that some 2,000 Tutsis were massacred in Taba, many of whom had sought refuge in the bureau communal (approximating a city hall and a community center)—the heart of

Jean-Paul Akayesu, a former teacher, school inspector, and mayor, became the first person convicted of the crime of genocide when the International Criminal Tribunal for Rwanda issued its verdict on September 2, 1998. (Alexander Joe/AFP/Getty Images)

Akayesu's domain. It has been alleged that Akayesu did not provide support or help for those his position had entrusted him to protect; not only this, but he actively encouraged the Interahamwe militias who had come to Taba, as well as the local Hutu population, to participate in the mass murder, rape, and torture of the Tutsis.

In addition, numerous Tutsi women were the victims of sexual violence in the bureau communal. They were mutilated and systematically raped, often by more than one attacker and in public. Armed police, as well as Akayesu himself, were reportedly present when some of these acts took place. Akayesu was also suspected of having ordered several murders, and to have stood by while they were carried out. In addition, he allegedly gave a death list to Hutu extremists, and ordered house-to-house searches to locate Tutsis. It was later concluded that his actions in Taba amounted to direct participation in the crime of genocide.

In the aftermath of the genocide, Akayesu fled the country, first escaping to Zaire (now the Democratic Republic of the Congo), then to Lusaka, Zambia, where he was arrested on October 10, 1995. Zambia became the irst African nation to extradite an alleged *génocidaire* to the International Criminal Tribunal for Rwanda (ICTR) in Arusha, Tanzania. He was formally indicted on February 13, 1996, and transferred to ICTR jurisdiction on May 15, 1996. The trial began on January 9, 1997.

Akayesu's was the first genocide trial in history. Initially, Akayesu was charged with encouraging the killing of Tutsis, directly ordering the killing of numerous individuals, and supervising the interrogation, beating, and execution of people from Taba. Richard Goldstone, the chief prosecutor for the ICTR, charged Akayesu with 12 counts of genocide, crimes against humanity, and violations of Article II of the 1949 Geneva Conventions. Ultimately, three additional counts of genocide and crimes against humanity were added to the charges, alleging that he had ordered and condoned rape and sexual mutilation—and then, the murder—of hundreds of Tutsi women. The prosecutor for the Akayesu trial was an American attorney, Pierre-Richard Prosper.

Akayesu pleaded not guilty on all counts. His primary defense was that he had played no part in the killings, and that he had been powerless to stop them. His essential argument was that at the time of the genocide, he had not been in a position of authority, and his attorneys argued that Akayesu was being made a scapegoat for the crimes of the people of Taba.

The trial judges found that, in his role as mayor, Akayesu was responsible for maintaining public order and executing the law in the municipality of Taba and that, in this function, he had effective authority over the police. His criminal responsibility was based on his direct participation in acts of genocide and on his position as a hierarchical superior. Article VI, section III, of the statute setting up the ICTR states that a superior can be held responsible if he knew or had reason to know that a subordinate was about to commit criminal acts or had done so, and that the superior had failed to take the necessary measures to prevent such acts or punish the perpetrators.

On September 2, 1998, Akayesu was found guilty of 9 of the 15 counts with which he was charged regarding genocide and crimes against humanity (extermination, murder [three counts], torture, rape, and other inhuman acts). This made him the first person convicted of the specific crime of genocide in an internationally accredited courtroom, and thus the first occasion on which the 1948 UN Convention on Genocide was upheld as law. It was a landmark decision also in that it recognized the crime of rape as a form of genocide, and made the legal definition of rape more precise.

On October 2, 1998, Akayesu was sentenced to life imprisonment for each of the nine counts, the sentences to run concurrently. He immediately appealed, but the Appeals Chamber rejected this on June 1, 2001. On December 9, 2001, Akayesu was transferred to Bamako Central Prison in Mali to serve out his life sentence.

Paul R. Bartrop

See also: Interahamwe; International Criminal Tribunal for Rwanda; Mouvement

Démocratique Républicain; Prosper, Pierre-Richard Rape; Rwandan Patriotic Front

Further Reading

Bodnarchuk, Kari. *Rwanda: A Country Torn Apart*. Minneapolis, MN: Lerner Publishing Group, 1998.

Friedrichs, David O., ed. *State Crime*. Brookfield, VT: Ashgate/Dartmouth, 1998.

Akazu

During Rwanda's colonial period, the word *Akazu* (Kinyarwanda for 'little house') was used to describe the courtiers surrounding the king. In the years leading up to and during the genocide, Akazu was the term used to describe the secret network of Hutu extremists who helped shape, plan, and direct the Rwandan Genocide.

Thought to have emerged in the mid-1970s, the Akazu played a powerful role in fostering anti-Tutsi sentiment in Rwanda. Agathe Habyarimana (born Agathe Kanziga), the wife of President Juvénal Habyarimana, formed *le clan de Madame* ("her court within a court"), which later became known as the Akazu. All its members came from the northwest of Rwanda, most of whom originated in the Bushiru region. Along with the high-ranking and influential members of the military elite, some of the Akazu's most prominent members included President Habyarimana's wife and their close relatives and friends, such as Protais Zigiranyirazo (prefect of Ruhengeri), Elie Sagatwa (a colonel of the Forces Armées Rwandaises [FAR]), Séraphin Rwabukumba (general manager of La Centrale, a rice import company), Laurent Serubuga (the former vice chief of general staff and a FAR colonel), Dr. Séraphin Bararengana, Dr. Charles Nzabagerageza (former prefect of Ruhengeri), Alphonse Ntirivamunda (Director General of Public Works), Minister Joseph Nzirorera (a deputy of Ruhengeri), and Noel Mbonabaryi (godfather of Habyarimana). The Akazu collaborated with a wide-ranging network of contacts (the so-called *Réseau Zéro*) throughout Rwanda who held positions within local councils, embassies, the government, and military. These and other members of the Akazu collaborated to annihilate Rwandan Tutsis and moderate Hutus.

Théoneste Bagosora, a FAR colonel, became a key member of the Akazu in the years leading up to the genocide. After President Habyarimana was killed in a plane crash on April 6, 1994—an incident which most scholars point to as the event that started the genocide—Bagosora assumed control of the military and political affairs. He then directed the Interahamwe militia, the anti-Tutsi paramilitary group he had formed years earlier, to start murdering Tutsi.

The international community learned of the Akazu's anti-Tutsi agenda prior to the genocide. In August 1992, Christophe Mfizi, formerly a key official of President Habyarimana's political party, the National Revolutionary Movement for Development (French: Mouvement Révolutionnaire National pour le Développement, or MRND), published an open letter in France that described the activities of the *Réseau Zéro* (the Akazu's network of contacts). In December 1992, Filip Reyntjens, a Belgian Law professor and specialist on Rwanda, gave a press conference with Senator Willy Kuypers in the Senate in Brussels discussing the existence of the death squads directed by the Akazu. At that time, the professor and senator also identified, by name, some of the key members of the Akazu, including Bagosora. In mid-1993, a French journalist published an article in the newspaper *Libération* accusing the French government of supporting a

Hutu group in Rwanda that was planning an annihilation of Tutsis.

Alexis Herr

See also: Bagosora, Théoneste; Forces Armées Rwandaises; Habyarimana, Agathe Kanziga; Habyarimana, Juvénal; Interahamwe; Mouvement Révolutionnaire National pour le Développement

Further Reading

Gellately, Robert, and Ben Kiernan, eds. *The Specter of Genocide: Mass Murder in Historical Perspective.* New York: Cambridge University Press, 2003.

Grünfeld, Fred, and Anke Huijboom. *The Failure to Prevent Genocide in Rwanda: The Role of Bystanders.* Boston: Martinus Nijhoff, 2007.

Melvern, Linda. *Conspiracy to Murder: The Rwandan Genocide.* London: Verso, 2006.

Prunier, Gérard. *The Rwanda Crisis, 1959–1994: History of a Genocide.* Kampala: Fountain Publishers, 1995.

Scherrer, P. Christian. *Genocide and Crisis in Central Africa: Conflict Roots, Mass Violence, and Regional War.* Westport, CT: Praeger, 2002.

Albright, Madeleine

During the Rwandan Genocide (April-May, 1994), Madeleine Albright served as the U.S. ambassador to the United Nations (UN). In the aftermath of the genocide, and most profoundly in the Frontline documentary on the atrocity entitled *Ghosts of Rwanda* (2004), Albright's actions during the atrocity came under scrutiny.

Madeleine Albright (birth name: Marie Jana Korbel) was born in Prague, Czechoslovakia, in 1937, just two years before Nazi troops invaded her hometown. Ten days after the Nazi invasion, Albright and her family fled to England where they remained for the duration of the war. Only after Hitler's defeat did the Korbels return to Czechoslovakia. Although Albright had been raised Catholic, she later learned that her parents had converted from Judaism and that three of her grandparents perished in Nazi concentration camps. In the aftermath of the Holocaust, her parents once again were forced to flee oppression, this time the threat being the onset of communism. The Korbels moved in 1948 and resettled in Denver, Colorado. As a young student, Albright excelled and her academic achievements earned her a scholarship to Wellesley College in Massachusetts, where she graduated with honors in 1959. She went on to earn a certificate in Russian studies (1968) and later her master's (1968) and doctorate (1976) in public law and government from Columbia University. Her education served her well as she pursued professional positions in the public and private sectors.

Under President Bill Clinton, Albright became the U.S. ambassador to the United Nations on January 27, 1993. During the Rwandan Genocide (April-May 1994), Albright was the key negotiator within the UN for the United States, and her actions have received much criticism in recent years. A cache of previously classified documents released by the U.S. government in 2004 revealed that in the early days of the genocide, Albright had sent a cable to the U.S. State Department proposing that the United States urge the UN to recall the majority of its peacekeeping force. Ultimately, the UN did just that and the images of UN troops abandoning Tutsis to face their Hutu killers alone stands as a stark example of the international community's failure to save lives during the genocide. Many scholars of the genocide have claimed that the withdrawal

Madeleine Albright served as the U.S. ambassador to the United Nations (UN) during the Rwandan Genocide. She advocated for an early withdrawal of UN peacekeepers when the killing began, an action that has come to symbolize U.S. and UN failures during the genocide. (Sadık Güleç/Dreamstime)

of UN troops at the start of the genocide actually encouraged the perpetrators to kill Tutsis and moderate Hutus.

In the Frontline documentary *Ghosts of Rwanda*, Albright answers poignant questions about her actions during the genocide. When asked why she regretted Rwanda, she responded, "I wish it had been possible for us to do more ... I have reviewed the record a lot, and I don't think actually that we could have done more" (Frontline 2014). In short, while Albright lamented that more had not been done at the time, she remains uncertain if more could have been done. She explains that, given the time period, resources available, and overall approach of

the international community, the United States could not have done more. On a personal level, she regrets not having made a greater effort to push for intervention, but even if she had, she does not think anything would have come of it.

Alexis Herr

See also: Bystanders; International Reactions; Moderate Hutu; Rwandan Genocide, U.S. Response to the; Support Hope, Operation; Turquoise, Operation; United Nations Assistance Mission for Rwanda

Further Reading

"Interview: Madeleine Albright," Frontline (April 2004). http://www.pbs.org/wgbh/pages/frontline/shows/ghosts/interviews/albright.html.

Lander, Mark, "Declassified U.N. Cables Reveal Turning Point in Rwanda Crisis of 1994," *New York Times* (June 3, 2014).

Allen, Susan

Susan Allen is an American medical doctor who conducted research on HIV/AIDS in Rwanda both before and after the genocide of 1994.

Allen was born in 1958 in Caracas, Venezuela, to Irish American parents, and grew up in Brazil and Lebanon. Despite moving around as a child, her parents sought out French schools for Allen. Her parents reasoned that regardless of where they might be located, the curriculum would stay more or less consistent if she enrolled in French schools. As a result, Allen's school experience left her fluent in French.

In 1980, she graduated with a degree in chemistry, and four years later earned a medical degree, both from Duke University. During her residency at the University of

California in San Francisco (UCSF), she specialized in pathology (the science or study of diseases). While in San Francisco, she performed autopsies on gay men who were dying of unusual disease combinations that would soon be linked to the AIDS virus. While a resident doctor she also completed a Masters of Public Health at the University of California, Berkeley.

In 1984, Dr. Nathan Clumeck, a Belgian guest speaker then passing through San Francisco, addressed a group at Allen's hospital. From his talk, she learned that heterosexual African AIDS patients were also dying from typically treatable diseases. Approaching Clumeck later, she suggested that his hospital needed a pathology laboratory to diagnose the nature of the infections that were doing so much damage. He offered to write her a letter of introduction to the Rwandan Ministry of Health if she could obtain funding to set up such a laboratory in Kigali. In response, Allen wrote 150 grant applications, netting $30,000 to go to Kigali in order to test pregnant women for HIV antibodies. She moved to Rwanda in 1986 with seed money from UCSF and the state of California. Her initiative created the first mobile HIV-testing laboratory on the African continent.

In 1988, her research took a startling turn. While tracking HIV in pregnant Rwandan women, she found that 14 percent of her 1,500 research subjects did not share the same HIV status as their partners. To Allen, this discordance made these women and their partners an ideal cohort both to understand the factors that determine virus transmission and to identify strategies to prevent it. She began a program in which both partners received counseling about prevention strategies, and were routinely tested as a result. Soon it was shown that HIV incidence among counseled couples could be as much

as 50 to 70 percent lower than among those who were not counseled.

Despite the important progress of her research and her valuable contributions to Rwandan society, Rwandan president Juvénal Habyarimana proved an obstacle to Allen's success. The Rwandan government was wary about any discussion of HIV, fearful of its potential to kill off foreign investment and scare away tourists who came to see the country's gorillas. Allen was forbidden to publish any of her research results from 1986 until 1991, which placed pressure on her from her funding agencies in the United States who demanded to see her results. Partly in order to deflect Rwandan government attention, she began giving her work the official-sounding name of "Project San Francisco," cutting out any reference to Africa. The ploy worked, but only up to a point. She recalls having her phone tapped and her mail opened, and being shadowed by government agents spying on her activities. And, all too often, she could hear gunfire, as the Hutu Power campaign of hatred against the country's Tutsi population intensified throughout the early 1990s.

In April 1994, she traveled to Zambia to set up another research project, but returned to Kigali immediately after she learned that President Habyarimana's plane had been shot down and that interethnic violence had begun. Allen, along with her husband and son, were evacuated on convoys organized by Laura Lane of the U.S. embassy.

The Rwandan Genocide brought Allen's research to an abrupt halt. She and her team had been making good progress in terms of recruiting and educating people, until the genocide forced Allen to flee and the project to shut down. Hundreds of those involved in her study were murdered, together with about half of the staff of 70 assisting in the project. In August 1994, Allen returned alone to Kigali to learn the fate of her colleagues. The project was in tatters, and many of those who had survived were in mourning for lost family members. Allen herself concluded that she was suffering from the syndrome known as survivor guilt, as a result of which she required counseling back in San Francisco.

After a period of rest in the United States, she redeployed research funds that had previously been earmarked for Rwanda in order to develop a similar program in Zambia, where she had been when the genocide broke out in April 1994. Zambia, however, did not afford her the security she now craved. In Lusaka, she received death threats from Rwandan exiles that had been involved in the genocide, forcing her to carry a gun for her own protection.

In 1996, Allen joined the University of Alabama at Birmingham to continue her work, and in 2004, she was hired by Emory University in Atlanta, Georgia, where she became a professor of global health at the Rollins School of Public Health, with a joint appointment in epidemiology (a branch of science focused on the occurrence, transmission, and control of epidemic diseases). The project she directs, known around the world as the Rwanda Zambia HIV Research Group (www.rzhrg.org), includes the largest and longest-standing cohort of HIV-discordant couples in the world. It has helped to identify strategies that reduce HIV transmission and to uncover the effects of the host's genotype and immune response on the evolution of the virus.

In addition to her medical work, Allen is also active in genocide prevention and broadening awareness about Rwanda's genocidal past. One of her primary concerns is that the genocide of 1994 remains a wound that can only be healed by bringing to justice those who led it. Allen has directed her attention to raising consciousness to the fact that many of the organizers of the genocide are now living free in the United States and elsewhere, and that it is a matter of social concern the perpetrators be identified and brought to justice. She has noted that if the opportunity of trying perpetrators is passed by, it will render much more complex situations next to impossible to resolve.

Paul R. Bartrop

See also: Habyarimana, Juvénal; International Criminal Tribunal for Rwanda; Lane, Laura

Further Reading

Bodnarchuk, Kari. *Rwanda: A Country Torn Apart*. Minneapolis, MN: Lerner Publishing Group, 1998.

Evans, Glynne. *Responding to Crises in the African Great Lakes*. Oxford: Oxford University Press, 1997.

Anyidoho, Henry Kwami

Major General Henry Kwami Anyidoho was born in Tanyigbe, in the Volta Region of Ghana, on July 13, 1940, and is arguably Ghana's most distinguished and well-known military officer. A career soldier, he is a graduate of the Ghana Military Academy and the U.S. Marine Staff College in Quantico, Virginia. He received his commission with the Ghanaian army's Signal Corps in 1965, and served in various military capacities, including commanding officer of the Army Signal Regiment, commandant of the Ghana Military Academy and Training Schools, Director General of Logistics, Joint Operations and Plans at the General Headquarters of the Ghana Armed Forces, and general officer commanding Northern Command. Anyidoho is probably best known internationally as a leader and participant in a number of important United Nations (UN) peacekeeping missions, particularly in Rwanda in 1994 and Darfur, Sudan since 2005.

Prior to his deployments to Rwanda and Sudan, Anyidoho had already served with the UN Emergency Force (UNEF) in Sinai, Egypt with the UN Interim Force in Lebanon (UNIFIL) as chief military press and information officer, with the Economic Community of West African States Monitoring Group (ECOMOG) in Liberia in 1990, and with the UN Transitional Authority in Cambodia (UNTAC). In December 1993, he was appointed to serve as deputy force commander and chief of staff of the UN Assistance Mission for Rwanda (UNAMIR), under the command of Lieutenant General Roméo Dallaire. Anyidoho arrived in Kigali on January 15, 1994, less than three months prior to the start of the genocide. While serving as Dallaire's deputy force commander, he also commanded the Ghanaian contingent of the UNAMIR forces.

Anyidoho's experiences in previous peacekeeping missions did not provide him with a template of how to respond to the carnage that descended on Rwanda in April 1994, but he was quick to adapt to the situation as it developed. Organizing the Ghanaian troops under his command, and liaising closely with Dallaire, he found himself pulled in a dozen different directions at once, with calls to station soldiers at the homes of prominent moderate Hutu politicians, or to rescue others and bring them to safety. The forces under his command were quickly overwhelmed, yet he continued to try to fulfill his commitments with the highest level of professionalism and with the key aim of saving lives.

As the genocide developed in the first days of April 1994, however, the UN Security Council located in New York rapidly reduced the initial peacekeeping/monitoring mandate of UNAMIR. Countries that had originally contributed troops began to withdraw them, and on April 21, the UN Security Council passed Resolution 912, which called for a reduction of the UNAMIR force from 2,548 to just 270. Anyidoho was the first senior officer in Kigali to receive the news on the phone, as Dallaire was away at that time from the office, attempting to negotiate a ceasefire. His immediate reaction was to resist the reduction order, and defy the UN command to withdraw. He advised Dallaire along these lines. Dallaire, in turn, had received the news from his chief of staff, Major Brent Beardsley, and had already reached a similar conclusion. Pleading with New York not to close down the mission, Dallaire achieved a reprieve of sorts that allowed UNAMIR to remain, but only with a reduced force. Ultimately, 456 soldiers remained, 78 percent of whom were Anyidoho's Ghanaian battalion. The higher figure was not endorsed by the Security Council and instead it was simply adhered to by the personnel on the ground in Rwanda who refused to leave.

Anyidoho's decision to stay in Rwanda to try to save lives was his alone. He communicated the decision to his government in the Ghanaian capital of Accra as a self-evident fact, and the government agreed to it retrospectively. Anyidoho's decision to stay in combination with the efforts of Dallaire and his force, it has been estimated that up to 30,000 Rwandans lives were saved.

After leaving Rwanda in 1994, Anyidoho was reassigned to the post of special assistant to Ghana's minister of defence. He then embarked on a number of different appointments: as a member of the Organization of African Unity (OAU; later reconstituted as the African Union, AU) task force on the Mechanism for Conflict Prevention

Management and Resolution; as the UN expert who wrote the major discussion document at the initial meeting of the Heads of the Armed Forces of the OAU in Addis Ababa in June 1996; and in 2004, as the team leader of UN observers for the Cameroon-Nigeria Mixed Commission. Soon after this, Anyidoho was made team leader of another UN mission—an Assistance Cell providing strategic advice to the African Union on Darfur, following which he became coordinator of UN Support to the AU Mission in Sudan, or AMIS. This gave him a unique qualification for his next post; in 2005 he was appointed by the secretary-general of the African Union and the United Nations secretary-general as the joint special representative for the AU-UN Hybrid Operation in Darfur (UNAMID).

In 1997, Anyidoho published *Guns over Kigali,* his memoir of the Rwandan Genocide. Dallaire's own book on Rwanda, *Shake Hands with the Devil*, appeared in 2003, and corroborated much of what Anyidoho had recalled earlier. The conclusion to be drawn from both works is that the courage and resourcefulness of Anyidoho and his Ghanaian troops did a lot to keep the residual UNAMIR force in place in Rwanda, maintaining a UN presence in the country when the preference from New York was otherwise one of removing that presence altogether. Anyidoho, who was later decorated with the Distinguished Service Order for Gallantry, must thus be considered a major force behind the protection of tens of thousands of Rwandan Tutsis and moderate Hutus, who, through his actions, were saved from certain death.

Paul R. Bartrop

See also: Bystanders; Dallaire, Roméo; International Reactions; United Nations Assistance Mission for Rwanda (UNAMIR); Rwandan Genocide, French Response to; Rwandan Genocide, U.S. Response to the

Further Reading

Anyidoho, Henry Kwami. *Guns over Kigali: the Rwandese Civil War, 1994.* Accra: Woeli Pub. Services, 1997.

Dallaire, Roméo. *Shake Hands with the Devil: The Failure of Humanity in Rwanda.* Toronto: Random House, Canada, 2004.

Evans, Glynne. *Responding to Crises in the African Great Lakes.* Oxford: Oxford University Press, 1997.

Klinghoffer, Arthur Jay. *The International Dimension of Genocide in Rwanda.* New York: New York University Press, 1998.

Arusha Accords

The Arusha Accords were a set of comprehensive protocols signed in Arusha, Tanzania, on August 4, 1993, that were intended to end the three-year-long Rwandan Civil War. In October 1990, the Rwandan Patriotic Front (RPF) launched an attack from southern Uganda into Rwanda, which resulted in the Rwandan Civil War between Rwanda's Hutu government and exiled RPF members. The Arusha Accords intended to institute a governmental power-sharing arrangement in Rwanda. The accords were also designed to foster the formation of a popularly elected democratic regime in Rwanda. The talks took place chiefly between the sitting Rwandan government and the RPF. Most of the terms of the Arusha agreements, which were cosponsored by the Organization of African Unity (a United Nations coalition representing African interests), France, and the United States, were never carried out.

The main negotiations in Arusha commenced on July 12, 1992, and lasted until

June 24, 1993. From July 19 to July 25, 1993, concluding talks were conducted in Rwanda. Although the resulting accords covered a host of issues, including refugee resettlement and the makeup of the Rwandan military, the main focus was on neutralizing President Juvénal Habyarimana's dictatorial rule, cobbling together a broad-based transitional government, and preparing Rwanda for the transition to a permanent, popularly elected, multiparty, and multiethnic national government.

The RPF was to be included in the national assembly, and the Rwandan military was to be divided so that 60 percent of its forces came from the established government's army, and 40 percent from the RPF. Of the 21 cabinet posts in the proposed transitional government, the ruling party was granted 5; the RPF was also to receive 5; the remaining positions were to be divided among the 4 other major parties. The transitional government was to be in place within 37 days of the signing of the accord, and that regime would last no longer than 22 months, after which elections had to be held. As the negotiators attempted to implement the accords, which required numerous meetings in Arusha, it was clear that Habyarimana and the Hutu-dominated government intended to delay their implementation for as long as possible. Indeed, no transitional government was formed.

On April 6, 1994, as Habyarimana and Burundian president Cyprien Ntaryamira (a Hutu) were returning to Kigali from a meeting in Arusha, a missile shot down their plane and killed the presidents. Who fired the missile remains unknown, but Rwanda's Hutu-dominated government nevertheless blamed the Tutsis and the RPF. The incident was the tipping point that escalated the Rwandan Civil War into genocide.

Paul G. Pierpaoli Jr.

See also: Burundi; Burundi, Genocide in; Habyarimana, Juvénal; Rwandan Civil War; Rwandan Genocide, French Response to the; Rwandan Genocide, U.S. Response to the; Rwandan Patriotic Front

Further Reading

Ali, Taisier M., and Robert O. Matthews. *Civil Wars in Africa: Roots and Resolution.* Toronto: McGill-Queen's University Press, 1999.

Shaw, Martin. *War and Genocide: Organized Killing in Modern Society.* Cambridge, UK: Polity, 2003.

Smith, M. James, ed. *A Time to Remember. Rwanda: Ten Years after Genocide.* Retford, UK: The Aegis Institute, 2004.

AVEGA-AGAHOZO

AVEGA-AGAHOZO is a non-profit Rwandan organization formed in January 1995 to help survivors of the 1994 Rwandan Genocide. The name AVEGA-AGAHOZO is partly an acronym for *L'Association des Veuves du Génocide*, or Association of Genocide Widows. Founded by 50 Rwandan widows who lost their spouses during the genocide, the organization's initial mission was to extend financial, material, and moral support to the many thousands of Rwandans left widows and orphans after the genocide. AVEGA-AGAHOZO was formally recognized by the Rwandan government on October 30, 1995. In 1997, the organization expanded its reach by establishing regional and local offices throughout Rwanda. The headquarters remains in Kigali.

AVEGA-AGAHOZO sponsors many programs that benefit genocide victims such as medical care, psychological counseling, education, vocational training, legal aid, and housing and shelter. Medical care and counseling have been especially important for the hundreds of thousands of women and girls who were raped or abused during the genocide. At least 47,000 women are currently receiving medical services through AVEGA-AGAHOZO. These same medical facilities have also played a critical role in testing for HIV and treating patients with AIDS. The organization has also helped and encouraged victims to testify in trials against genocide perpetrators.

In more recent years, AVEGA-AGAHOZO has broadened its mission to support orphaned children who became the heads of households. AVEGA-AGAHOZO also seeks to bring together its members so that they may engage in mutual support and encouragement, foster closer cooperation with similar aid groups, memorialize the events and victims of the genocide, seek justice for victims, and pursue reconciliation and reconstruction efforts within Rwanda. In 2012, AVEGA-AGAHOZO's membership stood at some 25,000 widows and more than 71,000 orphans and dependents. At the time of writing this (2017), AVEGA-AGAHOZO membership is around 20,000, which includes 1,686 who are over 70 years

of age, 732 members who have lost all nuclear family members, 1599 individuals who contracted HIV from sexual assault during the genocide, and 1,122 children born out of rape that occurred during the genocide.

AVEGA-AGAHOZO has also successfully pressured the Rwandan legislature to do more to support women. The organization lobbied the government to reform its inheritance laws and as a result the government passed the Rwandan Succession Law of 1999 that established equal inheritance rights to land for women and men. In 2009, the Rwandan government enacted the country's first gender-based anti-violence law, which was accomplished largely through the efforts of AVEGA-AGAHOZO.

Paul G. Pierpaoli Jr.

See also: Kigali Genocide Memorial; Rape

Further Reading

Smith, M. James, ed. *A Time to Remember. Rwanda: Ten Years after Genocide.* Retford, UK: The Aegis Institute, 2004.

Waller, James. *Becoming Evil: How Ordinary People Commit Genocide and Mass Killing.* Oxford: Oxford University Press, 2002.

"Who we are," AVEGA AGAHOZO, http://avega.org.rw/who-we-are/.

B

Bagosora, Théoneste

During the 1994 Rwandan Genocide, Colonel Théoneste Bagosora held the position of Minister of Defence in the Rwandan government. A Hutu, Bagosora was born on August 16, 1941, in the Giciye commune of the Gisenyi prefecture, an area from which Rwandan president Juvénal Habyarimana also originated. From this background, he became linked to the Akazu, the so-called "Little Hut"—the inner circle of Habyarimana's associates, dominated by the president's wife, Agathe Habyarimana. During the genocide, Théoneste controlled elite units in the armed forces.

The son of a schoolteacher, Bagosora spent his whole career in the Rwandan Armed Forces (the *Forces Armées Rwandaises*, or FAR). In 1964, he graduated from Kigali's Officers' School (*École des officiers*), with the rank of second lieutenant. He then continued his studies in France, where he obtained a diploma in Advanced Military Studies from the French Military School. He was later appointed second-in-command of the *École supérieure militaire* (Higher Military School) in Kigali, after which he received promotion to the rank of colonel, with command over the important Kanombe military camp. He remained there until June 1992, when he was appointed as *directeur du cabinet* (director of the cabinet) in Rwanda's Ministry of Defence. Despite his official retirement from the military on September 23, 1993, he retained this position until fleeing the country in the final days of the genocide in July 1994.

Bagosora is widely considered the mastermind of the genocide and started planning for the annihilation of Tutsis years in advance. By 1990, he had reportedly developed a plan to eliminate Rwandan Tutsis. Despite being present at the discussions between the Rwandan government and the Tutsi-led Rwandan Patriotic Front (RPF), he was an impassioned opponent of the 1993 Arusha Accords, the ceasefire agreement brokered between the Rwandan government and the Tutsi-led Rwandan Patriotic Front. His opposition to the Accords was rooted in his hatred of Tutsis; he wanted nothing to do with the RPF and had no interest in allowing Tutsis to hold positions of power within the government. Bagosora publicly stated that the Tutsis would be wiped out if the RPF continued its fight against Rwanda and/or if the Arusha Accords were enforced.

On December 4, 1991, President Habyarimana set up a military commission to answer the question, "What must be done to defeat the enemy in military, propaganda and political terms?" Habyarimana appointed Bagosora to coordinate an appropriate response. The resultant report was nothing other than an incitement to hatred employed by high-ranking officers who encouraged and facilitated revulsion and ethnic violence. The widely circulated report referred to Tutsis and moderate Hutus as enemies of the state and the Hutu majority.

As early as 1992, Bagosora reportedly had the Rwandan army's general staff draw up lists of all those who were thought to be associated with the RPF. Ultimately, such lists were used by the military and the

Colonel Théoneste Bagosora, the alleged mastermind of the Rwandan Genocide, was found guilty by the International Criminal Tribunal for Rwanda on December 18, 2008. He was the most senior military official convicted by the Tribunal and his trial helped prove that the mass murder of Rwandan Tutsis constituted genocide. (Kennedy Ndahiro/AFP/Getty Images)

Interahamwe militias to locate, capture, and kill Tutsis and moderate Hutus during the genocide. Beginning in early 1993, Bagosora is known to have had weapons distributed to militias and other extremist Hutus.

Assuming effective control of Rwanda after April 6, 1994, most accounts consider Bagosora as being the man responsible for coordinating the genocide of Rwanda's Tutsi population following Habyarimana's assassination on that date. He is said to have issued the order on April 7, 1994, for the military to begin the killing. And he allegedly issued the order that roadblocks be set up

across Rwanda to capture and kill fleeing Tutsis and moderate Hutus.

Immediately after Habyarimana's assassination, Bagosora and a few other officers established a "Crisis Committee" to work out what to do next. The head of the United Nations Assistance Mission for Rwanda (UNAMIR), Canadian general Roméo Dallaire, contacted Bagosora in the hope of providing some direction and oversight for the country. Bagosora proposed having the military take control of the political situation until they could hand it over to the politicians, but Dallaire rejected this, emphasizing that Rwanda still had a working government led by the next in line to the succession, Prime Minister Agathe Uwilingiyimana. Within hours, however, Uwilingiyimana was murdered, one of the first casualties of the genocide. Bagosora and his associates then set up an interim government comprised of extremist Hutus dedicated to one essential objective—the elimination of the Tutsis and any Hutus who stood in their way.

With the end of the genocide and the victory of the RPF in July 1994, Bagosora disappeared. It was later learned that he had first fled to neighboring Zaire (now the Democratic Republic of the Congo), after which he moved to Yaoundé, Cameroon, where he lived from July 1995 until his arrest on March 9, 1996.

The International Criminal Tribunal for Rwanda (ICTR), based in Arusha, Tanzania, had long been interested in Bagosora, and indicted him soon after its inception in 1994. Upon being located and arrested in Cameroon, Bagosora was transferred to the UN prison quarters in Arusha on January 23, 1997, to face 13 counts of 11 different international crimes relating to genocide, crimes against humanity, and war crimes. At his first appearance before the Tribunal, he entered a plea of not guilty. The trial began on April 2,

2002, simultaneously with three others: Brigadier General Gratien Kabiligi, former chief of military operations in the FAR; Lieutenant Colonel Anatole Nsengiyumva, former military commander of Gisenyi Military Camp; and Major Aloys Ntabakuze, former commander of the Kanombe Paracommando Battalion, Kigali. The joint proceedings became known as "Military Trial 1."

Preparation for the trial took up an enormous amount of the Tribunal's time before finally getting underway. It was only on October 14, 2004, that the prosecution's case concluded, with the trial finishing on June 1, 2007. On December 18, 2008, the ICTR found Bagosora, Ntabakuze, and Nsengiyumva guilty of genocide, crimes against humanity, and war crimes. Overall, Bagosora was convicted of 10 counts of eight different crimes, including genocide, murder, extermination, rape, persecution, other inhumane acts, two counts of violence to life, and outrages upon personal dignity. Bagosora was sentenced to life imprisonment.

His trial was one of the most important cased heard before the Tribunal because it established the government's intent—a key component in proving genocide—to annihilate Tutsis and moderate Hutus. As such his trial addressed such points as to how the genocide was planned and carried out at the highest levels of the Rwandan military, as well as the relationship between the army and extremist Hutu politicians.

On December 14, 2011, Bagosora's life sentence was reduced to 35 years.

Paul R. Bartrop

See also: Arusha Accords; Forces Armées Rwandaises; Habyarimana, Agathe Kanziga; Interahamwe; Habyarimana, Juvénal; International Criminal Tribunal for Rwanda; Moderate Hutu; Rwandan Civil War; Rwandan Patriotic Front; Uwilingiyimana, Agathe

Further Reading

Melvern, Linda. *Conspiracy to Murder: The Rwandan Genocide.* London: Verso, 2006.

Off, Carol. *The Lion, The Fox and The Eagle: A Story of Generals and Justice in Rwanda and Yugoslavia.* Toronto: Random House Canada, 2000.

Bahutu Manifesto

The *Bahutu Manifesto* was a sociopolitical declaration issued on March 24, 1957, in Rwanda, which was then under Belgian rule. The 10-page manifesto was the work of nine Hutu intellectuals, including Catholic archbishop André Perraudin, and played a key role in fomenting anti-Tutsi sentiment among Rwanda's Hutu majority.

The declaration included decrees and goals that took aim at Tutsi power and privilege. First, it denounced the Tutsis' historic domination over the Hutu, which had begun in earnest under German rule. Second, it demanded the liberation of Hutu civilians from colonial European and Tutsi rule. Third, it called for the disenfranchisement of the Tutsis and a ban on intermarriage between Hutus and Tutsis. Fourth, it sought the imposition of racial quotas in all aspects of public life, including employment and education, which were to be advantageous to the Hutu. Fifth, it demanded the exclusion of Tutsi people from the Rwandan military. Finally, it argued that the Hutus were socially, culturally, and morally superior to the Tutsis. This claim was based upon faulty and outmoded thinking concerning racial differences and placed the blame for Rwanda's problems exclusively on the Tutsi people.

The *Bahutu Manifesto* certainly did not espouse many new ideas. In fact, it largely codified the thinking among many Hutus that had its origins dating back at least to the late 19th century. Both German and Belgian colonizers had historically favored the minority Tutsi, often ruling through the Tutsi-dominated monarchy. The Europeans typically viewed Hutu as inferior to the Tutsi because they generally had darker skin. This favoritism of the Tutsi deepened Hutu distrust of Tutsi.

Growing anger and frustration among the Hutus ultimately led to the *Bahutu Manifesto*. That document would become the ideological underpinning of the Hutus' drive to seize control in Rwanda and to eradicate the Tutsis and their influence. That effort began in earnest in 1959, when Hutu leaders ousted the Tutsi monarchy, a move that the Belgians tacitly supported. The Hutu Social Revolution spurred massacres of Tutsis and the forced exodus of at least 130,000 Tutsis from Rwanda. It also instituted a Hutu-dominated government for the next 30 years. In July 1962, the Belgians left the Rwandans to their own devices, freeing the nation of almost 80 years of colonial domination.

For decades thereafter, the Hutus dominated Rwandan politics and created an increasingly hostile environment for the Tutsis. This turn of events inspired the radicalization of exiled Rwandan Tutsis by the late 1980s, and in 1990 the Tutsi-led Rwandan Patriotic Front (RPF) launched an attack on Rwanda that sparked a three-year civil war between Rwanda's Hutu-led government and the RPF. The Hutus fought back, often brutally, creating a powder keg of racial tensions within the country. In April 1994, radicalized Hutus, employing the attitudes and language of the *Bahutu Manifesto*, commenced a mass genocide against Rwanda's Tutsis and moderate Hutus. In less than three months, 800,000 to a million persons had been murdered.

Paul G. Pierpaoli Jr.

See also: Hutu Social Revolution; Hutus; Rwandan Civil War; Rwandan Genocide, Role of Propaganda in the; Rwandan Patriotic Front; Tutsis

Further Reading

Kamukama, Dixon. *Rwanda Conflict: Its Roots and Regional Implications*. 2nd ed. Kampala, Uganda: Fountain Publishers, 1998.

Newbury, Catherine. *The Cohesion of Oppression: Clientship and Ethnicity in Rwanda, 1860–1960*. New York: Columbia University Press, 1988.

Straus, Scott. *The Order of Genocide: Race, Power, and War in Rwanda*. Ithaca, NY: Cornell University Press, 2008.

Barayagwiza, Jean-Bosco

Jean-Bosco Barayagwiza was an anti-Tutsi media executive in Rwanda, active before and during the genocide of 1994. He was born in 1950 in Mutura commune, in Gisenyi, western Rwanda. A lawyer by training who studied in the Soviet Union, he held the office of director of political affairs in Rwanda's Foreign Ministry. He was a cofounder, with Ferdinand Nahimana, of the "Steering Committee," (French: Comité d'initiative) which in turn established the anti-Tutsi radio station Radio-Télévision Libre des Mille Collines (RTLM). Prior to and during the genocide, the RTLM's broadcasts sustained the Hutu public's focus on the annihilation of the Tutsis and moderate Hutus.

Between 1990 and July 1994, Barayagwiza and others conspired to exterminate the civilian Tutsi population and eliminate members of the Hutu opposition. The components of their plan included the broadcasting of messages of ethnic hatred and incitements to violence, the training of militias, the distribution of weapons to anti-Tutsi militias, and the preparation and distribution of lists of people to be killed. Within his own district of Gisenyi, Barayagwiza allegedly presided over several meetings to plan these activities, and delivered weapons and money to help with the murders.

Barayagwiza's political party, the Coalition for the Defence of the Republic (the *Coalition Pour la Défense de la République*, or CDR), was established in February 1992. He set it up with his extreme racist Hutu colleagues Jean Shyirambere Barahinura, a former member of the Tutsi-led Rwandan Patriotic Front (RPF) who had defected, and Hassan Ngeze, the founder-owner of the radical newspaper *Kangura*. The CDR was intended exclusively for Hutus. Indeed, CDR members could not have parents or grandparents of Tutsi origin. Given the extremist outlook of its members, it almost seems befitting that the CDR established its own radical party militia movement in 1992, known as the Impuzamugambi ("those with the goal"). The CDR recruited its young members to join the militant group. Impuzamugambi was established to harass, assault, and ultimately murder Tutsis.

The CDR was fervently opposed to President Juvénal Habyarimana's negotiations with the RPF during 1993 and early 1994, and was in the forefront of those undermining his authority after the signing of the Arusha Peace Accords on August 4, 1993—the ceasefire agreement between the Rwandan Government and RPF. Unsurprisingly, after Habyarimana's assassination on April 6, 1994, the CDR entered into a coalition with the hastily formed interim government. Through the Impuzamugambi, the CDR was thus a major participant in the Rwandan tragedy. Working in concert with the Interahamwe, the Impuzamugambi killed thousands of Tutsis.

According to the prosecution of Barayagwiza by the International Criminal Tribunal for Rwanda (ICTR), he knew that members of the CDR killed Tutsis and moderate Hutus in Gisenyi, where he presided over the CDR since February 6, 1994. Furthermore, he allegedly conspired with Nahimana, Félicien Kabuga, and others to set up RTLM in order to promote the Hutu Power extremist ideology.

As Rwanda was progressively overrun by RPF troops in June and July 1994, Barayagwiza, along with most other high-ranking *génocidaires*, fled the country. He was arrested in Yaoundé, Cameroon, on March 27, 1996 on orders of the newly instated Rwandan government. After being jailed for 330 days without knowing the charges against him, he was transferred to Arusha, Tanzania, on November 19, 1997 to be tried by the ICTR. His previous lengthy imprisonment violated to ICTR standing orders, which stipulate that charges must be laid within 90 days of an arrest being made. Because of this breach of procedure, the ICTR was obliged to release him. He pleaded not guilty to all counts on February 23, 1998.

On March 31, 2000, the ICTR Appeals Chamber overturned its earlier decision, and directed that he stand trial. This, in turn, was consolidated into a larger proceeding, along with two other media executives involved in the genocide, Hassan Ngeze, former editor of the newspaper *Kangura*, and his cofounder of RTLM, Ferdinand Nahimana (who was also the former director of the Rwandan National Information Office, ORINFOR). Collectively known as the "Media Trial," the three were found responsible for creating a climate that implanted the idea of Tutsi annihilation onto the Hutu worldview long before the killing started.

All three were alleged to have conspired to set up RTLM to promote Hutu extremism and ethnic division, and to incite the murder and persecution of Tutsis. They were charged with several counts of genocide, public incitement to commit genocide, complicity in genocide, and crimes against humanity. According to the ICTR indictment, Barayagwiza allegedly presided over several meetings to plan the murder of Tutsis and moderate Hutus in Mutura commune, Gisenyi prefecture. He is also alleged to have assisted in the distribution of weapons and funds to the Interahamwe militia, and ordered murders and violent acts against Tutsis. Furthermore, it was stated that he knew or had reason to know that members of the CDR had participated in the killings of Tutsis and moderate Hutu in the Gisenyi prefecture.

Barayagwiza refused to participate in the trial, claiming that the judges were not impartial. On December 3, 2003, the trial chamber of the ICTR found him guilty on nine counts, and handed down a 35-year sentence. The Appeals Chamber affirmed his guilt on November 28, 2007, but only for the counts of instigating the perpetration of acts of genocide, for planning, ordering, or instigating the commission of a crime against humanity (extermination), and for instigating the perpetration of a crime against humanity (persecution). For this, his original sentence was reduced from 35 years in prison to 32 years, and on June 27, 2009, he was transferred to Akpro Missérété Prison in the Republic of Benin to serve out his sentence. He immediately appealed the sentence, and has continued to issue appeals in the intervening years. His last formal appeal was rejected by the ICTR on June 22, 2009.

Early on the morning of Sunday April 25, 2010, Jean-Bosco Barayagwiza died at the Centre Hospitalier Départemental de l'Ouémé, in Porto Novo, Benin. Earlier, on March 5, 2010, he had been admitted with an advanced case of hepatitis C. His family subsequently reported that he was denied adequate treatment, though this has yet to be verified.

Paul R. Bartrop

See also: Arusha Accords; Impuzamugambi; International Criminal Tribunal for Rwanda; *Kangura*; Media Trial in Rwanda; Moderate Hutu; Nahimana, Ferdinand; Ngeze, Hassan; Radio-Télévision Libre des Mille Collines

Further Reading

Barnett, Michael. *Eyewitness to a Genocide: The United Nations and Rwanda*. Ithaca, NY: Cornell University Press, 2002.

Beigbeder, Yves. *Judging War Criminals: The Politics of International Justice*. New York: St. Martin's Press, 1999.

Barril, Paul

Paul Barril is an expert in international security issues and special operations and for years worked in the French national police force (*Gendarmerie Nationale*), during which he was involved in a number of clandestine, and sometimes controversial, operations. He allegedly participated in the 1994 Rwandan Genocide, although the precise extent of his engagement remains unknown.

Barril was born on April 13, 1946, in Vinay, Isère, France, and earned a law degree from the University of Paris, Sorbonne. By the early 1970s, he had joined the Gendarmerie. Later he helped establish the National Gendarmerie Intervention Group (the *Groupement d'Intervention de la Gendarmerie Nationale*, or GIGN), which is a special forces unit usually involved in clandestine activities. From approximately 1974 until

1982, he served as the second officer of the GIGN, under Christian Prouteau, who commanded the unit. In 1982, Barril was tapped to establish and supervise a counterterrorist unit under orders of French president François Mitterand. He remained in this post until the early 1990s and left the Gendarmerie in 1995. In 1979, he helped the Saudi Arabian government quash an uprising by fundamentalist Muslims at the Grand Mosque in Mecca, the holiest site in all of Islam.

While working in the GIGN, Barril established several private security firms, beginning in 1984, through which he worked for several world leaders and foreign governments, including the Ivory Coast. Sometime in the late 1980s, Barril formed the private security firm Société d'Études de Conception et de Réalisation d'Equipements Techniques de Sécurité (known by the acronym SECRETS), which provided security consultations for foreign nations. Many of the operations performed by SECRETS took the form of covert armed intervention, special operations, and mercenary equipage and training.

Perhaps Barril's most controversial actions involved Rwanda. His company was reportedly retained in 1989 to reorganize Rwanda's intelligence service. According to some sources, his company was enlisted to provide an efficiency audit of Rwanda's army in 1990. Barril allegedly worked as a high-level military and security adviser to Juvénal Habyarimana, Rwanda's Hutu president from 1973 to 1994. At the same time, it has been suggested that Barril and other French agents were arming and training extremist Hutus who later on became the leaders of the Rwandan Genocide. Some of these Hutus likely set up the assassination of President Habyarimana, which provided the catalyst for the mass killings of Tutsis and moderate Hutus beginning in April 1994.

After Habyarimana's plane was shot down as it neared the airport in Kigali on April 6, 1994, Agathe, the president's widow, supposedly retained the services of SECRETS to find the perpetrators of her husband's assassination. Barril claimed publicly that he believed Rwandan Patriotic Front operatives, led by Tutsi Paul Kagame, took the plane down with shoulder-fired missiles. That helped stir Hutu outrage and sparked the genocide that would follow. After the genocide, Barril continued to work for the temporarily Hutu-led government. Much of Barril's involvement in the events in Rwanda remains sketchy and fragmentary, and some reports were based on Barril's own claims, which should be viewed with some skepticism.

Paul G. Pierpaoli Jr.

See also: Habyarimana, Agathe Kanziga; Habyarimana, Juvénal; Hutus; Kagame, Paul; Moderate Hutu; Rwanda; Rwandan Genocide, French Response to the; Rwandan Genocide, Role of Propaganda in the; Rwandan Patriotic Front; Tutsis

Further Reading

Des Forges, Alison. *Leave None to Tell the Story: Genocide in Rwanda.* New York: Human Rights Watch, 1999.
Straus, Scott. *The Order of Genocide: Race, Power, and War in Rwanda.* Ithaca, NY: Cornell University Press, 2008.

Beardsley, Brent

Brent Beardsley worked as an infantry offer in the Royal Canadian Regiment for over 25 years and retired at the rank of major. Prior to and during the 1994 Rwandan Genocide, Beardsley served as the Personal Staff Officer to General Roméo Dallaire, Force Commander of the United Nations

Assistance Mission for Rwanda (UNAMIR). As a staff officer in Rwanda, Beardsley witnessed the horrors of genocide and in its aftermath testified against Colonel Théoneste Bagosora (the alleged architect of the genocide) at the International Criminal Tribunal for Rwanda (ICTR).

Born in Ottawa on November 25, 1954, he was raised in Montréal, Canada. He graduated from a pre-Arts program at Sir George Williams University in 1974, completed a BA in history from Concordia University in 1977, and undertook a postgraduate diploma in education at McGill University in 1978. In the same year, he joined the Canadian army. As an officer in the Royal Canadian Regiment, he has held a wide range of command, staff, and training positions, and has served four tours of duty in Norway, Germany, and Cyprus. He has been employed as an instructor on the Basic Officer Training Course, helped author the first draft of the Canadian Forces Peacekeeping Manual, and was the chief instructor of the Canadian Forces Peacekeeping Training Centre.

During the 1990s, he served with the Canadian delegation to the United Nations in New York, prior to being sent in 1993 as operations manager (effectively chief of staff and personal assistant) to Dallaire. He was thus ideally placed as an eyewitness to the genocide in Rwanda, both as an observer and as a participant who tried to mitigate the suffering of those around him and stop the killing.

Beardsley was disgusted when the UN Security Council voted on April 21, 1994, to reduce UNAMIR from 2,500 troops to just 270. Together with Dallaire and his second-in-command, General Henry Kwami Anyidoho of Ghana, Beardsley watched with increasing frustration and anger as the UN Department of Peacekeeping Operations in New York consistently refused to see the genocide as anything other than a civil war into which the UN could not intrude. In an interview years later with Frontline Beardsley explained, "It was almost to the point where you know you want to get on the phone and just yell in to it 'Is there anybody alive out there?' The world just didn't care and it made no difference what you said or how you said it to them."

Many of the challenges Beardsley and Dallaire faced in Rwanda were later committed to paper in an award-winning memoir the two co-authored entitled *Shake Hands with the Devil: The Failure of Humanity in Rwanda* (2003). Beardsley is also active in promoting awareness of the Rwandan Genocide and its survivors. To this end he has spoken at universities and in other public forums, has taken part in numerous documentaries, written articles, and participated in commemorative events relating to the Rwandan Genocide. In February 2004, Beardsley testified at the ICTR in Arusha, Tanzania, in the trial of Théoneste Bagosora, the alleged architect of the Rwandan Genocide.

Building on his experiences in Rwanda and elsewhere, Beardsley continues to urge Canadians to re-examine the way they view national security. If environmental and humanitarian crises are left unchecked, Beardsley argues that they can have a profound effect on national security by becoming a source of conflict in the future. People living without hope or an opportunity to improve their lives, for whom survival is a day-to-day struggle, can become so frustrated that they turn to violence. While these issues are not of themselves a threat to comfortable middle-class security in the West, a failure to prevent or stop them can lead them to escalate to the point that humanitarian crises become security threats. An immediate and preferred solution, Beardsley argues, would be to begin the promotion of democracy in developing nations.

On July 18, 1995, Brent Beardsley was awarded the Meritorious Service Cross, presented by the governor-general of Canada, for his heroic actions in Rwanda. He is also a recipient of the Canadian Forces Decoration for his many years of military service. In September 2006, Beardsley was named as a fellow of the Montréal Institute of Genocide and Human Rights Studies, at Concordia University.

Paul R. Bartrop

See also: Anyidoho, Henry Kwami; Bagosora, Théoneste; Bystanders; Dallaire, Roméo; International Criminal Tribunal for Rwanda; Support Hope, Operation; United Nations Assistance Mission for Rwanda

Further Reading

Anyidoho, Henry Kwami. *Guns Over Kigali: The Rwandese Civil War, 1994. A Personal Account.* Accra: Woeli Publishing Services, 1997.

Dallaire, Roméo. *Shake Hands with the Devil: The Failure of Humanity in Rwanda.* Toronto: Random House, Canada, 2004.

"Interview: Major Brent Beardsley," Frontline (1 April 2004), http://www.pbs.org/wgbh/pages/frontline/shows/ghosts/interviews/beardsley.html.

Bicamumpaka, Jérôme

Jérôme Bicamumpaka was the minister of Foreign Affairs and Cooperation in Rwanda's interim government between April 9 and mid-July, 1994. The interim government was directed by Hutu extremists close to the so-called Akazu clique, an informal organization of relatives and close friends of President Juvénal Habyarimana and his wife Agathe. As foreign minister, Bicamumpaka was responsible for, and exercised authority over, all government policy on foreign affairs. In this position, he attended cabinet meetings where he was informed about the sociopolitical situation in the country and apprised of Hutu extremist policy.

Bicamumpaka, a Hutu, was born in 1957 in Mukono, Ruhondo commune, in Ruhengeri district. From late 1990 until July 1994, he is said to have become wholly dedicated to planning the annihilation of Rwanda's Tutsi population. In support of this aim, Bicamumpaka allegedly organized, ordered, and participated in the massacres that took place after President Habyarimana's death on April 6, 1994 sparked the genocide. Bicamumpaka has been accused of conspiring with other senior figures in Rwanda, notably Théoneste Bagosora, to plan the genocide.

It is alleged by the International Criminal Tribunal for Rwanda (ICTR) that Bicamumpaka knew—or from his position of power, should have known—that those in his department had committed or were about to commit crimes involving the massacre of Tutsis and moderate Hutus. Between April 8 and July 14, 1994, a wide variety of public officials working for Bicamumpaka, from ministers to civil servants and the police, ordered, encouraged, committed, and helped to commit these massacres, in such districts as Butare, Kibuye, Kigali, Gitarama, and Gisenyi, and did nothing to prevent them or punish the perpetrators. The ICTR has further alleged that between April 11 and July 14, 1994, Bicamumpaka and other ministers traveled to several of these same districts to supervise the implementation of the interim government's orders, particularly in matters of civil defense and security. The ICTR concluded that Bicamumpaka knowingly failed in his duty to ensure the security of all Rwandans and consciously participated in the massacres from a command position.

By mid-July 1994, the forces of the interim government were in full retreat before the advance of General Paul Kagame's Rwandan Patriotic Front. Bicamumpaka fled Rwanda, and sought sanctuary in Cameroon. It was here that he was arrested, at the request of the ICTR prosecutor, on April 6, 1999. On July 31, 1999, he was transferred to the UN prison complex in Arusha, Tanzania.

Bicamumpaka was indicted on May 7, 1999. The charges levied against him were

Jérôme Bicamumpaka, the Rwandan foreign affairs minister during the genocide, smiles at reporters on November 6, 2003, before his hearing in the International Criminal Tribunal for Rwanda in Arusha, Tanzania. Ultimately, the court found that it lacked sufficient evidence to convict Bicamumpaka and he was acquitted of all charges on September 30, 2011. Of the 93 individuals indicted, he was one of only 14 defendants acquitted by the court. (Stella Vuzo/AFP/Getty Images)

conspiracy to commit genocide, genocide, complicity in genocide, direct and public incitement to commit genocide, murder as a crime against humanity, extermination as a crime against humanity, rape as a crime against humanity, and war crimes. At his first court appearance, on August 17, 1999, he refused to plead either guilty or not guilty to any of the charges, and so, in accordance with the ICTR statute, the judges concluded that he had pleaded not guilty.

At the request of the prosecutor, Bicamumpaka's case was joined with those of three other members of the interim government: Casimir Bizimungu, the minister of health; Justin Mugenzi, the minister of trade and industry; and Prosper Mugiraneza, the minister of the civil service. The joint proceedings, referred to as the "Government II Trial," opened in Arusha, Tanzania on November 6, 2003, before the second trial chamber of the ICTR. By June 23, 2005, the prosecution had presented its arguments. Then, on October 31, 2005, with the trial still underway, Bicamumpaka was partially acquitted of various counts in the indictment, namely, rape as a crime against humanity, outrages upon personal dignity as a war crime, and conspiracy to commit genocide insofar as his superior responsibility was concerned.

On June 12, 2008, the evidence phase of the trial was closed and on November 22, 2008, the defense filed its closing brief. The case was completed in December 2008. The prosecutor called for the maximum penalty available to the ICTR—life imprisonment. On September 30, 2011, in a verdict that surprised many, the tribunal acquitted Jérôme Bicamumpaka of all charges. He was immediately released from custody, and reunited with his family.

Paul R. Bartrop

See also: Akazu; Bagosora, Théoneste; Habyarimana, Agathe Kanziga; Habyarimana, Juvénal; International Criminal Tribunal for Rwanda

Further Reading

Boot, Machteld. *Genocide, Crimes Against Humanity, War Crimes: Nullum Crimen Sine Lege and the Subject Matter Jurisdiction of the International Criminal Court.* Antwerp: Intersentia, 2002.

Melvern, Linda. *Conspiracy to Murder: The Rwandan Genocide.* London: Verso, 2006.

Bikindi, Simon

Simon Bikindi was a well-known composer, director, and singer of popular music in Rwanda before and during the Rwandan Genocide in 1994. He was born on September 28, 1954, to Hutu farmers in Akanyirabagoyi, a village in the Gisenyi Province in northwestern Rwanda. After the genocide, when on trial for his role in the killings, he recounted how he inherited his love of music from his parents. His mother was a singer, dancer, and narrator invited to perform at popular festivals and his father, a blacksmith, played the Rwandan sitar in his free time. At school, Bikindi made a name for himself among his peers by playing a combination of modern and regional music from his home province.

As a popular recording artist, Bikindi was in effect a propagandist for the extremist Hutu cause against the country's Tutsis. His songs included the following:

- *Twasezereye Ingoma Ya Cyami* (*We Said Good-Bye to the Monarchy*), which was performed for the first time in 1987 during the celebrations for the 25th anniversary of independence. Here, Bikindi criticized the monarchy that was overthrown in 1959, celebrating instead the end of feudalism and colonization that came with independence in 1962. This song, which was played constantly on Radio Rwanda and Radio Télévision Libre des Mille Collines (RTLM) in 1992 and 1993, was a public appeal for Hutus to band together to oppose the Arusha Accords, the power-sharing agreement signed in August 1993 between the Hutu Power president of Rwanda, Juvénal Habyarimana, and the Tutsi-led Rwandan Patriotic Front (RPF).

- *Akabyutso* (*The Little Awakening*) was a song expressing Bikindi's hatred of those Hutus who did not live up to the highest standards of proper behavior expected of a Hutu—those who did not look out for their fellow Hutus, who were mean with money, who forgot the old days of the Tutsi hegemony, or who were disparaging of other Hutus.

- *Bene Sebahinzi* (*The Descendants of Sebahinzi*) praised the significance and value of the 1959 Hutu revolution.

- *Impuruza* (*Warning*), composed in 1993, alerted listeners to the danger of a Tusi ascendancy.

Bikindi's songs were comprised of popular and catchy tunes that mixed Kinyarwanda (the official language of Rwanda) lyrics with French and English words in a style that combined rap and folk melodies, and through this he became Rwanda's most famous and popular singer. Prior to the genocide, he directed the famous Irindo ballet, and was also a civil service official in the Ministry of Youth and Sport, as well as a member of President Juvénal Habyarimana's ruling party, the National Republican Movement for Development and Democracy (the *Mouvement Républicain National pour le Développement et la Démocratie*, or MNRDD).

When the Rwandan Civil War between the Hutu-led government and the Tutsi rebels of the RPF began in October 1990, Bikindi was already the most popular singer in Rwanda. It has been alleged that from then on Bikindi contributed to a government-run media campaign designed to stir up anti-Tutsi hatred. He was said to have composed and performed songs that encouraged the Interahamwe and the civilian population to murder Tutsis. He recorded songs with anti-Tutsi lyrics that were in turn broadcast repeatedly across the radio. It has been further alleged that in the months prior to the genocide Bikindi consulted with President Habyarimana, Minister of Youth and Sports Callixte Nzabonimana, and officers from Rwanda's military forces about the lyrics of certain anti-Tutsi songs.

Although Bikindi left the country a few days before the start of the killing in April 1994, it was well known that throughout the genocide, Hutu killers sang Bikindi's songs as they slaughtered Tutsis. When groups of extremist Hutus went searching for Tutsis to kill, they often sang the songs they had heard on RTLM, and radio appeals to attack the Tutsis were often preceded or followed by Bikindi's music. His songs were therefore a crucial part of the genocidal project, as they helped incite the ethnic hatred of Tutsis and encouraged mass murder.

Bikindi returned to Rwanda later in June 1994, and it has been alleged that he participated actively in massacres of Tutsis, reportedly recruiting, training, and supervising the Interahamwe militia in Gisenyi. He was also said to have personally ordered the execution of some victims. With the advance of the RPF he fled to Zaire (now known as the Democratic Republic of the Congo), alongside most of Rwanda's Hutu militia,

military, and government officials. There, he continued singing and playing to Hutu groups.

On July 12, 2001, Bikindi was arrested in a center for asylum seekers in Leiden, Holland. He fought calls from Rwanda for his extradition and requested asylum, but on March 27, 2002, he was transferred to Arusha, Tanzania to await trial by the International Criminal Tribunal for Rwanda (ICTR). The ICTR indicted him with conspiracy to commit genocide; genocide, or alternatively complicity in genocide; direct and public incitement to commit genocide; and murder and persecution as crimes against humanity. On April 4, 2002, he appeared before the ICTR and pleaded not guilty on all counts.

The trial began on October 2, 2006, and took 61 days. Closing arguments were heard on May 26, 2008, when the prosecution demanded a sentence of life imprisonment, arguing that Bikindi should be convicted on the basis of his personal participation in planning and instigating acts of genocide and the murder of Tutsi civilians. The defense used the argument of Bikindi exercising his right of freedom of expression, but the judges rejected this argument. On December 2, 2008, Bikindi was found guilty on the count of direct and public incitement to commit genocide, and sentenced to 15 years in prison, with credit for the seven years he had already served in custody. This was the only count among the six for which he had been charged that could stick. The judges held that all the songs under discussion had been written before 1994, and thus before the period covered in the ICTR statute. They also found that there was not enough evidence to prove that Bikindi had played a role in the dissemination of the songs via RTLM, even though that radio station had played the songs throughout the genocide.

Bikindi appealed, arguing that he had never killed anyone and that he could not stop the *génocidaires* from singing his songs. The appeals chamber of the ICTR rejected Bikindi's appeal in its entirety on March 18, 2010 and upheld the original conviction and sentence.

Simon Bikindi was the first performing artist to have been brought before an international court and charged with using his creativity to incite genocide. For some legal and human rights commentators, this presented problematic elements of humanitarian justice, given that artistic expression and its influence is an extremely broad field leading to a variety of interpretations. It came as something of a relief, therefore, that a judgment was not rendered in this area, and that Bikindi was found guilty on other grounds.

In post-genocide Rwanda since 1994, his songs have been banned from national radio stations.

Paul R. Bartrop

See also: Arusha Accords; Habyarimana, Juvénal; Interahamwe; International Criminal Tribunal for Rwanda; Radio-Télévision Libre des Mille Collines; Rwandan Genocide, Role of Propaganda in the

Further Reading

Jokic, Aleksandar, ed. *War Crimes and Collective Wrongdoing: A Reader.* Malden, MA: Blackwell Publishers, 2001.

Kressel, Neil Jeffrey. *Mass Hate: The Global Rise of Genocide and Terror.* New York: Plenum Press, 1996.

Bisengimana, Paul

Paul Bisengimana was mayor of Rwanda's Gikoro Commune in the Kigali-rural Prefecture who was indicted and found guilty by the International Criminal Tribunal (ICTR) for his role in the Rwandan Genocide of 1994. Bisengimana was born circa 1945 in the commune of Gikoro. By the early 1990s, he had become its mayor and was allied with the Interahamwe, a Hutu paramilitary organization with strong ties to the Hutu-dominated government in Rwanda. This organization was a decentralized militia force that operated throughout the country, especially in provincial towns and the rural countryside.

As the mayor of the Gikoro Commune, Bisengimana was tasked with carrying out orders from the central government; he therefore exercised complete control over administrative subordinates as well as the local police force. Between late 1990 and mid-1994, he took part in the planning and implementation of policies designed to harass, persecute, and murder scores of Tutsis living in the area under his control. He helped arm local factions of the Interahamwe, established lists of those to be displaced or killed, and personally took part in the rape, mutilation, and mass murder of Tutsis.

Between January 1 and April 30, 1994, Bisengimana met repeatedly with other individuals implicated in the genocide, even holding some of the meetings at his home. At the same time, he helped procure arms for the Interahamwe and incited its members to kill Tutsis and others who opposed the national government. Around April 8, 1994, Bisengimana reportedly raped a Tutsi woman who worked in the commune's administrative offices. That same day, he exhorted Interahamwe members to rape and kill Tutsi women. Some two days later, he gave the order to kill at least 200 Tutsi refugees. Three days later, he led a group of Tutsi refugees to a church, assuring them that their safety would be guaranteed. Soon thereafter, he ordered their mass executions; the women were first mutilated, then raped, and finally killed. Bisengimana, who reportedly took part in the killings, then ordered that the corpses be discarded in a mass grave.

In June or July of 1994, as Tutsi opposition forces began closing in on the commune, Bisengimana fled the country, eventually settling in Mali, where he was arrested on December 4, 2001. At his trial, he pled guilty to the charges and was sentenced to 15 years in prison.

Paul G. Pierpaoli Jr.

See also: Interahamwe; International Criminal Tribunal for Rwanda; Rape

Further Reading

Melvern, Linda. *Conspiracy to Murder: The Rwanda Genocide*. Rev. ed. London: Verso, 2006.

Straus, Scott. *The Order of Genocide: Race, Power, and War in Rwanda*. Ithaca, NY: Cornell University Press, 2008.

Bizimungu, Augustin

Augustin Bizimungu was the chief of staff of the Rwandan Armed Forces (French: Forces Armées Rwandaises, or FAR) before and during the Rwandan Genocide of 1994. An ethnic Hutu, Bizimungu was born in Nyange, Byumba prefecture, in northern Rwanda on August 28, 1952. He was a career soldier and was steadily promoted. On April 6, 1994, the day President Juvénal Habyarimana's death sparked the start of the genocide, Bizimungu held the rank of lieutenant colonel and was responsible for military operations in the Ruhengeri prefecture. It was alleged that from late 1990 onwards Bizimungu conspired with other radical Hutus in planning the annihilation of Tutsi civilians and all Hutus who opposed it.

Bizimungu's hatred of Tutsis preceded the genocide. A clear example of his early prejudice was his opposition to the Arusha Peace Accords, a treaty signed between the Rwandan government and the Rwandan Patriotic Front (RPF) in August 1993 intended to end the Rwandan Civil War. In February 1994, he stated that if the RPF attacked again, he did not want to see one Tutsi left alive in his sector. According to the International Criminal Tribunal for Rwanda (ICTR) indictment of Bizimungu, Bizimungu had supervised the training of the soldiers and militia groups (the Interahamwe in particular) who carried out the genocide. Such training was conducted simultaneously in several prefectures around the country, including Bizimungu's zone of operations in the Ruhengeri prefecture. Bizimungu was alleged to have distributed weapons to militiamen either by personally handing them out or by issuing them through his subordinates, mayors, and district councilors.

On April 16, 1994 Bizimungu was promoted to major general and appointed as head of the army. The former army chief of staff, Déogratias Nsabimana, died in the same plane crash that had killed Rwandan president Juvénal Habyarimana on April 6, 1994. His promotion, which he retained until July 1994, crowned Bizimungu's military career. From this position, he was the leading military figure involved in negotiations with the United Nations Assistance Mission for Rwanda (UNAMIR).

From April to July 1994, officers of the army general staff, one of whom was Bizimungu, allegedly participated in daily briefings at which they were informed of the massacres of the civilian Tutsi population and of moderate Hutus. It has been further alleged that these higher echelon officers ordered, encouraged, and backed the massacres. Around May 18, 1994, during a

The International Criminal Tribunal for Rwanda sentenced Augustin Bizimungu, the former chief of staff of the Rwandan army, to 30 years in prison for his role in the 1994 Rwandan Genocide. Under Bizimungu's command, soldiers and national policemen massacred tens of thousands of Tutsi civilians, many of whom had taken shelter in churches, schools, and hospitals. His arrest and conviction were important steps on the path to justice after the genocide. (AFP/Getty Images)

meeting at which Bizimungu was present, these officers were reported to have been pleased with the performance of the Interahamwe and underlined the need to provide them with better weapons.

Within his own locality of Ruhengeri, Bizimungu was allegedly aware that his subordinates were about to commit (or had already committed) crimes, but did nothing to prevent them or punish the perpetrators. Between April 10–15, 1994, several Tutsis sought refuge in the Ruhengeri prefecture. On orders from Bizimungu, armed civilians killed some of these refugees. To cover up the massacre Bizimungu allegedly ordered

that a message be played on the radio that blamed the RPF for the death of the refugees.

In July 1994, faced with the advance of the RPF, Bizimungu fled Rwanda and found sanctuary in Angola among the National Union for the Total Independence of Angola (Portuguese: União Nacional para a Independência Total de Angola, or UNITA), an Angolan rebel group. The post-genocide government of Rwanda accused Bizimungu of various anti-Tutsi activities after the genocide had ended. The most damning charge was that, as the former head of the FAR and de facto head of the Interahamwe, he orchestrated various attacks against Rwandans while in exile in the Democratic Republic of the Congo after 1994.

On April 12, 2002, the ICTR issued an arrest warrant for Bizimungu, who was finally discovered hiding among demobilized UNITA militants. He was arrested by the Angolan government in Luena, northeastern Angola, on August 12, 2002, and transferred to the prison quarters of the United Nations in Arusha, Tanzania on August 14. The charges he faced were conspiracy to commit genocide, genocide or alternatively complicity in genocide, three counts of crimes against humanity, and war crimes. He was also charged with specific additional crimes and command responsibility for crimes committed by his subordinates. The acts covered within Bizimungu's indictment included murder, extermination, and rape; he was also charged with directly ordering acts to be committed against Tutsis and, by way of his omissions, in failing to halt the acts of his subordinates. At his initial court appearance on August 21, 2002, Bizimungu pleaded not guilty to all of the nine counts with which he was charged.

At the request of the chief prosecutor, the ICTR then ordered a combined trial for

Bizimungu and three other senior officers of the FAR on the same counts. They were: Augustin Ndindiliyimana, chief of staff of the National Gendarmerie; François-Xavier Nzuwonemeye, commander of the Reconnaissance Battalion of the Rwandan army; and Innocent Sagahutu, second-in-command of the Reconnaissance Battalion. According to a new indictment dated August 23, 2004, Bizimungu was also accused of having participated in a plan conceived in the early 1990s to exterminate the Tutsi population through acts which included the training of the Interahamwe.

The trial of Augustin Bizimungu and his co-accused, known as "Military Trial 2," opened on September 20, 2004, before the Second Trial Chamber of the ICTR. At the beginning of the trial, he once more pleaded not guilty to all charges. The trial was completed on June 29, 2009. On May 17, 2011, Bizimungu was sentenced to 30 years in prison.

Paul R. Bartrop

See also: Forces Armées Rwandaises; Habyarimana, Juvénal; Interahamwe; International Criminal Tribunal for Rwanda; Rape; Rwandan Civil War; United Nations Assistance Mission for Rwanda

Further Reading

Kressel, Neil Jeffrey. *Mass Hate: The Global Rise of Genocide and Terror.* New York: Plenum Press, 1996.

Neier, Aryeh. *War Crimes: Brutality, Genocide, Terror, and the Struggle for Justice.* New York: Times Books, 1998.

Booh-Booh, Jacques-Roger

Jacques-Roger Booh-Booh is a former foreign minister of Cameroon and Special Representative of the Secretary-General (SRSG) of the United Nations (UN) in Rwanda between November 1993 and June 1994. In the latter capacity, he was the senior UN civilian official in Rwanda during the time of the Rwandan Genocide.

Booh-Booh was born on February 5, 1938, in Manak, Cameroon, when the country was still a French colony. After Cameroon's independence on January 1, 1960, the country sought to develop an autonomous foreign policy within the Western bloc. In this context, Booh-Booh chose a career as a diplomat in the Ministry of External Relations. He rose through the ranks to become head of the Department of African Affairs, director for Asia and Africa, and deputy permanent representative to the UN. As a foreign representative, he was ambassador to Morocco, Greece, and the United Nations Educational, Scientific and Cultural Organization (commonly referred to as UNESCO), before his most prestigious postings as ambassador to the Soviet Union (1981-1983) and later France (1983-1988). On May 16, 1988, he became Cameroon's minister of external relations.

In November 1993 Booh-Booh took up his position as the head of the United Nations Assistance Mission for Rwanda (UNAMIR). The UN Security Council Resolution 872 had been established on October 5, 1993, for the purpose of helping to implement the Arusha Peace Agreement signed in Arusha, Tanzania, on August 4, 1993, by the primarily Hutu government of Rwanda and the Tutsi-led Rwandan Patriotic Front (RPF). The Arusha Accords were a set of five agreements intended to end the Rwandan Civil War. The talks leading to Arusha had been co-sponsored by the United States, France, and the Organization of African Unity, and addressed a variety of topics, including refugee resettlement, power-sharing between

Hutu and Tutsi, the introduction of an all-embracing democratic regime, the dismantling of the military dictatorship of President Juvénal Habyarimana, and the encouragement of a transparent rule of law throughout Rwanda.

In monitoring the Accords, UNAMIR's mandate was to supervise the cease-fire, establish and expand the demilitarized zone and demobilization procedures, provide security for the Rwandan capital city of Kigali, monitor the security situation during the final period of the transitional government's mandate leading up to elections, and assist in the coordination of humanitarian assistance activities in conjunction with relief operations. UNAMIR was under-resourced, and provided with poorly equipped and trained troops from a variety of small and impoverished nations. UNAMIR had a huge job to do, but only a small force of approximately 2,548 military personnel with which to do it.

As SRSG, Booh-Booh's role was to act as chief executive officer of the mission, reporting directly to Secretary-General Boutros Boutros-Ghali. His relationship with UNAMIR's force commander, General Roméo Dallaire, was far from effective. Handpicked by Boutros-Ghali, with whom Booh-Booh was a personal friend, the SRSG's role was supposedly to report back to New York jointly with Dallaire. It has been widely alleged, however, that Booh-Booh regularly undervalued and miscalculated the implications of Dallaire's reports that were in some instances based directly on intelligence gathered from Hutu informers. Other accusations have been that Booh-Booh refused to acknowledge the lethal nature of the Hutu Power threat, or how organized and centralized the killing arrangements were, and that he rarely showed up at the UN headquarters in Kigali. After the genocide began in April 1994,

moreover, some claim that he became less and less available to provide appropriate leadership when the military command was calling for it. Also, according to RPF claims based on secret message intercepts, Booh-Booh allegedly had close ties to the leaders of the Hutu militants.

Despite Dallaire's attempts to minimize deaths and participate actively as a peacekeeper during the genocide, he and Booh-Booh appeared to be working on different teams. In the aftermath of a series of murders of Tutsis in late February 1994, Booh-Booh reported to UN headquarters that there was no evidence that the killings had been "ethnically motivated," notwithstanding advice from Dallaire (operating on a tip from a former key member of the Interahamwe militia in January) that this was precisely what it was.

Booh-Booh considered that both the military and the civilian branches of UNAMIR were under the orders of the SRSG, and he did not see himself as being accountable to Dallaire. One of the points of the Arusha Accords was that neither side—the Tutsi rebels nor the Rwandan government—should rearm, but Booh-Booh held that Dallaire was not impartial when it came to the rearmament of the RPF. He informed Boutros-Ghali of these problems and criticized Dallaire for not sharing intelligence with him. He noted correctly that Dallaire's relationship with Habyarimana was strained, and held the force commander responsible for the diplomatic breakdown between UNAMIR and the Rwandan president.

Many in the international community voiced concern about just how impartial Booh-Booh really was for someone in his position. Not only were he and Habyarimana good friends, he was also close with the leadership of the extremist Hutu-dominated Republican Movement for National

Democracy and Development (French: Mouvement Républicain National pour Démocratie et le Développement, or MRNDD) and was associated some of the most notorious leaders of the 1994 Rwandan Genocide, including Théoneste Bagosora.

In April 2005, Booh-Booh responded to his critics by publishing *Le Patron de Dallaire Parle* (*Dallaire's Boss Speaks*). He denounced Dallaire's actions before and during the genocide. He accused Dallaire of aiding the RPF, and claimed that Dallaire did not report to him the events of the night April 6, 1994, when the plane carrying Habyarimana and the president of Burundi, Cyprien Ntaryamira, was shot down. It was this act that triggered the genocide of Rwanda's Tutsi population and the death of the Hutu liberal middle class over the next three months. And he claimed that Dallaire did not inform him that ten Belgian officers had been murdered on April 7, an act which ultimately inspired a wholesale pullout of UN military contributions to UNAMIR.

Booh-Booh's role in Rwanda as SRSG has been the subject of harsh criticism from Dallaire and many of his senior staff officers, foremost among whom have been Major Brent Beardsley and General Henry Anyidoho, who have contended that he played an instrumental role in forestalling preventive action against the Hutu *génocidaires* even before President Habyarimana's plane was shot down. Booh-Booh was eventually dismissed as SRSG, ostensibly because he left the country in May 1994 without UN permission. He was replaced as SRSG on July 1, 1994, by Shahryar Khan of Pakistan, who remained in this role until 1996.

Paul R. Bartrop

See also: Bystanders; Dallaire, Roméo; Habyarimana, Juvénal; International Reactions; United Nations Assistance Mission for Rwanda

Further Reading

Booh-Booh, Jacques-Roger. *Le Patron de Dallaire Parle: Révélations sur les dérives d'un général de l'ONU au Rwanda*. Paris: Duboiris, 2005.

Dallaire, Roméo. *Shake Hands with the Devil: The Failure of Humanity in Rwanda*. Toronto: Random House, Canada, 2004.

Burundi

Burundi is a landlocked country located in the African Great Lakes region of East Africa. It lies south of Rwanda, west of Tanzania, and east of the Democratic Republic of the Congo. It is slightly smaller than the U.S. state of Maryland and of its 11 million inhabitants, 85 percent are ethnic Hutus, 14 percent are Tutsis, 1 percent are Twa, 3,000 are Europeans, and 2,000 are South Asians.

The earliest inhabitants of Burundi are the Twa Pygmies. They were followed by the Bantu-speaking Hutus, who arrived between 500 BCE and 1000 CE and soon outnumbered the Twa. The Nilotic Tutsi migrated into the area from the northeast between the 1400s and 1600s and in the 1700s established a Tutsi kingdom and several states. The Tutsi king governed other Tutsis and the more-numerous Hutus in a feudal system.

German colonists seized Burundi (Urundi) in 1890, incorporating it and neighboring Rwanda (Ruanda) into German East Africa. At the time, Germany did not even have an outpost in the territory and it governed primarily through indirect rule. Following Germany's defeat in World War I, the League of Nations handed over control of Urundi-Ruanda to Belgium in 1919.

At the end of World War II, Urundi-Ruanda became a UN (United Nations) Trust Territory, with Belgium continuing as its administrator. In 1958, Prince Louis Rwagasore—a pro-independence prince with strong ties to the Hutu community—formed the Union for National Progress (French: Union pour le Progrès National, or UPRONA). In UN-supervised elections held in September 1961, UPRONA won 58 of the 64 seats. The king's son, Louis Rwagasore, served as prime minister for two weeks before being assassinated. His brother-in-law, Andre Muhirwa, succeeded him. Full independence came on July 1, 1962, following the granting of internal self-government and the establishment of Burundi and Rwanda as two separate states. The Tutsi king, Mwami Mwambutsa IV, headed the freshly independent Burundi nation.

Hutu-Tutsi tensions grew during the first years of independence. Despite overall Tutsi political dominance, Hutu candidates captured most seats in 1965 parliamentary elections. The king, however, appointed a Tutsi to serve as prime minister and a group of Hutu police responded by staging a coup attempt. Loyalist police put down the rebellion, but the king fled the country and was deposed in abstensia the following year by his son Charles. Charles later became Mwami Ntare V. In the wake of the coup attempt, almost all of the country's Hutu political elite were executed and most of the army's Hutu officers were purged.

In November 1966, Prime Minister Captain Michel Micombero ousted King Ntare V and declared Burundi a republic, with himself as president. Hutus staged another rebellion in 1972, again provoking a swift and harsh reaction from the Tutsi government, which proceeded to execute virtually all Hutus with higher education, as well as all remaining Hutu army officers. An estimated 100,000 to 200,000 people were killed in the massacres, which prompted thousands of Hutus to flee the country. Ntare

V was also killed during the unrest. The following year, Micombero formed a seven-member presidential bureau with himself as president and premier. In 1974, the government adopted a new constitution that declared UPRONA to be the sole governing party. Micombero became secretary-general of UPRONA and was reelected president.

For the next three decades, Burundi fell under the military rule of a group of Tutsi-Hima all from the Bururi province: Michael Micombero (1966–76), Jean-Baptiste Bagaza (1976–87), and Pierre Buyoya (1987–93). Throughout this period, UPRONA was the dominant party.

In 1976, Micombero was overthrown in a bloodless coup led by Lieutenant Colonel Jean-Baptiste Bagaza, his neighbor from Rutovu commune in Bururi. Burundi adopted a new constitution in November 1981, and in so doing reconfirmed Burundi's one-party system and mandated a popularly elected National Assembly. In October the following year, Burundi held legislative elections, and in July 1984, Bagaza was elected president. During this period, Hutus were all but excluded from government. By 1985, for example, out of 20 cabinet members, 4 were Hutu, out of 65 MPs, 17 were Hutu, out of the 52 members of UPRONA's Central Committee, only 2 members were Hutu, and out of 22 total ambassadors, only one was Hutu (Uvin 2009: 10).

In September 1987, Major Pierre Buyoya accused President Bagaza of corruption and took control of the country while the president was abroad. Buyoya suspended the constitution, dissolved the legislature, and formed a 30-member ruling party, the Military Committee for National Salvation.

Ethnic violence flared again in August 1988, when Hutus killed several hundred Tutsis in two northern towns, claiming they had been provoked. The government deployed soldiers of the Tutsi-dominated army to the region and widespread massacres of Hutus followed. Estimates of the number of Hutus killed range from 5,000 to 20,000. Several months later, Buyoya took steps to encourage national unity by appointing a Hutu majority to the Council of Ministers, including a Hutu prime minister. He also authorized an investigation into the August massacres, pledged to eliminate discrimination against Hutus, and announced new measures to give Hutus equal educational and employment opportunities.

Over the next few years, progress toward a more democratic political system continued, culminating in the adoption of a new multiparty Burundi Constitution in March 1992 and democratic presidential elections followed in June 1993. The winner of those elections, Melchior Ndadaye, became the nation's first Hutu president. Strongly committed to ethnic reconciliation, Ndadaye appointed a Tutsi prime minister and named Tutsis to several other cabinet posts. Just three and a half months after his inauguration, however, Ndadaye and a number of his government ministers were killed in a military coup led by Tutsi army officers. The coup collapsed within several days—with army leaders asking remaining government members to resume control—but not before setting off a new wave of ethnic violence that left as many as 100,000 to 200,000 people dead.

Foreign Affairs Minister Sylvestre Ntibantunganya, a Hutu and a close friend of Ndadaye, was chosen to serve as interim president for several months before the legislature elected Cyprien Ntaryamira as president in January 1994. Three months later, Ntaryamira and Rwandan president Juvénal Habyarimana were killed in a suspicious plane crash and consequently Ntibantunganya again assumed control of Burundi. The legislature elected him to fill the post of president on a permanent basis in October 1994, not long after the nation's various political factions had signed a new power-sharing agreement. But the power-sharing agreement did little to resolve the ongoing ethnic conflict and killings on both sides have been a constant in recent years.

The fighting reached a new peak in March 1995, when Tutsi extremists—allegedly backed by army troops—went on a rampage in the capital, killing hundreds of Hutus as Ntibantunganya proved unable to rein in the Tutsi-dominated army. Escalating violence throughout 1995 and into 1996 prompted fears of widespread massacres, similar to the ones in neighboring Rwanda during April–June 1994. Domestic and international observers expressed little hope about the chances of breaking the cycle of violence, but representatives of the Hutu-based Front for Democracy in Burundi and UPRONA opened talks on the issue in late April 1996.

In late July 1996, the Tutsi-dominated army staged a coup, ousting Ntibantunganya's government and naming Pierre Buyoya once again as president. Buyoya claimed that he accepted the position because he wanted to halt the escalating ethnic violence. The international community strongly condemned the coup, however, and several neighboring nations imposed an economic blockade.

In the following years, representatives of Hutu rebels and Buyoya's military government held talks, but the Hutu-Tutsi conflict endured. Both sides took steps toward peace after former South African president Nelson Mandela took charge of peace negotiations in December 2000, but still violence continued to plague the country. In July 2001, Buyoya and most of Burundi's political parties signed a power-sharing agreement that established a transitional government in which he would remain head of state for 18 months, after which a Hutu would assume the office. The country's two main rebel groups rejected the agreement, and fighting intensified just days after the transitional government was sworn in on November 1, 2001.

After a Hutu, Domitien Ndayizeye, assumed the office of president in a peaceful transfer of power in April 2003, the rebel Forces for the Defense of Democracy (French: Forces pour la Défense de la Démocratie, or FDD) began negotiating with Ndayizeye's government. However, the other main Hutu rebel group, the National Liberation Forces (French: Forces Nationales de Libération, or FNL) maintained that Ndayizeye's presidency made little difference as long as the military was still dominated by Tutsis. As a result of peace talks, FDD rebels joined Ndayizeye's government in November 2003, but the FNL continued to fight the government.

Paul R. Bartrop

See also: Burundi, Genocide in; Habyarimana, Juvénal; Hutus; Rwanda; Tutsis

Further Reading

Lemarchand, René. *Burundi: Ethnic Conflict and Genocide*. New York: Cambridge University Press, 1997.

Uvin, Peter. *Life After Violence: A People's Story of Burundi*. New York: Zed Books, 2009.

Webster, John B. *The Political Development of Rwanda and Burundi*. Syracuse, NY: Maxwell Graduate School of Citizenship and Public Affairs, Syracuse University, 1966.

Weinstein, Warren, and Robert Schrire. *Political Conflict and Ethnic Strategies: A Case Study of Burundi*. Syracuse, NY: Syracuse University Press, 1976.

Burundi, Genocide in

Sometimes referred to as Rwanda's "false twin," Burundi has a great deal in common with its neighbor to the south, including its small size (28,000 square kilometers), high population density (180 per square kilometers), traditional political systems (both were monarchies), colonial heritage, and ethnic map. Of a population of some eight million, 15 percent are Tutsi and 74 percent are Hutu. Furthermore, both Rwanda and Burundi have experienced bloodshed on a genocidal scale. Despite their similarities the violence in Burundi was by no means a carbon copy of the Rwandan Genocide: there are notable differences in the magnitude of the bloodshed, and unlike what happened in Rwanda, the victims were Hutu. Though largely forgotten by the outside world, the killing of anywhere from 200,000 to 300,000 Hutu in 1972 at the hands of a predominantly Tutsi army remains deeply etched in the collective memory of Burundians.

The roots of the genocide are inscribed in the particularities of the country's ethnic configurations and history. Its social structure, though strikingly like that of Rwanda, was more complex. Similar to Rwanda, Burundi's population was composed of Tutsi, Hutu, and Twa with the Hutu accounting for the vast majority of the population. In the 16th century, society was organized according to family and clan structures. The Tutsi monarchy was led by the king (*mwami*). A princely class, known as the *ganwa*, mediated between the king and the masses. The Tutsi minority was sharply divided into two separate sub-categories: the high-ranking *Banyaru-guru* clan (generally located in the north), and the lowly *Hima* clan (generally located in the south). Among Hutu, rank and privilege had a great deal to do with family origins. All this meant that the political system had none of the sharply defined fractures typical of Rwanda, ensuring a relatively smooth transition to self-government. With considerable support from both Hutu and Tutsi, the nationalist party Union for National Progress (French: Union pour le Progrès National, or UPRONA), founded in 1960 and led by Prince Rwagasore (King Mwambut-sa's eldest son), easily won a majority of the seats in parliament. The assassination of Rwagasore in 1961 by a Greek gunman in the pay of the opposition party, the Christian Democratic Party (French: Parti Démocrate Chrétien, or PDC), only enhanced the legitimacy of Rwagasore's party.

With Burundi's independence from its colonizers in 1962, the social landscape underwent a radical change. The emergence in Rwanda of a Hutu-dominated republic served as a powerful pole of attraction for the Hutu of Burundi and of repulsion for the Burundian Tutsi. As their efforts to gain a meaningful share of power proved unavailing, Hutu leaders in Burundi felt their only option was the use of force. On October 18, 1965, Hutu anger erupted in an abortive coup directed at the king's palace, followed by sporadic attacks against Tutsi elements in the interior. In reprisal, Tutsi units of the army arrested and shot 86 leading Hutu politicians and army officers, many affiliated with the pro-Hutu Party of the People (French: Parti du Peuple, or PP). Allegations by the government of a Hutu plot in 1969, led to the arrest of another 70 Hutu personalities, civilian and military, of whom 19 were executed. After the king's decision to leave the country in 1965, the Burundi National Army, led by

Colonel Michel Micombero, a Tutsi, emerged as the key player.

The turning point came in April 1972 with the outbreak of a local peasant uprising in the southern region of Rumonge and Nyanza-Lac, causing hundreds and possibly thousands of deaths among Tutsi civilians. In a matter of hours, terror was unleashed by Hutu upon Tutsi. The response of the Micombero government was immediate and unforgiving. Following a brutal repression in rebel-held localities, the army, assisted by the pro-UPRONA youth group, the Rwagasore Youth Revolutionists (French: Jeunesses Révolutionnaires Rwagasore, or JRR), proceeded to launch a nationwide manhunt, arresting and killing almost every Hutu male in sight. What began as a repression quickly morphed into genocide. Some of the most gruesome scenes of the genocide took place at the university in the capital, Bujumbura, and in secondary and technical schools. In a scenario that would repeat itself again and again, groups of soldiers and members of the JRR would suddenly appear in classroom, call students by name and take them away. Few ever returned. Additionally the Church, the civil service, the army were systematically purged of Hutu elements. Exactly how many died is impossible to determine. If the figure of 300,000 cited by Boniface Kiraranganiya, a Tutsi observer, may seem excessive, most informed observers would agree that at least 200,000 perished.

Although there is widespread agreement that the Hutu insurgents represented a tiny minority, and included a sprinkling of non-Hutu elements from eastern Congo, their underlying motives are a matter of controversy. The commonly accepted view that the insurrection can best be described as a local peasant rebellion with limited aims, i.e., the removal of specific grievances, such as bringing an end to Tutsi exactions and

The 1994 Rwandan Genocide is connected in countless ways to the 1972 genocide in Burundi. While the victims of the Rwandan Genocide were Tutsi, during the Burundian Genocide they were the perpetrators. Seen here is an example of the ethnically charged violence that plagued the Great Lakes region (Burundi, the Democratic Republic of Congo, Kenya, Rwanda, Tanzania, and Uganda) for decades. These murdered Hutu were discovered on a road near Bujumbura, Burundi, on May 27, 1972. (Bettmann/Getty Images)

privileges, has been challenged by two well-known experts, the French historian Jean-Pierre Chrétien and the Belgian journalist Jean-Francois Dupaquier. In their co-authored volume on the events of 1972, *Burundi 1972: Au bord des génocides*, they make the argument that the insurrection had as its ultimate objective the physical elimination of the Tutsi community. Put differently, they argue that what many described as a genocide of Hutu was really designed as a preventative measure intended to avert a genocide of Tutsi. Owing to the limited evidence offered by the authors, their argument is less than compelling.

Just as it is inaccurate to claim that all Hutu should be held responsible for the

killings of Tutsi, the genocidal response of the army and youth groups cannot be imputed collectively on all Tutsi. Only a small number of extremists in the government, the army, and the JRR were actively involved in the decision to carry out the carnage. The planning of the genocide was conducted by Artémon Simbabaniye, the Minister of Foreign Affairs at the time, Albert Shibura, the Minister of Interior and Justice, and André Yanda, the executive secretary of the ruling UPRONA party. As the social profile of the victims makes clear, the government's aim was to systematically kill all educated Hutu elements, including civil servants, teachers, agronomists (experts in soil management and the production of field crops), university students and school-children, and to eliminate any perceived challenge to Tutsi domination for the fore-seeable future.

One of the most puzzling questions raised by the Burundi bloodbath relates to the silence of the international community. Although the horrors sweeping across the country were accurately relayed to Washington by the U.S. embassy deputy chief of mission (DCM) Michael Hoyt, soon confirmed by a devastating report by The Carnegie Endowment for International Peace, *Passing-By: The United States and Genocide in Burundi* (1972), the reaction of the U.S. State Department was conspicuously low-key, reflecting U.S. Secretary of State Henry Kissinger's view at the time that, however regrettable, the mass killings of Hutu did not pose a major threat to the U.S. national interests. Hardly more edifying was the response of the UN secretary-general, Kurt Waldheim, who blandly expressed his fervent hopes that peace, harmony, and stability could be restored successfully and speedily. Even more astounding was the official statement released by the Organization of African Unity (OAU), through its secretary-general, Diallo Telli, who said that he and the OAU stood in total solidarity behind the government and the people of Burundi. Behind the silence of the international community lies the obvious fact that very little was known at the time about the circumstances of slaughter (not unlike what happened in Rwanda 21 years later), or for that matter about Burundi. Equally important to bear in mind is that human rights issues had yet to acquire the saliency they have today. Again, at a time when the international concerns of Western nations were largely centered on the Cold War, the international community did not consider upending the bloodshed in Burundi as politically, economically, or militarily strategic. Nor did they feel especially concerned by the aftermath of the crisis.

What emerged from the carnage was a state utterly dominated by Tutsi elements. It would take another 16 years before a localized Hutu revolt again erupted in the north, in turn setting in motion a process of democratization that led to multiparty presidential and parliamentary elections in July 1993. The election of Melchior Ndadaye, the first popularly elected Hutu president, seemed a beacon of hope after Burundi's recent history. The sense of elation felt by the Hutu masses, however, proved to be short-lived. On October 21, 1993, Tutsi extremists in the army, acting in collusion with their civilian counterparts, assassinated Ndadaye. Hardcore Tutsi politicians and extremist members of the army were unwilling to relinquish what had previously been unfettered control of state institutions by the Tutsi to a newly elected Hutu president.

If any event helps account for the radicalization of anti-Tutsi sentiment in Rwanda, it is the death of Ndadaye. The death of a Hutu president at the hands of radical Tutsi elements provided the ideal propaganda for Hutus in neighboring Rwanda who sought to paint Rwandan Tutsis as an internal enemy and threat to Hutus. To understand Ndadaye's death, however, it is important to remember that the 1972 genocide set in motion the events that would eventually bring a Hutu to power and why some Burundian Tutsis felt it prudent to murder a Hutu who they perceived as a threat to their own status.

René Lemarchand

See also: Burundi

Further Reading

Brown, Michael, Gary Freeman and Kay Miller. *Passing-By: The United States and Genocide in Burundi, 1972.* New York: The Carnegie Endowment for International Peace, 1973.

Lemarchand, René, ed. *Forgotten Genocides: Oblivion, Denial and Memory.* Philadelphia: University of Pennsylvania Press, 2011.

Totten, Samuel, William S. Parsons, and Israel W. Charny, eds. *Century of Genocide: Eyewitness Accounts and Critical Views.* New York: Garland Publishing, 1997.

Bushnell, Prudence

Prudence Bushnell was a senior American administrator and diplomat. During the Rwandan Genocide, she worked tirelessly to keep the genocide at the forefront of her government's attention.

Bushnell was born in 1946 in Washington, D.C. The daughter of American diplomat Gerald Bushnell, as a child she experienced life in a range of diverse countries and cultures owing to her father's many overseas postings. These included periods growing up in Iran, Germany, France, and Pakistan. She was educated at the University of Maryland and Russell Sage College (a women's college located in Troy, New York). Upon graduating she worked as a management consultant in Texas, prior to joining the U.S. Foreign Service in 1981 as an administrative track officer. Her first assignment was in Mumbai, India, prior to serving as deputy chief of mission under Ambassador George Moose at the U.S. embassy in Dakar, Senegal.

In April 1993, President Bill Clinton appointed George Edward Moose Assistant Secretary of State for African Affairs and Bushnell joined him as deputy assistant secretary at the Africa Desk. Ultimately, she rose to the position of principal deputy assistant secretary of state, at a time marked by heightening tension in Africa. In one country, Rwanda, attempts had been made at resolving violence between hard-line Hutu nationalists espousing a culture of ethnic purity, and Rwandan Tutsi *émigrés* based in Uganda. The result was a set of five agreements signed by the Hutu-dominated government of Rwanda and the Tutsi-led Rwandan Patriotic Front (RPF) in Arusha, Tanzania, on August 4, 1993.

The Arusha Accords—cosponsored by the United States, France, and the Organization of African Unity—sought to bring an end to fighting between Rwanda's Hutu-dominated government and the Tutsi-led RPF. The Accords addressed a variety of topics, such as refugee resettlement, power sharing between Hutu and Tutsi, the introduction of democracy throughout Rwanda, the dismantling of the military dictatorship of President Habyarimana, and the establishment of a transparent rule of law throughout the country. In the months that followed the signing of the Accords, the parties involved met to discuss its implementation. This involved the parties traveling to and from Arusha, sometimes by road and at other times by plane. It was after one of these meetings, on April 6, 1994, that the plane carrying President Habyarimana of Rwanda and President Cyprien Ntaryamira of Burundi was shot down by a missile as the plane neared Kigali airport. All on board were killed, triggering the genocide of Rwanda's Tutsi population and the death of the Hutu liberal middle class over the next three months.

Just weeks before the genocide began, Bushnell went to Rwanda to try to impress upon President Habyarimana the importance of seeing the Arusha Accords implemented successfully. She cautioned him that failure to do so could cost Rwanda U.S. support in the future. On the same day as the president's assassination, Bushnell issued a memorandum to the State Department in which she predicted the likelihood of widespread violence following Habyarimana's death and urged the U.S. government to take immediate action to prevent large-scale killings.

In the weeks that followed, Bushnell was the U.S. State Department official most closely connected to developments in Rwanda. As news of the killings came across her desk she began calling Rwandan military officials to try to persuade them to stop the carnage. For the most part, she was either ignored or her pleas were treated with contempt. She also spoke by phone to the chief of staff of the Rwandan Armed Forces (French: Forces Armées Rwandaises, or FAR), Major General Augustin Bizimungu, warning him that President Clinton was holding him personally responsible for the killings then taking place. On April 28, Bushnell rang the head of the interim Hutu Power government, Théoneste Bagosora, warning him that the State Department was fully apprised of what was happening in Rwanda and ordering him on behalf of the United States to stop the killing and immediately arrange a ceasefire. While Bushnell's action was clearly a case of foreign intervention in the domestic affairs of a sovereign state, she was unrepentant about exceeding her authority in this instance. Elsewhere, Bushnell proposed reducing the effectiveness of the Hutu killers by jamming

Radio-Télévision Libre des Mille Collines (RTLM)—the radio and television station responsible for organizing and inciting racial violence—but permission to do this was denied as it was both too expensive and contrary to international (as well as American) law.

During and after the genocide, Bushnell remained at her post as deputy assistant secretary. In 1996 she was nominated by President Clinton to serve as U.S. ambassador to Kenya. In this role, she and her embassy were targeted on August 7, 1998, when a car bomb was detonated next to the embassy by Al-Qaeda terrorists. Twelve embassy staff and 212 Kenyan civilians were killed and Bushnell was cut by flying glass. Then, in 1999, Bushnell was appointed as U.S. ambassador to Guatemala, where she served until July 2002 prior to becoming dean of the Leadership and Management School at the Foreign Service Institute (the U.S. government's main training institution for officers and support personnel of the U.S. foreign affairs community) in Arlington, Virginia.

In 2005, Bushnell was portrayed in a made-for-television movie about the Rwandan Genocide, *Sometimes in April*, directed by Haitian-born filmmaker Raoul Peck. In this film, three-time Academy Award–nominated American actress Debra Winger explored Bushnell's daily dilemmas as she agonized over the inaction of U.S. policy towards Rwanda despite her constant pleas and attempts to stop the killing.

Overall, Prudence Bushnell was the only high-ranking American official to keep attention focused on the killing in Rwanda throughout the genocide. At the time, she was derided for this by many in the U.S. government, but she has since been applauded for her efforts, both in and outside the corridors of government in the United States.

Paul R. Bartrop

See also: Bizimungu, Augustin; Burundi; Burundi, Genocide in; Forces Armées Rwandaises; Habyarimana, Juvénal; International Reactions; Radio-Télévision Libre des Mille Collines; Rwandan Genocide, U.S. Response to the

Further Reading

Gribbin, Robert E. *In the Aftermath of Genocide: The US Role in Rwanda.* New York: I Universe, 2005.

Ronayne, Peter. *Never Again? The United States and the Prevention and Punishment of Genocide since the Holocaust.* Lanham, MD: Rowman & Littlefield Publishers, 2001.

Carlsson, Ingvar

Ingvar Carlsson is a Swedish politician. A former leader of the Swedish Social Democratic Party and prime minister, he was born the son of a warehouse worker in Boras, Sweden, on November 9, 1934. He studied social sciences at Lund University, graduating in 1958. In 1965, after completing his studies in economics at Northwestern University in Illinois, he was elected as a member of the Swedish parliament.

His political rise accelerated over time and his portfolio accumulated: minister of Education, 1969–1973; minister of Housing, 1973–1976; deputy prime minister, 1982–1986; and, following the assassination of Olof Palme in 1986, prime minister. In 1990, Carlsson resigned after failing to gain political endorsement for his economic reforms, but his cabinet was immediately reinstated upon amending its program. The Social Democrats lost the 1991 elections, but Carlsson returned to office after new elections in 1994. He was succeeded by Goran Persson as prime minister and party leader in 1996, and subsequently retired from politics.

In March 1999, UN secretary-general Kofi Annan approached him with an invitation to chair an inquiry into the actions of the United Nations during the 1994 genocide in Rwanda. Carlsson accepted the invitation, and eventually established a working group which included Han Sung-Joo, the former foreign minister of the Republic of Korea, and Lieutenant General Rufus M. Kupolati of Nigeria.

Ingvar Carlsson, a Swedish politician who twice served as Sweden's prime minister, was hired by the United Nations (UN) to lead an independent inquiry into the UN's actions during the 1994 Rwandan Genocide. The so-called Carlsson Report concluded that the UN had ignored evidence that the genocide was premeditated and had failed to act once the genocide had begun. (Francis Joseph Dean/Dreamstime)

After an exhaustive consultation and research process, the final report, comprising more than 150 pages, was completed on December 15, 1999. Officially entitled "Report of the Independent Inquiry into the Actions of the United Nations During the 1994 Genocide in Rwanda," it was divided into five parts and analyzed the key events associated with the genocide. Some of the key events the report noted were the Arusha Peace Agreement, the establishment of the United Nations Assistance Mission for Rwanda (UNAMIR), and the so-called Genocide Fax of January 11, 1994 (a message sent by General Roméo Dallaire to UN Headquarters in New York alerting the UN to the possibility of a genocide). Furthermore, it provided a lengthy list of conclusions citing failures on the part of the United Nations. These included the inadequacy of UNAMIR's mandate, confusions and failures to respond to the genocide, the effect of earlier events in Somalia, the lack of political will on the part of UN member-states, failures in protection and evacuation, and impediments to the flow of information. Most importantly, with an eye to the future, the authors included 14 strongly worded recommendations:

1. An action plan to prevent genocide,
2. Improving the capacity of the UN to conduct peace keeping operations,
3. Military preparation on the part of contributing member-states to "prevent acts of genocide or gross violations of human rights wherever they may take place",
4. Improving the early-warning capacity of the UN,
5. Improving protection of civilians,
6. Improving protection of UN personnel and staff,
7. Improving cooperation of UN personnel,
8. Improving the flow of information in the UN system,
9. Improving the flow of information in and to the Security Council,
10. Improving the flow of information on human rights issues,
11. Improving coordinating evacuation operations,
12. Re-addressing what membership in the Security Council means (in this regard, it may be noted that Rwanda itself was a member of the Security Council during the period of the genocide),
13. Supporting efforts to rebuild Rwanda, and
14. UN acknowledgement of its own responsibility (i.e. failure) for not having done more to prevent or stop the genocide.

A lengthy "Chronology of Events," detailing happenings between October 1993 and July 1994, was annexed to the report.

Carlsson's own view was that the Security Council had the power to have prevented at least some of the Rwandan tragedy, and was able to ensure such a tragedy did not happen again. The Security Council's decision to reduce the strength of UNAMIR after the genocide started—despite its knowledge of the atrocities—was, he concluded, the cause of much current bitterness in Rwanda towards the UN. Further general conclusions he drew were that in future the UN Secretariat must tell the Security Council exactly what is needed to bring about effective action, and that the Council must ensure that short-term financial constraints do not prevent its realization. The Council, moreover, must give missions the mandate they need, mobilize the necessary troops and resources, and accept its responsibility irrespective of where problems occur.

Upon its release, Kofi Annan declared that he fully accepted the Inquiry's conclusions. He argued that its recommendations merited very serious attention, and urged member states to engage in reflection and analysis aimed at improving the capacity of the United Nations to respond to various forms of conflict.

As a fitting extension to his involvement with the United Nations through the Inquiry, in 1995 Carlsson and Sir Shridath ("Sonny") Ramphal, the former secretary-general of the Commonwealth of Nations, co-chaired a United Nations Commission on Global Governance. The commission was established with the full endorsement of UN secretary-general Boutros Boutros-Ghali. The commission's report, "Our Global Governance," caused a controversy in some quarters, as it called for increased UN involvement in international development, security, globalization, and governance with complete disregard to state sovereignty.

The Carlsson Report on Rwanda suggested that serious attention would be given in the future to UN involvement in peacekeeping and humanitarian intervention activities. In light of a new report in January 2005, however, entitled "Report of the International Commission of Inquiry on Darfur to the United Nations Secretary-General," the lessons of the earlier tragedy would seem not to have been learned. A decade further on from Rwanda, there was still a reluctance to label Darfur as a true genocide, rendering Carlsson's strong recommendations ultimately meaningless so far as future action was concerned.

Paul R. Bartrop

See also: Carlsson Report; International Reactions; Rwandan Genocide, French Response to the; Rwandan Genocide, U.S. Response to the; United Nations Assistance Mission for Rwanda

Further Reading

Eltringham, Nigel. *Accounting for Horror: Post-Genocide Debates in Rwanda*. Londres: Pluto Press, 2004.

Scherrer, P. Christian. *Genocide and Crisis in Central Africa: Conflict Roots, Mass Violence, and Regional War*. Westport, CT: Praeger, 2002.

Carlsson Report

The Carlsson Report was officially released on December 16, 1999, and was the product of an independent commission of inquiry established by United Nations (UN) secretary-general Kofi Annan that investigated events preceding and during the genocide (October 1993 to July 1994). The commission was chaired by Ingvar Carlsson, the former prime minister of Sweden. Also on the commission were Lieutenant General Rufus M. Kupolati of Nigeria and Hang Sung-Joo, former foreign minister of South Korea. The report, officially entitled, "Report of the Independent Inquiry into the Actions of the United Nations during the 1994 Genocide in Rwanda," offered three key findings. First, it outlined a detailed chronology of the genocide. Second, it analyzed the failings of the international community and the UN in preventing or stopping the genocide. And lastly, it made a long list of recommendations to avert genocides in the future.

The report begins by giving a detailed history of events, commencing with the 1993 Arusha Peace Agreement (also known as the Arusha Accords), which ended the Rwandan Civil War. It then details the establishment of the United Nations Assistance Mission for Rwanda (UNAMIR), the downing of the Rwandan president's aircraft on January 11, 1994, which served as the immediate catalyst to the genocide, and other key events during the genocide.

Next, the report cites deficiencies on the part of the UN and international community that permitted the genocide to proceed unabated. The authors describe the failure of the UN to act on pre-genocide intelligence that strongly suggested a genocide was about to occur. The report also points to the UN and international community's lack of will to intervene in the genocide. Additionally, the study details the weak and conflicting UNAMIR policies and rules of engagement and a lack of communication among various UN departments and its offices in the field.

The most important—and illuminating—section of the Carlsson Report detailed recommendations to prevent or stop future genocides, some of which have now been formally adopted by the UN. They include: drafting formal plans to prevent genocide; improving UN peacekeeping missions; preparing member states' militaries to deal more effectively with genocide or mass human rights abuses; fine-tuning the UN's ability to foresee impending genocides; bolstering protections for civilian populations and UN peacekeepers; improving inter-UN communications; enhancing UN-supervised evacuation operations; clarifying UN Security Council membership; supporting reconciliation and reconstruction in Rwanda; and formally acknowledging the UN's failures in preventing and halting the Rwandan Genocide.

Paul G. Pierpaoli Jr.

See also: Arusha Accords; Carlsson, Ingvar; Dallaire, Roméo; Habyarimana, Juvénal; International Reactions; United Nations Assistance Mission for Rwanda; Rwandan Genocide, French Response to the; Rwandan Genocide, U.S. Response to the

Further Reading

Eltringham, Nigel. *Accounting for Horror: Post-Genocide Debates in Rwanda.* Londres: Pluto Press, 2004.

Scherrer, P. Christian. *Genocide and Crisis in Central Africa: Conflict Roots, Mass Violence, and Regional War.* Westport, CT: Praeger, 2002.

Coalition Pour la Défense de la Rèpublique

The Coalition for the Defense of the Republic (French: Coalition Pour le Défense de la République, or CDR) was a radical, extremist, and right-wing Hutu political party formed in February 1992. An offshoot of the National Revolutionary Movement for Development (French: Mouvement Révolutionnaire National pour le Développement, or MRND), the CDR pursued a virulent anti-Tutsi agenda. The CDR went on to create its own militia named Impuzamugambi, which in Kinyarwanda means "those with a single purpose." The extremist ideology propagated by the CDR and acted upon by its militia contributed to the 1994 Rwandan Genocide.

The CDR was created by Jean Shyirambere Barahinyura—a well-educated man and author—and led by fellow anti-Tutsi ideologues Jean-Bosco Barayagwiza, Hassan Ngeze, and Martin Bucyana. Barayagwiza was a high-ranking official with *Radio-Télevision Libre des Milles Collines*, a virulent propaganda vehicle and anti-Tutsi media outlet. Ngeze owned and edited the anti-Tutsi *Kangura* newspaper. Bucyana helped found and lead the CDR, but was murdered before the genocide began.

The CDR refused to admit any members who were Tutsi or had close Tutsi relatives. It was a major purveyor of hatred and intolerance toward the Tutsis and openly encouraged its membership to oppress, harass, intimidate, assault, and kill Tutsis. The party's slogan, "Watch Out!" was meant to intimidate Tutsis into submission. The CDR called for Hutu cultural supremacy, complete Hutu domination of the Rwandan government and other national institutions, and strict segregation between Tutsis and Hutus. It condemned any intermarriage between

Hutu and Tutsi and branded Hutu women who married Tutsi men as traitors. The CDR also forbade its members from doing any business with Tutsi establishments and threatened to banish from the party anyone caught doing so.

Initially, the CDR had supported Rwandan president Juvénal Habyarimana, but by 1993, it withdrew its support because the party flatly rejected the president's attempts to seek compromise and to accommodate the Rwandan Patriotic Front (RPF). After Habyarimana signed the August 4, 1993 Arusha Accords, which was an attempt to end the ongoing Rwandan Civil War, the CDR actively attempted to undermine the president's regime and broke ties with the MRND, which had agreed to the Arusha Accords. The CDR was now entirely divorced from Rwanda's main political landscape and was shut out of the transitional government. About the same time, it formed Impuzamugambi, which carried out many Tutsi killings during the genocide and harassed or killed Tutsis prior to that time.

After Habyarimana was assassinated on April 6, 1994, the CDR once again allied itself with the MRND and gained power in the shaky transitional government. The two parties now conspired to perpetrate genocide by blaming the Tutsis for the president's death and by alleging that the Tutsis had deliberately provoked a nationwide confrontation with the Hutus. The Impuzamugambi, along with the Interahamwe militia, were major perpetrators of the Rwandan Genocide.

After the genocide ended, the CDR was permanently banned. Several CDR leaders were also indicted and convicted by the International Criminal Tribunal for Rwanda as perpetrators of the Rwandan Genocide. They included Barayagwize, Ngeze, and Ferdinand Nahimana (a historian and one of the founders of Radio-Télévision Libre des Mille Collines).

Paul G. Pierpaoli Jr.

See also: Arusha Accords; Barayagwiza, Jean-Bosco; Habyarimana, Juvénal; Hutus; Impuzamugambi; Interahamwe; International Criminal Tribunal for Rwanda; Media Trial in Rwanda; Mouvement Révolutionnaire National pour le Développement (MRND); Nahimana, Ferdinand; Ngeze, Hassan; Radio-Télévision Libre des Mille Collines; Rwanda; Tutsis

Further Reading
Kressel, Neil Jeffrey. *Mass Hate: The Global Rise of Genocide and Terror.* New York: Plenum Press, 1996.

Melvern, Linda. *Conspiracy to Murder: The Rwandan Genocide.* London: Verso, 2006.

Valentino, Benjamin A. *Final Solutions: Mass Killing and Genocide in the Twentieth Century.* Ithaca, NY: Cornell University Press, 2004.

Waller, James. *Becoming Evil: How Ordinary People Commit Genocide and Mass Killing.* Oxford: Oxford University Press, 2002.

Congo, Democratic Republic of the

No other event in the history of the Democratic Republic of the Congo (DRC) has had a more profoundly destabilizing impact than the 1994 genocide in Rwanda. Besides triggering the rebellion that led to the violent overthrow of President Mobutu Sese Seko's 30-year dictatorship, and then to the assassination of his successor Laurent-Désiré Kabila in January 2001, the Rwandan carnage is the central element behind two of the most devastating wars experienced by the DRC and Central Africa. No less critical have been the aftereffects of these deadly conflicts. Much of the violence sweeping across the eastern provinces of North and South Kivu is indeed traceable to the priorities and policies set by Rwanda's president, Paul Kagame, in the wake of the genocide.

The DRC's location in Central Africa as well as it natural resources have created many problems for the Congo. The DRC (formerly known as the Republic of Zaire from 1971 to 1997) is slightly less than one-fourth the size of the United States, making it the eleventh largest nation in the world. It is boarded by nine countries: Angola, Central African Republic, Burundi, Republic of the Congo, Rwanda, South Sudan, Tanzania, Uganda, and Zambia. The DRC is blessed and cursed by a wealth of minerals, such as cobalt, copper, niobium, tantalum, diamonds, gold, tungsten, uranium, and more.

The dynamics of violence in the DRC are inscribed in its ethnic map. Contrary to a widespread belief, Rwanda and Burundi are not the only states in the continent to claim Hutu and Tutsi populations. Tens of thousands of them are also found in eastern DRC. Even before the 1994 genocide, the civil war in Rwanda (1990–1994) drove a deep wedge between the two communities across the border. As the Tutsi-dominated Rwandan Patriotic Front (RPF) fought its way into Rwanda in the early 1990s, thousands of Tutsi exiles joined its ranks, many from the DRC. Conscious of the threat posed to his long-time friend, President Juvénal Habyarimana of Rwanda, and indeed to his own security, Mobutu gave his local allies in the east a free hand to turn against ethnic Tutsi. Even though many of them traced their roots in eastern Congo to pre-colonial days, such as the so-called Banyamulenge ("the people of Mulenge") of South Kivu, their foreign origins were often perceived as proof their pro-RPF sympathies. For many

self-styled "authentic" Congolese their alienness made it imperative to send them back to Rwanda, by force if needed. Countless outbreaks of anti-Tutsi violence were reported in the months preceding and following the seizure of power by the RPF in Rwanda in July 1994. Meanwhile, with the outpouring of some two million Rwandan Hutu across the border and into eastern DRC, including many perpetrators of the genocide, it was not long before eastern DRC served as a jumping off point for armed raids against Rwanda.

Kagame sensed with growing concern the danger rebels in the DRC posed to Rwanda's security, and in November 1996 the Rwandan Patriotic Army (RPA), assisted by ethnic Tutsi from the DRC, launched a deadly strike at the refugee camps strung along the border, killing thousands and sending an untold number running for their lives. Perhaps as many as 300,000 Hutu civilians were systematically killed by the RPA and its Congolese allies in the course of one of the most extensive exercises in ethnic cleansing recorded in the history of the Congo. Most of the young men who survived the onslaught later joined the militant pro-Hutu militia, the Democratic Forces for the Liberation of Rwanda (Forces Démocratiques pour la Libération du Rwanda, or FDLR), now the principal target of the Congolese army in eastern DRC.

The primary objective of the First Congo War (1996–1997)—at least from Rwanda and its allies' perspective—was to destroy the camps sheltering the Hutu perpetrators and their families and then to overthrow the Mobutist state. Both were accomplished with remarkable speed. Spearheaded by a Congolese rebel movement consisting largely of ethnic Tutsi, the Alliance of Democratic for the Liberation of the Congo (*Alliance des Forces Démocratiques pour la Libération du*

Congo, or AFDL), headed by Laurent Kabila, the rebellion enjoyed the military and logistical support of several regional players, among them Uganda, Angola, Zimbabwe, Namibia, and Eritrea. Although it took months before Kagame finally conceded his leading role in waging the war, the RPA was the backbone of the anti-Mobutist crusade. Predictably, once Kabila had been anointed the new head of the Congo, the kingmakers insisted on keeping a close watch on their client state. But having Tutsi advisors dictating to him what course of action to take is what Kabila categorically refused to accept—but not without creating a major crisis of confidence between himself and his former allies.

Thus began the Second Congo War (1998–2003), also known as Africa's World War, which was deadlier than the first. Despite Kabila's new government, eastern Congo remained a brutal conflict zone. Kabila abandoned his former backers (Uganda and Rwanda) in favor of allowing Hutu armies to regroup in eastern Congo. Uganda and Rwanda responded with a joint invasion in 1998. To fight off the Uganda-Rwanda soldiers, Kabila joined forces with Angola, Namibia, and Zimbabwe to force out soldiers and rebel groups backed by the Uganda-Rwanda alliance. The five-year war finally came to a conclusion in July 1999, when all seven countries signed the Lusaka Peace Accord. The United Nations (UN) created the United Nations Mission in the Democratic Republic of the Congo (*Mission des Nations unies en République démocratique du Congo*, or MONUC) on November 30, 1999, and sent in 5,000 peacekeepers to monitor the situation. Despite the accords and the ever-expanding peacekeeping force in Congo, violence, mass rape, slave labor, and corruption still dominate national affairs.

According to the International Rescue Committee (IRC), the death toll in DRC between 1998 and 2008 is estimated at 5.4 million. Although subsequent studies by the Canadian Human Security Report would downsize that figure by 50 percent, there can be no doubt about the appalling human losses. Nor is there any question about the responsibility of Kagame's army in contributing to the carnage, a fact made painfully clear in the 2010 UN Mapping Report which provides a detailed description of the killings of Hutu civilians in eastern DRC, going as far as to suggest a possible genocide.

Rwanda's extensive and unceasing support of pro-Tutsi secessionist militias in eastern Congo is one of the most dramatic of the many unanticipated consequences of the Rwandan Genocide. Kagame's "imperial" ambitions in eastern DRC have been remarkably consistent over the years. First by providing extensive military and political assistance to the Congolese Rally for Democracy (a rebel group that terrorized the eastern region of the DRC), until its gradual collapse after the 2005 Congolese elections, then by throwing his weight behind Laurent Nkunda's political armed militia National Congress for the Defence of the People (French: Conseil National pour la Défense du Peuple, or CNDP), until a deal was made to bring it into the fold of the Congolese army, and finally, after the deal went sour, by giving military and logistical aid to the newly created militia, the so-called M23, Kagame has consistently demonstrated his determination to control the rich Congo borderlands. Protecting the lives of the Tutsi minority is not his only motive; access to the Congo's mineral wealth, directly or through proxies, is the key imperative. Thus, if the past is anything to go by, there is every reason to believe that the spinoffs of the

Rwandan Genocide will be felt in eastern Congo for many years to come.

René Lemarchand

See also: Burundi; Kagame, Paul; Rwanda; Rwandan Civil War

Further Reading

Lemarchand, René. *The Dynamics of Violence in Central Africa*. Philadelphia: University of Pennsylvania Press, 2009.

Prunier, Gérard. *Africa's World War: Congo, the Rwandan Genocide, and the Making of a Continental Catastrophe*. New York: Oxford University Press, 2009.

Reyntjens, Filip. *The Great African War: Congo and Regional Geopolitics, 1996–2006*. Cambridge: Cambridge University Press, 2009.

Stearns, Jason. *Dancing in the Glory of Monsters: The Collapse of the Congo and the Great War of Africa*. New York: Public-Affairs, 2011.

Turner, Thomas. *The Congo Wars: Conflict, Myth and Reality*. London and New York: Zed Books, 2007.

Curic, Vjekoslav

Vjekoslav "Vjeko" Curic was a Bosnian Croat Franciscan priest and humanitarian, best known for his role in helping to save Rwandan Tutsis threatened with annihilation during the Rwandan Genocide of 1994. Born in Lupoglava, Bosnia-Herzegovina, on April 26, 1957, he studied in Visoko, central Bosnia, and in Sarajevo. He entered the Franciscan order on July 15, 1976, and was ordained to the priesthood in Sarajevo on June 21, 1982. Later in 1982 he went to Paris to train as a missionary, and on August 18, 1983, he began his missionary work in Rwanda. He was one of the first volunteers of the Franciscan Africa Project.

One of only two non-African Catholic priests to stay in Rwanda for the duration of the genocide, Curic's actions saved hundreds of lives. To help the victims evade capture by the Interahamwe and Impuzamugambi perpetrators, Curic secretly sheltered Tutsis and ferried them out of the country in the bottom of his truck. At the beginning of the genocide, he also saved the lives of numerous white clergy—many of them Belgian priests, monks, and nuns—whose lives were in danger. He allegedly received direct order from the Vatican to leave the country, but refused to do so, claiming that while his flock was in danger, he could not abandon them.

By 1994, Curic was a long-term resident of Gitarama in the Southern Province of Rwanda, working to help develop his neighborhood. He was well known and liked by those in his parish of Kivumu, and when the killings got underway in April and May, the local people looked to him as one who would offer them rescue. Curic decided to remain at a time when many expatriates were leaving. True to his ideal that he had come to Rwanda to serve the people, he made a stand with the people of Kivumu. He threw himself into the work of aiding all who reached him, as well as helping others to escape. He also continued to preach the Gospel, condemning the violence and calling for peace.

Among those he encountered were a BBC television news crew fronted by David Belton, a director, writer, and film producer. In early May 1994, Belton had arrived in Rwanda to cover the genocide for the current affairs program *Newsnight*. He traveled throughout the country, witnessing the horror and reporting it for British television. At one point, the violence became so bad that Belton and his team had to seek shelter, and it was to Curic that they turned. On several occasions, Curic protected the

Newsnight team from extremist violence, as the Hutu Power authorities became increasingly suspicious of their presence. This experience would later bring Curic's story to a much broader audience through the popular media.

After the genocide, Curic continued his work in Kivumu parish. He helped to resettle widows and re-establish their shattered lives and established educational projects for children. He remained impartial throughout, helping Hutus and Tutsis alike rebuild their communities.

For this, his efforts were not universally appreciated. He was viewed by many Hutus as a collaborator with the Tutsis who had come in with the Rwandan Patriotic Front in July 1994 to stop the genocide, and subsequently established a Tutsi-led government. In 1996, Curic escaped an attempt on his life, but still refused to leave against the advice of many of those around him. His attitude was that he had stayed with this congregation during the genocide, and would not abandon them now. Then, on January 31, 1998, he was shot in his car, murdered in the heart of downtown Kigali. His assailants remain unknown. The Catholic Church immediately declared that he had gone to a martyr's death after devoting himself to the rescue others for the glory of God and love of his neighbors. He was buried in Kivumu, the community he had served without interruption for 15 years, in a church that he and his congregation had built together. His funeral was attended by the prime minister of Rwanda, Pierre-Célestin Rwigema, and other members of the government, along with a vast number of Catholics and other Christians, as well as representatives from the Jewish and Islamic communities.

Several years later, the British director David Belton learned that Curic had been murdered. It forced him to revisit a period of his life that he had, in effect, put aside, and as a result he wrote down his recollections of his time in Rwanda during the genocide. In 2005, Belton's account of Curic formed the backdrop of a movie about Rwanda entitled *Shooting Dogs* (directed by Michael Caton-Jones), which was released in the United States as *Beyond the Gates*. Belton cowrote the original story and was the movie's producer; the screenwriter, David Wolsencroft, also knew Curic in Rwanda in 1994, and both men employed their memories of Curic as the inspiration for one of the film's leading characters, Father Christopher, played by John Hurt.

Paul R. Bartrop

See also: Impuzamugambi; Interahamwe; Roman Catholic Church; Rwandan Patriotic Front; Tutsis

Further Reading

Bodnarchuk, Kari. *Rwanda: A Country Torn Apart*. Minneapolis, MN: Lerner Publishing Group, 1998.

Eltringham, Nigel. *Accounting for Horror: Post-Genocide Debates in Rwanda*. Londres: Pluto Press, 2004.

D

Dallaire, Roméo

Lieutenant General Roméo Dallaire was the force commander of the United Nations Assistance Mission for Rwanda (UNAMIR) prior to, during, and after the 1994 Rwandan Genocide. Despite the decision of the United Nations (UN) to reduce the size of his force from 2,600 to 450 soldiers when the killings began in April 1994, he still managed to help save 30,000 people. His courageous efforts to protect those targeted for genocide as well as his continued self-directed mission thereafter to preserve the memory of that atrocity has earned him international praise, brought greater awareness to the genocide, and challenged politicians, the United Nations, and the international community to do more to prevent atrocity.

Dallaire was born to a French Canadian soldier and a Dutch nurse in Denekamp, Holland on June 25, 1946. Later that year, the family left Holland and returned to Canada. He was raised in Montreal. In 1963, Dallaire joined the Canadian army. He studied at the Royal Military College Saint-Jean (*Le Collège militaire royal de Saint-Jean*) in Quebec, and graduated as an artillery officer in 1970 with a Bachelor of Science degree. Rising over succeeding years, on July 3, 1989, he was promoted to brigadier general.

On October 5, 1993, the UN Security Council passed Resolution 872, which established UNAMIR and, in doing so, created the reason for Dallaire's journey to Rwanda. The UN had created and then deployed UNAMIR for the express purpose of helping to implement the Arusha Peace Accords signed on August 4, 1993, by the primarily Hutu government of Rwanda and the Rwandan Patriotic Front (RPF), the Tutsi-led rebel force. In late 1993, Dallaire was nominated as UNAMIR force commander. His mission's mandate included monitoring the ceasefire agreement; establishing and expanding the demilitarized zone and demobilization procedures; providing security for the Rwandan capital city of Kigali; monitoring the security situation during the final period of the transitional government's mandate leading up to elections; and assisting in the coordination of humanitarian assistance activities in conjunction with relief operations. It was Dallaire's first UN command, and for most of those involved, it was anticipated that this would be a relatively straightforward mission.

A reality to which Dallaire was not alerted prior to his posting was that the extremist Hutus were intent on annihilating the Tutsis and had said as much in media broadcasts, newspaper articles, and declarations. Dallaire's first major test—apart from trying to ensure that his force was equipped and ready to carry out its mission, despite an appalling lag time in the transfer of military supplies and equipment from donor countries—came in early 1994. On January 10, Dallaire received intelligence that a radical Hutu, codenamed "Jean-Pierre," was prepared to disclose information regarding a planned genocide of Tutsis. Jean-Pierre had been an officer in Rwanda's Presidential Guard, but had left to become one of the key men in the Interahamwe militia. It transpired that Jean-Pierre had much to say. He described in

Lieutenant-General Roméo Dallaire served as force commander of the United Nations Assistance Mission in Rwanda prior to and during the 1994 genocide. He and a small cadre of peacekeepers defied the United Nations directive to evacuate once the genocide began and instead stayed on to serve to the best of their abilities those targeted for annihilation. After the genocide, Dallaire founded the Roméo Dallaire Child Soldiers Initiative with the mission to end the recruitment and use of child soldiers. This photo was taken in the Democratic Republic of the Congo on April 2, 2012, while working on his documentary on child soldiers. (Eye Steel Film)

detail how the Interahamwe were trained, who trained them, and where they were trained, adding that the militia was in a state of permanent readiness sufficient to kill 1,000 Tutsis in Kigali within 20 minutes of receiving an order to do so. As a sign of goodwill and reliability, Jean-Pierre offered to reveal the location of a large stockpile of weapons somewhere in central Kigali.

Dallaire, operating within the terms of his mandate, assessed that these arms had to be confiscated. He decided to order an arms raid, and faxed the UN Department of Peacekeeping Operations (DPKO) in New York, headed at that time by Kofi Annan, for authorization. This cable outlined in detail Jean-Pierre's revelations.

Dallaire's fax was received negatively in New York. The DPKO ordered him not to carry out the raid for fear of exacerbating the situation. Under no circumstances was he authorized to conduct arms raids. He was taken to task for suggesting that he exceed his Chapter VI peacekeeping mandate, and was ordered to turn over what Jean-Pierre had disclosed to Rwanda's president, Juvénal Habyarimana—the very man whose anti-Tutsi agenda the Interahamwe was enforcing. The DPKO, together with the office of the then secretary-general, Boutros Boutros-Ghali, decided that process was more important, on this occasion, than action; not only this, but they were concerned for the image of the UN considering an earlier failed arms raid that took place with heavy loss of life in Mogadishu, Somalia, in October 1993. Dallaire protested the decision insistently, but New York would not budge.

As the crisis in Rwanda worsened, particularly in early 1994, Dallaire concluded that the constant stream of murders he and his soldiers were discovering and witnessing was not a result of warfare between two combatants, but, rather, crimes against humanity by one group (Hutus) against another (Tutsis). Initially he referred to such killing as "ethnic cleansing," and continued to fire one urgent message after another to UN headquarters requesting more forces and supplies, and the broadening of his mandate to quell the violence perpetrated by the Hutu extremists. Again, his requests were denied.

On April 6, 1994, Habriymana's plane was shot down as it was about to land in Kigali. Fighting between the Hutus and Tutsis broke out immediately, and genocidal mass murder quickly followed. Within a day, 10 of Dallaire's peacekeepers from Belgium had been murdered while trying to protect the interim head of state in Habyarimana's stead, Prime Minister Agathe Uwilingiyimana, but she, too, was murdered by the Presidential Guard. Dallaire attempted to broker a cease-fire between the RPF and the extremist Hutus, but to no avail. His immediate conclusion was that UNAMIR's mandate was untenable in light of the changed circumstances. Despite his repeated pleas for a Chapter VII mandate for more troops and arms that would have allowed the force to engage the *génocidaires* in combat, the UN retained its totally inadequate Chapter VI mandate and refused to provide him with additional troops.

Dallaire pleaded for additional logistical support, and for UNAMIR to be immediately reinforced with 2,000 more troops. He put forth a plan arguing that with an overall command of 5,000 well-equipped and highly trained troops, he could stop the killing and reimpose peace. The Security Council refused, and then dropped a bombshell of its own. On April 21, some two weeks into the killing, the Council voted to reduce UNAMIR to a force of just 270 peacekeepers, justifying its decision by saying that the mission to monitor the peace was now redundant. The peace had not held. UNAMIR was reduced, and Dallaire was ordered home. He, together with his deputy force commander, General Henry Kwami Anyidoho of Ghana, and ably supported by his chief of staff, Major Brent Beardsley, refused to obey this order.

Stripped of authority, manpower, resources, and logistical support, Dallaire concluded that he was witnessing genocide and as such had a duty to stay. He and what was left of UNAMIR did what they could to help people, Dallaire's command alone saving the lives of an estimated 30,000 Tutsis and moderate Hutus in safe areas established by UNAMIR, such as the Amahoro Stadium and the Mille Collines Hôtel.

Ultimately, the Security Council revised its earlier decision and, too late, voted to establish a revamped mission, UNAMIR II, with a troop complement of 5,500. It did not arrive until early July, however, only after the genocide had ended with the victory of the Rwandan Patriotic Front under General Paul Kagame. Estimates range between 800,000 and 1,000,000 Tutsis and moderate Hutus were murdered in 100 days.

Dallaire returned to Canada in August 1994, and was appointed to different commands in Québec and Ottawa. His experiences in Rwanda, however, had taken a terrible personal toll on him and he nearly lost his sanity. He was overwhelmed by what he witnessed and frustrated at not having been being able to stop the killing. He viewed his mission as a failure and felt personally responsible for failing to convince his superiors in New York and Ottawa of the gravity of the situation.

Despite praise for his efforts in Rwanda, Dallaire was haunted by all that he had seen. In 1996, two years after his return to Canada, Dallaire was made an Officer of the U.S. Legion of Merit, the highest military decoration awarded to foreigners. He was also diagnosed with post-traumatic stress disorder and his mental and physical health continued to deteriorate. He began to drink heavily to blot out what he had witnessed in Rwanda and attempted suicide on more than one occasion. On January 24, 2000, he commenced a period of extended sick leave. By mid-2000, he took early retirement from the

Canadian army, and a few months later, he combined alcohol with his antidepressant medication in another attempt to kill himself. He was found comatose under a park bench in Hull, Quebec.

In 2004, 10 years after the start of the UNAMIR mission to Rwanda, Dallaire and Brent Beardsley published *Shake Hands with the Devil: The Failure of Humanity in Rwanda*, in which Dallaire speaks about what happened in Rwanda and how it affected him. Given his trauma following the experience, it had taken this long for Dallaire to be able to gather his thoughts and reflect clearly on his understanding of what had happened and why. Awarded the Governor-General's Literary Award for Non-Fiction in 2004, the book became a bestseller in Canada and several other parts of the world.

On the tenth anniversary year of the genocide, a documentary film, *Shake Hands with the Devil: The Journey of Roméo Dallaire* (dir. Peter Raymont, 2004), was released showing Dallaire's return to Rwanda. The same year saw the appearance of the first major motion picture on the genocide, *Hotel Rwanda* (director/writer/producer, Terry George). The film starred Don Cheadle in a celebration of the actions of the manager of Kigali's Hotel Mille Côllines, Paul Rusesabagina, and offered a controversial portrayal of the head of the UN peacekeeping forces, a Canadian officer named "Colonel Oliver," played by Nick Nolte. It showed a character very much at variance with the reality of who Dallaire was and what he had been able to achieve. He was also portrayed—much more empathetically—in a Canadian movie that took its title from Dallaire's book. *Shake Hands with the Devil* (dir. Roger Spottiswoode, 2007) starred Canadian actor Roy Dupuis in the role of Dallaire.

Dallaire has become a national hero for Canadians, despite his own views about his inadequacy in Rwanda. On October 10, 2002, he was made an Officer in the Order of Canada (OC), and in 2005 a Grand Officer of the National Order of Quebec (GOQ). On March 24, 2005, he was appointed to the Canadian Senate by Prime Minister Paul Martin, representing Quebec.

Since his retirement from the military, Dallaire has become increasingly involved in the world of education and academia. In 2004–2005, he served as a Fellow at the Carr Center for Human Rights Policy at Harvard University's John F. Kennedy School of Government, and on September 8, 2006, he joined the Montreal Institute for Genocide and Human Rights Studies (MIGS) at Concordia University as a senior fellow and codirector of the MIGS "Will to Intervene" project. This is a research initiative that seeks to find ways to set in practice the UN-endorsed set of principles known as Responsibility to Protect. As part of this, Dallaire and the MIGS Director, Professor Frank Chalk, were among the authors of a study in 2010, *Mobilizing the Will to Intervene: Leadership to Prevent Mass Atrocities.*

In 2010, Dallaire, pursuing an additional humanitarian interest of his own, published *They Fight Like Soldiers, They Die Like Children*, a passionate study of the militias and governments that turn of children into "child soldiers."

Throughout the entire period since Rwanda, Roméo Dallaire has sought to draw the world's attention to the dangers of genocide, describing Darfur as "Rwanda in slow motion," and calling on NATO (the North Atlantic Treaty Organization, also called the North Atlantic Alliance) to intervene in Sudan. A featured speaker wherever he goes, he will long be remembered for a maxim that has come to characterize his humanitarian vision: "All humans are human, and there are no humans more human than others."

Paul R. Bartrop

See also: Anyidoho, Henry Kwami; Arusha Accords; Beardsley, Brent; Habyarimana, Juvénal; Moderate Hutu; United Nations Assistance Mission for Rwanda

Further Reading

Dallaire, Roméo. *Shake Hands with the Devil: The Failure of Humanity in Rwanda.* Toronto: Random House, Canada, 2004.

Smith, M. James, ed. *A Time to Remember. Rwanda: Ten Years after Genocide.* Retford, UK: The Aegis Institute, 2004.

Day of Reflection on the Genocide in Rwanda (International)

The International Day of Reflection on the Genocide in Rwanda has occurred on every April 7 since 2004. The United Nations (UN) General Assembly declared the Day of Reflection to coincide with the tenth anniversary of the beginning of the Rwandan Genocide.

The Day of Reflection occurs on what is considered the anniversary of the start of the genocide. On April 6, 1994, a plane carrying Rwandan president Juvénal Habyarimana was shot down while attempting to land in the Rwandan capital of Kigali. Hutu extremists blamed the president's death on Tutsis. The death of Habyarimana quickly became the catalyst for the Rwandan Genocide when violence broke out the next day.

While the UN failed to stop the genocide, it became more engaged in Rwanda when the killings ended. In 1995, less than a year after the genocide, the UN called for an outreach program to help the survivors and

victims of the Rwandan catastrophe. It also called for educational efforts to prevent such occurrences in the future. The UN General Assembly adopted resolution 58/234 on December 23, 2003, which designated April 7 the International Day of Reflection on the Genocide in Rwanda. The Day of Reflection is observed in varying ways around the world. Observances usually take the form of material/historical exhibitions, scholarly or student conferences, and ceremonies honoring the dead. The UN outreach program and remembrance activities are organized and sponsored by the UN Department of Public Information.

Paul G. Pierpaoli Jr.

See also: Habyarimana, Juvénal; International Reactions; United Nations Assistance Mission for Rwanda

Further Reading

Melvern, Linda. *Conspiracy to Murder: The Rwandan Genocide.* London: Verso, 2006.

United Nations General Assembly Resolution 58/234, *International Day of Reflection on the 1994 Genocide in Rwanda* (23 February 2004), available from undocs.org/A /RES/58/234.

de Saint-Exupéry, Patrick

Patrick de Saint-Exupéry is a French journalist who has spent much of his career covering major stories in various parts of Africa (Liberia, South Africa, Rwanda), the Middle East (the Gulf War, Iran, Libya, Saudi Arabia), as well as Cambodia, Canada, and the Soviet Union. He was born in 1962, the son of Count Jacques de Saint-Exupéry and his wife, the Countess Martine d'Anglejan. The writer Antoine de Saint-Exupéry was his grandfather's cousin.

De Saint-Exupéry began his career as a journalist at the age of 19 after winning a competition for young reporters. In 1983 he joined *France Soir* magazine, moving to its foreign desk in 1987. In 1988 he freelanced for *L'Express* and *Grands Reportages*, prior to becoming a foreign reporter with *Le Figaro* in 1989. Between 2000 and 2004 he was *Le Figaro*'s permanent correspondent in Moscow.

During the 1994 Rwandan Genocide, de Saint-Exupéry was one of the few journalists who managed to send reports out of the country while the killings were in progress. His articles on Operation Turquoise and the Bisesero resistance and massacres cast immense doubt on the role played by the French military, leading to an intense reaction on the part of the French government.

Operation Turquoise was the name given to UN Security Council Resolution 929 of June 22, 1994, in which France set in motion an intervention in Rwanda with an initial deployment of 2,500 French and Senegalese troops. They set up a block of so-called Safe Areas in the southwest of Rwanda, claiming that this was the best way to prevent vast numbers of refugees moving into northern Zaire (now the Democratic Republic of the Congo), while at the same time safeguarding the refugees' lives. Much speculation has taken place regarding the possible ulterior motives of the French in setting up the safe areas where they did, given that nearly all of those who fled to them were Hutus rather than Tutsis, and that among these were substantial numbers of genocidal killers. It has also been suggested that France decided to defend these Hutus from the advance of the army of the Rwandan Patriotic Front (RPF), a force that was largely English speaking in a Francophone country. An important consequence of Operation Turquoise was that the French troops did not completely disarm the Hutus. Extremists still possessing weapons were thus able to operate effectively within the safe area, continuing to kill any Tutsis they could find, unhindered by any fears of being caught by the RPF. French troops did intervene between Hutu killers and Tutsi victims whenever contact was obvious, but this was infrequent.

In his newspaper columns, de Saint-Exupéry left little room for doubt as to his view that Operation Turquoise was helping the Hutu killers rather than purely assisting the Tutsi victims. He was in Rwanda when the French troops arrived and witnessed the deployment in person. But the general observations he had on Operation Turquoise were enhanced by his witnessing of the French behavior over the Tutsi resistance at Bisesero in late June 1994.

Located in the Kibuye district of western Rwanda, Bisesero was in an area with the highest proportion of Tutsis in Rwanda. Soon after the genocide began, Tutsis from the surrounding area numbering up to 50,000 converged on Bisesero for refuge. They sought safety in numbers, making the most of the few weapons they had. For the most part, they possessed only farm tools and stones, which were far less effective than the Hutus' grenades and guns. Nonetheless, the people of Bisesero managed to stave off Hutu assaults until mid-May, killing some of their attackers and deterring others. But it was bitterly cold in the hills and raining heavily, and they were short of food. Each Hutu attack claimed hundreds of Tutsis.

On May 13, the attackers returned in full force, armed with weapons the Tutsis could not match. Although the struggle continued throughout May and into early June, the remaining Tutsis succumbed to wounds, hunger, and exposure. Eventually Hutu reinforcements from the Republican Guard and Interahamwe militiamen, armed with modern powerful weapons, organized a serious attack against the Tutsis. Under this new attack, the people of Bisesero could not survive.

The final assault, known by some today as the Bisesero Hill Massacre, took place on June 27, 1994. The Tutsis' last stand saw them throwing rocks and fighting hand to hand against powerfully armed army and Interahamwe forces who had been sent to finish them off. French soldiers from Operation Turquoise had been to Bisesero a few days before the final massacre and talked many of the Tutsis into coming down from the hills, saying the genocide was over and that additional French forces would provide humanitarian aid. Before the French arrived in force, however, Hutu military and Interahamwe moved in and thousands more Tutsis were killed. In the end, those too weak to resist could only attempt to hide and hope not to be discovered, or, in a last desperate encounter with the *génocidaires* (French: "those who commit genocide"), try to rush towards those with guns to at least secure a swifter end. By the time the French forces returned to impose order on whatever population was left, only around 1,300 of the 50,000 Tutsis were still alive.

De Saint-Exupéry witnessed these events directly, and in his reports, did not hold back from describing what he saw. This included the arrival of French Special Forces and an air deployment of troops to Bisesero on June 27, 1994. At no stage did he see the French troops helping the survivors—though he did observe them fighting against the RPF.

In covering the genocide, he stirred up a hornet's nest within the French political and military establishment, as well as in the media. His articles in *Le Figaro* had an enormous impact on opinion at home, and these, followed by a series of follow-up pieces in

1998, triggered the establishment of a Parliamentary Commission of Inquiry on Rwanda chaired by Paul Quiles, the then president of the National Assembly's Commission of National Defense and the Armed Forces. The Commission delivered its report in December 1998. It found that France was not responsible for the genocide, and did not bear liability for the annihilation of the Tutsis. The Commission did not come to a conclusion as to who actually was responsible, but was careful to emphasize that, whoever it was, it was not France.

After the genocide and his return to other duties, de Saint-Exupéry decided to pursue a fuller account of what had happened. His main interest was to try to discover the extent to which the French government and military assisted the Hutu killers, and how extensive their responsibility in the genocide actually was. Ten years after the genocide, in 2004, he published his findings in a book, *L'inavouable: La France au Rwanda* (*The Unspeakable: France in Rwanda*) published by Editions Les Arènes. It was reissued in April 2009, with a new preface in which he provided a fresh assessment of the record of France in Rwanda. To date, these works have not yet appeared in English.

It was a matter of conjecture as to whom he considered to be "the unspeakable"; it could have been the Hutu killers, but it could just as easily have been the French politicians. He specifically singled out Foreign Minister Dominique de Villepin, and began with a powerful indictment of Villepin's rhetoric in which he framed France's intervention in Operation Turquoise in terms of the Rwandan "genocides," pointedly using the plural and thus indicting the RPF in some sort of equation of moral equivalence between Hutu Power and the RPF. De Saint-Exupéry's book was an indictment of French foreign policy in Rwanda, in which he also argued that France armed and trained those who were guilty of committing the genocide. He named many political leaders, military figures, and institutions as accomplices in the genocide, which in turn prompted law suits against him and his publisher for defamation. In one key case, where former Foreign Legion commander Colonel Jacques Hogard sued de Saint-Exupéry, the Paris Criminal Court acquitted the journalist on December 11, 2009, taking much of the sting out of his opponents' hostility.

In January 2008, Patrick de Saint-Exupéry took extended leave without pay from *Le Figaro*. He used this time to establish a new news magazine, *XXI*, with his colleague Laurent Beccaria. De Saint-Exupéry currently serves as the magazine's editor-in-chief.

Paul R. Bartrop

See also: Rwandan Genocide, French Response to the; Rwandan Patriotic Front; Turquoise, Operation

Further Reading

Eltringham, Nigel. *Accounting for Horror: Post-Genocide Debates in Rwanda*. Londres: Pluto Press, 2004.

Smith, M. James, ed. *A Time to Remember. Rwanda: Ten Years after Genocide*. Retford, UK: The Aegis Institute, 2004.

Denial of the Rwandan Genocide

No genocide is immune to denial and Rwanda is no exception. In the case of the Rwandan Genocide, many unanswered questions surrounding the circumstances of the bloodshed have helped shape denial of the Rwandan Genocide, such as: To what extent are the Tutsi invaders directly or indirectly responsible for the massive retribution exacted by the Hutu extremists? Who is responsible for the crash of President Juvénal Habyarimana's plane? How do the crimes committed by the Rwandan Patriotic Front (RPF) measure up to those attributed to the Hutu perpetrators? The temptation to deny the genocidal quality of the carnage has been particularly pervasive.

In his groundbreaking analysis, *States of Denial*, Stanley Cohen draws a distinction among three types of denial: literal ("nothing is happening"), interpretive ("what is happening is really something else"), and implicatory denial ("what is happening is justified"). The first has little to do with the case at hand; the evidence is too massive to be shoved under the rug. Literal and interpretive denial is where the Rwanda bloodbath has generated its richest harvest of disavowals.

Interpretive denial in Rwanda hinges on the notion that the term "genocide" does not apply to the Rwandan case. Rather than a calculated attempt to physically eliminate Tutsi, those practicing interpretive denial contend that the killings can best be described as a spontaneous outburst of popular anger. The argument draws attention to the collective fear generated by the invasion of the country by the Tutsi-dominated Rwandan Patriotic Front (RPF) on October 1, 1990, a terror that reached an apex following the death of President Habyarimana, on April 6, 1994. Widely perceived by Hutu leaders at that time as a planned RPF assassination of the president, government officials claimed the RPF shot down the plane carrying President Habyarimana. From this vantage point, the Rwandan tragedy is the direct consequence of the mortal threats posed by the RPF to state security and Hutus.

Implicatory denial is an attempt to justify the genocide of Tutsi by blaming the RPF for the genocidal crimes committed against the Hutu community. Here, attention shifts to the "double genocide thesis," with the emphasis placed on the equivalence, in terms of numbers killed, between the horrors committed by the Hutu *génocidaires* and those attributed to the RPF during the Rwandan civil war. The thrust of the argument is that the Tutsi are themselves too morally compromised by their human rights violations to accuse the Hutu of having committed a genocide.

The first type of denial is frequently set forth by domestic and international actors wishing to exonerate Hutu perpetrators. Among Rwandan politicians and intellectuals, it finds its clearest expression in the statements issued by the refugee-based party Republican Rally for Democracy in Rwanda (RDR), well known for its efforts to spread genocide revisionism and denial. The contention that the Tutsi bear much of the onus of responsibility for the Rwanda tragedy is a frequent theme of its propaganda, along with references to "a civil war," "tragedy," and/or "crisis" to designate what others call genocide. What Tom Ndahiro, a Rwandan journalist and human rights activist, calls "genocide laundering" recurs time and again in the political discourse of the RDR; the aim is to deflect attention from the "g-word" by making the Rwandan tragedy appear as the unfortunate by-product of the RPF aggression. As the French historian Jean-Pierre Chrétien has shown, this is also a central theme in the commentaries offered by some French and Belgian human rights activists, journalists, and missionaries.

Implicatory denial, best illustrated by the "double genocide" thesis, is typical of the attitude displayed by representatives of Rwandan opposition parties in the months following the seizure of power by the RPF. In 1996, a coalition of opposition members in exile identified with the Resistance Forces for Democracy, issued a political platform with an entire section devoted to "*le double génocide.*" The same theme finds a powerful echo in the statements made by a number of Western human rights activists, including missionaries and journalists. Its most authoritative formulation came from the late French president François Mitterrand, in 1995, when he famously corrected his interpretor to pluralize the Rwandan Genocide.

Regardless of the arguments mustered to defend one type of denial or another, the Rwandan Genocide will continue to generate considerable controversy. Too many facets of this tragedy have yet to be fully investigated, actors to be interrogated, events to be explored, and responsibilities to be established before a broader consensus of opinion can be reached. Once all is said and done, the substantial body evidence available makes it is clear that what happened in Rwanda over the course of 100 days in the spring and summer of 1994 was one of the largest genocides of the last century.

René Lemarchand

See also: Hutus; Rwandan Civil War; Rwandan Genocide, French Responses to; Rwandan Genocide, Role of Propaganda in the; Rwandan Patriotic Front; Tutsis

Further Reading

Cohen, Stanley. *States of Denial: Knowing About Atrocities and Suffering.* Cambridge: Polity Press, 2001.

Ndahiro, Tom. "Genocide-Laundering: Historical Revisionism, Genocide Denial and the Rassemblement Républicain pour la Démocratie au Rwanda," in Clark, Phil, and Zachary Kaufman, eds., *After Genocide: Transitional Justice, Post-Conflict Reconstruction and Reconciliation in Rwanda and Beyond* London: Hurst Publishers, 2008.

Shaw, Martin. *What Is Genocide?* Cambridge: Polity Press, 2007.

Des Forges, Alison

Alison Des Forges was a human rights researcher and historian, and the leading American voice for human rights in Rwanda. She was born in Schenectady, New York, on August 20, 1942, studied at Radcliffe College, and earned a MA (1966) and a PhD (1972) at Yale University. For her masters and doctoral studies, Des Forge examined the history of Rwanda under German and Belgian colonial rule. She was drawn into human rights work when colleagues and friends in Rwanda and Burundi began suffering discrimination, harassment, and in some cases, death at the hands of repressive governments.

Des Forges dedicated her life's work to understanding Rwanda, exposing the serial abuses suffered by its people, and to helping bring the positive change needed to establish a peaceful and prosperous future for that country. She spent most of her adult life working on Africa's Great Lakes region (Burundi, the Democratic Republic of Congo, Kenya, Rwanda, Tanzania, and Uganda), despite a short period in China with her husband, Roger, a professor of Chinese history at the University of Buffalo.

In the 1980s Des Forges began working as a volunteer for the New York–based nongovernmental organization Human Rights Watch (HRW), and from the early 1990s onwards she served as HRW's senior adviser on Africa. Where Rwanda was concerned, she worked almost exclusively at trying to draw attention to what she saw as genocide in the making. She cochaired an international commission that scrutinized the rise of ethnic violence in the region, and was part of a group organized by HRW and other such organizations that examined human rights abuses in Rwanda from 1990 to 1993. The

inquiry published a report of its findings several months before the genocide.

Prior to the start of the genocide in April 1994, she labored to warn the world that Rwanda was sliding into genocide. When the actual killing began she watched in horror from the United States. Unable to do anything directly for the people she knew in Rwanda, she lobbied diplomats in the United States to at least try to give some form of assistance to those most directly threatened. Thus, on the first day of the genocide, she spent long hours on the phone calling her friend Monique Mujawamariya, a human rights associate in Kigali, as the first actions of the *génocidaires* (French: "those who commit genocide") were being carried out. Mujawamariya managed to escape by crossing the border, and she received sanctuary thanks in part to Des Forges's help. Upon her arrival in the United States, Mujawamariya then lobbied the White House, albeit unsuccessfully, to intervene during the early weeks of the genocide.

In April 1994, Des Forges was one of the first foreigners to claim that genocide was under way in Rwanda, and a month later, in May, she called for the killings to be officially declared as such. By then, already 200,000 people had been murdered.

Once the genocide was over, Des Forges set herself the important task of writing a definitive account of what had happened. She spent four years interviewing both the organizers and the victims of the genocide and gathering government documents. The final product, *Leave None to Tell the Story: Genocide in Rwanda* (1999), was a meticulously detailed description of the methods by which the Hutu Power killers implemented an anti-Tutsi campaign.

The book also analyzed the failure of the international community to intervene. Des Forges offered extensive analysis on the many warnings preceding the genocide, the redistribution of the victims' property, the Hutus who tried to resist participation in the slaughter, and—importantly and controversially—the killings that took place in retaliation by the Tutsi-led Rwandan Patriotic Front (RPF). Her insistence that RPF forces should also be held accountable for their crimes, including the murder of 30,000 people during and immediately after the genocide, placed her at odds with the new RPF-led government.

After publishing *Leave None to Tell the Story*, the MacArthur Foundation recognized her work with a "Genius Grant," in which Des Forges won $375,000 to enable her to continue her research on the Great Lakes region. In 2008, however, she was banned from the country after HRW published an extensive analysis of Rwanda's judicial reform. The report drew attention to problems of inappropriate prosecution and external influence on the judiciary that resulted in trials and verdicts that failed to conform to the facts of the cases.

With a commitment to postgenocide justice for the victims, Des Forges appeared as an expert witness in 11 genocide trials at the International Criminal Tribunal for Rwanda, three trials in Belgium, and at trials in Switzerland, the Netherlands, and Canada. She also provided documents and other assistance in judicial proceedings involving genocide in four other national jurisdictions, including the United States. Her expertise was sought on numerous occasions, and she provided assistance to investigations undertaken by the French National Assembly, the Belgian Senate, the United States Congress, the Organization of African Unity, and the United Nations.

After the Rwandan Genocide, Des Forges turned her attention to the killings then known to be taking place in the eastern region of the Democratic Republic of the Congo (DRC), and she was among a number of critics who accused the RPF government of killing civilians and refugees in the eastern Congo in 1996 and 1997. Des Forges then began working on a HRW report about these killings, and in doing so she became an authority on DRC human rights violations.

On February 12, 2009, Alison Des Forges was killed in an air crash, when Continental Connection flight 3407, flying from Newark, New Jersey, crashed into a home near Buffalo, New York (where Des Forges lived). She was among the 50 passengers who died in the crash.

Paul R. Bartrop

See also: Congo, Democratic Republic of the; Denial of the Rwandan Genocide; Kagame, Paul; *Leave None to Tell the Story: Genocide in Rwanda*; Rwandan Patriotic Front

Further Reading

Des Forges, Alison. *Leave None to Tell the Story: Genocide in Rwanda*. New York: Human Rights Watch, 1999.

Gribbin, Robert E. *In the Aftermath of Genocide: The US Role in Rwanda*. New York: I Universe, 2005.

Diagne, Mbaye

An army officer from the African country of Senegal, Mbaye Diagne worked as a United Nations (UN) Military Observer in Rwanda before and during the 1994 genocide. One of nine children, he studied at the University of Dakar before joining the Senegalese army. In 1993, as a young captain, he was assigned to the UN Assistance Mission for Rwanda (UNAMIR) as a military observer (MILOB) covering the implementation of the Arusha Accords. He was stationed at the Hôtel des

Mille Collines, one of Kigali's luxury hotels and the scene of a major sustained rescue of Tutsis throughout the genocide.

Within hours of the start of the genocide on April 6, 1994, Diagne decided that his orders not to intervene were unacceptable given the lives that were at stake. The morning after the assassination of President Juvénal Habyarimana, the next in line of succession, the moderate Hutu prime minister Agathe Uwilingiyimana, was murdered along with her husband by Presidential Guards. Learning of Uwilingiyimana's murder, Diagne decided to investigate the scene of the murder. In the process, he discovered the prime minister's five children hiding in the adjoining housing compound of the United Nations Development Program. After a fruitless wait for UN evacuation vehicles that never arrived, he decided to load the children into his own vehicle, hide them with blankets, and then return to the relative safety of the Mille Collines. Despite the dangers involved, they soon departed the hotel and miraculously managed to cross through various roadblocks enforced by the Interahamwe militias without the children being discovered, reach the airport, and obtain passage for all five children out of the country. Thanks to Diagne, the children boarded a Canadian transport to Nairobi, Kenya.

It was a reckless and risky move, but it was only the first of many occasions on which the young officer would ignore the standing orders from UN headquarters to remain neutral and not get involved. As a MILOB, his job was to try to find ways to prevent conflict and report on what he witnessed. It was essentially a liaison and investigation role, in which the military observer could find himself involved in a variety of situations designed to facilitate a peaceful outcome. This was not what Diagne did. In the weeks following the start of the genocide, Diagne worked hard to save the lives of hundreds of Rwandans, charming his way past roadblocks, smiling, joking, sharing cigarettes with the murderers, and over and over again talking his way through the checkpoints. In this way he personally saved hundreds of lives. His solo rescue missions, nearly always at great peril to himself, attained legendary status among the UN forces in Kigali.

Diagne's strength lay in his ability to persuade others of his friendliness and comradeship. His disposition helped him to obtain the confidence of families, groups, and leaders of all parties in the conflict. It was calculated that he had to pass through 23 Interahamwe checkpoints to get to most of the people he was trying to save. The Interahamwe, who, depending on the time of day, could be drunk or drugged, had to be convinced on each occasion that he was not harboring Tutsis. Diagne would find Tutsis who were hiding, drive them back through the same checkpoints, and then hide them—often in the Amahoro Stadium, from which he would then ferry them to some other place of refuge. He engaged in countless such missions, as he could only carry three to four (or sometimes, five, though this was extremely hazardous) at a time. On one occasion, he spent an entire day operating in precisely this format after he came across a group of 25 Tutsis hiding in a house in Nyamirambo, Kigali. On each occasion, he bluffed his way through the roadblocks. He relied on his extensive contacts among the Hutu military and militias; his ability to defuse tense situations owing to a sharp sense of humor; and, from time to time, bribery in the form of cigarettes or money. His dynamism saw him seemingly everywhere at once.

It certainly helped that in his position as a MILOB he had access to most of the city, and was known widely by all sides of the conflict. But in engaging in his acts of selfless bravery, he was repeatedly forced to flout his operational orders—which were, put simply, not to intervene in the conflict. UNAMIR's commander, General Roméo Dallaire, was aware of what Diagne was doing, but neither stopped him nor reprimanded him for disobedience. While everyone in the UN establishment seemed to know of Diagne's actions, some believed that Dallaire would not discipline him owing to him undertaking a role that Dallaire himself would have preferred to be doing.

On May 31, 1994, Diagne was driving alone, back to UN headquarters in Kigali with a message for Dallaire from the chief of staff of the Rwandan Armed Forces, Augustin Bizimungu. At this time, the rebel Rwandan Patriotic Front (RPF) was closing in on Kigali, and engaged in fierce fighting with the Rwandan army. A random mortar shell, fired by the RPF towards a Hutu extremist checkpoint, accidentally landed behind his jeep. Shrapnel entered through the rear window and hit Diagne in the back of the head, killing him instantly.

Mbaye Diagne was universally recognized as a real-life hero of the Rwandan Genocide. Upon learning of his death, UNAMIR Force Headquarters held a minute of silence in his honor, and a small parade took place at Kigali airport on June 1. A devout Muslim, he was buried in Senegal with full military honors. Later, his wife and two small children accepted on his behalf the UMURINZI award, Rwanda's Campaign against Genocide Medal.

Paul R. Bartrop

See also: Bizimungu, Augustin; Dallaire, Roméo; Hotel des Mille Collines; Rwandan Patriotic Front; United Nations Assistance Mission for Rwanda; Uwilingiyimana, Agathe

Further Reading

Barnett, Michael. *Eyewitness to a Genocide: The United Nations and Rwanda*. Ithaca, NY: Cornell University Press, 2002.

Dallaire, Roméo. *Shake Hands with the Devil: The Failure of Humanity in Rwanda*. Toronto: Random House, Canada, 2004.

F

Forces Armées Rwandaises

The Rwandan Armed Forces (French: Forces Armées Rwandaises, or FAR) existed prior to and after the 1994 Rwandan Genocide. It began in 1962 as the national military establishment of Rwanda and then was dissolved and then retooled after the genocide.

The FAR participated in the genocide. At the time of the genocide, the FAR numbered some 40,000–50,000 men, many of whom were Hutus. The force was administered by the ministry of defence but reported solely to the Rwandan president. The FAR included a small air force as well as an elite Presidential Guard Reserve Force, a National Guard, the Armée Rwandaise (AR), which was the main body of ground troops, and the Gendarmerie Nationale (GN), which functioned as a police and internal security force. The AR and GN were heavily involved in the killings that constituted the Rwandan Genocide.

The size of the FAR increased exponentially beginning in the early 1990s, when the Rwandan government began fighting the Rwandan Patriotic Front (RPF). The RPF had been formed by the Tutsi diaspora in Uganda during the late 1980s. The French government helped the FAR received much help and training from the French government, which dispatched as many as 1,200 troops to Rwanda after 1990.

When the Rwandan Genocide began in April 1994, the FAR was a principal perpetrator of mass murder against Rwanda's Tutsi minority and moderate Hutus who either objected to the killing of Tutsis or tried to protect them. Although the brunt of the genocide lasted for only 100 days, as least 800,000 people died in the bloody calamity, and 75 percent of the Tutsi population was murdered.

When a new Tutsi-led RPF government was installed in Rwanda in July 1994, the FAR was substantially recast, reduced in size, and renamed the Rwandan Defense Forces (RDF), which continues to this day as Rwanda's military establishment. Thousands of Hutus who had been in the FAR fled from Rwanda in the aftermath of the genocide, fearing arrest or revenge by Tutsis or the RPF government. Most went to the Democratic Republic of the Congo (DRC), from which they staged raids against Rwanda. It should be noted, however, that RPF was not guilt-free in the Rwandan Genocide, because it perpetrated atrocities against Hutus. It is also responsible for the deaths of as many as 200,000 Hutu refugees in the DRC after the genocide ended.

The International Criminal Tribunal for Rwanda (ICTR), based in Arusha, Tanzania, has indicted and tried key members of the FAR.

Paul G. Pierpaoli Jr.

See also Congo, Democratic Republic of the; Forces Armées Rwandaises; Hutus; International Criminal Tribunal for Rwanda; Moderate Hutu; Rwandan Civil War; Rwandan Genocide; Rwandan Patriotic Front; Tutsis

Further Reading

Ali, Taisier M., and Robert O. Matthews. *Civil Wars in Africa: Roots and Resolution.* Toronto: McGill-Queen's University Press, 1999.

Dallaire, Roméo. *Shake Hands with the Devil: The Failure of Humanity in Rwanda.* Toronto: Random House, Canada, 2004.

G

Gacaca Courts

Since the 1994 genocide, the international community and Rwanda have pursued four types of trials: international trials in Arusha, Tanzania sponsored by the United Nations International Criminal Tribunal for Rwanda (ICTR); transnational trials held in Belgium, Canada, Switzerland, the Netherlands, and Finland; civilian and military trials in Rwanda's domestic courts; and gacaca community courts throughout Rwanda. Gacaca represented the most voluminous and widespread attempt at justice within Rwanda. Conceived by the Rwandan transitional government in the late 1990s and implemented widely throughout Rwanda between 2005 and 2012, gacaca addressed a backlog of genocide related cases and in so doing became a cornerstone of post-genocide mediation, justice, and healing. These community-run tribunals, however, are not without criticism and ultimately raise important questions about the achievability of justice after genocide.

Historically, villages and towns across Rwanda used the gacaca system to resolve disputes among family and neighbors, conflicts over land, and the like. Gacaca (pronounced "ga-cha-cha"), translated as "justice on the grass," is derived from the Kinyarwanda (Rwandan) word *guacaca*, meaning 'the lawn' or 'the grass.' Traditionally, a town's male elders would sit under the shade of a tree and render judgments on local disputes.

The Rwandan government reconceived gacaca in the aftermath of the genocide to deal with a backlog of prisoners. In 1994 and 1995 the new Rwandan government—composed of members of the Rwandan Patriot Front (RPF) that ended the genocide—hunted down and arrested an estimated 120,000 persons suspected of involvement in the genocide. Lacking a prison infrastructure large enough to accommodate such a great number of persons, the 120,000 accused were forced into overcrowded facilities intended to hold 45,000 people. The national courts could not move quickly enough and Hutus continued to be arrested. As way of example, as of August 2003, the national courts had tried just over 6,000 of the 130,000 prisoners arrested (Totten and Bartrop 2009, 485).

Before the start of gacaca, most of the genocide suspects were incarcerated for years before being charged formally for any crime. The existing national courts and ICTR lacked the time, space, and money needed to try the estimated 100,000 incarcerated Rwandans still awaiting trials in the late 1990s. The international community and many Rwandans criticized the government for continuing to hold prisoners without charging them and for keeping them in inhumane and squalid conditions.

In 1999, the government proposed a reshaping of the traditional gacaca model of local justice to attend to the tens of thousands of prisoners languishing in overcrowded facilities. Although the goals of gacaca were numerous, in the broadest terms, it aimed to prosecute genocide suspects and to triage a divided and mourning society. While the ICTR had a mandate to

After the genocide, the government of Rwanda instituted a form of locally driven justice rooted in Rwandan tradition called *gacaca*. This billboard located in Kigali, Rwanda, promoted the gacaca court system, which has earned praise and condemnation both at home and abroad. (Robin Kirk)

prosecute persons bearing the greatest responsibility for the genocide and Rwanda's national court was charged with prosecuting those accused of committing grave atrocities, rape, and planning the genocide, local judges in gacaca courts heard cases of genocide suspects accused of all crimes, which as of 2008 expanded to include individuals accused of planning the genocide on the local level, inciting others to participate, rapists and sexual torturers. The first pilot phases of gacaca began on June 18, 2002, and became fully operational three years later. From 2005 to 2012 an estimated 12,000 community-based courts staffed by a quarter million lay judges tried 1,003,227 individual Hutu in 1,958,634 cases. The gacaca appeals court accounts for approximately 9 percent of these cases (Chakravarty 2015, 7).

Because the genocide had left the country with only 12 prosecutors and 244 judges, the first order of business was to elect judges or *inyangamugayo* (which loosely translates into "trustworthy person") to serve in the gacaca community courts. Candidates had to be 21 years or older, have no prior criminal convictions, could not have served in the government or held a political leadership role, and could not have participated in the genocide. Through a series of community elections held between October 2001 and April 2002, more than 250,000 men and women were elected and began training shortly thereafter.

The accused were divided into three different categories per a newly enacted law known as Organic Law 08/96 adopted by the domestic courts on August 30, 1996 to try perpetrators. Category 1 suspects included the planners and organizers of the genocide, notorious murderers, and perpetrators of sexual violence. Category 2 defendants were charged with participating in killings and committing other forms of physical violence. Category 3 encompassed those committing crimes against property.

The gacaca courts operated at two levels of geographical administration and divided cases per the categories defined by Organic Law 08/96. The cell (*akagari*) level courts presided over a jurisdiction of about 400 persons dealt with Category 3 crimes (theft and plunder) committed within their area. The sector (*umurenge*) level courts attended to Categories 1 and 2 (planners, instigators, and physical violence) and appeals. Rwanda set up 9,013 courts at the cell level and 1,545 courts at the sector level (Bornkamm 2012, 46).

Gacaca trials required the widespread participation of Rwandans as judges, witnesses, and defendants. Both the cell and sector courts took place in classrooms, conference rooms, or outdoors. At each trial the judges (*inyangamugayo*) were outfitted in the colors of the Rwandan flag (green, yellow, and blue sashes) and typically sat together on a bench. Early on, 19 judges oversaw the trials, but this number was reduced over time to 14, 9, and ultimately 5. And while in the beginning attendance at the gacacas was optional, after low turnout rates the government required the local community to attend. Scholars estimate that by 2012, the courts had tried one in three of the adult Hutus who had resided in Rwanda during the genocide (Chakravarty 2015, 3). Every

Rwandan was touched in some way by the gacaca proceedings.

The trials encouraged and required dialogue between witnesses, victims, perpetrators, and judges. Instead of having lawyers represent their interests, victims and perpetrators spoke for themselves. Perpetrators that confessed to their crimes at these public hearings and asked for forgiveness could have their sentences reduced by half. Those who did not provide a genuine or full confession often received a lengthier sentence. Gacaca courts did not seek capital punishment and could only impose custodial sentences, such as imprisonment.

The confession-based trial system had strengths and weaknesses and as such has been praised and criticized. Human rights groups applauded the Rwandan government for attending to the judicial backlog; however, they also lamented the obvious procedural deficiencies of gacaca, such as not affording the defendants a lawyer. Gacaca has also received substantial criticism for the political nature of the tribunals. To put it succinctly, even though Tutsis killed Hutus during and after the genocide, gacaca trials only processed Hutu crimes and as such Tutsi crimes have gone unpunished. And yet, despite all its challenges, gacaca has encouraged conversation, reconciliation, and helped move the country forward.

Justice cannot be fully achieved after genocide because it is impossible for any punishment to fit the crime. As a result, gacaca could never offer true justice. Yet, gacaca did propose a way for Rwandans to confront their violent past. It is unclear whether gacaca has fulfilled its goals or if it has helped heal the country, but it is a remarkable achievement and historical in its scope and implementation.

Alexis Herr

See also: International Criminal Tribunal for Rwanda (ICTR); Rape; Rwandan Patriotic Front (RPF)

Further Reading

Bornkamm, Paul Christopher. *Rwanda's Gacaca Courts: Between Retribution and Reparation.* Oxford: Oxford University Press, 2012.

Chakravarty, Anuradha. *Investigating in Authoritarian Rule: Punishment and Patronage in Rwanda's Gacaca Courts for Genocide Crimes.* Cambridge: Cambridge University Press, 2015.

Clark, Philip. *The Gacaca Courts, Post-Genocide Justice and Reconciliation in Rwanda: Justice Without Lawyers.* Cambridge: Cambridge University Press, 2011.

Totten, Samuel and Paul R. Bartrop, eds. *The Genocide Studies Reader.* New York: Taylor & Francis, 2009.

Straus, Scott and Lars Waldorf, eds. *Remaking Rwanda: State Building and Human Rights after Mass Violence.* Madison, WI: University of Wisconsin Press, 2011.

Gaillard, Philippe

Philippe Gaillard is a Swiss Red Cross worker who headed the mission of the International Committee of the Red Cross (ICRC) in Rwanda during the 1994 Rwandan Genocide. Born in Valais, Switzerland, on July 6, 1956, Gaillard studied literature at the universities of Geneva, Freiburg-in-Breisgau, and Salamanca. Joining the ICRC in 1982, he worked for more than 10 years in Latin America and two in the Middle East, as well as a year spent at ICRC headquarters in Geneva.

The ICRC opened a delegation in Rwanda in 1990, prior to which it covered the country from a larger regional headquarters in Kinshasa, Ziare (now known as the Democratic Republic of the Congo). In mid-July 1993 Gaillard went to Rwanda at his own request, just as the Arusha Peace Accords were being signed between the Hutu Power government of President Juvénal Habyarimana and the rebel Rwandan Patriotic Front (RPF), led by General Paul Kagame. Gaillard was appointed head of the ICRC's Rwanda delegation, a post he was to hold for a year. On July 20, 1993, Gaillard met Habyarimana as part of a larger ICRC delegation to Rwanda. At this time people around the country were nervous about what the future might hold, and despite the Arusha Accords being signed on August 4, there were signs that the situation was not going to be easily remedied.

Soon after Gaillard's arrival, the United Nations Assistance Mission for Rwanda (UNAMIR) was established with Canadian general Roméo Dallaire as force commander. Within weeks, more than 50 people were killed in the so-called "demilitarized zone" between the government forces and those of the RPF. Radio and television propaganda, encouraging Hutus to kill Tutsis with machetes, was broadcast daily. In January 1994 Dallaire invited Gaillard to the residence of UN special representative of the secretary-general Jacques-Roger Booh-Booh. Dallaire told Gaillard at this time of the news he had received about the impending genocide, and that he had sent a fax to UN headquarters in New York, seeking permission to go on a raid against Interahamwe arms caches. With the raid forbidden by UN headquarters in New York, it was from here onwards that Gaillard realized that the so-called peace process was not feasible.

Once the genocide began in April 1994, Gaillard labored to facilitate both safety and medical support for thousands of sick and wounded Rwandans, regardless of their ethnicity. At the outset of the massacres, he called the Red Cross office in Geneva to explain what was happening, and after discussing the pros and cons of going public with the story it was decided that the ICRC would go against its past record of confidentiality to let the world know. Gaillard sent out a very short press release of about five lines regarding a single incident involving the treatment of ICRC wounded, and the next day the story was spread worldwide. After this, with the support of the ICRC in Geneva, Gaillard was tireless in his efforts to get the word out to the international media about the ongoing slaughter. Gaillard felt he had to speak out in the context of such horror. His attitude was that by remaining silent he would be complicit in the genocide, thus he felt he had a responsibility to make his views known, even if only so that the international community could not say that it was unaware of the bloodshed in Rwanda. This was probably the first occasion in the 20th century when the Red Cross had made a public announcement of atrocities taking place while its delegates were still in the field.

While many of the other nongovernmental organizations and expatriate communities were evacuating, there was little hesitation about staying as far as the ICRC was concerned. Gaillard was later to comment that the main reason the ICRC decided to stay was because its local staff. He reduced the expatriates to six key workers (mainly doctors), but owing to the respect paid by all sides to the Red Cross only one out of the 120 local staff who remained at their posts was killed during the genocide. Gaillard received a lot of support for his efforts from Geneva, and spoke with headquarters daily. Needing more and more help with the medical side of the crisis, he found that all he had

to do was ask, and within days there would be more surgeons, nurses, and other specialized staff on their way to Kigali.

Towards the end of April 1994, the UN sent the recently appointed High Commissioner for Human Rights José Ayala Lasso to Rwanda. On May 12, he met with Gaillard and Dallaire to be briefed on the situation. Upon being asked approximately how many people had been killed to date, Gaillard replied that his best estimate would be at least 250,000. Dallaire did not think the figure was as high as that, but Gaillard later concluded that he in fact had better intelligence sources than Dallaire owing to the ICRC's reach throughout the whole country.

One of the major challenges in providing humanitarian aid is to help victims without also helping their murderers. The ICRC gave the militias fuel to remove the corpses of their victims, and rarely named killers publicly in order to be able to continue its humanitarian activities. During the genocide, however, Gaillard found himself talking to and dealing with the killers all the time. He would visit the Ministry of Defence twice and sometimes three times a week to discuss the situation, and one day even confronted the mastermind of the genocide, Colonel Théoneste Bagosora, and demanded that something be done to stop the killing.

At an early date in the genocide—around April 10 or 11—Gaillard went to the Ministry of Defence to speak directly with the minister, Augustin Bizimana, with whom Gaillard had previously been in close touch. He asked for a government-appointed liaison officer, the better to be able to coordinate contact between the ICRC and the Rwandan Armed Forces. Later that same day Bizimana appointed Colonel François Munyengango, a Hutu colonel affected by

HIV-AIDS. By all accounts, in his new role, Colonel Munyengango helped to save hundreds of defenceless civilians. He assisted ICRC delegates and medical workers to cross the checkpoints, and would browbeat the Interahamwe into giving way. On one occasion, he learned that the Interahamwe were threatening an orphanage in Butare with Tutsi children. Colonel Munyengango immediately drove to Butare, alone, and organized the evacuation of 1,619 orphans from Butare to Burundi. Sadly, by the end of 1994, his illness took his life.

Despite Gaillard's own life being threatened on numerous occasions by the Interahamwe, he has concluded that the Red Cross saved somewhere between 60,000 and 70,000 people. Ten thousand people were taken care of in Gaillard's hospital alone. Perhaps thousands more orphans were saved, either directly by the Red Cross or through its initiatives.

Throughout the time of the genocide, Gaillard maintained his psychological balance through poetry. He had with him *A Season in Hell* by the French poet Arthur Rimbaud, and before having dinner every evening, around seven o'clock, he would read a poem from the collection to his colleagues, who listened in silence.

After the genocide, he remained with the ICRC, but he found himself to be somewhat inured to horror. Gaillard has concluded that simple beauty should be enjoyed more and while he and his wife had previously not wanted children, after the genocide both wanted to create life. Now as a father and senior humanitarian aid worker, he is attracted to beauty in all its forms.

Paul R. Bartrop

See also: Arusha Accords; Bagosora, Théoneste; Booh-Booh, Jacques-Roger; Dallaire, Roméo; Habyarimana, Juvénal; Interahamwe; Kagame, Paul; Rwandan Genocide, Role of Propaganda in the; Rwandan Patriotic Front

Further Reading

Eltringham, Nigel. *Accounting for Horror: Post-Genocide Debates in Rwanda*. Londres: Pluto Press, 2004.

Evans, Glynne. *Responding to Crises in the African Great Lakes*. Oxford: Oxford University Press, 1997.

Gisimba, Damas

When the Rwandan Genocide began in April 1994, Damas Mutezintare Gisimba was the director of the Gisimba Memorial Centere orphanage in Nyamirambo. Despite the imminent dangers helping Tutsis posed to Hutus, Gisimba risked his life by sheltering 400 Tutsi children and adults.

Gisimba was born in Rwanda in 1950. In 1980, his father and mother founded the orphanage, and Damas and his brother Jean-François both worked to serve the children there. In 1986, after his father's death, Gisimba became director of the facility. The orphanage was well run and respected within Rwanda.

When the genocide began the Gisimba Memorial Center housed about 65 orphaned children. The larger community in Kigali, by way of donations and support of staffing, supported it. When the carnage began in April, Gisimba, a Hutu, was determined to shield as many Tutsis as he could. Gisimba later stated in interviews that his parents had taught him not to focus on ethnicity, to respect all people equally, and to help them in times of need. Over the proceeding 100 days, encouraged by the Hutu-dominated government, the Interahamwe militia, a de facto mass killing organization, massacred hundreds of thousands of people—mainly

Tutsis and moderate Hutus—in cities, villages, and the countryside within Rwanda. Hutu civilians also heeded their government's call, and a sizable number became caught up in the violence; Hutu neighbors killed Tutsi neighbors and friends, and some hardline Hutus even murdered members of their own family, if they happened to be moderate Hutus or Tutsis.

It was amid this bloodshed that Gisimba and his brother Jean-François decided to hide as many people as they could at the orphanage, knowing full well that if they were discovered they would be killed. Within a week or so after the genocide began, more than 400 children and adults had flooded into the orphanage. They were all Tutsis or moderate Hutu. The huge influx taxed Gisimba's already meager food supplies, but he managed to scavenge what he could without raising undue suspicions. Several times, Interahamwe fighters threatened the orphanage, but the Gisimba brothers managed to keep them at bay, using a combination of bribes and threats. In the end, all those who had sought refuge with Gisimba survived the terrible ordeal.

Damas and his brother have since received numerous accolades, awards, and honors for their selfless courage from the Rwandan government as well as a wide variety of international organizations and foreign nations. Today, the orphanage continues to be directed by Gisimba and houses some 150 children. Until about a decade ago, nearly all the facility's children were victims and/or survivors of the genocide. In recent years, that profile has shifted to children orphaned because of poverty or disease, especially AIDS.

Gisimba continues to instill in his children the importance of not judging people because of their ethnicity or other outward appearances.

Paul G. Pierpaoli Jr.

See also: Hutus; Interahamwe; Moderate Hutu; Rape; Rwanda; Tutsis

Further Reading

Des Forges, Alison. *Leave None to Tell the Story: Genocide in Rwanda*. New York: Human Rights Watch, 1999.

Melvern, Linda. *Conspiracy to Murder: The Rwandan Genocide*. London: Verso, 2006.

Habyarimana, Agathe Kanziga

Agathe Kanziga Habyarimana she was Rwanda's first lady for more than 20 years until her husband, President Juvénal Habyarimana, was killed in a plane crash on the evening of April 6, 1994. Despite her likely involvement in the planning of the atrocity, she has yet to be tried by a court of law for her role in the genocide.

Agathe was born in 1942 to a prominent Hutu family in northern Rwanda. Her family could trace its lineage back to the Hutu leaders that had presided over an independent principality until the late 1800s. Her ancestral prestige is said to have helped bolster the political aspirations of her husband who had a far more modest family history.

Madame Agathe, as Rwandans commonly knew her, is said to have had a strong personality that attracted the respect of her fellow Hutu extremist northerners. Know at first as *le clan de Madame* ("her court within a court") and later as Akazu (Kinyarwanda for "little house"), Agathe and her comrades are thought to have planned and orchestrated the Rwandan Genocide. Via Akazu, it is also alleged that she played a powerful role in state affairs during the Rwandan Civil War (1990–1994). Among those in her inner circle were three of her brothers, a cousin, and other senior army officers. The Akazu commanded considerable political, economic, and military influence, which allowed it to play a key role galvanizing the Hutu Power movement.

Following the assassination of her husband President Habyarimana in April of 1994, French soldiers evacuated Agathe to Paris, an action (among many) that has caused much scrutiny of France's connection to the genocide. After the genocide, she spent 1995 to 1997 in Africa, where she resided in Gabon, Zaire (now known as the Democratic Republic of the Congo), and Kenya. Fearing retribution from the Rwandan Patriotic Front (RPF), Agathe returned to France where she has continued to live for the past two decades. She filed for asylum in France in January 2004, however, the French Office for the Protection of Refugees and Stateless Persons rejected her application two years later owing to her suspected role in the Rwandan Genocide. France's Council of State confirmed this decision in 2009.

The Rwandan government issued an international arrest warrant for Agathe in October 2009 for her alleged role in planning the genocide. The arrest warrant spurred the French police to arrest Agathe on March 2, 2010. After being interviewed, she was released and ordered to not leave France and to appear monthly to the police. France has chosen not to extradite Agathe back to Rwanda.

Alexis Herr

See also: Akazu; Habyarimana, Juvénal; Rwandan Genocide, French Response to the; Rwandan Patriotic Front

Further Reading

Gourevitch, Philip. "The Arrest of Madame Agathe," *The New Yorker* (2 March 2010), accessed July 7, 2017. http://www.new

yorker.com/news/news-desk/the-arrest-of
-madame-agathe.

Gourevitch, Philip. We Wish to Inform You
That Tomorrow We Will be Killed With
Our Families: *Stories from Rwanda*. New
York: Picador, 1999.

Melvern, Linda. *A People Betrayed: The Role
of the West in Rwanda's Genocide*. New
York: Zed Books, 2000.

Meredith, Martin. *The Fate of Africa: A History
of the Continent Since Independence*.
New York: PublicAffairs, 2011.

Scherrer, Christian P. *Genocide and Crisis in
Central Africa: Conflict Roots, Mass Violence,
and Regional War*. Westport, CT:
Praeger, 2002.

Habyarimana, Juvénal

Juvénal Habyarimana was president of
Rwanda from 1973 until his death on
April 6, 1994. He was born into an aristocratic
Hutu family on March 8, 1937, in
Gasiza, Gisenyi, the son of a landowner,
Jean-Baptiste Ntibazilikana, and his wife
Suzanne Nyirazuba. He was educated in
Ziare (now known as the Democratic Republic
of the Congo), and studied medicine
before entering Rwanda's Officer Training
School in Kigali in 1960. He graduated in
1961 and two years later became chief of
staff in the Rwandan Armed Forces (French:
Forces Armées Rwandaises or FAR). In
1965, at the age of 28, he was made minister
for the armed forces and police in the government
of his cousin, Grégoire Kayibanda.
In 1973, he was promoted to major general,
and then overthrew Kayibanda in a military
coup on July 5, 1973.

Habyarimana's military regime remained
in office until 1978, when a referendum
established a new constitution. Habyarimana,
setting himself up as the only candidate,
was elected to a five-year term as

At the time of his death, Juvénal Habyarimana
had spent 21 of his 57 years as president of the
Republic of Rwanda. During his long tenure,
tensions between Hutu and Tutsi intensified
and his death on April 6, 1994, is widely viewed
as the catalyst of the genocide. (Frederic
Neema/Sygma via Getty Images)

president, which was renewed in subsequent
sham elections. Under Habyarimana, the
quality of life for most Rwandans improved:
there was political stability, and the economy
improved. This "golden age" came at a price,
however. Every Rwandan citizen, including
babies and the elderly, had to be a member
of Habyarimana's political party (the only
one permitted), the National Revolutionary
Movement for Development (French: Mouvement
Révolutionnaire National pour le
Développement, or MRND). The MRND
sought to elevate the status of Hutus, which
in turn disenfranchised Tutsis.

Habyarimana relied heavily on an inner clique of the MRND, the so-called Akazu (Kinyarwanda for "Little Hut"), a euphemism given to an informal but tightly knit (and highly corrupt) network of Habyarimana's closest family members, friends, and party associates. It was said to be so thoroughly dominated by Habyarimana's wife Agathe (née Kanziga) that, at times, even her husband could be frozen out of the decision-making process. The name *Akazu* was originally, in precolonial times, a term given to the inner circle of courtiers to the royal family. The Akazu was an oligarchy that not only obliterated any possibility of Rwanda returning to democracy, but also worked assiduously to promote the interests of northern Rwanda (the Akazu base) over those of the south. This further destabilized the position of the minority Tutsis throughout the country, and, through its extensive network of supporters in the bureaucracy, the financial sector, and society generally, the Akazu skimmed off vast amounts of public money for the greater good of the extended Habyarimana family. It even went so far as to institute its own death squad, recruited from members of the Presidential Guard.

The late 1980s saw Rwanda experience an economic downturn, as world coffee prices—upon which the Rwandan economy relied—dropped sharply. This destabilized Habyarimana's regime, forcing him to introduce an economic austerity program that led to widespread unrest. In hopes of curbing unprecedented antigovernment sentiment, he convened a national commission to study how best to implement a multiparty democracy in Rwanda. While army control ensured that he still held the country in an iron grip, the forced budget cuts of 1989—accompanied by a drought from 1988 to 1989 and a plea for

financial assistance to the World Bank—saw pressure brought against Habyarimana to open Rwanda's political system to other political parties. And contrary to portraying an image of one who would not be averse to a liberalization of his government, he was and remained a Hutu supremacist.

In late 1990, the Rwandan Patriotic Front (RPF), a large and well-equipped rebel Tutsi army located in nearby Uganda, invaded Rwanda. The RPF engaged the Rwandan army in heavy fighting that came close to the Rwandan capital city of Kigali and threatened to destroy Habyarimana's regime. Only the intervention of French paratroopers, units of which stood physically between the RPF and the government forces, stopped the invasion. The civil war continued intermittently for another three years, further damaging Rwanda's already vulnerable economy, and led Habyarimana inevitably to the conclusion that he would have to be open to some form of a negotiation process if his administration was to survive. Thus, in 1992, the country held its first multiparty elections and Rwanda's political structure changed to allow for both a prime minister and a president.

By August 4, 1993, delegates from the RPF met with officials of the Habyarimana administration and representatives of the United States, France, and the Organization of African Unity (a organization of UN African states established in 1963 to promote unity and solidarity among African states), to negotiate a settlement. The resulting agreement, signed in Arusha, Tanzania, saw a set of five accords agreed to between the two parties. The aptly named Arusha Accords addressed a variety of topics, including refugee resettlement, power sharing between Hutus and Tutsis, the introduction of an all-embracing democratic regime, the dismantling of Habyarimana's dictatorship, and the encouragement of a transparent rule of law throughout Rwanda. The Arusha Accords guaranteed the RPF half of the officer corps and 40 percent of the enlisted men in a reorganized Rwandan army, as well as Tutsi representation in key government posts.

In the months that followed, the parties involved continue to meet and negotiate the implementation of the Accords. This required government leaders and representatives traveling to and from Arusha, sometimes by car and at other times by plane. Some observers considered that Habyarimana purposely allowed these negotiations to drag on to buy time and thereby reinforce his position at home. Some of the Hutu extremists in Rwanda viewed Habyarimana's willingness to negotiate with the RPF as little more than his capitulation to the rebel forces.

On April 6, 1994, while returning to Kigali from one of the negotiation rounds in Arusha, the jet carrying Habyarimana, President Cyprien Ntaryamira of Burundi, the chief of staff of the Rwandan military, and a few others, was shot down by two missiles fired from just outside the Kigali airport. The plane crashed into the grounds of the presidential palace, and everyone onboard was killed. Within hours the news of Habyarimana's assassination spread through Rwanda and acted like an alarm bell, calling Hutu extremists to begin murdering Tutsis.

It has never been proven conclusively who was responsible for the missile attack. A French investigating team blamed the RPF and its leader (and later president of Rwanda), General Paul Kagame. Others have argued that it was Hutu extremists who decided to kill Habyarimana and blame it on the RPF to force a final reckoning with the RPF and the Tutsis. Yet others have even suggested that it was members of the Akazu—and thus, Habyarimana's own family—who arranged for the plane to be shot down.

Whatever the case, the assassination certainly served as an opportunity for extremist Hutus to begin genocide. Within hours, the militias, the FAR, the Presidential Guard and the Gendarmerie Nationale (the national police force) begin murdering Rwanda's Tutsis and moderate Hutus. At least 800,000 people—though by several estimates, nearly a million—were killed over the next three months, in one of the fastest genocides in recorded history.

Three days after the plane crash, French forces escorted the slain president's widow, Agathe Habyarimana, out of the country, evacuating her to France. Reports of her living a life of luxury in Paris surfaced frequently over the next several years, rubbing salt into the wounds of the RPF-dominated government that came to power in Rwanda after the genocide. As one of the leading members of the Akazu (also known in some circles as the "Clan de Madame"), Agathe Habyarimana was alleged by the RPF to have been one the genocide's masterminds. After many years in exile, Madame Agathe was denied political asylum in France on January 4, 2007, (though incongruously, she was permitted to remain in the country).

Then, on March 2, 2010, she was arrested by the government of French president Nicolas Sarkozy on suspicion of her involvement in the genocide. The move against her followed a visit to Rwanda by Sarkozy during which he promised that those responsible for the genocide must be found and punished. She was detained at her home in the southern Paris suburbs by police executing a Rwandan-issued international arrest warrant issued in October 2009. Immediately, the Rwandan government urged Paris to extradite her for trial, though it is assumed that

France will never actually do so. French judges have consistently refused to extradite genocide suspects to Kigali on the grounds that the alleged perpetrators would not receive a fair trial.

Paul R. Bartrop

See also: Akazu; Arusha Accords; Forces Armées Rwandaises; Habyarimana, Agathe; Interahamwe; Kayibanda, Grégoire; Moderate Hutu; Mouvement Révolutionnaire National pour le Développement; Rwandan Civil War; Rwandan Genocide, French Response to the; Rwandan Patriotic Front

Further Reading

Davies, Lizzy and Chris McGreal, "Widow of assassinated Rwandan president arrested," *The Guardian* (2 March 2010), https://www.theguardian.com/world/2010/mar/02/widow-assassinated-rwandan-president-arrested.

Jokic, Aleksandar, ed. *War Crimes and Collective Wrongdoing: A Reader.* Malden, MA: Blackwell Publishers, 2001.

Melvern, Linda. *Conspiracy to Murder: The Rwandan Genocide.* London: Verso, 2006.

Hamitic Hypothesis

Stock-in-trade of early colonial historians, the Hamitic Hypothesis lies at the core of racist theories purporting to show the innate superiority of the Tutsi people as the ideal embodiment of the Hamitic race. According to historian David Newbury, it is founded on the following assumptions: ethnic categories are defined by biological criteria; the origin of each group is traceable to a distinct geographical area; each group possesses a specific corporate history; and the history of the region can best be explained in terms of the conquest of one race by another.

The linguistic and theoretical origins of the Hamitic Hypothesis are found in the Bible in chapter five of Genesis. According to this text, Noah cursed his youngest son Ham and his descendants. In the sixth century, the Babylonian Talmud (a central work of rabbinic teachings in the Jewish faith) suggested that the curse of Ham's offspring was to have black skin. Early colonists and anthropologist theorized that Tutsis appeared more European than Hutu and therefore concluded that Tutsis were scions of Ham who had emigrated from Ethiopia.

Such ideas can be found in germ, as it were, in the writings of early European explorers who saw in the somatic traits of Tutsi and Hima people unmistakable proof of their Ethiopian origins. After encountering the people of Uganda in the 1850s, John Henning Speke was one of the first to propose that people of Hamitic descent were racially superior to lesser breeds of Africans. His views were later echoed in Count Gustav Adolf von Goetzen's description of the Tutsi of Rwanda in 1894. According to the German explorer, the Tutsi were exceptionally gifted, physically and culturally distinct from the great mass of Hutu agriculturalists, and must have migrated with their long-horned cattle from Abyssinia to Rwanda. Father A. Pagès gave further respectability to the term in the title of his book, *Au Rwanda: Un royaume hamite au centre de l'Afrique* (1933). Writing in the 1920s, the British anthropologist C. G. Seligman captured the gist of the myth in his book on *The Races of Africa* (1922) when he referred to the Hamites as "pastoral Europeans." For all the critical responses voiced by more serious observers, the Hamitic Hypothesis showed a surprising capacity to survive in one form or another throughout the colonial period and after.

The Hamitic frame seemed ideally suited to legitimize the Belgian version of indirect rule. Though later appropriated by Rwandan historians of Tutsi origins, most notably Alexis Kagame, to reclaim self-rule, on the eve of independence Hamitic references became a familiar theme in the discourse of Hutu politicians anxious to discredit the monarchy and its feudal supporters. It eventually surfaced as a notoriously noxious ideology during the genocide, when it was used as a tool in the hands of Hutu extremists to insist on sending the Tutsi back to their "original homeland" of Ethiopia.

As a hypothesis, a myth or an ideology the Hamitic frame of reference has had a profound influence on the destinies of Africans. It has added a strongly racist coloration to the writings of early historians; it has shaped the ideas and practices of colonial administrators and missionaries in many parts of Central Africa, including Rwanda and Burundi; and, most importantly, it has given a spurious halo of respectability to the proponents of genocidal ideas during the Rwandan carnage.

René Lemarchand

See also: Hutus; Rwandan Genocide, Role of Propaganda in the; Tutsis

Further Reading

Chrétien, Jean-Pierre. *The Great Lakes of Africa: Two Thousand Years of History.* Translated by Scott Strauss, New York: Zone Books, 2003.

Newbury, David. *The Land Beyond the Mists: Essays on Identity and Authority in Precolonial Congo and Rwanda.* Athens: Ohio University Press, 2011.

Prunier, Gérard. *The Rwanda Crisis, 1959–1994: History of a Genocide.* Kampala: Fountain Publishers, 1995.

Sanders, Edith. "The Hamitic Hypothesis: Its Origins and Functions," *Journal of African History* 10, no. 4, (1960): 521–532.

Hotel Rwanda (Film, 2004)

Hotel Rwanda was a critically acclaimed U.S.-made movie released in 2004 based on real events that occurred during the spring of 1994 during the Rwandan Genocide. The film is based on Paul Rusesabagina (played by Don Cheadle), who managed a small hotel in the Rwandan capital of Kigali, and his family. *Hotel Rwanda* also stars Sophie Okonedo, Joaquin Phoenix, Nick Nolte, and Jean Reno. As the Rwandan Genocide begins, Rusesabinga, who is a Hutu, and his wife Tatiana, who is a Tutsi, are increasingly horrified by the violence they see unfolding around them. To complicate matters, the Hutu-led Interahamwe militia frowns upon their mixed marriage. Despite their increasing fears that one or both of them will be killed, Rusesabinga negotiates with and bribes local officials to leave the hotel alone, and before long it becomes a refuge for nearly 1,300 Rwandan refugees, mostly Tutsis. Many critics have called *Hotel Rwanda* an African-based version of *Schindler's List*, a 1993 movie about a rescuer during the Holocaust.

Like *Schindler's List*, *Hotel Rwanda* deals with the causes and results of mass violence and genocide, societal and political corruption, hypocrisy, and the redeeming value of human kindness during unspeakable human suffering. An independent film, the movie had a limited release in December 2004 but was more widely released in February 2005. *Hotel Rwanda* earned moderate financial success and received many accolades. It accepted awards at the Toronto

Film Festival and the Berlin Film festival, among others.

In a subtle way, *Hotel Rwanda* also deals with the unwillingness—or inability—of the international community to stop the bloodshed. United Nations (UN) peacekeeping troops are portrayed as being deeply concerned about the mass killings, but essentially unable to take any offensive action against the Hutus or the Interahamwe because the UN Security Council had forbidden them from intervening in the genocide. The film ends with Rusesabinga's family, along with the refugees he shielded, successfully leaving the hotel after joining a UN convoy and reaching Tutsi rebel protection.

Paul G. Pierpaoli Jr.

See also: Dallaire, Roméo; Hotel des Mille Collines; Ibuka; Interahamwe; Rusesabagina, Paul

Further Reading

Dallaire, Roméo. *Shake Hands with the Devil: The Failure of Humanity in Rwanda.* Toronto: Random House, Canada, 2004.

Melvern, Linda. *Conspiracy to Murder: The Rwandan Genocide.* London: Verso, 2006.

Hutu Social Revolution

Lasting from 1959 to 1962, the Hutu Social Revolution (also called the Hutu Peasant Revolution, Social Revolution, and *muyaga*, a Kinyarwanda word for a strong but variable wind) had a lasting impact on ethnic relations within post-colonial Rwanda. The revolution occurred during a period of imminent political change and destabilization caused by the withdrawal of Belgian colonial forces from Rwanda. Any understanding of

the Hutu Social Revolution requires an analysis of the pre-and post-colonization power dynamics in Rwandan and its impact on Hutu and Tutsi identity politics. The Hutu Social Revolution encapsulates a series of events that informed the social dynamics that some scholars have argued helped motivate the 1994 genocide.

Prior to the arrival of Europeans in the region now known as Rwanda, Hutus, and Tutsis lived together without major conflict. While there were two main groups of people, the identity of "Hutu" and "Tutsi" did not indicate separate nationalities. Instead, the categories in the broadest sense referred to social castes based on profession and wealth. The Hutus typically tilled the land and Tutsi owned cattle, however, these occupations were not set in stone. Building on the Hamitic Hypothesis (a biblical justification for the alleged superiority of Tutsi over Hutu), the German and then Belgian colonizers constructed a more rigid social structure that elevated the status of Tutsis (composing 14 percent of the population) over Hutus (approximately 85 percent of the population). Colonizers placed Tutsi in leadership roles and other positions of power, provided Tutsis with greater access to education, and increased legal protections. The Belgian colonial government's introduction of identity cards with ethnic classifications (for example, Hutu) in 1933 helped facilitate these new ethnic identity strata in Rwanda.

The 1957 publication of the Bahutu Manifesto (also referred to as the Hutu Manifesto) by Hutu intellectuals voiced the anger and frustration that many Hutus felt regarding their disadvantaged social standing and helped set the scene for the Hutu Social Revolution two years later. The manifesto asserted that Tutsis and white Europeans were foreign invaders and that the Hutu majority should run the country. This racially charged document was given a new life during the genocide.

Events in 1959 created real opportunities for Hutus to shift the balance of power in Rwanda. When the Belgians made known their intention to withdraw from neighboring Congo in January 1959, Hutus in Rwanda saw a chance to change their suppressed status. Hutus assumed that it was only a matter of time before the Belgians left Rwanda, too. The sudden death of Rwanda's king on July 25, 1959, created another opening for Hutu advancement. While Tutsis quickly installed a new monarch without first consulting the Belgians, Hutu politicians called for the establishment of a republic. In a republic, Hutus, who vastly outnumbered Tutsis, would have the chance to achieve greater representation in government.

Violence erupted in early November 1959 before democracy had a chance to take root. The alleged murder of Dominique Mbonyumutwa, an administrative subchief in the central Rwandan province of Gitarama, by Tutsi political activists inspired roving bands of Hutus to attack Tutsi authorities across the nation. Belgian colonists' failure to intervene and protect Tutsis allowed Hutu violence to continue unchecked. Hutu bands burned, pillaged, and killed Tutsis. Belgian colonizer Colonel Guy Logiest supported the replacement of Tutsi chiefs with Hutu chiefs and even encouraged Hutu actions.

In mid-1960, an election was held and with Hutus presiding over the polling stations Hutus won 90 percent of the top government posts. By this time, some 20,000 Tutsis had been displaced by Hutu violence and thousands had sought refuge in Rwanda's neighboring countries. Less than a year later, on the eve of the Belgian colonial forces departure from Rwanda, the Belgians met with the new Hutu leaders to abolish the monarchy and declare Rwanda a republic. And by the time Rwanda declared independence in 1962, Rwanda was firmly in the hands of an ethnic Hutu leading party.

Alexis Herr

See also: Bahutu Manifesto; Hamitic Hypothesis; Identity Cards, Rwanda

Further Reading

Gourevitch, Philip. We Wish to Inform You That Tomorrow We Will be Killed With Our Families. New York: Picador, 1999.

Straus, Scott. *The Order of Genocide: Race, Power, and War in Rwanda*. New York: Cornell University Press, 2006.

Jones, Adam. *Genocide: A Comprehensive Introduction*. London and New York: Routledge, 2011.

Hutus

The Hutu most commonly reside in the region of Rwanda and Burundi. Although during the Rwandan Genocide in 1994 the Hutu government murdered their Tutsi countrymen and denigrated them by calling them cockroaches, it is most commonly thought that Hutus and Tutsis originate from the same ancestors and their perceived ethnic divisions are more fiction than fact.

The Hutu and Tutsi are descended from ancestors sharing a common language, Kinyarwanda, who settled the Rwanda-Burundi area of east Central Africa more than 1,000 years ago. The early settlers took up two main occupations. One group became farmers and the other raised cattle. Over time, the farmers came to be known as Hutus and the pastoralists as Tutsis. In this culture, the ownership of cattle was a marker of wealth. With time, Hutu and Tutsi became class markers with the pastoral Tutsi as the wealthier members of the society. Despite the propaganda during the colonial period and in the propaganda leading up to and during the genocide, the distinctions of Hutu and Tutsi have little to do with race.

At the time of the German conquest in the 1880s, Rwandan society and class distinctions were polarized. The majority Hutu occupied the peasant, or subject, position to the Tutsi minority holding the tribal leadership positions. The German colonizers did little to interfere with the social makeup of the indigenous people. When Belgium assumed control over Rwanda at the close of World War I, the situation changed. The Belgians relied heavily on indigenous Tutsi leaders to govern the colony. This served to reinforce Tutsi control

and provided an apparatus to repress the approximately 85 percent of Rwandans considered Hutus. Belgian leaders excluded Hutus from government service and from higher education.

During the 1950s, the Hutus pushed for greater representation and prominence in Rwandan society by using the decolonization programs of the United Nations to gain access to education and public office. Hutu leaders were successful in exploiting the decolonization process to gain power throughout Rwanda. When Rwanda revolted against Belgium and secured its independence between 1961 and 1962, the class roles were reversed, and the Hutus held the positions of power.

Tutsi rebels challenged Hutu rule immediately. In response to cross-border rebel

The Rwandan Civil War, which plagued Rwandans during the four years leading up to the 1994 genocide, impacted Hutus and Tutsis alike. To escape military and militia violence, many civilians fled their homes. Pictured here are young Hutu refugees carrying water containers. (MSGT Rose Reynolds/U.S. Department of Defense for Defense Visual Information Center)

incursions, the Hutu government massacred some 20,000 Rwandan Tutsis and forced 300,000 to flee. In the aftermath, a military dictatorship solidified its power in Rwanda. Over the next two decades, the standard of living in Rwanda declined steadily.

As the economic weakening in Rwanda continued, the power base of the military leadership eroded. Rebel groups, most notably the Rwandan Patriotic Front, began to challenge the government from camps in neighboring states. According to Rwanda's Hutu government, Rwandan Tutsi participation with the rebels justified the further repression of the Tutsis. The government began planning the genocide of the Tutsis as a way of repolarizing the population.

The assassination of President Juvénal Habyarimana on April 6, 1994, provided the catalyst for action against the Tutsis. During the next 13 weeks, military forces compelled the Hutu population of Rwanda to massacre the Tutsis. In the end, three-quarters of the Tutsi population were murdered.

Rob Coyle

See also: Arusha Accords; Habyarimana, Juvénal; Radio-Télévision Libre des Mille Collines; Rwandan Patriotic Front; Tutsis

Further Reading

Adelman, Howard, and Astri Suhrke, eds. *The Path of a Genocide: The Rwanda Crisis from Uganda to Zaire.* New Brunswick, NJ: Transaction Publishers, 1999.

Webster, John B. *The Political Development of Rwanda and Burundi.* Syracuse, NY: Maxwell Graduate School of Citizenship and Public Affairs, Syracuse University, 1966.

Ibuka

Ibuka, which means "remember" in Kinyarwanda, formed in 1995 in the aftermath of the Rwandan Genocide with the goal of achieving justice, preserving memory, supporting survivors, and encouraging peacebuilding. Acting as an umbrella network for 15 other organizations in Rwandan concerned with the same objectives, Ibuka has pursued projects that support survivors. Although Ibuka has done much to help Tutsi victims of the genocide, some scholars and human rights practitioners have criticized it for its involvement in national politics.

Ibuka and its member organizations have achieved a lot since its formation after the genocide. According the organization's website, it has pursued projects that support education, participated in the construction of 416 memorial sites, conducted statistical research on victims, rescuers, and perpetrators of the genocide, held five international conferences, provided shelter to vulnerable groups, and trained many people to provide counseling services to victims. Ibuka has also helped supply logistical and financial support to orphans and orphan headed households. In addition to the work conducted at its headquarters in Kigali and throughout Rwanda, Ibuka has groups in Europe, Canada, and the United States.

Despite its humanitarian efforts, Ibuka's human rights work is not the only reason why it has received international attention. In 2005, François Xavier Ngarambe, president of Ibuka, spoke out to discredit Paul Rusesabagina, the protagonist of the 2004 film *Hotel Rwanda*. Starting Don Cheadle as Rusesabagina, the film depicts the heroic efforts of hotel manager Rusesabagina and his wife Tatiana to provide shelter to over a thousand Tutsis in Hôtel des Mille Collines in Rwanda during the genocide. Rusesabagina has since spoken out against Rwandan president Paul Kagame and claimed that he has remained in power since the genocide because of election fraud. Rusesabagina has also stated that Ibuka has colluded with Kagame's government to lead a smear campaign of his activities during the genocide. According to Rusesabagina, Ibuka members have encouraged survivors to discredit him.

Perhaps it should come as no surprise that an organization focused on preserving memory of the Rwandan Genocide has become involved in the modern bureaucracy of remembrance. The politics of memory with regard to the Rwandan Genocide are ongoing and as such, so are the activities of Ibuka on the ground in Rwanda, with survivor networks abroad, and in newspapers discussing current events tied to memory.

Alexis Herr

See also: AVEGA-AGAHOZO; *Hotel Rwanda*; Kigali Genocide Memorial; Rusesabagina, Paul

Further Reading

George, Terry, "Smearing a Hero," *Washington Post* (May 10, 2006).

"IBUKA," SURF Survivors Fund, http://survivors-fund.org.uk/what-we-do/local-partners/ibuka/.

Khor, Lena. *Human Rights Discourse in a Global Network: Books beyond Borders.* New York: Routledge, 2013.

Identity Cards, Rwanda

Identification cards resembling passports were issued to all Rwandans beginning in the early 1930s. They were mandated by Belgian colonial authorities, whom had been ruling the country since World War I. The identity cards indicated an individual's ethnicity—Tutsi, Hutu, or Twa—and contained the bearer's address or place of residence and other personal information. All Rwandans were required to carry their cards with them always and present them to authorities when asked. The cards helped the Belgians and their Tutsi allies, who then dominated Rwanda, to control the movement of people within the country. Indeed, no Rwandan could move to a new address or location without seeking permission from the government ahead of time. If the move was approved, a new identity card would be issued.

The identity cards were a major point of contention among Rwandans, especially the majority Hutu, whom the Belgians relegated to second-class citizenship. Most Hutus were barred from government service, had separate educational institutions that were patently subpar to those for Tutsis, and were routinely discriminated against in most public venues, including employment and housing. The identity cards drove a wedge between the Tutsis and Hutus and created a corrosive atmosphere of distrust and dislike between Rwanda's two principal ethnic groups. This atmosphere was reinforced by Belgian policies that clearly favored the minority Tutsis.

Amid this environment, the Hutu rebelled against the Tutsi monarchy and Tutsi elites in 1959. Thousands of Tutsis died in the violence, and at least 130,000 were forced to flee the country. By 1961, the Hutus had formed their own government, which shut out the Tutsis. In 1962, the Belgians left and Rwanda became an independent nation under a Hutu-dominated government. Thereafter, race relations in the country remained poor, and the Hutu led government continued to mandate the identity cards, but now the tables were turned and they were used chiefly to single out, ostracize, and repress the Tutsis. When the Rwandan Genocide commenced in April 1994, the Hutu government and allied militia groups like the Interahamwe used the cards to single out Tutsis for murder. Thus, the cards made the process of mass killing based on ethnicity much faster and simpler. Some have argued that the identity cards also helped some Hutus distance themselves psychologically from the genocide by reinforcing long-ingrained but faulty ideas about ethnic superiority and ethnic vilification.

Paul G. Pierpaoli Jr.

See also: Habyarimana, Juvénal; Hamitic Hypothesis; Hutu Social Revolution; Hutus; Interahamwe; Rwanda; Tutsis; Twas

Further Reading

Melvern, Linda. *Conspiracy to Murder: The Rwandan Genocide.* London: Verso, 2006.

Prunier, Gérard. *The Rwanda Crisis, 1959–1994: History of a Genocide.* Kampala: Fountain Publishers, 1995.

Straus, Scott. *The Order of Genocide: Race, Power, and War in Rwanda.* Ithaca, NY: Cornell University Press, 2008.

Impuzamugambi

The Impuzamugambi (Kinyarwanda word meaning "those with the same goal") was the youth group created in 1992 by the Coalition for the Defense of the Republic (French: Coalition Pour le Défense de la République, or CDR), a right-wing, radical, and extremist Hutu political party. The Impuzamugambi, along with the Interahamwe, was one of the main anti-Tutsi militias that hunted, tortured, and murdered Tutsis and moderate Hutus during the Rwandan Genocide in 1994.

During the genocide, little distinction can be made between the actions of the Interahamwe and the Impuzamugambi. Both played key roles in the annihilation of hundreds of thousands of Tutsis and moderate Hutus. Although their activities were alike during the genocide, they got their orders from different political groups. The Interahamwe (Kinyarwanda word meaning "stand, fight, or work together") formed earlier than the Impuzamugambi, had more members, and was led by ruling members of the National Republic Movement for Development (French: Mouvement Révolutionnaire National pour le Développement, or MRND). The Impuzamugambi were overseen by Jean-Bosco Barayagwiza, a founding member of the CDR and a member of the Free Radio and Television of the Thousand Hills (French: Radio Télévision Libre des Mille Collines, or RTLM), the broadcast company that used propaganda and hate speech during the genocide to direct and fuel the brutal annihilation of Tutsis and nonconforming Hutus. Its members were by and large unemployed young men trained by the Presidential Guard (soldiers that while smaller in number than the Impuzamugambi and Interahamwe also participated in the genocide).

During the genocide, Barayagwiza ordered the Impuzamugambi to create and run roadblocks. Such blocades helped the Impuzamugambi to fulfill Barayagwiza's next directive, which was to kill all the Tutsis they discovered. At the roadblocks, they checked identity cards and relied on ethnic stereotyping (Tutsis were portrayed by propaganda as uniformly slender and tall with narrow noses and high cheekbones) to identify their victims. The Impuzamugambi were often drunk and smoking marijuana and in addition to murdering their victims they also robbed and sexually assaulted them.

The Impuzamugambi, along with the Interahamwe, are responsible for the murder of tens of thousands of Rwandan civilians and their activities were examined in part during the International Criminal Tribunal for Rwanda (ICTR) during the trials of key perpetrators like that of Barayagwiza. After the genocide, Barayagwiza and members of the Impuzamugambi fled the country to escape civilian retribution or judicial punishment for their involvement in the killings. Barayagiwza was later tried by the ICTR in the so-called Media Trial.

Alexis Herr

See also: Barayagwiza, Jean-Bosco; Coalition Pour le Défense de la République; Identity Cards, Rwanda; Interahamwe; International Criminal Tribunal for Rwanda; Media Trial in Rwanda; Moderate Hutus; Mouvement Révolutionnaire National pour le Développement; Radio-Télevision Libre des Mille Collines

Further Reading

Stearns, Jason. *Dancing in the Glory of Monsters: The Collapse of the Congo and the Great War of Africa.* New York: PublicAffairs, 2011.

Thompson, Allan ed. *The Media and the Rwanda Genocide.* Ann Arbor, MI: Pluto Books, 2007.

Ingando

Ingando were political reeducation camps for Hutu rebels returning from the Democratic

Republic of the Congo, Rwandan prisoners who had confessed to committing genocide, and others the government considered a hindrance to unity. The camps were orchestrated and run by members of the Rwandan government. From 1999 to 2009, an estimated 90,000 Rwandans participated in Ingando.

As part of the Rwandan government's attempt to create unity and encourage reconciliation between Hutu perpetrators and Tutsi victims, Ingando focused on using education to unearth the roots of genocide ideology. Participants received detailed lessons on the historical misconceptions that led to the genocide, learned to identify the signs of trauma, and to respect Tutsi victims experiencing trauma. The history lessons stressed that perceived notions of ethnic identity (Hutu and Tutsi) were created by European colonists and intensified by post-colonial Hutu regimes. Participants stayed for weeks to months in Ingando camps and were isolated from their communities and families.

The success of the Ingando project—as well as the pros and cons of its operations—is still debated. Those who have gone through Ingando have mixed opinions about their experience. Some found the reeducation model confusing. Others felt the camp administers' promise to support the participants after they were released never materialized. Critics of Ingando have noted the authoritarian character of the reeducation project as an attempt by the Rwandan Patriot Front to brainwash Hutus. And some participants have expressed frustration that although they had participated in Ingando, upon their release their communities still did not accept them.

The Ingando camps used education to try and repair a shattered society and while their methods of doing so have been questioned, the goal was to include former perpetrators in a re-imagined Rwanda. Instead of giving up on perpetrators as a lost cause, the Ingando camps attempted to bring Hutu back into society and in so doing promote peace and reconciliation. The tenor of that peace and reconciliation is still under debate.

Alexis Herr

See also: Congo, Democratic Republic of the; *Gacaca* courts; Hamitic Hypothesis; Identity Cards, Rwanda; Rwandan Patriotic Front

Further Reading

Chakravarty, Anuradha. *Investing in Authoritarian Rule: Punishment and Patronage in Rwanda's Gacaca Courts for Genocide Crimes*. New York: Cambridge University Press, 2016.

Hoeksema, Suzanne, "Re-educating the Perpetrators in the Aftermath of the Rwandan Genocide," in *Genocide: New Perspectives on its Causes, Courses, and Consequences*, ed. Ugur Ümit Üngör. Amsterdam: Amsterdam University Press, 2016: 195–215.

Thomson, Susan, "Reeducation for Reconciliation: Participant Observations on *Ingando*," in *Remaking Rwanda: State Building and Human Rights after Mass Violence*, eds. Scott Straus and Lars Waldorf. Madison, WI: University of Wisconsin Press, 2011: 331–339.

Interahamwe

The Interahamwe was the largest and most potent anti-Tutsi paramilitary group in Rwanda. The term *Interahamwe* comes from the Kinyarwanda word meaning "stand, fight, or work together." The Interahamwe started to attack and kill Tutsis during the Rwandan Civil War and later helped accelerate the Rwandan Genocide in 1994. The militia group helped organize, perpetrate, and lead genocidal efforts that resulted in the annihilation of some 800,000 Tutsis and moderate Hutus.

The militia group grew out of a youth-oriented soccer club during the early 1990s, under the tutelage of Robert "Jerry" Kajuga, who turned the club into a brutal killing machine; he served as its president during the Rwandan Genocide. Ironically, Kajuga was an ethnic Tutsi whose father had illegally acquired Hutu identification papers. The Interahamwe cultivated a deep hatred of Tutsis, and often recruited its members at gunpoint from among the Hutu peasantry. By 1994, the Interahamwe had a membership approaching 6,500 well-armed men.

Many Interahamwe fighters were trained by French forces under the direction of President Juvénal Habyarimana between 1991 and 1994. When Habyarimana signed the 1993 Arusha Accords, the Interahamwe criticized the president for negotiating and accused him of accommodating the Rwandan Patriotic Front (RPF), a Tutsi group. From 1992 until the outbreak of the genocide in April 1994, the Interahamwe, in conjunction with other anti-Tutsi militias like the Impuzamugambi, waged a virulent guerrilla-style media campaign designed to rally Hutus against the Tutsis and to force Tutsis to flee Rwanda. The Rwandan government and armed forces supported the Interahamwe's activities and Rwandan vice president Georges Rutaganda directed many of the group's attacks.

The downing of Habyarimana's presidential plane in Kigali on April 6, 1994, provided the Interahamwe, along with other like-minded groups, and the Rwandan military, a pretext to launch a campaign of genocide against Tutsis, who were blamed for the president's death. In just 100 days, as many as 800,000 Tutsis and Hutu sympathizers were dead.

Once the bloodletting was over, many Interahamwe members fled to the Democratic Republic of the Congo; some then made their way to other neighboring countries, including Burundi and Uganda. From there they launched raids against Rwanda, now governed by the Tutsi-dominated RPF. In 1999, Interahamwe refugees in Uganda were responsible for the murders of 14 foreign tourists in Uganda's Bwindi National Park.

Since the RPF takeover of the Rwandan government, several members of the Interahamwe senior cadre have been tried and convicted by the International Criminal Tribunal for Rwanda (ICTR), based in Arusha, Tanzania. Some Interahamwe leaders have also been tried in Rwandan courts. The ICTR has indicted at least 20 Interahamwe leaders since 1995.

Paul G. Pierpaoli Jr.

See also: Arusha Accords; *Gacaca* Courts; Habyarimana, Juvénal; Hutus; International Criminal Tribunal for Rwanda; Kajuga, Jerry; Rutaganda, Georges; Rwandan Patriotic Front; Tutsis

Further Reading

Valentino, Benjamin A. *Final Solutions: Mass Killing and Genocide in the Twentieth Century.* Ithaca, NY: Cornell University Press, 2004.

Waller, James. *Becoming Evil: How Ordinary People Commit Genocide and Mass Killing.* Oxford: Oxford University Press, 2002.

International Criminal Tribunal for Rwanda

The United Nations Security Council (UNSC) created the International Criminal Tribunal for Rwanda (ICTR) in 1994 to prosecute individuals whom it considered responsible for the Rwandan Genocide and other violations of international humanitarian law. The landmark trials indicted 93 individuals of whom 62 were sentenced, 14 acquitted, 10 referred to national jurisdictions for trial, 3 are still at large, 2 died prior to judgment, and 2 indictments were withdrawn before trial.

Resolution 955 (1994) was adopted by the UNSC on November 8, 1994, and outlines the structure and objectives of the ICTR. Rwanda's ambassador to the United Nations (UN) opposed the ICTR in 1994 because Resolution 955 ruled out the use of the death penalty. The ICTR, however, forged ahead and established its court in Arusha, Tanzania.

The ICTR had three trial chambers, an Office of the Prosecutor (in charge of the investigation and prosecution of alleged crimes), and a Registry (which handled administrative matters). It shared an Appeals Chamber with the International Criminal Tribunal of Yugoslavia based in The Hague.

The UN General Assembly elected 16 judges from a list of candidates submitted by the UNSC. In 2002 the UNSC formed a pool of 18 *ad litem* judges in accordance with Resolution 1431 to help expedite the

trials. The *ad litem* judges acted as reserve judges who could step in if needed to fulfill the needs of the court. The judges held four-year terms and each represented a different country.

The Tribunal's jurisdiction was clearly defined. It prosecuted genocide, crimes against humanity, and other crimes defined in Article 3 of the Geneva Convention and its Additional Protocol II. It litigated crimes committed between January 1 and December 31, 1994. Those indicted included military, government, religious, militia, and media leaders, as well as politicians and businessmen. The alleged crimes had to have been committed by Rwandans within Rwanda or its neighboring states, or by non-Rwandans who committed crimes in Rwanda. The Tribunal also had a Witness and Victims Support Section to protect the anonymity of Rwandans who testified against those accused of genocide.

The tribunal detained accused individuals before and during their trials. The United Nations Detention Facility in Arusha was the first UN-built prison ever created. The defendants could communicate with family and friends and receive visits. They were also allowed to mingle with one another and have full access to legal counsel. Individuals convicted by the trial chambers could appeal their convictions to the appeals chamber. The maximum sentence meted out by the Tribunal was life imprisonment.

The ICTR had landmark cases that set new milestones in international law. Jean-Paul Akayesu was the first person ever convicted of genocide. In the same judgment, the ICTR recognized rape as a tool of genocide and in so doing defined the crime of rape in international law. The so-called Media Case was the first international trial to prosecute members of the media for

Individuals indicted by the ICTR	93
Sentenced	62
Acquitted	14
Referred to national jurisdictions for trial	10
Fugitives referred to the MICT*	3
Deceased prior to judgment	2
Indictments withdrawn before trial	2

*The Mechanism for International Criminal Tribunals or MICT was created by the United Nations Security Council on December 22, 2010. Initially it operated in parallel with the ICTR and it continued to operate after the ICTR closed on December 31, 2015.

Source: "The ICTR in Brief," United Nations Mechanism for International Criminal Tribunals (Accessed 16 September 2017), http://unictr.unmict.org/en/tribunal.

inciting the public to commit genocide. When Jean Kambanda, the former interim government prime minster of Rwanda, pleaded guilty he became the first person to admit having committed genocide. At the end of 2014, the ICTR concluded its operations.

Amy Hackney Blackwell

See also: Akayesu, Jean-Paul; Barayagwiza, Jean-Bosco; Kabuga, Félicien; Jean, Kamuhanda; Kambanda, Jean; *Kangura*; Kayishema, Clement, Trial of; Karamira, Froduald; Media Trial in Rwanda; Nahimana, Ferdinand; Ndindiliyimana, Augustin; Ngeze, Hassan; Nowrojee, Binaifer; Ntakirutimana, Elizaphan; Ntamabyariro, Agnes; Nyiramasuhuko, Pauline; Prosper, Pierre-Richard; Radio-Télévision Libre des Mille Collines; Ruggiu, Georges; Rutaganda, Georges, Trial of

Further Reading

Boot, Machteld. *Genocide, Crimes Against Humanity, War Crimes: Nullum Crimen Sine Lege and the Subject Matter Jurisdiction of the International Criminal Court.* Antwerp: Intersentia, 2002.

"The ICTR in Brief," United Nations Mechanism for International Criminal Tribunals (February 2017). http://unictr.unmict.org/en/tribunal/.

Schabas, William A. *Genocide in International Law: The Crime of Crimes.* Cambridge, UK: Cambridge University Press, 2000.

K

Kabuga, Félicien

Félicien Kabuga is a multimillionaire Rwandan businessman alleged to have been the chief financier of the 1994 Rwandan Genocide. On the run since 1994, he is one of the most wanted men in Africa.

Kabuga was born in 1935 in Muniga, in the commune of Mukarange, Byumba, and had close ties to the long-serving president of Rwanda, Juvénal Habyarimana, and his ruling party, the National Revolutionary Movement for Development (French: Mouvement Révolutionnaire National pour le Développement, or MRND). He was one of the main financial contributors to MRND, and to the Coalition for the Defense of the Republic (French: Coalition pour la Défense de la République, or CDR), an extremist anti-Tutsi Hutu party emerging from within the MRND.

It has been alleged that from the end of 1990 until July 1994, Kabuga played an important role in the preparation and execution of a plan aimed at the extermination of the Tutsis. This plan encouraged hatred and ethnic violence, trained and armed anti-Tutsi militias, and drafted lists of people to be murdered.

Kabuga also became president of the ruling committee of the rabidly anti-Tutsi radio station Radio-Télévision Libre des Mille Collines (RTLM), helping to indoctrinate the Rwandan people with extremist Hutu ideologies. In November 1993, and again in February 1994, the Habyarimana government, which was at that time attempting to project an image of pluralism and tolerance, publicly urged Kabuga to stop the distribution of messages that would incite interracial hatred, but Kabuga countered by declaring that RTLM should become the official voice of the Hutu Power regime. Throughout the genocide, RTLM subsequently played a vital propaganda and directing role to help facilitate the killing.

Kabuga also wielded considerable influence because of his wealth. On April 25, 1994, it is reported that Kabuga and others met in Gisenyi to create the National Defence Funds Acting Committee (French: Comité Provisoire du Fonds de Défense Nationale, or FDN), of which he became president. The FDN was created to provide assistance to the radical Hutu-dominated interim government to help destroy Tutsis and moderate Hutus. The purpose of the FDN was to buy weapons, vehicles, and uniforms for the Interahamwe militia and the national army. Kabuga was granted signatory power over the fund's bank accounts. It was in this capacity that he became known as the chief paymaster of the Interahamwe militias that undertook the task of carrying out and directing the Rwandan Genocide.

It is alleged that he exercised authority over organizations aligned with Hutu Power, enabling him to organize, order, and even participate in the mass murders. Certainly, he employed his wealth to outfit the Interahamwe. Before and during the genocide, Kabuga is alleged to have participated in the provision of weapons to the militia, purchasing vast quantities of machetes, hoes, and other agricultural tools for Interahamwe use. From 1992, one of Kabuga's companies,

ETS, was reported to have bought massive stocks of machetes, hoes, and other farm tools, in the belief that they would function as weapons during the genocide. In March 1994, just before the killings began, Kabuga was reported to have imported 50,000 machetes from Kenya. Kabuga has also been accused of continuing to supply machetes and other weapons during the genocide. Additionally, it has been alleged that he suppled uniforms and transportation to the Interahamwe through his company-owned vehicles. Kabuga has always claimed he is innocent of the accusations leveled against him.

In June 1994, as troops from the Rwandan Patriotic Front (RPF) advanced on Kigali, and then took over most of the country, Kabuga fled Rwanda. On July 22, 1994, he sought asylum in Switzerland. He was expelled, at Swiss government expense (with his wife and seven children), on August 18, 1994, and flew immediately to Kinshasa in the Democratic Republic of the Congo (DRC). Before leaving Switzerland, it is alleged, he withdrew funds from his Swiss bank account with UBS at the Geneva airport. He then spent time in the DRC, arranging sanctuary in a third country, widely believed to be Kenya. He took up residence in Nairobi, where he allegedly found protection from senior government officials of then president Daniel Arap Moi. This protection enabled him to evade a number of attempted arrests by Kenyan police and international bodies.

In 1995, when the International Criminal Tribunal for Rwanda (ICTR) was established, Kabuga was one of the first of those for whom the Tribunal planned to investigate. In August 1998 he was indicted by the ICTR on 11 counts that included genocide, conspiracy to commit genocide, complicity in genocide, and violations of the laws and customs of war.

One year later, in August 1999, an international warrant for his arrest was issued.

Despite these efforts, as of this writing, Kabuga has eluded capture. He is said to be a frequent traveler to various African nations where he buys protection. A 1999 report of a United Nations (UN) commission of inquiry into arms purchases by the former militia of the Rwandan government reported that Kabuga had been seen in Southeast Asia in September 1998, and in 2000, he was said to have transited through Belgium, where his wife was living at that time.

From this time on, concerted efforts were made to capture Kabuga. On June 11, 2002, the United States offered a reward of up to $5,000,000 for any information leading to his capture, and later that year the United States formally accused Kenyan security authorities of having given sanctuary to Kabuga and of using governmental infrastructures to prevent him from being arrested. On August 28, 2003, in Security Council Resolution 1503, the UN urged all member states (and Kenya in particular) to intensify their cooperation to find Kabuga and bring him to justice. The ICTR also arranged to have Kabuga's financial assets confiscated, and to block access to his bank accounts in France, Switzerland, and Belgium.

In November 2009 the U.S. ambassador for war crimes issues, Stephen Rapp, told reporters in Nairobi that he was convinced Kabuga was still living in Kenya, and that he had seen pictures of Kabuga in Kenyan neighborhoods. By way of response, Kenyan prime minister Raila Odinga claimed that Kabuga was not in the country. Then, on a visit to the ICTR in Arusha, Tanzania, in February 2010, Rapp once more announced that Kabuga was still in Kenya, notwithstanding government declarations to the contrary.

As of this writing, Félicien Kabuga remains on the run. The Kenyan government continues to deny he is in the country, but has reaffirmed its pledge to arrest him if he is located.

Paul R. Bartrop

See also: Coalition Pour la Défense de la Rèpublique; Habyarimana, Juvénal; Interahamwe; International Criminal Tribunal for Rwanda; Moderate Hutu; Radio-Télévision Libre des Mille Collines; Rwandan Genocide, Role of Propaganda in the; Rwandan Patriotic Front

Further Reading

Friedrichs, David O., ed. *State Crime*. Brookfield, VT: Ashgate/Dartmouth, 1998.

Neier, Aryeh. *War Crimes: Brutality, Genocide, Terror, and the Struggle for Justice*. New York: Times Books, 1998.

"Wanted: Félicien Kabuga," U.S. Department of State (June 2002), accessed 17 July 2017. https://www.state.gov/j/gcj/wcrp/206033.htm.

Kagame, Paul

Paul Kagame is a Rwandan politician, who, as the leader of the Tutsi-led Rwandan Patriotic Army (RPA), the military arm of the Rwandan Patriotic Front (RPF), defeated Hutu extremist forces to end the 1994 Rwandan Genocide. In 2000, he became president of Rwanda, a position he holds to this day.

A Tutsi, Kagame was born in Gitarama on October 23, 1957, and as a child became a refugee as his family (among tens of thousands of other Rwandan Tutsis) fled to Uganda in 1960 in the face of Hutu attacks on Tutsis. In 1962, they settled into an Ugandan refugee camp, where Kagame spent the rest of his childhood. He was educated in the Ugandan education system, was taught in English rather than French (as spoken in Rwanda), and studied for a time at Makerere University in Kampala. For the next 30 years after 1960, he lived his life as an exile.

Determined to resist oppressive regimes, as a young man Kagame decided on a rebel military career, and he joined with a Ugandan dissident leader, Yoweri Museveni, who had formed his own National Resistance Army (NRA). Together, the two spent five years waging guerrilla warfare against the government of Ugandan prime minister Apollo Milton Obote. When Museveni took power in 1986, he sent Kagame to Cuba for training with several other intelligence officers then under Kagame's command. Then, in 1989, Museveni sent Kagame on a training course at the U.S. Army Command and Staff College at Fort Leavenworth, Kansas.

In 1985, as a young, English-speaking Tutsi refugee burning to return to Rwanda, Kagame and his best friend, Fred Rwigyema, established the Rwandan Patriotic Front (RPF), a political organization with an armed wing named the RPA composed mostly of Tutsis who had fought in Uganda with Museveni's NRA in the overthrow of President Idi Amin in 1979. By October 1990, the movement was strong enough to launch an invasion of Rwanda from Uganda, supported by Museveni. Rwigyema was killed during the invasion, which failed after a French-led intervention force stopped its advance following an appeal for help from Rwandan president Juvénal Habyarimana. After Rwigyema's death, Kagame became the head of the RPF. Kagame's role in negotiations with the Habyarimana regime throughout the 1990s was important, and certainly contributed to the signing of the Arusha Accords, a peace settlement between the RPF and the Rwandan government signed on August 4, 1993. Habyarimana's assassination on April 6, 1994, however, destroyed any possibility that these accords would be implemented.

Controversy has since dogged Kagame over Habyarimana's assassination, with several accusations made against him for his alleged responsibility for having shot down Habyarimana's plane—an event which killed not only the president, but also the president of Burundi, Cyprien Ntaryamira, and the plane's French pilot and crew. In January 2000, three Tutsi informants told United Nations (UN) investigators that they were part of an elite hit squad that had assassinated Habyarimana. Their confession implicated Kagame in his capacity as

President Paul Kagame took office in April 2000, and has since helped rebuild and refinance Rwanda. In August 2017, Kagame was reelected to serve a third term, but only after a constitutional amendment which upended a two-term limit for presidents. (Government of Rwanda)

overall commander, though nothing was proven and no official allegations were made. According to Lieutenant Aloys Ruyenzi, a member of the RPA, Kagame was primarily responsible for shooting down the plane, while the French government launched its own investigation, leading to a conclusion by Judge Jean-Louis Bruguière that Kagame in fact ordered the shooting. In response, in November 2006, Rwanda severed all diplomatic ties with France and ordered its entire diplomatic staff out of Rwanda within 24 hours. Relations between the two countries remained strained for several years after this, but in an attempt to establish better relations with France, Kagame visited Paris in mid-September 2011, reciprocating a visit to Rwanda by French president Nicolas Sarkozy in February 2010.

All accusations against Kagame have been met with vigorous denials by Kagame and his supporters, who have argued that the plane was shot down by Hutu extremists furious with Habyarimana for arranging a peace settlement with the Tutsis, and who exploited the events in order to commence the already-well-planned genocide. In 2007, the Rwandan government launched a formal investigation into the plane crash. The results were released in 2010, concluding that Hutu extremists were responsible for shooting down the plane in an effort to derail Habyarimana's peace negotiations with Kagame and the Tutsi rebels.

With the onset of the genocide in April 1994, Kagame and the RPF renewed their war against the government, and by the end of May, they controlled most of Rwanda. Kigali was captured on July 4, 1994, and the remnants of the extremist Hutu Power government of Jean Kambanda fled. Once the conflict was over, Kagame became vice president and defence minister under Pasteur

Bizimungu, but many believed that Kagame was the real power behind the presidency. Bizimungu, who was a deputy commander of the RPF and an ethnic Hutu, eventually came into conflict with Kagame over the direction of postgenocide policy-making. He resigned in March 2000, and Kagame became caretaker president. He was then elected in a landslide victory on August 25, 2003, in the first national elections since the genocide. Kagame won 95.5 percent of all votes cast, and was sworn in for a seven-year term on September 12, 2003. Then, on August 9, 2010, Kagame was re-elected for a second seven-year term as president. In an outcome questioned by many observers from around the world as thoroughly unimaginable for a free and fair election, Kagame received 93.08 percent of the vote.

After the genocide, many of the Hutus responsible for the killing fled to neighbouring Zaire (now known as the Democratic Republic of the Congo, or DRC) using the country as a base from which to continue attacking Rwanda. Kagame sent Rwandan troops into the country in late 1996 to pursue these Hutus, many of whom were in refugee camps on the Rwandan-DRC border, in what was a clear violation of the larger country's sovereignty. Kagame now found himself embroiled in a confusing conflict in which a Congolese civil war involving forces either supporting or opposing Zairean president Mobutu Sese Seko and his adversary Laurent-Désiré Kabila—and all these forces were inconsistent in which side they championed—had fragmented into a series of smaller conflicts involving competing local warlords and the government. Into this mix came the Rwandan Hutu exiles, the invading Rwandan forces, as well as an army from Museveni's Uganda. Some parts of the DRC were then occupied by Rwandan troops for the next five years. In

the course of the war, the Rwandan army financed its invasion through an illegal trade in Congo's natural resources, namely tin, tungsten, tantalum, and gold.

Kagame's invasion of the DRC has been severely criticized in several quarters, as the army was known to have committed a series of brutal (and often systematic) massacres against fleeing and unarmed Hutus. Also, to finance the campaign, the Rwandan military allegedly plundered vast amounts of precious minerals from the areas in eastern Congo it occupied. Kagame was known to support the rebel forces in the DRC until 2002, when he signed a peace accord and agreed to remove Rwandan troops in exchange for the disarmament and repatriation of Hutu forces. This notwithstanding, a Rwandan presence—sometimes quite active and violent—remained throughout the next few years, further confusing an already complex and disastrous situation which some estimates claim have cost up to 5.4 million lives.

In the aftermath of the genocide and the 34 years of exile that preceded it, a major focus of Kagame's presidency has been to build Rwandan national unity. Accordingly, his preference for postgenocide Rwanda is for the nation's citizens to downplay all references to their separate ethnic identities. During the 2003 presidential campaign he portrayed himself as a Rwandan rather than a Tutsi, and has since made it illegal for any politician or citizen to make statements encouraging ethnic animosity or expressing ethnic solidarity. Some have seen this as the tip of an antidemocratic iceberg that suppresses human rights, and Kagame has been criticized as an authoritarian leader who often disregards and stifles public opinion. The international humanitarian monitoring organization Human Rights Watch has accused Rwandan police of several instances

of extrajudicial killings and deaths in custody, and Kagame has been accused of
being a ruthless and repressive leader intol-
erant of criticism. Some have pointed out
that he favors Tutsis over Hutus in senior
positions.

On the other hand, Kagame's leadership
style has enabled him to devote much of his
attention to issues of postgenocide justice,
reconciliation, and building peace, often
without dissent. Other areas of priority
have included economic development,
good governance, women's empowerment,
and advancement of education. Kagame
has received international recognition for
his leadership of what was a broken country,
and he is considered by many to be one of
the most dynamic and effective leaders in
Africa in the early 21st century.

Paul R. Bartrop

See also: Arusha Accords; Congo, Democratic
Republic of the; Habyarimana, Juvénal; Kambanda, Jean; Rwandan Patriotic Army; Rwandan Patriotic Front

Further Reading

Bodnarchuk, Kari. *Rwanda: A Country Torn
Apart*. Minneapolis, MN: Lerner Publishing Group, 1998.

Eltringham, Nigel. *Accounting for Horror:
Post-Genocide Debates in Rwanda*. Londres: Pluto Press, 2004.

Prunier, Gérard. *Africa's World War: Congo,
the Rwandan Genocide, and the Making
of a Continental Catastrophe*. New York:
Oxford University Press, 2010.

Kajuga, Jerry Robert

Jerry Robert Kajuga was the founder and
national president of the Rwandan youth
militia known as the Interahamwe ("those

who stick together"). Born in 1960, Kajuga
was the child of a mixed Hutu-Tutsi marriage. His father was a highly respected
Episcopal priest of Tutsi background who
had married a Hutu woman, and it is believed
that the family at first disguised their official
identity as Tutsi and "passed" as Hutus.

The genesis of the Interahamwe movement originated in junior soccer clubs.
Some of the first Interahamwe recruits came
from *Loisirs* ("Leisure"), a Sunday soccer
club headed by Kajuga. The Interahamwe
was founded in 1990 and evolved into a radical Hutu killing machine as the anti-Tutsi
campaign of hatred spread by Rwandan
president Juvénal Habyarimana intensified
throughout 1992 and 1993. After Habyarimana was killed in a plane crash on April 6,
1994, it was the Interahamwe, together with
the Rwandan army and the Presidential
Guard, which took the lead in the massacre
of Tutsis throughout the country.

The Interahamwe was comprised of young
males who were connected with the youth
wing of Habyarimana's National Revolutionary Movement for Development (French:
Mouvement Révolutionnaire National pour le
Développement, or MRND) party. They were
among the most active killers during the 1994
Rwandan Genocide. As a paramilitary unit,
Interahamwe was fundamental to the Rwandan Genocide, and the most important of the
anti-Tutsi militias during the atrocity.

Originally trained by the French at
Habyarimana's request, the Interahamwe
were the most radical of the many factions
opposed to the Arusha peace process of
1992. In the years prior to the genocide,
the Interahamwe engaged in lethal street
fights hoping to upset the social order. Their
source of weapons was provided through the
army, allowing them to engage in daily
murder sprees employing machetes and other
implements. On January 26, 1994, MRND

leaders, including Kajuga, reportedly met to discuss ways to create conflict between the Interahamwe and Belgian soldiers serving with the United Nations Assistance Mission for Rwanda (UNAMIR). The militias were ordered to never obey orders from the Belgians, to call for support from surrounding areas whenever confronted by Belgians, and to get as many people as possible from the surrounding area to witness the confrontation. Then, on February 25, 1994, Kajuga presided over a meeting of Interahamwe leaders that recommended greater vigilance against Tutsis in Kigali; this resulted in lists of Tutsis in the city being drawn up, presumably for any future action that might be taken. The leaders decided on a system of communications using telephones, whistles, runners, and public criers. They ordered militia members to be ready to act at any moment using traditional weapons and firearms. The meeting ordered the Interahamwe to be ready to come to the aid of members of the militias of other radical Hutu political parties such as the Impuzamugambi of the extremist Coalition for the Defense of the Republic (French: Coalition pour la Défense de la République, or CDR).

To keep the Interahamwe in check, there were periodic purges of the most zealous members, who wished to proceed at a pace faster than that preferred by their political leaders; thus, when the call for action came after Habyarimana's assassination on April 6, 1994, none were more bloodthirsty than the Interahamwe. From this time on, Interahamwe killing units were left largely to their own devices. They knew their instructions, and required little prompting.

Right up to the end of the genocide, all members and cells of the Interahamwe were carefully monitored by Joseph Nzirorera (b. 1950), the secretary-general of the MRND,

even though its vice president, Georges Rutaganda, coordinated the day-to-day affairs of the Interahamwe. The Interahamwe forcefully recruited peasants to popularize their role as mass killers. When the killing ceased, many of the Interahamwe members managed to escape to eastern Congo. The Interahamwe's actions during the genocide demonstrate that the genocide had been planned prior to President Habyarimana's death. Indeed, it was a carefully planned campaign of extermination that had its executioners prepared and waiting to go into action long before the bloodshed began in April 1994.

Kajuga justified the role of the organization of which he was national president on the grounds that Rwanda's Tutsis were waging a concerted offensive, through the Tutsi-led Rwandan Patriotic Front (RPF), to destroy Hutus. A fanatic of the most extreme calibre, Kajuga was active throughout the genocide not only in running the Interahamwe, but also in his negotiations with Rwanda's Hutu Power interim government.

During the genocide, Kajuga kept his brother Wyclif at the Hôtel des Mille Collines in Kigali as a safeguard due to the family's hidden Tutsi identity. This may have contributed to the success of the Mille Collines in remaining safe from the genocide. The Mille Collines stood as an island of refuge for a select few Tutsis threatened with annihilation, largely at the initiative of the hotel manager, a Hutu named Paul Rusesabagina. Throughout the genocide, the hotel in central Kigali was protected by UNAMIR troops.

In July 1994, as the RPF forces conquered more and more of Rwanda and began to close in on Kigali, the Interahamwe fled in advance of their arrival. Kajuga retreated along with many thousands of his militia members. He evaded capture within

Rwanda until 1996, and then slipped into Zaire (now known as the Democratic Republic of the Congo), where he lived for another two years. In 1998 he was arrested by UN security forces, and was taken to Kigali, where he stood trial before a Rwandan national court. He was sentenced to life imprisonment for war crimes.

Paul R. Bartrop

See also: Coalition Pour la Défense de la Rèpublique; Dallaire, Roméo; *Hotel Rwanda*; Interahamwe; Rwandan Patriotic Front; Rusesabagina, Paul; United Nations Assistance Mission for Rwanda

Further Reading

Dallaire, Roméo. *Shake Hands with the Devil: The Failure of Humanity in Rwanda*. Toronto: Random House, Canada, 2004.

Melvern, Linda. *Conspiracy to Murder: The Rwandan Genocide*. London: Verso, 2006.

Shaw, Martin. *War and Genocide: Organized Killing in Modern Society*. Cambridge, UK: Polity, 2003.

Kambanda, Jean

Jean Kambanda was the prime minister of Rwanda during the genocide that took place between April and July 1994. After President Juvénal Habyarimana and Prime Minister Agathe Uwilingiyimana had been assassinated—the former as the result of a missile attack on his plane by unknown attackers on April 6 and the latter, a Hutu moderate, murdered by Hutu extremists— Kambanda was sworn in as head of an interim government on April 9.

A member of the Democratic Republican Movement (French: Mouvement Démocratique Républicain, or MDR), Kambanda remained prime minister throughout the genocide, directing general government policy with regard to the genocide of Rwanda's Tutsi population. He broadcast messages on Radio-Télévision Libre des Mille Collines (RTLM) inciting Hutus to kill Tutsis, and urged Hutus to construct roadblocks throughout Rwanda to prevent Tutsis from fleeing the country. He also traveled throughout Rwanda for the express purpose of rousing the Hutu population to undertake genocide, while at the same time providing weapons and ammunition to Hutu militia movements such as the Interahamwe and the Impuzamugambi. As the head of the government he also contributed indirectly to the killing by failing—or rather, refusing—to condemn the militias when they broke the law by killing Tutsis and destroying vast amounts of property.

Born on October 19, 1955, Jean Kambanda was an educated member of Rwanda's dominant Hutu middle class and held a degree in commercial engineering. He was director of the Union of Popular Banks of Rwanda from May 1989 to April 1994, and, with an interest in politics, had become vice president of the Butare section of the MDR by the time the genocide broke out in April 1994. The MDR had earlier been promised the position of prime minister in the negotiations that led to the signing of the Arusha Accords of August 4, 1993. This was a series of agreements made between Habyarimana's government of Rwanda and the rebel Rwandan Patriotic Front (RPF), and was designed to end the country's civil war and help bring about a democratic Rwanda. In the transitional government that would follow, the MDR and other parties were guaranteed certain compromises, one of which involved earmarking specific positions in any future administration. Owing to a series of internal party intrigues, however, Kambanda, who then remained prime minister for the entirety of the genocide, bypassed the party's first choice, Faustin Twagiramungu, for the job. Twagiramungu became prime minister after Kambanda at the end of the genocide. He retained that position until his resignation in 1995. When the forces of the RPF defeated the army of the interim government on July 19, 1994, Kambanda fled Rwanda and his government collapsed.

He was on the run for three years, until he was arrested in Nairobi, Kenya, on July 18, 1997, after a seven-week stakeout by a multinational team of police investigators. He was transferred immediately to the jurisdiction of the International Criminal Tribunal for Rwanda (ICTR) in Arusha, Tanzania, and was arraigned on a variety of charges relating directly to genocide and crimes against humanity. The charges against him included: genocide, and conspiracy to commit genocide; public and direct incitation to commit genocide; aiding and abetting genocide; failing in his duty to prevent the genocide which occurred while he was prime minister; and two counts of crimes against humanity. Acknowledging his responsibility, on May 1, 1998, he pleaded guilty on all counts. The court sentenced him to life imprisonment, the maximum penalty that can be imposed by the ICTR, on September 4, 1998.

After this, however, he rescinded his confession and appealed his conviction. His claimed his original confession had been in error, and that his legal counsel had misrepresented him. Indeed, there was no little controversy surrounding the appointment of Kambanda's counsel, who was chosen by the ICTR Registrar from a limited list that excluded French and Canadian Francophone lawyers. This forced Kambanda to defend himself for four months, effectively denying him the same

This photo captures former Rwandan prime minister Jean Kambanda speaking at his headquarters in Gitarama on May 27, 1994. After the genocide, the ex-premier plead guilty to charges of genocide and in 1998 became the first person in history to be sentenced for the crime of genocide. (Alexander Joe/AFP/Getty Images)

access to legal process available to all other accused. Some alleged that the trial was for show—to make the ICTR look good—rather than achieving to justice. After receiving legal counsel, his attorneys argued that Kambanda had been nothing more than a sham figurehead, a puppet in the hands of a genocidal military led by such figures as Colonel Théoneste Bagosora. They claimed that Bagosora had used Kambanda to legitimize the government and military's control of the country by cloaking their murderous action under the mantle of constitutional respectability. The defense petitioned the Tribunal to reduce

Kambanda's sentence to two years' imprisonment owing to his having been forced to act "under duress with limited responsibility." The ICTR, for its part, concluded that this defense against a charge of genocide was irrelevant, and dismissed the appeal on October 19, 2000. The original verdict was upheld on all counts, and he was transferred to Bamako Central Prison, Bamako, Mali, where he is currently serving his sentence.

The significance of the Kambanda verdict is that it was the first occasion on which a head of government had pleaded guilty to committing genocide, and the first such conviction. As the highest-ranking political leader in the custody of the ICTR, Kambanda's verdict has further enhanced the legal principle that refuses to recognize state immunity as a legitimate defense against genocide. This principle, first set down as one of the "Nuremberg Principles" adopted by the United Nations International Law Commission in 1950, accepts that every person is responsible for their own actions, and that, as a result, no one stands above international law. The defense of "following superior orders" is nullified by these principles, and in the specific case of Kambanda the third principle prevails: being a Head of State or a government official does not absolve a person from the responsibility of having committed a criminal act, if the act committed is criminal within international law.

Paul R. Bartrop

See also: Arusha Accords; Bagosora, Théoneste; Habyarimana, Juvénal; Impuzamugambi; Interahamwe; International Criminal Tribunal for Rwanda; Radio-Télévision Libre des Mille Collines; Rwandan Civil War; Uwilingiyimana, Agathe

Further Reading

Melvern, Linda. *Conspiracy to Murder: The Rwandan Genocide*. London: Verso, 2006.

Prunier, Gérard. *The Rwanda Crisis, 1959–1994: History of a Genocide*. Kampala: Fountain Publishers, 1995.

Kamuhanda, Jean, Trial of

On November 26, 1999, Jean de Dieu Kamuhanda was arrested in France and soon extradited to Arusha, Tanzania, to sit trial for his involvement in the 1994 Rwandan Genocide. In April 2001, Kamuhanda, former minister of higher education and scientific research in the Rwandan interim government during the genocide, was placed on trial in the International Criminal Tribunal for Rwanda (ICTR) on nine counts of genocide and crimes against humanity. The court accused Kamuhanda of leading the massacre of 800 Tutsis at a church in the Gikomero commune, Kigali-Rural Prefecture, in April 1994. He was also charged because the interim government in which he held high office either directed or failed to stop many of the 1994 massacres during the Rwandan genocide.

The trial witnessed numerous delays: first, two of the presiding judges had to be replaced because one died and another was promoted. Subsequently, scheduling conflicts arose with other trials that were sharing the same court space. After almost two years, the trial had met in session for only 73 days. Initially, the prosecution hoped to try Kamuhanda along with seven other former government officials, but the ICTR rejected the idea of a joint trial. Some critics argued that Kamuhanda's prosecution was less important than other government officials and that his suit was being driven by political pressure. The prosecution portrayed Kamuhanda as the instigator of the events at Gikomero, as well as an influential member of the Movement of the Republic for National Development (French: Révolutionnaire National pour le Développement, or MRND). He was reportedly promoted to minister in May 1994 because of his support for the ongoing massacres. The defense countered that Kamuhanda had been in Kigali at the time of the Gikomero attacks and could not possibly have traveled there given the fighting in the region. The defense also argued that he was never influential in the government and that, based on previous legal precedents; he could not be convicted simply for being part of an organization engaged in killings.

Kamuhanda was tried in the reconstituted Trial Chamber II, with Judge William Sekule of Tanzania presiding; Winston Matazima Maqutu of Lesotho and Arlette Ramaroson of Madagascar also served on the judicial panel. Douglas Moore of Ireland led the prosecution team, while Aicha Conde of Guinea directed Kamuhanda's defense. In August 2002, as the defense opened its case, it successfully argued that the count of conspiracy to commit genocide should be dropped for lack of evidence, so Kamuhanda now faced a total of eight counts.

In presenting its case, the prosecution called 27 witnesses. Most testified about events that took place in Gikomero in mid-April 1994. According to their accounts, Kamuhanda delivered weapons to local Hutu gendarmes and members of the Interahamwe. He then visited the church compound where many Tutsis were seeking refuge and told officials "to begin work." Hours later, hundreds were killed in the compound. The prosecution portrayed Kamuhanda as an influential party official who had been a

presidential adviser even before his appointment as minister. This claim of previous advising was crucial because Kamuhanda did not become minister until May 25, 1994, almost two months after large-scale killings had begun.

The defense did not deny that genocide had occurred, but questioned the reliability of the witnesses that placed Kamuhanda in Gikomero. Several of the witnesses reported only what they had heard from others. Such hearsay evidence was allowed by the Tribunal, but was considered weak. Other witnesses stated that they saw a man at Gikomero, but only later identified him as Kamuhanda. The defense questioned these identifications. Some witnesses identified Kamuhanda in court, but he was the only male on his side of the courtroom. The defense also presented Kamuhanda's testimony, supported by that of some two dozen friends and relatives, that he was in Kigali from April 6 until April 18 and thus could not have been responsible for events that took place in Gikomero during that time. To answer the question of whether he might have briefly visited Gikomero, the defense presented witnesses who testified that fighting in the area made it impossible to travel between Kigali and Gikomero. The defense also tried to counter the portrayal of Kamuhanda as a key party figure. In their accounts, Kamuhanda never had close ties to the interim president or other high-ranking officials. Defense lawyers claimed that he had risen quickly in the government because of his talent and efficiency, not as a reward for his support of massacres. Furthermore, the defense argued that he accepted the promotion to minister because he feared for his life and was never more than a figurehead leader.

Kamuhanda was ultimately convicted of genocide and of extermination as a crime against humanity, but was acquitted of conspiracy to commit genocide, rape as a crime against humanity, and war crimes and other inhumane acts. He was sentenced to life imprisonment. Following an appeal, his sentence was affirmed in 2005 and on December 7, 2008, he was transferred to Mali to serve his sentence.

John Dietrich

See also: International Criminal Tribunal for Rwanda; Mouvement Révolutionnaire National pour le Développement

Further Reading

Cruvellier, Thierry. *Court of Remorse: Inside the International Criminal Court for Rwanda.* Madison, WI: University of Wisconsin Press, 2010.

Des Forges, Alison, and Timothy Longman. "Legal Responses to Genocide in Rwanda." In *My Neighbor, My Enemy: Justice and Community in the Aftermath of Mass Atrocity*, edited by Eric Stover and Harvey M. Weinstein, 49–63. Cambridge: Cambridge University Press, 2004.

Kangura

Kangura, a virulent anti-Tutsi newspaper and a vehicle for pro-Hutu propaganda, played a major role in laying the ideological and social foundations of the 1994 Rwandan Genocide. *Kangura*, which translates from Kinyarwanda (Rwandan) as "Wake Them Up," was owned and edited by Hutu businessman and journalist Hassan Ngeze. As the title implies, the publication was intended to "educate" and "inform" the Hutu majority about the alleged dangers posed by the minority Tutsi population. It also exposed and thus endangered moderate Hutus (those who did not support or were opposed to violence against Tutsis).

From May 1990 to February 1994, *Kangura* denigrated Tutsis and fanned the flames of inter-ethnic hatred among Rwandans. The paper released its first edition in May 1990, to coincide with the start of the Rwandan Civil War and the rise of a political movement called Hutu Power (a group that defined Rwanda as a Hutu nation). In December 1990, *Kangura* published some of its most inflammatory material, the "Hutu Ten Commandments." Many of the so-called commandments echoed long-standing Hutu prejudices while encouraging Hutu distrust of Tutsis. The Hutu Commandments forbade marriage and friendship between Tutsi and Hutu; extolled the superiority of Hutu women; exhorted Hutus to abandon Tutsi spouses or relatives; asserted that Tutsis could not hold any positions in government or the military; argued that education should be dominated by Hutus; instructed all Hutus to show no mercy toward Tutsis; ordered Hutus to band together to fight the "Tutsi menace"; and encouraged educators to instruct all Hutus in "Hutu ideology," including the social revolution of 1959. The last published newspaper came out in February 1994, less than two months prior to the beginning of the genocide.

Through the constant repetition of the commandments and the venomous anti-Tutsi articles and editorials, *Kangura* served to dehumanize the Tutsis while giving Hutu readers the impression that oppressing and hurting Tutsis was acceptable. The newspaper frequently referred to the Tutsis as *inyenzi* (a Kinyarwanda word meaning "cockroach"), with the implication that like cockroaches, the Tutsis were dirty vermin that had to be exterminated. The paper also issued frequent (and entirely unfounded) warnings that Tutsis were out to enslave or eradicate Hutus. Because of its clever manipulations and the fact that Hutus, who made up roughly 85 percent of the population, outnumbered Tutsis, who accounted for just 14 percent of Rwandans, *Kangura* propaganda was widely devoured by the masses. Although only three in 10 Rwandans could read, articles were commonly read out-loud in public and later during Interahamwe (Hutu paramilitary organization) rallies (Melvern 2004, 49).

Not surprisingly, the newspaper vilified the Tutsi-dominated Rwandan Patriotic Front (RPF) and exhorted Hutus to support the government in the ongoing civil war with the RPF. It refused to support President Juvénal Habyarimana's efforts to bring an end to the conflict or to seek any accommodation with the RPF. *Kangura* bitterly denounced the August 1993 Arusha Accords (a set of protocols signed between RPF and the Rwandan government to end the three-year Rwandan Civil War) and claimed that they pandered to the RPF and Tutsis. The newspaper worked closely with other pro-Hutu propaganda media outlets, especially Radio-Télévision Libre des Mille Collines (RTLM), with whom it frequently coordinated its propaganda and sensationalist reporting. Ngeze was in fact one of the main program directors of RTLM.

In the months leading up to the genocide, *Kangura* continued to wage a violent propaganda war against Tutsis and the United Nations. After the United Nations Assistance Mission for Rwanda (UNAMIR) was dispatched to help Rwanda implement the terms of the Arusha Accords and to prevent a flare-up in violence, *Kangura* savagely debased the UN mission. These attacks included spurious claims that UNAMIR was a tool of the Tutsis and was sent to Rwanda to aid in a Tutsi takeover of the government. By early 1994, the newspaper was openly advocating the mass annihilation of Tutsis, especially those in the RPF. *Kangura*

also published the names of Hutus whose "loyalty" to their ethnicity was questionable. Later, when the genocide began in April 1994, many of these Hutus were murdered as "traitors."

Although *Kangura* ceased publication in February 1994, there is no doubt that it contributed greatly to the anti-Tutsi hatred and hysteria that ultimately manifested itself in the Rwandan Genocide. In December 2003, the International Criminal Tribunal for Rwanda (ICTR) convicted Ngeze of various crimes associated with the genocide. He was given a life sentence, which in 2008 was reduced to 35 years in prison.

Paul G. Pierpaoli Jr.

See also: Arusha Accords; Hutus; International Criminal Tribunal for Rwanda; Media Trial; Moderate Hutu; Ngeze, Hassan; Radio-Télévision Libre des Mille Collines; Rwanda; Rwandan Genocide, Role of Propaganda in the; Rwandan Patriotic Front; Tutsis

Further Reading

Kressel, Neil Jeffrey. *Mass Hate: The Global Rise of Genocide and Terror.* New York: Plenum Press, 1996.

Melvern, Linda. *Conspiracy to Murder: The Rwandan Genocide.* New York: Verso, 2004.

Valentino, Benjamin A. *Final Solutions: Mass Killing and Genocide in the Twentieth Century.* Ithaca, NY: Cornell University Press, 2004.

Karamira, Froduald

Froduald Karamira was a radical Rwandan politician prior to and during the Rwandan Genocide in 1994. Born on August 14, 1947, in Mushubati, central Rwanda, to a mixed Tutsi-Hutu family, he could have claimed either identity and ultimately, he did. He began life as a Tutsi, but started to identify as a Hutu as he grew older. As an adult, he was accepted as such by other Hutus. Entering Hutu society allowed him to gain importance both politically and economically, and he managed to advance to such an extent that by the late 1980s, he was the owner of several properties in downtown Kigali.

Karima became vice president of the Democratic Republican Movement (French: Mouvement Démocratique Républicain, or MDR)—a party that formed in 1991 and became the chief threat to President Juvénal Habyarimana's party—and a leader in the party's extremist wing, MDR-Power. He represented a faction that was hostile to any cooperation with the rebel Rwandan Patriotic Front (RPF), and was vehemently opposed to the Arusha Accords, the peace settlement between the Rwandan government and the RPF signed on August 4, 1993.

While the mainstream MDR, led by Agathe Uwilingiyimana and Faustin Twagiramungu, supported negotiations with the Tutsi-led RPF, Karamira was appalled by it. In July 1993, as the negotiations leading to Arusha were taking place, Karamira engineered a split within the MDR. Karamira's perspective was that the party was that the mainstream MDR party was not sufficiently pro-Hutu, and that any form of negotiation with the RPF was an intolerable ethnic betrayal. On October 23, 1993, he made a highly inflammatory speech at the Nyamirambo Stadium in Kigali, in which he called on the Hutus to "look within ourselves for the enemy which is amongst us," and rise up to "take the necessary measures" to target that enemy. In this speech he first introduced the concept of "Hutu Power," which, from then on, designated the coalition of the Hutu extremists and became

their slogan. Karamira was now recognized as the principal ideologue of the Hutu Power idea.

After the death of President Habyarimana on April 6, 1994, Karamira participated in the creation of Rwanda's interim government, a regime that quickly became radicalized along pure ethnic Hutu lines. Karamira's party, MDR-Power, participated actively in the genocide of Rwanda's Tutsis that began almost immediately. Karamira went on the air daily on Radio-Télévision Libre des Mille Collines, the rabidly anti-Tutsi private radio station, delivering messages that were hate-filled incitements to commit mass murder against the Tutsis.

It has been alleged that he was personally responsible for hundreds of murders, and directly answerable for the deaths of at least 13 Tutsi members of his own family. He was, indeed, well placed to commit such atrocities as a local leader of the anti-Tutsi Interahamwe militia. As the rebel forces of the RPF closed in on the interim government in June and July 1994, Karamira fled Rwanda. In June 1996 he was arrested in Mumbai, India, and extradited, via Addis Ababa, back home.

While he was on the run, the newly installed RPF Rwandan government indicted Karamira for genocide, murder, conspiracy, and nonassistance to people in danger. On January 13, 1997, with Karamira now incarcerated, his trial got underway in a Special Trial Chamber in Kigali. The indictment was amended by this stage to also include crimes against humanity and inciting genocide through his daily radio speeches, as well as playing a key role in the creation and arming of the Interahamwe and in providing them with arms. Karmira's defense attorney asked for a deferment of the hearing, stating that he had not had the possibility of meeting with Karamira before the start of the trial. The trial judge granted this request, and postponed the start of the trial until January 28, 1997.

The trial, when it came, was short. On February 14, 1997, Froduald Karamira was found guilty of the crimes of genocide, murder, conspiracy, and nonassistance to people in danger, and in organizing the implementation of the 1994 genocide. He was sentenced to death. He appealed to the Kigali Appeals Court, but on September 12, 1997, the court rejected the appeal.

On April 24, 1998, in a public event at the same Nyamirambo Stadium in Kigali where he had made his most inflammatory public speeches, Karamira was publicly executed by firing squad. The event was carefully stage-managed before thousands of cheering spectators, and was met with considerable protest from human rights groups around the globe. Karamira was not alone when facing the execution squad; a number of other *génocidaires* convicted of involvement in the genocide were also shot on or around April 24, in similar circumstances. On the same day as Karamira's execution, for example, a schoolteacher, Virginie Mukankusi (the first woman to be executed for the Rwandan Genocide), a former medical assistant, Déogratias Bizimana, and a farmer, Egide Gatanazi, were also publicly executed.

The trials and executions took place pursuant to a new postgenocide Rwandan law, Organic Law 08/96, dated August 30, 1996. Special Trial chambers, such as that which tried Karamira, were set up specifically to deal with alleged *génocidaires*, as it was felt that courts that existed before the genocide did not have the legal competence to try cases related to genocide and crimes against humanity. Karamira was thus subjected to a new and special form of justice, with the death penalty a viable outcome.

For its part, Rwanda abolished the death penalty in 2007. Those executed in 1998, including Karamira, were among the very last to have been executed in Rwanda in accordance with Rwandan courtroom procedures.

Paul R. Bartrop

See also: Interahamwe; International Criminal Tribunal for Rwanda; Mouvement Démocratique Républicain; Radio-Télévision Libre des Mille Collines; Rwandan Patriotic Front; Uwilingiyimana, Agathe

Further Reading

Melvern, Linda. *Conspiracy to Murder: The Rwandan Genocide.* London: Verso, 2006.

Prunier, Gérard. *The Rwanda Crisis, 1959–1994: History of a Genocide.* Kampala: Fountain Publishers, 1995.

Kayibanda, Grégoire

Grégorie Kayibanda served as the first elected prime minister, and later president, of Rwanda from 1960 to 1973. During his tenure as the nation's top leader, he guided Rwanda as it moved from colonialism to independence. He came to power on the heels of great historic change and took control of the nation at a crucial time in its history. His actions during this period helped set the scene for the ethnic tensions between the Hutu majority and Tutsi minority that intensified during and in the years leading up to the genocide.

Born a Hutu in 1924 during the period of colonial rule, Kayibanda had limited options due to his ethnic standing. Rwanda had been under the control of foreign European powers since the late 19th century. During colonialism, the Europeans favored Rwanda's Tutsi minority (approximately 14 percent of the population) over the Hutu majority (approximately 85 percent of the population). Bolstered by European support, Tutsis achieved greater economic, political, social, and educational standing. The main avenue for social advancement open to him was seminary school, a career he pursued. Prior to his political endeavors in the late 1950s, he served as a seminarist at Nyakibanda and a primary schoolteacher from 1948 to 1952. He left his teaching position in 1953 and was hired as a secretary and editor of *L'Ami*, a monthly periodical published by the Catholic seminary at Kabagyi. His career in journalism continued and by 1956 he was the editor-in-chief of the Church-owned newspaper *Kinyameteka*.

His close relationship with Belgian Catholic missionaries—both as an educator and writer—helped shape his worldview and political outlook. Thanks to his involvement with the missionaries, he was exposed to the pro-Hutu Christian Socialist movement that called for greater rights for Hutus. In 1957, he formed the Hutu Emancipation Movement (French: Parti l'émancipation du people Hutu, or Parmehutu). Then, he spent 1958 to 1959 in Brussels working for the missionary press center there. The mounting tensions between Hutu activists, Tutsis, and colonists prompted his return to Rwanda on the eve of the Hutu Social Revolution.

During the 1950s, Hutus' dissatisfaction with the status quo intensified. They called for more influence on Rwandan affairs and demanded an end to the Tutsi-dominated feudal structure. Hutu anger over their disadvantaged status increased when King Muratara III died and was succeed by his son Kigeri V in 1959. Many Hutus viewed the prince's accession as unfair and voiced their anger through violence, thus igniting the Hutu Social Revolution with Kayibanda as one of its key instigators. As the leader of the

Grégoire Kayibanda has the distinction of being the first elected president of Rwanda. He led the charge for Rwandan independence from its Belgian colonizers and helped assert Hutu power after the Europeans departed. (AFP/Getty Images)

Parmehutu, Kayibanda's anti-Tutsi party gained greater support during the revolution. During the fighting that ensued, thousands of Tutsis fled Rwanda, including King Kigeri V and the Belgian colonists shifted their support of the Tutsis to the Hutus.

During the elections that followed in 1960 and 1961 Kayibanda's status continued to climb. Rwandans elected him as prime minister in 1960. In 1961, the monarchy was abolished and the people elected Kayibanda president on October 26. By the time the Belgian colonialists left Rwanda and granted it full independence on July 1, 1962, Kayibanda had gone from schoolteacher to leader of the country.

Under Kayibanda's rule, the ethnic divides between Tutsis and Hutus deepened, however, now Hutus were on top. While the Hutu Social Revolution concluded with the departure of the Belgians, Hutu violence against Tutsis endured and more and more Tutsis fled Rwanda for the countries along its borders. To solidify the Hutus' dominance, Kayibanda created a quota system that restricted Tutsis to a small percentage of jobs in education and government. And church appointments were reserved for Hutus. Among Hutus, Kayibanda's regime elevated Hutus coming primarily from central Rwanda, which in turn caused discontent among Hutus in the north. As Kayibanda's isolationist policies robbed Rwanda of economic opportunities, Hutu-led resistance cells sprouted up in the north, the most prominent of which was that led by future president Juvénal Habyarimana.

Kayibanda's political reign came to an end on July 5, 1973, when Habyarimana and his followers from the north seized control of the Rwandan government in a coup. Under Habyarimana, many of the Parmehutu party leadership were executed and Kayibanda was placed under house arrest. He was sentenced to death, but later his sentence was changed to life imprisonment. He died of heart failure in 1976.

Alexis Herr

See also: Habyarimana, Juvénal; Hutu Social Revolution; Hutus; Mouvement Révolutionnaire National pour le Développement; Roman Catholic Church; Rwanda; Tutsi

Further Reading

Akyeampong, Emmanuel K. and Henry Louis Gates, Jr., eds. *African Biography*. Oxford, UK: Oxford University Press, 2012.

Prunier, Gérard. *The Rwanda Crisis, 1959– 1994: History of a Genocide*. Kampala: Fountain Publishers, 1995.

Kayishema, Clement, Trial of

With the help of local authorities, international investigators tracked down and arrested Clement Kayishema in Lusaka, Zambia on May 2, 1996. He was given over to the United Nations International Criminal Tribunal for Rwanda (ICTR) and flown to Arusha, Tanzania later that month. From 1997 to 1999 the ICTR investigated all 24 accounts of genocide and crimes against humanity that the prosecution levied against him. At the end of his three-year trial, the court convicted him on most of the charges and sentenced him to four life sentences.

Kayishema had been a physician who became prefect of Kibuye in 1992. As prefect, he was the top government official in the region and had command of several law enforcement groups. He also reportedly had some influence over the Interahamwe, an unofficial paramilitary group of extremist Hutus. When ethnic tensions and killings mounted in April 1994, many Tutsis sought refuge in churches and other communal locations. Kayishema reportedly ordered and led attacks on three of the major refuges: Home St. Jean, the local Catholic Church; a local stadium; and a church in Mubuga. Additionally, Kayishema, along with businessman Obed Ruzindana, reportedly helped organize and direct a major effort to kill tens of thousands of Tutsis who had fled into the hills of Bisesero.

In December 1995, Kayishema became one of the first Rwandans indicted by the ICTR. For each of the three refuge attacks and the fighting in Bisesero, he was indicted for genocide, crimes against humanity (murder, extermination, and other inhumane acts) and violations of the Geneva Conventions. The charges were based on four separate incidents, three occurrences in which Kayishema reportedly led attacks on Tutsis who had sought refuge in churches and other communal locations, and one incident of a more sustained effort to kill Tutsis in the hills of Bisesero. On the latter charge, Ruzindana was tried along with Kayishema. The trial was one of the first conducted by the ICTR and was therefore watched carefully for legal precedents. It was also hoped that indicting and convicting local officials would serve as a stepping-stone to convictions of higher-level Rwandan officials.

The trial began on April 11, 1997, in trial chamber II. Judge William Sekule of Tanzania presided and was joined by Judge Yakov Ostrovsky of the Russian Federation and Tafazzal Hossain Khan of Bangladesh. There were three prosecutors, including Brenda Sue Thornton, who made many of the key arguments. Andre Ferran, who many regarded as the rhetorical star of the trial, defended Kayishema.

The prosecution employed more than 50 witnesses, 400 pieces of physical evidence, and 3,400 pages of files to demonstrate Kayishema's knowledge of and direct control over the massacres. The prosecution also relied heavily on forensic evidence from the killing sites. The prosecution countered with several witnesses who reported seeing Kayishema at the sites discussing plans, signaling the start of the attacks, and participating in the attacks. The defense also tried to portray Kayishema as a man under threat from extremists and powerless to stop the violence. Ferran tried to win sympathy for his client by pointing out the extreme disparity of available resources for the prosecution and defense. He also argued that Kayishema was

not even at the sites of the massacres. Kayishema's wife and others stated that Kayishema had gone into hiding between April 16–20, and thus could not possibly have been involved.

The highlight of the trial was Kayishema's six days of testimony, during which he vigorously rejected the prosecution's contentions. Kayishema based his defense on claims that he was not physically at some of the massacre sites and that, given the chaos of the period, the prefect and government was powerless to stop local mobs. The judges rejected Kayishema's account and found him guilty of genocide in each of the four incidents. Kayishema was given a life sentence. Ruzindana was also found guilty of genocide, but was given a 25-year sentence. The judges, however, dealt the prosecution a severe blow by ruling, for various legal reasons, that Kayishema could not be found guilty on any of the 24 counts of crimes against humanity. Both sides appealed the case. While the genocide rulings were upheld, the prosecution was embarrassed by having its appeal on the crimes against humanity charges thrown out after missing a filing deadline.

The trial concluded on May 21, 1999. In its judgment, the ICTR judges largely echoed the prosecution's view of events. They rejected Kayishema's alibi and ruled that there was clear evidence that he had led a systematic effort to destroy the Tutsi people. Therefore, they found him guilty on all four counts of genocide. They then ruled that the prosecution had not shown a direct link between the specific crimes and the existing armed conflict in Rwanda, so the Geneva Convention did not apply. Next, they ruled that the indictment for "other inhumane acts" did not stipulate the crimes the prosecution intended to prosecute, so they found Kayishema not guilty on those counts.

Finally, in a controversial split decision, they ruled that, because the genocide counts and the crimes against humanity counts for murder and extermination were based on the same incidents and same evidence, finding Kayishema guilty on all counts would mean sentencing him twice for the same crime. They therefore rejected the crimes against humanity counts on a vote of two to one. On appeal, the judgments were upheld and Kayishema began serving his life sentence.

John Dietrich

See also: Interahamwe; International Criminal Tribunal for Rwanda; Roman Catholic Church

Further Reading

Cruvellier, Thierry. *Court of Remorse: Inside the International Criminal Court for Rwanda*. Madison, WI: University of Wisconsin Press, 2010.

Des Forges, Alison and Timothy Longman, "Legal Responses to Genocide in Rwanda," in *My Neighbor, My Enemy: Justice and Community in the Aftermath of Mass Atrocity*, eds. Eric Stover and Harvey M. Weinstein. Cambridge: Cambridge University Press, 2004, 49–63.

Kigali Genocide Memorial

The Kigali Genocide Memorial (KGM) is a memorial museum located in Rwanda's capital city of Kigali. The KGM extends a place for survivors to remember, visitors to learn about the Rwandan Genocide, and for Rwandans to work towards social reconciliation. The site also serves as the final resting place for some 250,000 victims of the 1994 Rwandan Genocide.

The KGM was designed with multiple purposes in mind. As stated on its website, its five primary objectives are the following:

1. To provide a dignified place of burial for victims of the Genocide against the Tutsi.
2. To inform and educate visitors about the causes, implementation and consequences of the genocide.
3. To teach visitors about what we can do to prevent future genocides.
4. To provide a documentation centre to record evidence of the genocide, testimonies of genocide survivors, and details of genocide victims.
5. To provide support for survivors, in particular orphans and widows.

The city of Kigali provided the land in 1999 for a place of remembrance and a space for Tutsi victims to be buried. The Memorial was developed by Aegis Trust (a non-profit government organization that works to prevent mass atrocities and genocide through education) in cooperation with the Kigali City Council. Building of the KGM broke ground in 1999 and the process of burying victims began in 2001. The Memorial opened its doors to the public in April 2004 to coincide with the 10th anniversary of the genocide. At the request of the Rwandan authorities, the Memorial is run by Aegis Trust who is under contract to Rwanda's National Commission for the Fight Against Genocide. Since opening, hundreds of thousands of people have visited the Memorial.

In addition to being a burial ground for victims, the KGM also includes three permanent exhibitions, a children's memorial, Education Centre, gardens, and an archive. The first exhibition entitled "The 1994 Genocide Against the Tutsi" provides an overview of Rwandan society prior to European colonization of Rwanda and details the planned nature and horror of the genocide. It includes stories of rescue and survival and

When the Kigali Genocide Memorial opened its doors in 2004 it became a place of mourning, education, and remembrance. Far more than a museum, the Memorial also serves as the resting place for the remains of more than 250,000 Tutsi. (Karen Foley/Dreamstime)

describes how the genocide unfolded. In the second exhibition, "Wasted Lives," visitors learn about other atrocities including those in Namibia, Armenia, Cambodia, and the Balkans, as well as the Holocaust. The third exhibition, "Children's Room," is dedicated to the memory of the Tutsi children killed during the genocide and in it are the pictures of murdered children.

The KGM is home to the Genocide Archive of Rwanda. The archive's physical holdings include testimonies, audio and video materials, photography, physical objects, documents, and publications. In 2015 the Genocide Archive of Rwanda launched a state of the art website that allows people from around the world to view primary source material and listen to testimony. Like the KGM, the Genocide Archive of Rwanda was created with support from Aegis Trust.

Alexis Herr

See also: AVEGA-AGAHOZO; Ibuka; Tutsis

Further Reading

"About KGM," Kigali Genocide Memorial, http://www.kgm.rw/about/.

"About Us," Genocide Archive of Rwanda, http://genocidearchiverwanda.org.rw/index.php/About_Us.

"Kigali Genocide Memorial," Aegis Trust, accessed July 5, 2007, https://www.aegistrust.org/what-we-do/activities/kigali-genocide-memorial/.

Williams, Paul. *Memorial Museums: The Global Rush to Commemorate Atrocities.* New York: Berg, 2007.

Kovanda, Karel

Karel Kovanda is a Czech diplomat who served as the permanent representative of the Czech Republic to the United Nations. At the UN Security Council in 1994, during the Rwandan Genocide, he worked tirelessly to bring the world's attention to the genocide as it was taking place.

Kovanda was born on October 5, 1944, in the northern English village of Gilsland, Cumbria. Active in the Czech student movement opposed to the communist regime between 1964 and 1969, he studied as an undergraduate at the Prague School of Agriculture and became president of the National Students' Union. In November 1968, during the period of government liberalization known as the Prague Spring, he was chairman of the student strike organized by the Action Committee. In the spring of 1969 he was elected chairman of the Association of University Students of Bohemia and Moravia, but in the communist clampdown after the Prague Spring, his position became untenable, such that in 1970 he left Czechoslovakia as a political exile and moved to the United States. There, he earned a PhD in political science at the Massachusetts Institute of Technology in 1975, a subject he taught at a number of southern California colleges between 1975 and 1977. From 1977 to 1979 he worked in China as a consultant to Radio Beijing, and from 1980 to 1990, back in the United States, he worked in private business as a manager with international responsibilities. He also worked as a freelance journalist and translator (he is fluent in Czech, English, Slovak, Spanish, and French, and is conversant in German and Russian). In 1985 he completed an MBA at Pepperdine University in Malibu, California.

In November 1989 the communist government of Czechoslovakia fell, and by 1990 Kovanda had returned from exile. Joining the civil service, between 1991 and 1993 he headed the administration section at the Ministry of Foreign Affairs, and in 1993 became a political director at the ministry with responsibility for European and North American affairs. In June 1993 he was appointed the Czech Republic's ambassador to the United Nations, aligning with his country's membership of the Security Council in 1994–1995.

In January 1994 the Czech Republic assumed the presidency of the Security Council, with Kovanda in the chair. In this capacity, he received a visit from Claude De Saide, who was representing the Rwandan Patriotic Front (RPF). It was the first connection Kovanda had had with any problems in the tiny African country. Later that month, the Department of Peacekeeping Operations, led by Kofi Annan, received the so-called "Genocide Fax" from the UN force commander in Rwanda, General Roméo Dallaire. In subsequent comments, Kovanda wrote that the secretary-general, Boutros Boutros-Ghali, did not share the information received from Dallaire with the Security Council. This was a prelude of things to come, as succeeding weeks and months were to show. Kovanda later recalled that the Secretariat constantly refused to pass information on to the Security Council, severely inhibiting the Council's capacity to act to stop the crisis. Kovanda later wrote that after the genocide exploded, there was a long time during which events in Rwanda were far from clear.

The Security Council was constantly frustrated about the lack of information coming from the secretariat, information on which it depended in order to be able to assess the situation. Moreover, Rwanda, governed by the Hutu Power administration of Juvénal Habiyarimana and the interim government that followed his death on April 6, 1994, was, ironically, also a serving member on the Security Council at the same time as the genocide. Overall, factors such as these led to a real lack of understanding being conveyed to the Council as to what was happening in Rwanda and how it should be handled.

While it was very difficult for Kovanda and the Security Council (and in particular, the states that were not permanent members, such as the Czech Republic) to obtain full or accurate information, that did not stop some from trying to do so. At one point, Kovanda invited an expert from Human Rights Watch, Alison Des Forges, to meet with the Czech delegation to share with his colleagues from the Security Council what she knew about Rwanda.

Kovanda was motivated to try to do something to stop the killing in Rwanda for personal as well as international reasons. With the memory of many members of father's family having been murdered in the Holocaust, Kovanda at one point told the Security Council that the suggestion that the RPF should negotiate a ceasefire with the Hutu Power government was akin to asking Hitler to reach a ceasefire with the Jews.

His frustration at having to sit in Security Council meetings to discuss Rwanda, where no action was ever contemplated to help the Tutsis, was intense. All around him, he saw evidence from nonofficial sources of the immensity of the killing that was taking place in Rwanda. In an interview for the 1999 *Frontline* documentary *The Triumph of Evil* (produced by Mike Robinson and Ben Loeterman), reporter Steve Bradshaw asked Kovanda if he felt that "lives were at stake" during Security Council meetings. Kovanda's emotional response was unequivocal: "Oh, heaven—heaven knows, yes. Yes! There were lives at stake! Lives that were

just like sand disappearing through our hands day after day. You've got 10,000 today, 12,000 tomorrow, and if you don't do something today, then tomorrow there will be more. If you don't do something this week, then next week there will be more, with no end in sight at the time. No end in sight."

Moreover, he was personally informed by his superiors in Prague not to call what was happening in Rwanda by the name "genocide." From where this order originated he was not sure, but he recalled being informed that it was the United States that had approached the Czech government with the request that Kovanda "lay off pushing Rwanda," and especially referring to "genocide." Kovanda was not sure whether the pressure was coming from the U.S. representatives in Prague or from the State Department in Washington, but he was certain the United States had communicated this to the Czech leadership.

Kovanda was bitterly disappointed that his own small country, with its history of having been abandoned by the international community during the Holocaust, was willing to do the same thing to another small country, this time in the center of Africa. Despite the instructions he received from Prague, he did what he could to disseminate the information being received from the nongovernmental organizations operating in Africa, and led the Czech delegation in being the first to articulate the word genocide in connection with Rwanda publicly at a Security Council meeting concerning Mozambique on May 5, 1994. At the same meeting, he expressed shock that neither the Security Council nor the secretariat had so far used the word describing the events that were taking place. Taking a leadership role in the absence of one, he then directed the sessions which resulted not only in the Council adopting a statement using the UN Genocide

Convention to describe what was happening in Rwanda as genocide, but led to the eventual deployment of UNAMIR II, a force that would have much more authority than Dallaire's United Nations Assistance Mission for Rwanda (UNAMIR) possessed originally.

After Kovanda left the United Nations in February 1997, he held a number of other important positions in the Czech Foreign Ministry, including deputy minister of foreign affairs (1997–1998) and ambassador to NATO (1998–2005). In April 2005, he went to Brussels to become deputy director general for external relations of the European Commission. From then until he left the post in 2010, he was responsible for the Common and Foreign Security Policy (CFSP), multilateral relations and human rights, and relations with North America, East Asia, Australia, New Zealand and (non-EU) Western Europe, and the European Free Trade Association (EFTA).

On July 4, 2010, Kovanda received Rwanda's Campaign against Genocide Medal, the UMURINZI award, in recognition of his efforts to bring the world's attention to the genocide during 1994.

Paul R. Bartrop

See also: Des Forges, Alison; Rwandan Genocide, U.S. Response to the; United Nations Assistance Mission for Rwanda

Further Reading

Des Forges, Alison. *Leave None to Tell the Story: Genocide in Rwanda.* New York: Human Rights Watch, 1999.

Klinghoffer, Arthur Jay. *The International Dimension of Genocide in Rwanda.* New York: New York University Press, 1998.

L

Lane, Laura

Laura Lane was a Foreign Service officer in the U.S. embassy in Kigali, Rwanda, prior to and during the earliest days of the Rwandan Genocide of 1994. Born in Evanston, Illinois, on February 1, 1967, she attended Loyola University, Chicago, where she graduated summa cum laude in political science and history, and then received a Master's degree in Foreign Service and international economics at Georgetown University, Washington, D.C. This strong Jesuit education assisted in providing her with a strong moral compass to guide her in her future work, and in many ways influenced her decisions during the fateful early days of the crisis in Kigali in 1994.

One of the youngest women in the Foreign Service when she went to Rwanda, she was also one of the youngest women to have passed the Foreign Service examination. Her first posting as a consular officer was to Bogotá, Colombia (1990–1992), at a time when the drug culture, violence, and corruption were making the lives of average Colombians difficult and dangerous. Lane volunteered to go to that country, believing that often in the worst of situations, the greatest good can be achieved through persistent effort and determination.

At the age of 26, in the fall of 1993, she undertook her second posting to Kigali. She had requested to go to Rwanda to learn French and have a larger role in a small embassy. She was also conscious that the country was going through some momentous times, with the Arusha Agreement having just been signed between the Hutu-led government of Juvénal Habyarimana and the Tutsi-led Rwandan Patriotic Front (RPF) directed by General Paul Kagame. In view of the political situation, Lane saw the possibility of helping the people in their transition through what was going to be a difficult—though hopefully uplifting—period.

The mission in Kigali was quite small and Lane found herself to be one of only six full-time Foreign Service staff, including the ambassador. She became, in her own words, the "everything else" officer, responsible for issues relating to economics and trade, visas and passports, military security assistance and training, and many other areas. As her strength was in economic reporting, she had a huge learning curve in the other technical areas, even participating in military security assistance training and studying all she could about military command and control functions. The embassy, being a Special Embassy Program post, was not protected by U.S. Marines, though her husband, Greg, was a former U.S. Marine, so as an added measure of personal protection they both carried weapons in Kigali when they thought the situation required it.

In her military assistance role, Lane's task was to liaise with the various military parties to the Arusha Agreement, as a consequence of which she spent many hours travelling to and from Kigali and the RPF headquarters in Mulindi in northern Rwanda, making the hazardous trip crossing the demilitarized zone to see Kagame. Her task required building trust between the parties, with the United States as an impartial but friendly presence. Americans were generally viewed as being trustworthy and neutral by all sides, unlike the Belgians and French, who, it was believed, were closely aligned with the Hutu government and/or the Tutsi RPF.

Within the embassy, almost everyone was aware that the Arusha Accords could collapse at any moment, and that just one small incident could destabilize the fragile emerging peace. The precarious situation was felt especially keenly by the deputy chief of mission, Joyce Leader, who was intimately involved with the negotiations involving the major actors.

Beginning in February 1994, the situation began visibly to deteriorate, and the cable traffic between the embassy in Kigali and the State Department in Washington flowed thick and fast. The embassy staff tried hard to explain the situation at the ground level in Rwanda, and the cables sent from Kigali played a very important role in informing the United Nations (UN) and the U.S. government of what was happening. They reported to the UN and the U.S. government that Arusha might be unraveling. The ambassador, deputy chief of mission, and Lane were fully aware that there were strong factions within the Rwandan government that were more than just anti-Tutsi; they were opposed to anyone in favor of the peace process. The embassy staff knew a number of moderate Hutus who were likely to run up against these strong factions within the Hutu led government, and it was recommended that a high-level response should be made from Washington and the United Nations to the Habyarimana government to step in and quell the poisonous atmosphere that was making deep inroads on the political culture of the country. Unfortunately, these reports failed to stimulate action and thus failed to prevent the cycle of escalating violence from spiraling out of control.

After Habyarimana's plane was shot down on the night of April 6, 1994, and the genocide plan began swiftly to be executed, Lane took over responsibility for coordinating the evacuation of all Americans from Rwanda. She had already done a great deal of work in the lead-up to that day in identifying where all Americans were located throughout the country, and, if at all possible, photographing them to assist with identification in the event of such an evacuation. She sincerely felt that she had a responsibility for every single American in Rwanda (which at the start of the crisis numbered 257, but ended with 258—with the birth of an American along the evacuation route), and she was determined that she would be the one to supervise their safe passage out of the country.

Examples of killing or destruction were everywhere, with the eerie sounds of piped-in classical music over the city's public speaker system as the Interahamwe and Presidential Guard pulled moderate Hutus and Tutsis from their homes and hiding places and killed them. At first most of the violence was in Kigali, and the terror was obvious just by looking out the window or stepping onto a sidewalk.

Washington's response to the mounting violence forced an early decision at the State Department to close the embassy. Lane then made an extraordinary request: to keep the embassy open, even if she and her husband were the only ones there, so as to maintain an American presence that could serve as a safe haven to those who could get through the lines of fighting to the embassy and thereby be protected from the killing. Never thinking about her own personal safety, she only thought about the prospect of keeping alive whoever could make it to the embassy. Every waking minute was spent trying to work out how to help. For as long as there was an official American presence in the country prior to the evacuation of the embassy itself, she didn't sleep. She wanted to use the embassy as a base of operations not only for the evacuation of the American community, but also for anyone in need. Her attitude was that if just one life could be saved, that was one life worth saving. Yet despite her pleas, Lane was forced to obey the order to leave, and begin the process of closing down the embassy. The Americans were to evacuate overland to Bujumbura, the capital of Burundi.

Before the embassy shutdown was complete and the evacuation convoys launched, Lane drafted personal, handwritten notes and left them on the desks of each one of the Foreign Service nationals (FSNs)—local Rwandan employees at the embassy—to the effect that she would do all in her power to ensure they were looked after and that she would return to Kigali as soon as possible. Tragically, only one of Lane's FSN staff would survive the genocide.

Lane helped organize multiple American evacuation convoys over the next couple of days. The last was the longest, with some 100 vehicles carrying over 600 people, only nine of whom were American. The rest included Kenyans, Tanzanians, Germans, Belgians, and French. Lane had been in touch with the other embassies, and many of their nationals came forward for protection under the aegis of the American evacuation. The convoy also included Rwandans. Not all were Tutsis; some of them were of mixed Hutu and Tutsi background. The question of who could be saved was largely ad hoc; there was little time to plan for anything in detail, and it was difficult enough for anyone to reach the embassy in any case. Attempts were made to accommodate all who could reach the embassy compound seeking sanctuary.

The embassy had requested that the U.S. government not send in protection from the Marines stationed in Burundi and Kenya, as this could have been seen as a hostile act and/or drawn fire on the convoys thus making a complicated support mission even more challenging. Instead, unarmed UN escorts were provided. Without weapons, the escorts could do nothing but watch when the Presidential Guard stopped and tried to pull people out of their cars. One convoy coming to the embassy to fuel up cars included the wife of Ambassador David Rawson. A car in her convoy was stopped, and attempts were made to force out a visiting African American aid officer who was mistaken for a Tutsi. Lane heard the commotion over the radio network and sprinted several blocks through the city streets of Kigali to intervene. Dressed in red track pants and a Mickey Mouse sweatshirt, she was visible and identifiable to all from a long distance away. When she arrived on the scene, she faced down the Interahamwe and Presidential Guards, asserting that this was the convoy of the wife of the U.S. ambassador, that every vehicle in it had diplomatic immunity, and that they were not to be stopped again. Stunned in many ways at this young white woman's effrontery, they gave way to her orders and never stopped any other cars coming to the embassy again if they carried the American flag or a white flag of neutrality (be it a ripped-up sheet or t-shirt), agreed on as the identifying symbols for the American convoys.

And as each of the convoys were being assembled and headed to the embassy for fuel, there were some Rwandans who were given "honorary American" status in the convoys with travel papers indicating that they were on official U.S. business. Lane's position was a simple one: if people could make it through the roadblocks and to the American embassy, she would find a way to help get them safe passage out of Kigali. While this was hardly proper procedure, Lane stretched the bounds of legality a long way in order to ensure that people could be granted sanctuary. She knew that with travel documents in hand, the Rwandans would be able to enter Burundi with the rest of the convoy, as the Burundian authorities, suspicious of anyone who was undocumented, respected documents of this kind. The possession of travel documents thus gave desperate people more hope than if they had nothing at all. Lane did not claim they were Americans, but the protection she provided nonetheless vouched for them sufficiently to guarantee their safe passage across the border. In this way, she was able to arrange for the survival of several innocent Rwandans caught in the crossfire who otherwise would have had next to no chance of staying alive (in some cases, she even hid them in car trunks in order to get them through the checkpoints).

The road trip between Kigali and Bujumbura normally should have taken about five hours, but given the length of the final convoy, the constant stopping, the roadblocks, and the checkpoints, the evacuation took between 18 and 20 hours. Lane and her husband were the last Americans out, in the last car in the last convoy. She had insisted that they would be the last out, as she wanted to be sure that no one who wanted to leave be left behind.

Once in Bujumbura, Lane and the others provided an on-the-ground assessment of the situation for the State Department. They stayed there for almost a week, and were then flown back to Washington, D.C., where Lane joined a task force established to field calls from Rwanda regarding the situation and find ways to assist those who were able to establish contact. While in Washington, Lane worked closely with Deputy Assistant

Secretary for Africa Prudence Bushnell, who was herself striving to raise consciousness within the administration about the Rwandan situation. Lane did all she could to help both in providing information for the government, and in establishing and maintaining contact with any of the FSNs back in Rwanda whose phone numbers she still had. The calls, however, were far from encouraging, and over time, fewer and fewer came.

By mid-summer—with more than a million Rwandans dead and the RPF having won control of the country—the State Department decided the embassy should be reopened, and that people were needed to go back to Kigali. Without hesitation, Lane immediately jumped at the offer, wanting to make good on her promise to her Rwandan staff and friends. She flew back to Kigali at the end of July 1994, and during August acted as a political adviser to U.S. forces providing humanitarian relief. The evidence of killing and destruction was everywhere. Returning to her former home, Lane saw that the house had taken several hits during the fighting, and that the destruction throughout the city had been massive and wanton, with ransacking of homes and commercial establishments in a highly personal—and vicious—manner.

To her dismay, Lane was not allowed to stay long in Kigali, as new Foreign Service officers had been commissioned to resume the embassy's daily functions. She stayed long enough to provide for the few survivors among the Rwanda staff, ensuring that they received the benefits and support to which they were entitled. She then closed this chapter in her life and returned to Washington, where she worked in the Trade Policy and Programs office in the Bureau of Economic and Business Affairs at the U.S. State Department (1995–1997) and subsequently moved to the U.S. Trade Representative's office and then on to the private sector.

As the years passed, however, Lane kept an active interest in Rwanda, most importantly through her support of Emory University professor of public health Susan Allen, who set up a foundation to raise awareness that the criminals responsible for the genocide are still at large. The foundation's focus has been on collecting evidence about their activities, and meeting with the Departments of Justice and State to try to find ways to ensure that *génocidaires* are not allowed to travel, can be extradited from the United States when found, and made to stand trial for their crimes. Lane also worked on a documentary with the U.S. Holocaust Memorial Museum to ensure that no one ever forgot what happened in Rwanda and how the world watched passively as a million people were killed in the space of three months.

Looking back, Laura Lane's reflections on her time in Rwanda have been that more of a difference could have been made if more people took the decision to make that difference. Instead, politics intruded on a situation where lives were at stake, crippling the human dimension from the start. Of her experiences, her feelings are mixed. On one hand, she regrets the closure of the U.S. embassy at a time when it was needed more than ever to stay open as a refuge for those escaping the violence and evil. On the other hand, she knows that her actions at least saved some lives—even though she wishes every day since then that it could have been more.

Paul R. Bartrop

See also: Allen, Susan; Bushnell, Prudence; Habyarimana, Juvénal; Interahamwe; Kagame, Paul; Rwandan Genocide, U.S. Response to the; Rwandan Patriotic Front

Further Reading

Barnett, Michael. *Eyewitness to a Genocide: The United Nations and Rwanda*. Ithaca, NY: Cornell University Press, 2002.

Melvern, Linda. *Conspiracy to Murder: The Rwandan Genocide*. London: Verso, 2006.

Leave None to Tell the Story: Genocide in Rwanda

Leave None to Tell the Story: Genocide in Rwanda was a comprehensive report on the 1994 Rwandan Genocide published by Human Rights Watch in 1999 and authored principally by the American historian Alison Liebhafsky Des Forges. Des Forges was among the first individuals outside Rwanda to recognize that genocide in Rwanda was occurring. After the mass killings stopped, she traveled to Rwanda with a group of researchers to collect evidence on the genocide. She used Rwandan government documents, UN (United Nations) documents, local news reports, interviews, and other elements to assemble a meticulously detailed book. Des Forges also testified eleven times at the International Criminal Tribunal for Rwanda (ICTR) and presented evidence to the United Nations, the Organization of African Unity, and the national legislatures of Belgium, France, and the United States, among others.

Both *The New York Times* and *The Economist* termed *Leave None to Tell the Story* the "definitive account" of the Rwandan tragedy. While the book does not dedicate much attention on the meaning and interpretation of the genocide, it does offer unparalleled narratives of the killings, and is unabashed in assigning blame to various types of perpetrators. The genocide was not simply an ad hoc explosion of tribal conflicts, argues Des Forges; rather, it was a well-orchestrated plan conceived and carried out by Rwanda's Hutu-led government. She also points out that the Tutsi-dominated Rwandan Patriotic Front (RPF) had blood on its hands because it engaged in retaliatory killings once the genocide was underway. The United Nations Security Council is excoriated for its limp reaction to the crisis, as are the governments of France, Belgium, and the United States. The book offers important insights on the warning signs that preceded the crisis, and offers a detailed treatment of the plight of Hutus who attempted to resist participation in the genocide.

Paul G. Pierpaoli Jr.

See also: Des Forges, Alison; International Criminal Tribunal for Rwanda; Rwandan Genocide, U.S. Response to the; Rwandan Patriotic Front

Further Reading

Des Forges, Alison. *Leave None to Tell the Story: Genocide in Rwanda*. New York: Human Rights Watch, 1999.

M

Media Trial in Rwanda

The Media Trial took place between October 23, 2000, and December 9, 2003, and was conducted by the International Criminal Tribunal for Rwanda (ICTR), based in Arusha, Tanzania. The trial was so named because it involved three Rwandan defendants who had been involved in media outlets in Rwanda both before and during the Rwandan Genocide of 1994. Although they were indicted separately, the ICTR decided to try them together because they had interconnected roles in the genocide. The presiding judge was Navanethem Pillay. The charges against the defendants included crimes against humanity, complicity to commit genocide, incitement to commit genocide, and conspiracy to commit genocide.

The first defendant, Ferdinand Nahimana, had co-founded the Radio-Télévision Libre des Mille Collines (RTLM), a virulently anti-Tutsi Rwandan radio/television station that incited hatred toward Tutsis, and supervised RTLM's radio programming. The second defendant, Jean-Bosco Barayagwiza, belonged to the radical Coalition for the Defence of the Republic (French: Coalition pour la Défense de la République, or CDR), a Hutu-dominated and anti-Tutsi political party and was the director of RTLM radio. The third defendant, Hassan Ngeze, had co-founded the anti-Tutsi newspaper *Kangura* and the CDR and was a principal investor in RTLM.

The ICTR indicted the three men under the provisions of the 1948 United Nations Convention on the Prevention and Punishment of the Crime of Genocide (UNCG). The Rwanda Media Trial was the first of its type to indict and try defendants who had not taken part in mass killings themselves, but instead had encouraged genocide through their positions as media personnel. The defense team argued that convicting the men based solely on messages they had devised for print and media broadcasts was a fundamental violation of free speech. The prosecution, however, successfully countered that the men's actions went far beyond free expression or even hate speech, and that they had in fact helped incite a genocide in which at least 800,000 people died. This was accomplished by rabid anti-Tutsi rhetoric and propaganda, as well as actual directives to a mass audience encouraging Hutus to kill Tutsis and moderate Hutus.

The verdict, rendered on December 9, 2003, was unambiguous. It found the three defendants responsible for the deaths of thousands of Rwandans, and that the RTLM had indeed directly compelled listeners to engage in the mass killing of Tutsis and Hutu sympathizers. The court also determined that Ngeze's *Kangura* newspaper had created an atmosphere toward the Tutsis that was so toxic that it was a de facto incitement to genocide, even though the paper had ceased publication several months before the start of the genocide.

Ngeze and Nahimana were given life-long prison sentences, while Barayagwiza was given a 35-year prison term. Lawyers for the three men appealed both the verdicts and sentences, but on November 28, 2007, the ICTR affirmed the verdicts as valid. The court did, however, alter the sentences. Ngeze's sentence was reduced to 35 years, while Nahimana's sentence was reduced to 30 years. Barayagwiza's sentence was reduced to 32 years.

Paul G. Pierpaoli Jr.

See also: *Kangura*; Barayagwiza, Jean-Bosco; Hutus; International Criminal Tribunal for Rwanda; Nahimana, Ferdinand; Ngeze, Hassan; Radio-Télévision Libre des Mille Collines

Further Reading

Valentino, Benjamin A. *Final Solutions: Mass Killing and Genocide in the Twentieth Century*. Ithaca, NY: Cornell University Press, 2004.
Waller, James. *Becoming Evil: How Ordinary People Commit Genocide and Mass Killing*. Oxford: Oxford University Press, 2002.

Micombero, Michel

Michel Micombero was the first president of the Central African state of Burundi, serving in that role between 1966 and 1976. A Tutsi, he was born in Rutovu, Bururi province, southern Burundi, in 1940, and educated in local Catholic schools. In 1960 he joined the Belgian colonial army, and was sent to Brussels for officer training. In 1962, he returned to Burundi with a commission as captain, and took up a position in the armed forces of what had by then become an independent state.

A large Hutu majority dominated the population of Burundi, with a much smaller Tutsi minority. Upon independence from Belgium in 1962, the Tutsis, who had been the traditional rulers before and during Belgian colonialism, retained their ascendancy—largely by force of arms and a tightly controlled bureaucracy. Upon his return from Belgium,

Micombero joined the Unity for National Progress party (French: Unité pour le Progrès National, or UPRONA), the ruling party dominated by the Tutsi elite. Rising quickly in the party ranks, Micobero became secretary of state for defense in 1963. The country, however, was about to enter a period of anarchy. In 1965, legislative elections gave Hutu parties a resounding victory, winning 23 out of 33 seats in the National Assembly. This victory was overthrown, however, when the Tutsi *mwami* (King), Mwambutsa IV Bangiricenge, appointed a Tutsi from the royal family as prime minister. Soon thereafter, on October 19, 1965, an attempted coup was suppressed, but this served only to intensify Hutu anger at their second-class status, and in some parts of the country, massacres of Tutsis erupted.

In mid-1966, Micombero conspired with others in arranging for a palace coup. While the coup failed, it did result in King Mwambutsa leaving the country. In his place, Mwambusta appointed his son Charles Ndizeye to rule in his absence. On July 11, 1966, Micombero formed a government, with himself as prime minister. Then, on November 28, 1966, he overthrew the monarchy, declared Burundi a republic, and placed himself at its head as president.

Micombero now became an advocate of what became known as African socialism. This was a vague ideology asserting that economic resources should be shared in what he called a "traditional African" manner. Within the Cold War context, both the Soviet Union and communist China courted African states professing African socialism, and Micombero's Burundi fell under the patronage of China as a result. Micombero imposed a tight law-and-order regime throughout the country, and did all he could to repress any possibility of a Hutu ascendancy. He also cracked down on Hutu militancy.

It was against this backdrop that on April 29, 1972, Hutu radicals in the southern provinces of Burundi launched an uprising against Micombero's military government, massacring several thousand Tutsi civilians. They were supported (and in some instances, organized) by Hutu refugees outside Burundi itself. This was viewed as a final challenge for supremacy by many Tutsi leaders, in particular Micombero. On the same day as the Hutu rising, he dissolved the government.

The country descended into chaos. Ethnic hostility between Hutus and Tutsis appeared more overtly than beforehand, and regional factionalism between Tutsi politicians and other members of the elite divided the government. Micombero adopted harsh measures to bring the country to heel, beginning with the brutal repression of Hutu suspects in Bururi (a city located in southern Burundi), the physical elimination of all Hutu troops in the army, and the transformation of regionally based measures into country-wide repression. A number of public sector purges were also carried out. Hutu hopes looked to the now-exiled ex-king Ntare to return and overthrow Micombero; he did return, but was killed soon thereafter while in government custody. It is widely believed that it was Micombero himself who personally ordered Ntare's assassination.

Micombero was now unchallenged in the measures he could adopt to suppress the Hutus, and he began to institute a series of deliberately targeted campaigns that can only be described as genocide. The intention of these killings was the elimination of all Hutu political aspirations once and for all. A series of deliberate campaigns took place against specific categories of Hutus, such as those in government employment, intellectuals (who could include any Hutu with a university education, whether completed or in process; secondary school students; and teachers), and the Hutu middle and upper classes. Estimates of the number killed between April and October 1972 vary, but most settle at somewhere between 100,000 and 200,000. Hundreds of thousands more fled the country to escape the violence.

The overall impact of these events took a personal toll on Micombero. Although he could claim to have saved the country (or at least, the Tutsi advantage within it), it was reported that he began drinking heavily and slipped into a psychological netherworld, paranoid and delusional. His administration henceforth became increasingly corrupt and inefficient. By November 1976, some members of the army, anxious to restore order to Burundi (though without necessarily seeking to come to the aid of the Hutus), staged a coup led by the chief of staff (and Micombero's distant cousin and clan member), Jean-Baptiste Bagaza. Micombero was apprehended and, after a brief imprisonment, he went into exile in Somalia, where he died of a heart attack in 1983.

The killing, however, did not end there. Subsequent large-scale massacres of Hutus by Tutsi government forces took place in 1988 and by Hutus against Tutsis in 1993. Accompanying these savage assaults was the wholesale exodus of thousands of refugees to neighboring countries, leading to an intensifying destabilization of the Great Lakes region (Burundi, the Democratic Republic of Congo, Kenya, Rwanda, Tanzania, and Uganda), which culminated in the Rwandan Genocide of April to July 1994. Until the early 1990s, successive Burundian governments had refused to acknowledge that genocide had even taken place in Burundi .

Paul R. Bartrop

See also: Congo, Democratic Republic of the; Hutus; Nahimana, Ferdinand; Tutsis

Further Reading

Jennings, Christian. *Across the Red River: Rwanda, Burundi and the Heart of Darkness*. Londres: Phoenix, 2000.

Scherrer, P. Christian. *Genocide and Crisis in Central Africa: Conflict Roots, Mass Violence, and Regional War*. Westport, CT: Praeger, 2002.

Moderate Hutus

The term "moderate Hutu" stands out in the history of genocide. Scholars do not discuss moderate Nazis when talking about the Holocaust, nor do they say moderate Ottomans when analyzing the Armenian Genocide. Scholars and journalists often use the term "moderate Hutu" when discussing the Rwandan Genocide to refer to an individual who identified as Hutu, but did not support the Hutu hardliners, plan to annihilate Tutsis. Examining how the first publications on the Rwandan Genocide use the term helps illuminate the opacity of this descriptor.

In We Wish to Inform You That Tomorrow We Will be Killed With Our Families: Stories from Rwanda, journalist Philip Gourevitch explains the genocide, drawing upon his travels in the immediate aftermath of the atrocity through the documents and interviews he collected. The first mention of moderate Hutus comes from one such testimony early on in the book. Survivor Etienne Niyonzima describes how more than 600 people in his neighbor died at the hands of the Hutu perpetrators. "They had the number of everyone's house," he explained, "and they went through with red paint and marked the homes of all the Tutsis and the Hutu moderates" (Gourevitch 1998: 22). As indicated by Gourevitch,

moderate Hutus often faced the same fate as Tutsis. This implies that Hutus who had openly criticized President Juvénal Habyarimana and his party the National Revolutionary Movement for Development (French: Mouvement Révolutionnaire National pour le Développement, or MRND) faced the same fate as Tutsis. According to the perpetrators, both moderate Hutus and Tutsis were enemies of the Hutu hardliners.

In the 1999 Human Rights Watch Report—the earliest large-scale research publication on the genocide—entitled *Leave None to Tell the Story: Genocide in Rwanda*, author Alison Des Forges first mentions moderate Hutus when discussing the disagreement within the Rwandan government over the Arusha Peace Accords in 1993. The Arusha Accords were the product of negotiations between the Rwandan government and the Rwandan Patriotic Front (RPF) who had been engaged in the Rwandan Civil War since 1990. Some within the Rwandan government argued that the RPF—a Tutsi rebel group composed predominately of exiled Rwandan Tutsis—got more in the peace agreement than Rwanda's Hutu-led government. In her discussion of the varying views of the Accords within the Rwandan political sphere, Des Forges explains that hard-liners pushed ahead with plans for violence in the name of Hutu "self-defense" whereas the so-called moderate Hutus did not. This does not mean, however, that they were not concerned about the Accords being unbalanced, only that moderate Hutus did not respond with violence.

In *The Order of Genocide: Race, Power, and War in Rwanda* Scott Straus argues that an analysis of the actions of moderate Hutus prior to and during the genocide suggests that an outside intervention that placed moderates in positions of power and offered them support might have upended the genocide altogether. He views the actions of moderate Hutus as evidence, in part, that "most Hutu men would have just as easily complied with orders for peace as with orders for violence" (Straus 2008: 13). Instead, the hardliners gained the upper hand and once the genocide began they quickly eliminated moderate Hutu leaders in order to make sure ordinary Hutus followed the commands to kill Tutsis. While some have challenged Straus's conclusion, it does raise the point that some Hutus who might have identified politically as moderate prior to the genocide only became killers to avoid retribution when the killings began in earnest. Newspapers and radio broadcasts would have only confirmed a moderate Hutu's fear of reprisal killings because propaganda at that time urged Hutus to attack Hutus sympathetic to Tutsis.

The term "moderate Hutu" requires further attention in order to clarify its origin prior to and during the genocide and its use thereafter. In short, the term functions as a blanket term to describe any Hutu who became a victim of the Hutu militia and/or resisted the killings. But ultimately, not all Hutus killed during the genocide actively resisted the genocide and are labeled as moderates nonetheless. For example, some Hutus were the victims of circumstance. In some cases, a Hutu hardliner labeled his Hutu neighbor a moderate and killed him to steal his livestock even though there was no evidence to prove the perpetrator's accusation against his neighbor. In other cases, the children of moderate Hutus, who were too young to have acted against the Hutu hardliners or have formed a political outlook, were murdered because of the views of their parents. Despite the fact that not all Hutu victims during the genocide held moderate views, for better or worse they are considered as one group of victims.

Alexis Herr

See also: Arusha Accords; Des Forges, Alison; *Leave None to Tell the Story: Genocide in Rwanda*; Mouvement Révolutionnaire National pour le Développement; Mugesera, Léon; Rwandan Civil War; Rwandan Patriotic Front; Rwandan Genocide, Role of Propaganda in the; We Wish to Inform You That Tomorrow We Will be Killed With Our Families: *Stories from Rwanda*

Further Reading

Des Forges, Alison. *Leave None to Tell the Story: Genocide in Rwanda*. New York: Human Rights Watch, 1999.

Gourevitch, Philip. We Wish to Inform You That Tomorrow We Will be Killed With Our Families: *Stories from Rwanda*. New York: Picador, 1998.

Straus, Scott. *The Order of Genocide: Race, Power, and War in Rwanda*. Ithaca, NY: Cornell University Press, 2008.

Mouvement Démocratique Républicain

The Democratic Republican Movement (French: Mouvement Démocratique Républicain, or MDR) formed in 1991 and quickly became the largest pre-genocide opposition party in Rwanda. The creation of the MDR reflects the changing political processes in Africa following the end of the Cold War (1947–1991). The MDR's actions before and during the genocide illuminate the history and strength of anti-Tutsi sentiment in Rwanda.

Rwanda, like most other African nations, had operated as single-party state since the end of colonialism. While opposition parties would have formed earlier, Article VII of the 1978 Rwandan Constitution prevented them from doing so. The fall of communism (starting in 1989) inspired Rwandans and other international powers (predominately France) to push for a multiparty state. Thus, Rwandan president Juvénal Habyarimana finally allowed other political parties to form. The MDR, among others, emerged shortly thereafter to challenge the president and his party, the National Revolutionary Movement for Development (French: Mouvement révolutionnaire national pour le développement, or MRND). The MRND held an extraordinary congress on April 28, 1991, and adopted a statute that would allow for a multiparty state.

Although MDR officially formed in 1991, its roots predated Habyarimana's entry into office in 1973. According to French historian Gérard Prunier, the MDR of 1991 was an outgrowth of the Party for Hutu Emancipation (French: Parti du Mouvement et d'Emancipation Hutu, or Parmehutu), a political group that formed in 1959. Parmehutu added Mouvement Démocratique Rwandais (making it MDR-Parmehutu) to its name after the anti-Tutsi pogroms that lasted from 1959 to 1961, of which Parmehutu had played a key role. Following the Habyarimana coup in 1973, the new president outlawed the MDR-Parmehutu party. But when Habyarimana approved a new constitution on June 10, 1991, that included a provision for a multiparty state, the MDR quickly registered as an official political party of Rwanda. Although another 15 parties formed, MDR was the chief threat to Habyarimana's MRND.

Following massive street demonstrations, Habyarimana was pressured to create a coalition government in April 1992 and consequently MDR's power increased. To better combat political and physical aggression from other parties, the MDR formed a youth wing called *Inkuba*, meaning "thunder." The Rwandan Civil War between the Hutu-led Rwandan government and the Tutsi-led Rwandan Patriotic Front (RPF) rebel group caused the MDR to split in two.

While the mainstream MDR, led by Agathe Uwilingiyimana and Faustin Twagiramungu, continued to support negotiations with the RPF and advocate for a pluralist government, other MDR members took a different approach. Led by Frodauld Karamira, the Hutu extremist members of the MDR formed MDR-Power. Championing Hutu superiority, the MDR-Power movement played an active role in the genocide by supporting the genocidal government and participating in the killing. Following a radio announcement on April 12, 1994, by Karamira, members of the *Inkuba* youth wing of MDR joined the Interahamwe in hunting down and annihilating Tutsi and moderate-Hutu.

To distinguish between the two factions— the MDR and MDR-Power—one has only to look at what happened to the leaders of each group. Uwilingiyimana, one of the leaders of the MDR, served as the interim prime minister (April 7, 1993 to April 7, 1994). Because she had worked during the Rwandan Civil War to try and broker peace between the warring factions, she was killed at the outset of the genocide. Karamira, leader of MDR-Power, was found guilty of organizing the implementation of the genocide and sentenced to death by a Rwandan court.

Alexis Herr

See also: Habyarimana, Juvénal; Interahamwe; Kambanda, Jean; Karamira, Froduald; Mouvement Révolutionnaire National pour le Développement; Rwanda; Uwilingiyimana, Agathe

Further Reading

Straus, Scott. *The Order of Genocide: Race, Power, and War in Rwanda*. Ithaca, NY: Cornell University Press, 2008.

Totten, Samuel and Paul R. Bartrop. *Dictionary of Genocide*, Volume II. Westport, CT: Greenwood Press, 2008.

Mouvement Révolutionnaire National pour le Développement

Former Rwandan president Juvénal Habyarimana created the National Revolutionary Movement for Development (French: Mouvement Révolutionnaire National pour le Développement, or MRND) in 1975, two years after the coup that landed him in office. The MRND came to symbolize Habyarimana's dictatorship because soon after he formed it, he outlawed all other political parties within Rwanda. As the only party, it claimed wide membership—everyone had to be a member of the MRND no matter their age—and Rwanda's national congress included representatives from all its communes. Over time, Habyarimana solidified his position using the MRND branches throughout the country to do his bidding. During the genocide in 1994, Habyarimana's MRND cadres played a key role in inspiring, executing, and planning the killing of some 800,000 Tutsis and moderate Hutus. And the Interahamwe ("Those who fight together"), the main militia responsible for the genocide, was a product of the MRND.

Habyarimana's single-party state—officially enacted following Habyarimana's election and institution of a new constitution that confirmed the MRND as the sole party—ensured his absolute control of government, military, and social affairs. Serving jointly as the country's president and the president of the MRND, he mobilized the government and his party to enact his vision. With hundreds of party prefects, sub-prefects, and burgomasters (the heads of communes, which ranged in population from less than 30,000 to more than 100,000 and numbering 145 in 1991), all of whom were members of the MRND, the president had a mobilized force willing to execute his demands throughout the country. In his groundbreaking book, We Wish to Inform You That Tomorrow We Will be Killed With Our Families, Philip Gourevitch went so far as to describe this network of MRND officials as like that of the mafia.

The *umganda,* unpaid and communal labor, exemplifies how the MRND network enacted government policies. Rwandans were required by the MRND representatives in their community to do manual labor, such as dig ditches and repair roads. Those who failed to report for umganda had to pay a fine. The umganda was intended to propel Rwanda's infrastructure, and Habyarimana used his office as president of the state and his party to require all Rwandans to work to fulfill his goals.

As an advocate of Hutu supremacy himself, the MRND reflected Habyarimana's own prejudices towards Tutsis, an ethnic minority making up 14 percent of Rwanda's population. Habyarimana, a member of the Hutu majority (approximately 85 percent of the population), created a government and put in place an administration that severely diminished Tutsi advancement in all realms of society. To help restrain Tutsis' status, for example, their access to education was restricted. The steady stream of regulations placed on Tutsis coincided with the MRND's desire to elevate Hutus and denigrate Tutsis.

Events in the 1980s and during the first few years of the 1990s challenged the MRND's absolute control of Rwanda. In the

1980s, Rwanda's economic decline—caused by a devastating drought, an influx of thousands of Burundi refugees, and a decades-long mismanagement of government funds—sowed discontent with Habyarimana's leadership nationally and abroad. International aid donors threatened to withdraw their financial support of the country unless the government opened the parliament to other political parties. Then, in 1990, the Rwandan Patriotic Front (RPF), made up largely of Rwandan Tutsi refugees in the countries surrounding Rwanda, launched an attack against Habyarimana's government. The Rwandan Civil War that followed lasted until the government and the RPF signed the Arusha Peace Accords in 1993.

Although President Habyarimana had bowed to pressure from France to end his exclusive rule of the MRND in 1991, it was not until April 1992 that Habyarimana caved to international and domestic demands to create a coalition government and allow other the creation of other political parties. As a result, his party's name changed from the National Revolutionary Movement for Development to the National Republican Movement for Democracy and Development (French: Mouvement Républicain National pour la Démocratie et le Développement, or MRNDD). Despite outward appearances of change, the president and the inner circle of the MRND (of which his wife Agathe was front and center) secretly made moves to keep power.

Key to maintaining its monopoly of power, the MRND organized, funded, and trained a youth militia in 1992 and 1993 known as the Interahamwe. While the Interahamwe might have begun as a political youth movement within the MRND, it quickly became a breeding ground for Hutu extremism. And by the time the genocide began in April 1994, several thousand Interahamwe militias had been formed throughout Rwanda. These militia groups became the main executers of the genocide. Jerry Robert Kajuga served as the national president and leader of the MRND-affiliated Interahamwe.

In addition to creating and arming a militia that would murder hundreds of thousands of Tutsis during the genocide, prominent members of the MRND leadership helped spread propaganda in print media, on the radio, and during public rallies to incite hatred and mistrust of Tutsis. The weekly magazine *Kangura*, for example, which was run by Hassan Ngeze and supported financially by the MRND, claimed that Tutsis were vermin that needed to be exterminated. And the anti-Tutsi radio station Radio-Télévision Libre des Mille Collines (RTLM) also helped voice the MRND's destructive and hateful messages.

Alexis Herr

See also: Akazu; Habyarimana, Agathe; Habyarimana, Juvénal; Interahamwe; *Kangura*; Kajuga, Jerry Robert; Ngeze, Hassan; Radio-Télévision Libre des Mille Collines; Rwandan Patriotic Front; Rwandan Civil War

Further Reading

Des Forges, Alison. *Leave None to Tell the Story: Genocide in Rwanda*. New York: Human Rights Watch, 1999.

Gourevitch, Philip. *We wish to inform you that tomorrow we will be killed with our families: Stories from Rwanda*. New York: Picador, 1999.

Melvern, Linda. *Conspiracy to Murder: The Rwandan Genocide*. New York: Verso, 2004.

Straus, Scott. *The Order of Genocide: Race, Power, and War in Rwanda*. Ithaca, NY: Cornell University Press, 2008.

Mugesera, Léon

Léon Mugesera is a former Rwandan Hutu Power politician and ideologue counted among the central politicians responsible for planning the Rwandan Genocide. He served as a senior adviser to Rwandan president Juvénal Habyarimana prior to the genocide, and despite being the country during the bloodshed, his actions before his departure in 1993 allegedly helped to incite the killings.

Mugesera was educated in Rwanda and in Canada. Born in 1954 in Kibilira, Gisenyi Prefecture in Rwanda, Mugesera studied under Canadian missionaries during the 1970s and abroad at Laval University in Quebec City in the 1980s. While in Canada, he completed internships with the Canadian and Quebec governments, and later became a professor at the University of Rwanda.

Prior to the genocide (which began in April 1994), he was a member of the ruling Hutu party, the National Revolutionary Movement for Development (French: Mouvement Révolutionnaire National pour le Développement, or MRND)—the MRND changed its name to the National Republic Movement for Democracy and Development (French: Mouvement Révolutionnaire National pour le Démocratie et le Développement, or MRNDD) in 1992—and was the party's vice chairman for his home prefecture in Gisenyi in 1992.

On November 22, 1992, Mugesera made a 15-minute speech to a thousand party members at a political meeting in Kabaya, in which he allegedly said that Rwandan law permitted the death penalty for traitors, and that if the judicial system did not carry out this punishment against the Tutsi *inyenzi* ("cockroaches"), the people must do it themselves. "Know that the person whose neck you do not cut," he exclaimed, "is the one who will cut yours." He stated that "we the people are obliged to take responsibility ourselves and wipe out this scum," and that Hutus should kill Tutsis and "dump their bodies into the rivers of Rwanda" and send them back to Ethiopia. The speech was recorded and circulated repeated across radio waves and the like. In the eyes of many, this speech helped to form the ideological rationalization for the genocide that would follow in 1994.

The Rwandan minister of justice, Stanislas Mbonampeka, at that time a human rights activist and member of the Liberal Party, opposed to the regime of President Juvénal Habyarimana, studied Mugesera's speech, and issued an arrest warrant against him for inciting racial hatred. Mugesera was hidden by the army, and then spirited out of the country. He first went to Zaire (now known as the Democratic Republic of the Congo), then Spain, before he was granted refugee status in Canada in 1993. Meanwhile, Mbonampeka was soon forced to resign from his post as minister of justice, and in 1993, he joined with Hutu Power, and sought to resume his political career.

As Mbonampeka was switching sides, Mugesera and his family were granted permanent resident status in Canada, which critics allege was made possible by political connections between the Quebec establishment and Rwanda's Hutu ruling elite. Mugesera secured a job teaching at Laval University in Quebec, where he began postdoctoral work.

In 1995, the government of Rwanda sought Mugesera's extradition on the grounds that his 1992 speech had incited genocide and that the hatred it had engendered was a crime against humanity. The Canadian government commenced deportation proceedings against him for having lied about his background in his refugee application, along with the war crimes allegations. Article 318 of the Canadian Criminal Code, dealing with those who advocate genocide, provides for five years' imprisonment for anyone who "advocates or promotes genocide," and Section 7 of the Code provides for universal jurisdiction over crimes against humanity or war crimes committed by non-Canadians found in Canada for acts undertaken outside of Canada. The preference on this occasion, however, was to deport Mugesera rather than prosecute him, and in 1996 it was ordered that he be deported from Canada.

Upon appeal, Mugesera denied the accusations against him, despite the evidence shown in a video of him making his speech in November 1992. In a surprise ruling on April 12, 2001, after Mugesera was ordered to be deported by two Immigration Board tribunals, the Canadian Federal Court of Appeal overturned these verdicts. Federal Court justices Marc Nadon and Robert Décary concluded that there was no proof linking the November 1992 speech to genocide in the spring of 1994. Nadon requested that the Immigration Board tribunal review its claim that Mugesera incited racial hatred and thereby helped to foment genocide, and asked the board's appeals tribunal to re-examine the conclusions it had drawn about Mugesera's culpability. Nadon also ordered that deportation proceedings against Mugesera's wife and five children be halted immediately. Then, on August 1, 2001, Mugesera requested a trial under Canada's new Crimes against Humanity and War Crimes Act.

In 2003 the Federal Court of Appeal again found that the allegations against Mugesera were without foundation, winning him a further reprieve. Then two years later, on June 28, 2005, the Supreme Court of Canada

Léon Mugesera used his platform as vice chairman of the MRND in the years leading up to the 1994 Rwandan Genocide to spread racist propaganda targeting Tutsis and was widely considered to have played a key role in planning the genocide. (Steve Terrill/AFP/Getty Images)

voted unanimously to overturn the Federal Court of Appeal's decision, thus upholding the original deportation order. The Supreme Court ordered Mugesera out of the country, but the government in Ottawa showed reluctance to enforce the order on the grounds that he would likely be subjected to mistreatment from a regime whose judicial system might not meet international standards. Also, Canada had a long record of reluctance to deport persons to places carrying the death penalty.

In 2007, however, Rwanda abolished the death penalty, removing this long-standing Canadian legal concern over Mugesera's deportation. In 2009, Ottawa agreed to restart deportation proceedings, though the federal government also said it needed more time to review Mugesera's case. While it did so, Mugesera would remain in the country. In mid-2010, the Rwandan government filed hundreds of pages of previously unseen documents to the Canada Border Services Agency, responsible for enforcing decisions of the Immigration and Refugee Board, to make its case in favor of Mugesera's deportation. Ultimately, Mugasera was deported to Rwanda on January 23, 2012.

In early February 2012, Mugesera was formally charged with planning genocide, inciting genocide, planning and preparing genocide, conspiring in the crime of genocide, and incitement of hatred among Rwandans. While the High Court intended to start the trial in September 2012, they granted Mugesera's request to postpone the start date to allow him more time to prepare his defence. The trial proceedings were again postponed twice in total and finally began on December 17, 2012. Initially, Mugesera refused to plea guilty or innocent in protest of his trial. Only on February 15, 2013 did he enter a plea of not guilty to all the charges levied against him.

More than two decades after the Rwandan Genocide, in 2016 the Rwandan High Court convicted Mugesera of genocide and crimes against humanity. He was given a life sentence, which he plans to appeal.

Paul R. Bartrop

See also: Habyarimana, Juvénal; Mouvement Républicain National pour le Développement; Rwanda; Rwandan Genocide, Role of Propaganda

Further Reading

Kressel, Neil Jeffrey. *Mass Hate: The Global Rise of Genocide and Terror.* New York: Plenum Press, 1996.

"Leon Mugesera," Trial International (1 June 2016), https://trialinternational.org/latest-post/leon-mugesera/.

Schabas, William A. *Genocide in International Law: The Crime of Crimes.* Cambridge, UK: Cambridge University Press, 2000.

Munyenyezi, Beatrice, Trial of

On February 21, 2013, a jury in a U.S. federal court in Concord, New Hampshire, found Beatrice Munyenyezi, a Hutu who had fled Rwanda in the aftermath of the Rwandan Genocide, guilty of having lied about her involvement in that tragedy when she applied for U.S. citizenship.

In 1998, Munyenyezi and her three daughters settled in Manchester, New Hampshire, where she secured a job with the Manchester Housing Authority. Munyenyezi had initially sought refugee status, claiming that she would be persecuted if she returned to Rwanda. She subsequently applied for permanent resident status (a green card), which was granted, and in 2003, she was awarded full citizenship. On her application for naturalization as an American citizen (N-400 naturalization form), Munyenyezi claimed that she had never committed a crime leading to her arrest or conviction, never been belonged to a political organization, party, club of the like; and never lied to or misled federal agents.

Back in Arusha Tanzania, Munyenyezi's husband and mother-in-law stood trial at the International Criminal Tribunal for Rwanda. Munyenezi traveled to Arusha in 2006 as a witness for her husband. In June 2011, her husband and mother-in-law, both alleged members of the Interahamwe (a Hutu militia group responsible for instigating and perpetrating the Rwandan Genocide), were sentenced to life imprisonment for war crimes, crimes against humanity, and genocide. Those trials brought to light Munyenyezi's activities in 1994, and federal prosecutors decided to investigate her role in the genocide. At approximately the same time, Munyenyezi's sister, Prudence Kantengwa, stood trial for having lied about her political affiliations in Rwanda before emigrating to the United States in the 1990s. A U.S. court found her guilty of immigration fraud, perjury, and misuse of visas, permits, or other documents in 2012. She was given a 21-month prison sentence.

Federal prosecutors brought two charges against Munyenyezi. The first alleged that she had lied about her role in the genocide and her ties to the Interahamwe and the Mouvement Révolutionnaire National pour le Développement (Hutu groups responsible for the genocide). The court accused her of participating in and instigating killings and rapes at a roadblock near Hotel Ihuriro where she and her husband lived. Federal prosecutors also claimed that she had entered the United States illegally by lying about her political associations and activities on her refugee and green card applications.

Her first trial ended with a deadlocked jury in March 2012. The second trial, which saw her convicted of both charges in February 2013, witnessed new prosecutorial tactics and witnesses, which proved more convincing. Several witnesses testified that Munyenyezi had been stationed at a roadblock during the 1994 genocide where she singled out Tutsis to be murdered; others claimed that she had worn the uniform of an extremist Hutu group implicated in its involvement in the mass killings. Munyenyezi vehemently denied these claims, but chose not to testify in either of her trials. She was found guilty and given a ten year sentence.

Paul G. Pierpaoli Jr.

See also: Hutus; Interahamwe; International Criminal Tribunal for Rwanda; Mouvement Révolutionnaire National pour le Développement; Tutsis

Further Reading

Melvern, Linda. *Conspiracy to Murder: The Rwandan Genocide*. London: Verso, 2006.

United States v. Munyenyezi, No. 13–1950 (United States Court of Appeals, First Circuit, 2015.

N

Nahimana, Ferdinand

Ferdinand Nahimana is a former Rwandan professor of history, and was a leading propagandist for the radical Hutu cause against the Tutsi minority prior to and during the Rwandan Genocide of 1994. He was born on July 15, 1950, in the commune of Gatonde, Ruhengeri Prefecture. He obtained a PhD in history from the University of Paris VII, and taught at the National University of Rwanda. While pursuing his doctorate, he became involved in Hutu supremacist politics. He developed a number of theories concerning the racial origins of the Rwandan population—theories he was later to popularize when promoting the cause of ethnic Hutu superiority over Tutsis via the Rwandan airwaves. Between 1979 and 1994 he allegedly wrote and published articles encouraging Hutus to revolt against the Tutsis and moderate Hutus.

In late 1990, Nahimana became director of the Rwandan National Information Office (French: Office Rwandais d'Information, or ORINFOR), and served as the overseer of the state-owned Radio Rwanda, the newspaper press, and all other media related activities. He left this position in February 1992, but in 1993 he and some of his colleagues—most of whom were members of the then ruling party, the Mouvement Révolutionnaire National pour le Développement, or MRND—the party of Rwandan president Juvénal Habyarimana—established the first approved private radio station in Rwanda, Radio-Télévision Libre des Mille Collines (RTLM).

As a senior executive of this anti-Tutsi radio station, Nahimana was largely responsible for the propagandistic content of the station's programming. He performed a vital role as an anti-Tutsi ideologue and Hutu apologist. Nahimana was also a founding member of a radical breakaway from the MRND, the Coalition for the Defence of the Republic (French: Coalition pour la Défense de la République, or CDR), an openly progenocide Hutu Party.

Soon after the genocide began in April 1994, Nahimana was given sanctuary in the French embassy, escaping the fighting in Kigali between units of the Tutsi-led Rwandan Patriotic Front (RPF) and the government forces. On April 12, 1994, the French subsequently allowed him to escape to Bujumbura, Burundi. During Operation Turquoise—a French military operation under the auspices of the United Nations—he returned to Rwanda and hid in a "safe zone" created by the French that ultimately acted as a sanctuary for Hutus escaping the RPF. He left again after the RPF had defeated the perpetrators and overcame the government in July. By August 30, 1994, Nahimana arrived in Cameroon, where he settled into a semipermanent exile.

On March 26, 1996, he was arrested there, pursuant to a request for extradition issued by Rwanda's RPF government. On April 15, 1994, the prosecutor of the International Criminal Tribunal for Rwanda (ICTR) requested the Cameroonian government not to proceed with the extradition—though still holding Nahimana in custody—while a formal indictment was prepared against him.

On July 22, 1996, the indictment was produced. Nahimana was charged with genocide, conspiracy to commit genocide, direct and public incitement to commit genocide, and crimes against humanity. He was transferred from Cameroon to the ICTR in Arusha, Tanzania, in January 1997, and his initial court appearance took place on February 19, 1997. At his first appearance, he pleaded not guilty.

Nahimana's trial was quickly consolidated into that of two other anti-Tutsi propagandists, Jean-Bosco Barayagwiza, the former director of political affairs at the Ministry of Foreign Affairs, a cofounder of the CDR, and a board member of the RTLM, and Hassan Ngeze, the former editor of the hateful newspaper *Kangura*. It commenced on October 21, 2001. Collectively known as the "Media Trial," the three were held responsible for creating a climate that implanted the idea of Tutsi annihilation onto the Hutu worldview long before the genocidal killing had begun. In addition, Nahimana was accused of chairing meetings at which MRND leaders discussed how to annihilate Tutsis and moderate Hutus. He also allegedly gave direct orders to murder Tutsis, and helped to distribute weapons to the anti-Tutsi Interahamwe militia.

After three years of testimony, the trial culminated in August 2003 when the tribunal retired to consider its verdict. The prosecutor demanded the maximum sentence, life imprisonment, for Nahimana, Barayagwiza, and Ngeze. On December 3, 2003, the Trial Chamber announced its verdict. Nahimana was sentenced to life imprisonment for genocide; conspiracy to commit genocide; incitement, directly and publicly, to commit genocide; complicity in genocide; and persecution and extermination as crimes against humanity.

Nahimana appealed his sentence, and a subsequent trial before the ICTR Appeals Chamber opened on January 16, 2007. On November 28, 2007, the Appeals Court affirmed his guilt, but only for the counts of direct and public incitement to commit genocide and persecution as a crime against humanity. It overturned several charges, notably those that touched on events taking place or articles he had written before 1994. It also overturned the conclusion of the initial trial judges that there had been a conspiracy between the RTLM, the CDR, and *Kangura* with a view to committing genocide. Accordingly, his sentence was reduced from life imprisonment to 30 years.

On December 3, 2008, Nahimana was transferred from Arusha to Bamako Central Prison, Mali, where he would serve his sentence.

Paul R. Bartrop

See also: Barayagwiza, Jean-Bosco; International Criminal Tribunal for Rwanda; Interahamwe; *Kangura*; Mouvement Révolutionnaire National pour le Développement; Ngeze, Hassan; Radio-Télévision Libre des Mille Collines; Turquoise, Operation; Rwandan Patriotic Front

Further Reading

Kagan, Sophia, "The 'Media case' before the Rwanda Tribunal: The Nahimana et al. Appeal Judgement," The Hague Justice Portal (24 April 2008), http://www.hague justiceportal.net/index.php?id=9166.

Midlarsky, Manus I. *The Killing Trap: Genocide in the Twentieth Century.* Cambridge, MA: Cambridge University Press, 2005.

Neier, Aryeh. *War Crimes: Brutality, Genocide, Terror, and the Struggle for Justice.* New York: Times Books, 1998.

Ndadaye, Melchior

Melchior Ndadaye, a Hutu engineer, was elected president of Burundi in June 1993 by 64.8 percent of Burndians and in so doing became the first democratically elected head of state. When he beat his Tutsi opponent Pierre Buyoya, Ndadaye became the first Hutu president in Burundi's history. His tenure, however, was short-lived. He was killed on October 21, 1993, during an unsuccessful coup attempt by units of the Tutsi-dominated military.

Ndadaye was born on March 28, 1953, and was still in secondary school when he fled the country for Rwanda in 1972 to escape a round of ethnic massacres by the army. He sought refuge in Butare, in the south of Rwanda, where he attended the Group Scolaire before going to France to study banking. He was active in political affairs in Rwanda's refugee community and was one of the founding members of a student movement, as well as the Labor Party of Burundi. He was a lecturer in Rwanda from 1980 to 1983.

Ndadaye returned to Burundi in 1983 and entered the banking sector, heading up a credit organization from 1983 to 1988. Following further ethnic massacres in 1988, Ndadaye called for the nomination of a Hutu prime minister, a democratic charter, and the restructuring of the army; he was subsequently imprisoned for close to three months. The following year, as the country made strides toward democracy and ethnic reconciliation, Ndadaye joined the rural development ministry as a counselor. He later was named to a constitutional commission but resigned from that body in 1991. Ndadaye's Front for Democracy in Burundi was legalized in 1992 and Ndadaye went on to win the June 1993 presidential elections. He assumed office on July 10, 1993, and was assassinated, along with several his cabinet members, three and a half months later.

Lynn Jurgensen

See also: Burundi; Burundi, Genocide in

Further Reading

Africa South of the Sahara 1994. London: Europa Publications Limited, 1994.

Prunier, Gérard. *The Rwanda Crisis: History of a Genocide.* New York: Columbia University Press, 1995.

Ndindiliyimana, Augustin

Augustin Ndindiliyimana was the chief of staff of the Rwandan Gendarmerie Nationale, the national police force, during the Rwandan Genocide of 1994. As chief of staff from September 2, 1992, he was responsible for the maintenance of peace and public order and ensuring the observance of law throughout Rwanda. Ndindiliyimana was born in Nyaruhengeri commune, Butare prefecture, in 1943. A career soldier in the Rwandan Armed Forces (French: Forces Armées Rwandaises, or FAR), at the time of the genocide he held the rank of major general.

According to the indictment issued by the International Criminal Tribunal for Rwanda (ICTR)—the justice system installed after the genocide by the United Nations to try leading perpetrators—sometime prior to his appointment as chief of staff of the Gendarmerie Nationale, he conspired with other high-level FAR officers to plan the logistics of what would become the annihilation of the Tutsi minority in Rwanda at the hands of the Hutu Power government.

On the night of April 6, 1994, Rwandan president Juvénal Habyarimana was assassinated when his plane was shot from the sky upon its approach to Kigali airport. A Crisis Committee was immediately set up, comprised of senior FAR officers led by Colonel Théoneste Bagosora, Tharcisse Renzaho, the governor of Kigali prefecture and president of the Civil Defense Committee for Kigali, and Ndindiliyimana in his capacity as chief of staff of the Gendarmerie Nationale. The force commander of the United Nations Assistance Mission for Rwanda (UNAMIR), General Roméo Dallaire, was invited to the initial meeting of the Crisis Committee, and arrived to find only senior military and paramilitary figures present. None of the civilian leadership was there. Dallaire rejected Bagosora's proposal of having the military take control of the political situation until they could hand it over to the politicians, reminding him that Rwanda still had a government headed by Prime Minister Agathe Uwilingiyimana. Bagosora responded that she was incapable of governing the nation. A few hours later, members of the Presidential Guard murdered Uwilingiyimana, along with her husband.

The ICTR also accused Ndindiliyimana of preventing UNIMAR's disarmament program, known as the 'Kigali Weapon Security Area' (KWSA). UNIMAR set up KWSA at the start of 1994 with the goal of collecting an overabundance of weapons in the Kigali town prefecture. Ndindiliyamana supposedly compromised the disarmament program by tipping off Mathieu Ngirumpatse (the president of Habyarimana's political party), thus giving his colleagues an advanced warning of the weapon searches. These weapons, hidden away as a result of the Ndindiliyamana's intel, were then used in the genocide. According to the ICTR prosecutor, Ndindiliyimana thus bears responsibility not only for the atrocities committed by the forces under his control, but also indirectly for making these weapons available to the militias.

Augustin Ndindiliyimana made headlines when the United Nations-backed war crimes tribunal in Arusha, Tanzania, first found the ex-paramilitary police chief guilty of genocide and later acquitted him of all charges. Prior to his trial, he had already spent 11 years behind bars awaiting his day in court. (Herwig Vergult/AFP/Getty Images)

Ndindiliyimana has been accused of sexual violence and rape of Tutsi women, and has been charged with participating in the murder of 10 Belgian UNAMIR peacekeepers that were guarding Prime Minister Uwingiliyimana at the time of her assassination on April 7, 1994. The death of the Belgian soldiers precipitated the withdrawal of all Belgian troops from UNAMIR.

There are some, despite this, who have found Ndindiliyimana's behavior during the genocide to be something less than fanatical in comparison to so many of those around him. Dallaire, among others, thought Ndindiliyimana might have been initially a moderate voice in the Crisis Committee. For example, Ndindiliyimana was known to be responsible for dismantling a potentially disastrous roadblock in front of the Hôtel des Mille Collines, at a time when the hotel manager, Paul Rusesabagina, employed the hotel as a United Nations–protected safe zone. Some have suggested that Ndindiliyimana was ambivalent towards the extreme measures being taken by the interim government.

After the genocide concluded in July 1994, Ndindiliyimana fled Rwanda for Belgium, where he was granted the status of a political refugee. On January 29, 2000, however, he was apprehended and extradited to the custody of the ICTR in Arusha, Tanzania, to face charges of conspiracy to commit genocide, genocide or complicity in genocide in the alternative, crimes against humanity, and war crimes. The ICTR had earlier issued an indictment against Ndindiliyimana and three other former FAR officers. Ndindiliyimana has, from the outset, pleaded not guilty to all charges against him. Known as the "Military II" trial, the indictment also groups together the former chief of staff of the FAR, General Augustin Bizimungu, and two commanding officers in the reconnaissance battalion, Major François Xavier Nzuwonemeye and Captain Innocent Sagahutu. According to the indictment of August 23, 2004, Augustin Ndindiliyimana was alleged to have conspired with his co-accused in the planning and commission of a plan to exterminate Tutsis in Rwanda. He was charged with ten counts of genocide, crimes against humanity, and violations of the Geneva Conventions on the treatment of combatants and civilians in wartime. Proceedings against Ndindiliyimana began on September 20, 2004.

Ndindiliyimana's defense attorney is a Canadian lawyer, Christopher Black, who has for a long time argued that the foundation upon which the ICTR was established is questionable, at best. Black has argued that the ICTR's interpretation of the events in Rwanda in 1994 as genocide is not a correct reading of what really transpired, and that there was no genocide of the country's Tutsis at the hands of the government. The case against Ndindiliyimana was completed on June 29, 2009. On May 17, 2011, Ndindiliyimana was sentenced by the ICTR to 11 years, 3 months, and 19 days' imprisonment, the equivalent of his time served since his arrest. The Tribunal found that Ndindiliyimana had limited control over the men he commanded and was personally opposed to the killings.

Paul R. Bartrop

See also: Bagosora, Théoneste; Bizimungu, Augustin; Dallaire, Roméo; Forces Armées Rwandaises; Rusesabagina, Paul; United Nations Assistance Mission for Rwanda; Uwilingiyimana, Agathe

Further Reading

"Augustin Ndindiliyimana," Trial International (10 June 2016), https://trialinternational.org/latest-post/augustin-ndindiliyimana/.

Dallaire, Roméo. *Shake Hands with the Devil: The Failure of Humanity in Rwanda.* Toronto: Random House, Canada, 2004.

Strozier, Charles B. and Michael Flynn, eds. *Genocide, War, and Human Survival.* Lanham, MD: Rowman & Littlefield Publishers, 1996.

Ngeze, Hassan

Hassan Ngeze was a Rwandan journalist responsible for writing, publishing, and spreading anti-Tutsi propaganda prior to the

Rwandan Genocide of 1994. Born on December 25, 1957, in Rubavu commune, Gisenyi, Ngeze is a Muslim and Hutu supremacist. His early life history is difficult to track down. His education seems to have been restricted only to primary school, after which he scratched out a living as a shoeshine boy and then a bus conductor. It does not appear that Ngeze had any formal apprenticeship or education as a journalist, though it is known that he worked as a columnist for different Rwandan newspapers from 1978 onwards. Prior to 1990, he was a correspondent and distributor in Gisenyi for *Kanguka*, a newspaper critical of the ruling regime of President Juvénal Habyarimana, especially of the military.

In 1990, Ngeze and other radical Hutus from the family entourage of the Habyarimana clan (a clique known as the *Akazu*, or "Little Hut") founded *Kangura* (Kinyarwanda for "Wake Them Up"), an anti-Tutsi, pro-Hutu popular newspaper intended as a counterweight to *Kanguka*, a newspaper sponsored by the Tutsi-led Rwandan Patriotic Front (RPF). The first issue was entirely financed by the Information Bureau of the Presidency. It continued publication with ongoing financial assistance from high-level members of Habyarimana's ruling party, the Mouvement républicain national pour la démocratie (MRND), and, later, from the extremist The Coalition for the Defense of the Republic (French: Coalition pour la Défense de la République, or CDR) party, of which Ngeze was a cofounder.

The creation of *Kangura*, for which Ngeze was made the chief editor, was part of a much wider strategy on the part of the State. Its first issue appeared in May 1990, and its last in February 1994—two months before the start of the genocide. During its tenure, *Kangura* spread and incited racial hatred of Tutsi.

Ngeze has always asserted that he was a businessman and entrepreneur rather than a Hutu Power ideologue, but the pages of *Kangura* constantly showed him to be much more than what he claimed to be. Perhaps the most infamous piece he authored for *Kangura* was a catalogue of 10 admonitory instructions—the "Hutu Ten Commandments"—that were to be followed by every Hutu in order to destroy Tutsi influence in Rwandan society, and guarantee Hutu hegemony. Their repetition through the pages of *Kangura* served as an important conditioning agent for the Hutus. Published in issue number six of *Kangura*, in December 1990, Ngeze claimed later that the list had been circulating for some years before, and was not in fact composed by him alone.

Kangura also published material that referred constantly to Tutsis as *Inyenzi*—cockroaches—and drove home the message that these *Inyenzi* (including those from outside, the *Inkotanyi*, or rebels, from the Rwandan Patriotic Front) were about to enslave all the Hutus and/or exterminate them. The answer to this "problem," it put rhetorically (and frequently), was to wipe out the Tutsis. Prior to ceasing publication, *Kangura* also published the names of Hutus deemed to be politically suspected—with the insinuation that they should suffer the same fate as the Tutsis—and exhorted "true" Hutus to take all measures to ensure that they would dominate now and into the future. Employing sensationalism at every turn, and with a readership many times greater than its circulation figures suggested, *Kangura* was a crucial instrument in developing a consciousness for genocide, notwithstanding that it had ceased publication by the time the genocide actually began.

Along with Jean-Bosco Barayagwiza and Jean Shyirambere Barahinura, Ngeze cofounded the extremist CDR party, and in

1993 became a founder, shareholder, correspondent, and leading director of the anti-Tutsi radio station Radio-Télévision Libre des Mille Collines (RTLM), which was to some extent a radio equivalent of *Kangura*. Although *Kangura* did not play any direct role in the genocide while it was in progress (having ceased publication in February 1994), Ngeze played a very active role in the genocide nonetheless.

As a former member of the MRND and one of the founders of the CDR, Ngeze also exercised political control over the Interahamwe militias, and was an organizer of the CDR's Impuzamugambi militia. During the genocide, he provided RTLM with the names of people to be killed in his prefecture of Gisenyi, which were broadcast on air. He is also alleged to have personally supervised and taken part in torture, mass rape, and killings within the prefecture.

In June 1994, Ngeze fled Rwanda as the RPF forces advanced, and on July 18, 1997, upon the demand of the prosecutor of the International Criminal Tribunal for Rwanda (ICTR), he was arrested in Mombasa, Kenya. He was transferred to the United Nations penitentiary in Arusha, Tanzania, the same day.

The ICTR charged Ngeze with several counts of genocide, public incitement to commit genocide, complicity in genocide, and crimes against humanity. His trial, which opened on October 23, 2000, was consolidated into that of two other anti-Tutsi propagandists, Barayagwiza and Ferdinand Nahimana; collectively known as the "Media Trial," the three were found responsible for creating a climate that implanted the idea of Tutsi annihilation onto the Hutu worldview long before the killings actually began.

From the beginning, Ngeze boycotted the trial for several days, protesting at the way in which his newspaper articles had been translated for the ICTR. He also demanded a complete translation of seventy-one issues of *Kangura* from Kinyarwanda into English and French. He then pleaded not guilty to all counts in the indictment against him.

When the trial got underway, his lawyer argued that it was not Ngeze himself who was on trial, but, rather, freedom of the press. The trial thereby assumed a special importance, since it was the first time since the trial of Adolf Hitler's propagandists at Nuremberg that journalists were appearing in the dock of an international tribunal—and, no less, for the crime of genocide. While the main elements of the trial were conducted on this important democratic principle, the Tribunal judges were ultimately not moved by such arguments. All three defendants were found guilty in December 2003. Ngeze was found guilty on the counts of genocide; conspiracy to commit genocide; direct and public incitement to commit genocide; and crimes against humanity (persecution and extermination). Although he was acquitted on the charges of complicity to commit genocide and of crimes against humanity (murder), the court still sentenced him to life imprisonment.

Ngeze appealed his conviction, and a further trial before the Appeals Chamber opened on January 16, 2007. On November 28, 2007, the Appeals Chamber affirmed his guilt, but only for the counts of aiding and abetting the commission of genocide, for direct and public incitement to commit genocide through publication, and for aiding and abetting crimes against humanity. His sentence was reduced to 35 years' imprisonment. On December 3, 2008, he was transferred to Bamako Central Prison, Mali, to serve out his sentence.

Paul R. Bartrop

See also: Barayagwiza, Jean-Bosco; Coalition Pour la Défense de la Règpublique; Habyarimana, Juvénal; Interahamwe; International Criminal Tribunal for Rwanda; *Kangura*; Media Trial in Rwanda; Nahimana, Ferdinand; Radio-Télévision Libre des Mille Collines; Rwandan Patriotic Front

Further Reading

Friedrichs, David O., ed. *State Crime*. Brookfield, VT: Ashgate/Dartmouth, 1998.

Valentino, Benjamin A. *Final Solutions: Mass Killing and Genocide in the Twentieth Century*. Ithaca, NY: Cornell University Press, 2004.

Niyitegeka, Felicitas

Sister Felicitas Niyitegeka, a member of the Hutu ethnic group, gave her life to protect and shelter Tutsis during the Rwandan Genocide. Now recognized as a national heroine of Rwanda, Sister Niyitegeka's efforts to save those most vulnerable stand out as story of courage, faith, and conviction. Furthermore, her endeavors as a religious leader to save Tutsis offers a welcome contrast to the countless other stories that have emerged since the genocide, which depict Christian priests and nuns as collaborators and perpetrators.

When the genocide broke out in April 1994, Sister Niyitegeka was about 60 years old and was serving as the director of the Centre Saint Pierre, an orphanage in the remote town of Gisenyi, Rwanda. When the killing of Tutsis began in earnest, Tutsis in the area flocked to Centre Saint Pierre to seek shelter and help from Niyitegeka and her sisters. Niyitegeka opened the doors of her home and sheltered more than 30 Tutsis.

Despite the inherent dangers that helping Tutsis posed, the sisters of Centre Saint Pierre labored to help dozens of Tutsis cross Lake Kivu to relative safety in neighboring Zaire (now known as the Democratic Republic of the Congo). Sister Niyitegeka knew that her actions and those of her sisters posed a great threat to their lives. Sister Niyitegeka's brother even went so far as to urge her to abandon the Tutsis and leave Centre Saint Pierre immediately. A colonel in the army, Sister Niyitegeka's brother knew what awaited so-called moderate Hutus like his sister. Instead, Sister Niyitegeka wrote a letter to her brother in which she defended her decision to stay, writing that she would rather die than abandon her charges.

When the Interahamwe militia arrived at Centre Saint Pierre they told Sister Niyitegeka that she would be spared because of her brother, however, she refused to abandon the Tutsi victims she sought to protect. Instead, the Interahamwe transferred her and her sisters to a freshly dug mass grave and shot six of her sisters and some 20 refugees in front of her. Still, she refused to leave her sisters and the Tutsi victims and so, she, too, was murdered.

In the aftermath of the genocide, the story of Sister Niyitegeka has resonated with many as an example of resilience and resistance in a time of lawlessness and infectious hatred. She is one of several heroes celebrated every year by Rwandans on the first of February for National Heroes' Day.

Alexis Herr

See also: Interahamwe; Roman Catholic Church; *Rwanda: The Preventable Genocide*; Victims

Further Reading

Katongole, Emmanuel. *Resurrecting Faith after Genocide in Rwanda*. Grand Rapids, MI: Zondervan, 2009.

Rittner, Carol, John K. Roth, and Wendy Whitworth, eds. *Genocide in Rwanda: Complicity of the Churches.* St. Paul, MN: Paragon House, 2004.

Nowrojee, Binaifer

Binaifer Nowrojee's upbringing and youth in Kenya shaped her interest in human rights. She grew up under an autocratic and dictatorial government in a household where her father worked as a human rights lawyer representing detainees. Following in her father's footsteps, Nowrojee went on to get a law degree and pursue a legal career in human rights. She has worked as a Lecturer on Law at Harvard Law School, held numerous prestigious fellowships, served as legal counsel with Human Rights Watch, as a staff attorney at the Lawyers Committee for Human Rights, and before becoming the Regional Director for Asia Pacific for the Open Society Foundation's work in Asia, she served as the founding director of the Open Society Foundations' Initiative for East Africa for a decade. Over the course of her career, Nowrojee's research has focused primarily on sexual violence. She has authored numerous articles, briefs, and books on the subject, including the 1996 report *Shattered Lives: Sexual Violence during the Rwandan Genocide and its Aftermath.*

Working as a consultant to the Women's Rights Project, Nowrojee traveled to Rwanda after the genocide with the intention of interviewing women who had survived rape during the Rwandan Genocide in 1994. In partnership with Janet Fleischman, Washington director of the nonprofit organization Human Rights Watch Africa, Nowrojee conducted research and interviewed survivors in March and April 1996. The resulting report, entitled *Shattered*

In the aftermath of the genocide, Binaifer Nowrojee worked with female victims whose experiences of rape had been silenced. Thanks in part to her work in Rwanda, aid workers are now better equipped to help genocide survivors who have experienced sexual trauma. (Mark Sagliocco/Getty Images for Hamptons International Film Festival)

Lives: Sexual Violence during the Rwandan Genocide and its Aftermath, demonstrated that rape was a key component of the victimization and brutalization of women during the Rwandan Genocide. Her research drew attention to the gendered experiences of victims and the gendered dynamics of post-genocide reconciliation and reconstruction. With women accounting for an estimated 70 percent of the population after the genocide, she explained, "the future of Rwanda is largely in the hands of its women." In her report, she noted that "many of these women have lived through unimaginable suffering . . . many have lost everything . . . Despite the overwhelming odds facing them, Rwandan women have begun to organize themselves and rebuild their shattered lives" (Binaifer 1996). She then offers her recommendations for how the international community and the Rwandan government can best serve the women of Rwanda who lacked the necessary services and institutions to help them recover and rebuild their lives.

In *Shattered Lives*, Nowrojee charges the International Criminal Tribunal for Rwanda (ICTR)—the judicial body set up in Arusha, Tanzania, by the United Nations after the Rwandan Genocide to prosecute key perpetrators of that genocide—to investigate and prosecute sexual violence. "Rape, sexual slavery and sexual mutilation," she asserted, "should be recognized and prosecuted, where appropriate, as crimes against humanity, genocide crimes, or war crimes." This report and the testimony she collected encouraged the ICTR to consider rape as an act of genocide, a charge that had never been pursued before. She helped make this a reality when she testified as an expert witness before the International Criminal Tribunal for Rwanda on sexual violence.

Alexis Herr

See also: Akayesu, Jean-Paul; International Criminal Tribunal for Rwanda; Rape

Further Reading

Nowrojee, Binaifer. *Shattered Lives: Sexual Violence during the Rwandan Genocide and its Aftermath*. New York: Human Rights Watch, 1996. Available online at https://www.hrw.org/reports/1996/Rwanda.htm.

The Uncondemned, directed by Michele Mitchell and Nick Louvel. 2015. Film at Eleven. Documentary Film.

Ntaganda, Bosco

Bosco Ntaganda is a Congolese military leader indicted by the International Criminal Court (ICC) for war crimes and crimes against humanity for acts he committed or condoned between July 2002 and December 2003. Ntaganda, a Tutsi, was born in 1973 in the Rwandan village of Kiningi. As a teenager, he went to Ngungu, in the eastern region of the Democratic Republic of the Congo (DRC), to escape the persecution of Tutsis then taking place in Rwanda. In 1990, he joined the leftist Tutsi Rwandan Patriotic Front, which was operating in southern Uganda. He saw action with the armed wing of that group during the 1990s, and following the 1994 Rwandan Genocide, he participated in the movement that ousted the Hutu-dominated government.

Later, Ntaganda became a member of the Patriotic Forces for the Liberation of Congo, which was the military wing of the Union of Congolese Patriots (French: Union des Patriotes, or UPC). He soon rose to chief of military affairs. Later still, he joined the National Congress for the Defense of the People (French: Congrès national our la defense du peuple, or CNDP), a militia force active in the DRC, serving as its chief of staff. In recent years, Ntaganda and the UPC have controlled several lucrative mineral mines in the eastern part of the DRC. It has been reported that Ntaganda has personally profited from these operations and has repeatedly engaged in the illicit mineral trade that continues to play a significant role in destabilizing the DRC. Some have likened his control over eastern Congo to that of a mafia kingpin. Most recently, he led the Mouvement du 23-Mars (commonly referred to as M23), an armed militia movement that tried unsuccessfully to seize the city of Goma, DRC, adjacent to the Rwandan border.

In August 2006, the ICC issued an arrest warrant for Ntaganda, based upon his actions during from 2002 to 2003. The specific charges included: employment of child soldiers; murder; rape; sexual slavery; and ethnic-based persecution. In April 2012, Congolese president Joseph Kabila called for the arrest of Ntaganda, citing his virtual war against the DRC's government.

In a stunning turn of events, following infighting within M23, Ntaganda surrendered to the U.S. embassy in Kigali, Rwanda, on March 18, 2013. He then requested that he be transferred to the ICC. He was then flown to The Hague where his trial began in September 2015. At the time of writing, his trial is still underway.

Paul G. Pierpaoli Jr.

See also: Congo, Democratic Republic of the; Rwandan Patriotic Front

Further Reading

"Rebel Leader in the Congo is Flown to The Hague," *The New York Times*, March 22, 2013.

"Why did Infamous War Criminal Bosco Ntaganda Just Surrender at a US Embassy?," *Washington Post*, March 18, 2013.

Ntakirutimana, Elizaphan

Elizaphan Ntakirutimana was a Rwandan minister who was convicted of genocide in 2003. Ntakirutimana, a Hutu, was born in Kibuye Prefecture, Rwanda in 1924. He eventually became a minister in the Seventh-day Adventist Church in Rwanda and then a pastor at the Mugonero church located in Ngoma. In mid-April 1994, at the height of

the Rwandan Genocide, several Seventh-day Adventist ministers sent a letter to Ntakirutimana in which they relayed the plight of the hundreds of Tutsi refugees under their care. The following day, well-armed Hutu militiamen converged on the refugees, murdering several hundreds of them.

Ntakirutimana apparently was complicit in the massacre of the refugees because he had transported and aided the militia. His crime was first brought to international attention in 1998 in Philip Gourevitch's book, *We wish to inform you that tomorrow we will be killed with our families*. Indeed, the title was taken from the letter written to Ntakirutimana by the besieged ministers at Mugonero. Prior to the publication of that book, however, Ntakirutimana had fled Rwanda, knowing that he had already been implicated in the massacre and that Rwandan and international law enforcement officials were pursuing him.

Ntakirutimana ultimately found his way to the United States, via Mexico, and was apprehended in Laredo, Texas, in 1996. Already wanted by the International Criminal Tribunal for Rwanda (ICTR), he was detained in a federal penal facility while he fought extradition. In January 2000, the U.S. Supreme Court ruled that Ntakirutimana had exhausted all legal avenues to fight extradition. This permitted his transfer to a detention facility run by the ICTR in Arusha, Tanzania.

The ICTR charged Ntakirutimana with genocide, conspiracy to commit genocide, three counts of crimes against humanity, and one count of violating Common Article 3 of the Geneva Conventions. Meanwhile, his son Gérard, a physician, was also put on trial for his role in the Rwandan Genocide. Ntakirutimana the elder was found guilty of genocide but not guilty of the other charges. On

February 19, 2003, he became the first cler-
gyman to be convicted for his role in the
genocide. He appealed the decision, but
the genocide charge remained and he was
imprisoned until December 6, 2006, when he
was released. All told, Ntakirtutiman spent
ten years detained or imprisoned. He died in
Arusha, Tanzania, on January 22, 2007.

Paul G. Pierpaoli Jr.

See also: International Criminal Tribunal for
Rwanda; *We wish to inform you that tomorrow we will be killed with our families*

Further Reading

Gourevitch, Philip. *We wish to inform you that
tomorrow we will be killed with our families: Stories from Rwanda.* New York: Picador, 1999.

Straus, Scott. *The Order of Genocide: Race,
Power, and War in Rwanda.* Ithaca, NY:
Cornell University Press, 2008.

Ntamabyariro, Agnes

Agnes Ntamabyariro was 60 years old when
she was arrested in Zambia on May 27, 1997
and extradited to Rwanda to face charges for
helping plan and incite the 1994 Rwandan
Genocide. Ntamabyariro's role in the mass
killing offers an example of a prominent
female perpetrator's participation in the
mass murder of Rwandan Tutsis. She also
has the distinction of being the most senior
official to be tried in Rwanda for the crime
of genocide.

Ntamabyariro was born in 1937 to a Hutu
father and a Tutsi mother. She excelled in
school and earned a law degree. She put her
education to use working for the government,
first as the minister of Commerce, Industry,
Mines and Artisans, and later as a minister of

Justice. Along with Pauline Nyiramasuhuko,
minister of Women and Family, and Agathe
Uwilingiyimana, Rwanda's first female
prime minister, Ntamabyariro was one of
three female ministers in the government at
the time of the genocide.

When President Juvénal Habyarimana's
plane was shot down on April 6, 1994, Ntamabyariro, along with the president's other
close advisors, quickly gathered to plan their
next steps. In an interview with Hazel Cameron conducted in 2005 for his book *Britain's
Hidden Role in the Rwandan Genocide: The
Cat's Paw*, Ntamabyariro explained that on
the night of the president's murder, she, along
with the other remaining government ministers and an assortment of Hutu extremists, "gathered together to form an 'interim
government' in which she played an instrumental role" (Cameron 2013: 48).

Ntamabyariro's role in the Rwandan Genocide came under investigation shortly after
the genocide. In the aftermath of the atrocity,
Ntamabyariro, along with her family, had
fled to Zambia. According to Ntamabyariro,
in 1997 Rwandan commandos had discovered her whereabouts and then proceeded to
drug, kidnap, and deport her back to Rwanda
where she awoke to find herself in a prison.
More than a decade later, she was finally
tried by a Rwandan court and sentenced to
life imprisonment in January 2009.

The court accused her of having of having
planned, incited, and perpetrated genocide.
Along with two other magistrates in the
Gitarama province, she was charged with
having perpetrated massacres in the Kabgayi
parish where Tutsis seeking refuge had gathered. And she was also accused of having
ordered the murder of Jean Baptiste Habyarimana, the former prefect of Butare, a Tutsi
who made a stand against the genocidal killings and paid for it with his life.

Ntamabyariro's trial, which began on October 18, 2006, in Kigali, Rwanda, before the high Court of the Republic, made history. While 15 other Rwandan government officials had stood trial for their crimes, all were tried in Arusha, Tanzania at the International Criminal Tribunal for Rwanda (ICTR). Although Ntamabyariro had traveled to Arusha, Tanzania in August 2006 to testify before the ICTR for the defense of another minister, her pleas to the ICTR to not force her to return to Rwanda fell on deaf ears. The Rwandan High Court found her guilty and on November 18, 2008, and recommended that she serve a lifelong imprisonment. Ntamabyariro contested the circumstances of her arrest as in breach with international conventions, but her claims were rejected on September 8, 2009. The Nyarugenge Court of First Instance sentenced Ntamabyariro to life in prison on January 19, 2009. Although Ntamabyariro appealed for a reduction of her sentence on February 21, 2014, Rwanda's High Court chose to uphold her sentence a year later.

Alexis Herr

See also: Habyarimana, Juvénal; International Criminal Tribunal for Rwanda; Nyiramasuhuko, Pauline; Perpetrators; Uwilingiyimana, Agathe

Further Reading

"Agnes Ntamabyariro," Trial International (13 June 2016), https://trialinternational.org/latest-post/agnes-ntamabyariro/.

Cameron, Hazel. *Britain's Hidden Role in the Rwandan Genocide: the Cat's Paw.* New York: Routledge, 2013.

Leatherman, Janie L. *Sexual Violence and Armed Conflict.* Malden, MA: Polity Press, 2011.

Mageza-Barthel, Rirhandu. *Mobilizing Transnational Gender Politics in Post-Genocide Rwanda.* New York: Routledge, 2015.

Nyirabayovu, Thérèse

When the Rwandan Genocide began in April of 1994, Thérèse Nyirabayovu, a Hutu, was sixty-seven and a widow. Despite the inherent dangers helping Tutsis posed, she risked her life to sheltered as between 18 and 20 Tutsis in her house.

Little is known of her life before or after the Rwandan Genocide. Nyirabayovu was born around 1927 in Kigali, the capital city of Rwanda. As a young woman, she became a midwife and was well respected in the Nyarugenge neighborhood of Kigali. Sometime prior to the start of the genocide, her husband died, leaving her to raise four children on her own (she had several other children, who had died in childhood) with meager resources. Although Nyirabayovu was not as poor as some Rwandans, she lived a very frugal life.

Even though protecting, hiding, or aiding Tutsis during the genocide was punishable by death, Nyirabayou decided to hide Tutsis in her modest home. With the help of her children, she sheltered Tutsis and did her best to feed them. Local members of the Interahamwe suspected her of hiding Tutsis, but they did not unduly bother her because she was elderly and was one of the most well-respected people in the neighborhood. Her home was searched multiple times, and someone threw a grenade at it, which fortunately caused no damage.

Nyirabayovu stated later that she did what she did because she always believed in helping other people who were in danger. During the genocide, she also provided food to refugees who had sought shelter in a nearby church, Sainte-Famille. After the killing ended, Nyirabayovu volunteered in refugee camps in Zaire (now the Democratic Republic of the Congo), even though several militiamen there had known about her actions in Kigali and did not approve of them.

Paul G. Pierpaoli Jr.

See also: Congo, Democratic Republic of the; Interahamwe; Roman Catholic Church; Rwandan Patriotic Front

Further Reading

Des Forges, Alison. *Leave None to Tell the Story: Genocide in Rwanda.* New York: Human Rights Watch, 1999.

Melvern, Linda. *Conspiracy to Murder: The Rwandan Genocide.* London: Verso, 2006.

Nyiramasuhuko, Pauline

Pauline Nyiramasuhuko served as the minister of Family Welfare and Women's Affairs in Rwanda before and during the genocide of 1994. She was born in 1946 in the commune of Ndora, Butare prefecture, into a poor farming Hutu family. Despite the many disadvantages of coming from a disadvantaged family, Nyiramasuhuko was a bright student and still managed attend the Karubanda School of Social Studies. It was there that she became friends with Agathe Kanziga, who later would marry President Juvénal Habyarimana.

After completing her studies, Nyiramasuhuko became a social worker and took up a post in the Ministry for Social Affairs in Kigali. Because of her connections with Kanziga, Nyiramasuhuko rose quickly in the civil service. In 1968, she married Maurice Ntahobali, who later went on to become a government minister, president of the National Assembly, and finally rector of the National University of Rwanda (French: Université Nationale du Rwanda, or UNR), Butare. The couple had four children, one of whom, Arsène Shalom Ntahobali, was later indicted on crimes against humanity and genocide charges owing to his role as an Interahamwe commander during 1994. After working in social services for many years, in 1986, Pauline Nyiramasuhuko became one of the few women to take up law studies at the UNR, and in 1990, she graduated with a law degree.

In 1992 she was appointed Minister of Family Welfare and Women's Affairs in Rwanda's first multiparty government. Her appointment was a random decision so far as the public was concerned; yet she retained her post until July 1994, when she fled Rwanda in the aftermath of the genocide. From the end of 1990 until July 1994, Nyiramasuhuko was said to have adhered to—and then participated in—the detailed development of a plan aimed at exterminating Rwanda's Tutsis. Then, when the genocide began, Nyiramasuhuko allegedly publicly incited the Hutu population to annihilate the Tutsi population.

Between April 9 and July 14, 1994, during various meetings of the Council of Ministers, Nyiramasuhuko and other ministers requested that arms be distributed within their home prefectures to perpetrate massacres. Nyiramasuhuko was made responsible for Butare. Ministers were instructed to incite hatred and ethnic violence, and to facilitate the training of anti-Tutsi militias and provide them with arms. They were also to assist in drafting lists of those to be eliminated.

In pursuit of this, Nyiramasuhuko reportedly planned, ordered, and participated in massacres in Butare. Here, she allegedly orchestrated a trap for the Tutsi population as word got out that the Red Cross at the Butare football stadium was providing food and shelter for the Tutsis. On April 25, the trap was sprung, and large numbers were instead raped, tortured, and killed by militias lying in wait. In a much-quoted incident, Nyiramasuhuko is said to have told the Interahamwe, "before you kill the women, you need to rape them." Soon afterward, Nyiramasuhuko reportedly went to a camp where a group of Interahamwe was holding some 70 Tutsi women and young girls as prisoners. It was later alleged that she then ordered the Interahamwe to rape the women before dousing them with gasoline and burning them to death. This was among a number of occasions when Nyiramasuhuko was reported to have encouraged (and sometimes ordered) the Interahamwe to rape and murder women.

Between April 19 and the end of June 1994, Nyiramasuhuko supervised the Interahamwe as they searched for Tutsi victims in the University district within Butare. When located, they would often be transported to different places within the prefecture for their execution. It was said that there were occasions when the victims were forced to strip off their clothes before being moved, at which point Nyiramasuhuko is said to have selected which Tutsi women would be raped.

The ferocity with which she allegedly urged the Interahamwe to slaughter Tutsis extended also to old women and unborn babies. It was said that she was sometimes seen dressed in military fatigues and boots, and carrying a rifle over her shoulder.

In July 1994, as the forces of the Rwandan Patriotic Front advanced on Kigali and the grip of the Hutu Power government became more and more tenuous, Nyiramasuhuko fled Rwanda for Zaire (now the Democratic Republic of the Congo). After first going into hiding in a refugee camp run by the Catholic charity Caritas, she made her way to Kenya, where she lived for the next three years. On July 18, 1997, she was arrested in Nairobi at the request of the chief prosecutor of the International Criminal Tribunal for Rwanda (ICTR). She was transferred the same day to the jurisdiction of the ICTR in Arusha, Tanzania, and charged with conspiracy to commit genocide, genocide (or, alternatively, complicity in genocide), public and direct incitement to commit genocide, and crimes against humanity including murder, extermination, rape, persecutions on political, racial, and religious grounds, other inhumane acts, and war crimes. At her initial court appearance on September 3, 1997, Nyiramasuhuko pleaded not guilty to all five charges.

She was the first woman to be indicted by the ICTR and the first woman brought to trial by any international tribunal. She also became the first woman ever to be indicted for rape as a crime against humanity, and the first woman to face genocide charges before an international tribunal. Moreover, she was the first woman ever charged with encouraging rape as an instrument of genocide.

On October 6, 1999, the ICTR, on request of the prosecutor, ordered a combined trial for Nyiramasuhuko and five other people accused of crimes committed in the Butare prefecture in 1994. They were: Nyiramasuhuko's son Arsène Shalom Ntahobali; Joseph Kanyabashi, the Hutu Power mayor of Ngoma; Sylvain Nsabimana, the *préfet* of Butare; Elie Ndayambaje, the mayor of Muganza; and Alphonse Nteziryayo, the *préfet* of Butare during the genocide.

The "Butare Six" trial, so called, became the longest and most costly trial in the history of international criminal justice. It opened on June 12, 2001, and closing arguments finished only on April 30, 2009, with the prosecutor seeking life imprisonment for all the accused. Judgment was delivered on June 24, 2011, with Nyiramasuhuko found guilty by the ICTR of genocide, conspiracy to commit genocide, crimes against humanity (extermination, rape, and persecution) and several serious violations of the Geneva Conventions. She was sentenced to life imprisonment. Nyiramasuhuko's son Arsène Shalom Ntahobali and four others of the "Butare Six" were also found guilty, with Ntahobali also sentenced to life imprisonment.

Paul R. Bartrop

See also: Habyarimana, Agathe; Habyarimana, Juvénal; Interahamwe; International Criminal Tribunal for Rwanda; Rape

Further Reading

Eller, Jack David. *From Culture to Ethnicity to Conflict: An Anthropological Perspective on International Ethnic Conflict*. Ann Arbor, MI: University of Michigan Press, 1999.

Kressel, Neil Jeffrey. *Mass Hate: The Global Rise of Genocide and Terror*. New York: Plenum Press, 1996.

Sjoberg, Laura. *Women as Wartime Rapists: Beyond Sensation and Stereotyping*. New York: New York University Press, 2016.

P

Prosper, Pierre-Richard

Pierre-Richard Prosper is a U.S. attorney and former ambassador-at-large within the Office of War Crimes Issues. He attracted worldwide attention when he successfully prosecuted the first case at the International Criminal Tribunal for Rwanda (ICTR) to bring in a guilty verdict for the crime of genocide. Born in Denver, Colorado, in 1963, Prosper is the son of two medical doctors who were refugees from Haiti. Raised in New York State, he graduated with a BA at Boston College in 1985 and earned his law degree from Pepperdine University in 1989.

Upon graduation in 1989, Prosper became a deputy district attorney for Los Angeles County, California, where he remained until 1994. He then began working in the federal government as an assistant U.S. attorney for the Central District of California in Los Angeles, where he investigated and prosecuted major international drug cartels while assigned to the narcotics section of the Drug Enforcement Task Force.

It was a colleague in the U.S. Attorney's office, Steve Mansfield, who was to draw Prosper's attention to Rwanda. Returning from a trip to that country, Mansfield briefed the staff about the 1994 genocide, which in turn motivated Prosper to learn more about that atrocity and find a way to help. From this moment on, he saw that he could make a difference in the broken society Rwanda had become, though he was aware of the pitfalls involved and the good life as an assistant U.S. attorney he might well have to give up. Throwing off his concerns, he first went to

Rwanda in April 1995 as part of a fact-finding mission to examine the national justice system. He was appointed as a special legal consultant of the U.S. government mission in Kigali where he assessed the post-genocide Rwandan justice system and assisted in developing an action plan to

Pierre-Richard Prosper served as a war crimes prosecutor for the United Nations International Criminal Tribunal for Rwanda from 1996 to 1998. As the lead trial attorney in the case against Jean-Paul Akayesu, he made history when he convinced the Tribunal to recognize rape as an act of genocide and crime against humanity. (Mark Sagliocco/Getty Images for Hamptons International Film Festival)

reinstate some form of judicial operation in a country that had been stripped of its legal infrastructure. To do so he consulted with Rwandan, United Nations, and donor country representatives and coordinated activities to maximize international efforts. He remained in this position until May 1995.

Building on this experience, and given that he was then working and living in Rwanda, he was offered a position by the United Nations to be one of two American prosecutors at the ICTR in Arusha, Tanzania. The more he learned, the more he came to regard the horrors committed in Rwanda as not just a crime against Rwandans, but against all humanity. It was while in this position that he successfully prosecuted the ICTR case against the former mayor of the town of Taba, Jean-Paul Akayesu. For Prosper, serving as lead prosecutor became a life-transforming experience. He and the judges on the Tribunal were confronted with the task of having to determine, for the very first time, what constitutes genocide in a legal sense. Reviewing the language of the 1948 Genocide Convention and half a century of legal scholarship, Prosper and his team had to establish how the concept of genocide applies in the contemporary context. They studied legal precedent, investigated the astonishing circumstances not only of the situation in Rwanda, but also regarding the specific case being tried, met with victims and survivors, and stood before mass graves—all prior to even starting the trial process.

The result saw a powerful prosecution that resulted in the first-ever conviction of the ICTR with Akayesu sentenced to life imprisonment. The trial was also the first-ever case of genocide under the 1948 Convention on the Prevention and Punishment of the Crime of Genocide. An important part of the judgment saw the further development of genocide case-law, as the three trial judges—Laity Kama from Senegal presiding; Navanethem Pillay from South Africa; and Lennart Aspegren from Sweden—ruled that rape could henceforth be considered within a general legal definition of genocide and crimes against humanity. In the 14-month trial, Prosper won additional life-sentence convictions against Akayesu for crimes against humanity. In developing his case, Prosper traveled widely, supervising investigations throughout Africa, Europe, and North America.

Reflecting on his Rwanda experience, Prosper said it both altered his professional life and challenged his fundamental assumptions about human nature. It changed his views concerning human evil, and of how important it is that all people contribute to making the world a better place.

Prosper remained a trial attorney with the ICTR until October 1998. In January and February of 1999 he became a special assistant to the assistant U.S. attorney general (where he helped with the development of international justice initiatives), prior to a secondment to the State Department as special counsel and policy adviser to the Office of War Crimes Issues within the Office of the Secretary of State. Here, he worked directly with the first U.S. ambassador-at-large for war crimes issues David Scheffer, developing policy and assisting in formulating U.S. responses to serious violations of international humanitarian law around the world. He traveled to affected areas in Europe, Africa, and Asia to promote initiatives and build coalitions, as well as engage in negotiations in support of U.S. government positions.

On May 16, 2001, President George W. Bush nominated Prosper to succeed Scheffer as ambassador-at-large for war crimes issues. After being confirmed by the U.S. Senate, he was sworn in on July 13, 2001, thereby becoming an official who served in high office in the administrations of both a Democrat (Bill Clinton) and a Republican (George W. Bush). He would serve in this capacity until October 2005, and, as such, was responsible to two secretaries of state—Colin Powell and Condoleezza Rice—on all matters relating to violations of international humanitarian law around the world. His role was important in that he advised not only the secretary of state, but also the president of the United States, secretary of defense, attorney general, national security adviser, chairman of the Joint Chiefs of Staff, director of the Central Intelligence Agency, White House Counsel, and other senior U.S. government officials.

The human rights violations that formed the centerpiece of Prosper's brief included genocide, crimes against humanity, and war crimes. Prosper was often required to speak publicly on behalf of the United States, as the face of U.S. war crimes, genocide, and crimes against humanity policies around the world. As with his earlier appointments, Prosper traveled extensively, conducting diplomatic negotiations and consultations with heads of state, foreign ministers, and senior government officials from over 60 different countries. He regularly visited conflict zones in efforts to secure peace, stability, and the rule of law. After the World Trade Center terrorist attacks in New York on September 11, 2001, Prosper played a key role in helping to develop antiterrorism policies, within a legal human rights framework.

In October 2005, Prosper resigned from his position in order to run for the Republican nomination for attorney general of California in the 2006 primaries. He withdrew his candidacy in February 2006, and did not proceed with his campaign.

In November 2006 and April 2007, he headed an International Republican Institute Election Observation Mission to observe and monitor the 2007 Nigerian presidential and National Assembly elections. He led a team of 59 international observers, meeting and consulting with candidates, political leaders, voters, and international observers. In February 2007, the United Nations General Assembly elected Prosper to serve as an independent expert to the UN Committee on the Elimination of Racial Discrimination, a human rights treaty body located in Geneva, Switzerland. This monitors compliance by state parties to the Convention on the Elimination of All Forms of Racial Discrimination. Then, in April 2008, he was appointed by President Bush to serve as a member of the United States Holocaust Memorial Council.

As of this writing, Prosper is an attorney in the Los Angeles office of the California law firm Arent Fox LLP, having joined on January 1, 2007, after his time in public service.

Paul R. Bartrop

See also: Akayesu, Jean-Paul; International Criminal Tribunal for Rwanda

Further Reading

Jokic, Aleksandar, ed. *War Crimes and Collective Wrongdoing: A Reader.* Malden, MA: Blackwell Publishers, 2001.

Neier, Aryeh. *War Crimes: Brutality, Genocide, Terror, and the Struggle for Justice.* New York: Times Books, 1998.

R

Radio-Télévision Libre des Mille Collines

Radio-Télévision Libre des Mille Collines (RTLM), meaning "One Thousand Hills Free Radio and Television" in French, was an independent Rwandan radio station that operated with the tacit approval and support of the Hutu-dominated Rwandan government prior to and during the 1994 Rwandan Genocide. RTLM played a central role in the genocide because it broadcast virulent anti-Tutsi propaganda that condoned and encouraged mass violence against Tutsis and Hutus who were sympathetic to the Tutsis.

The radio station began broadcasting on July 8, 1993 from Kigali, the Rwandan capital. It was organized and operated by supporters of President Juvénal Habyarimana. Since its inception, the RTLM endeavored to widen the divide between Hutus and Tutsis. Its earliest broadcasts attempted to undermine peace negotiations being held in Arusha, Tanzania between the Rwandan government and the Tutsi-led Rwandan Patriotic Front (RPF). Although the station was supposedly independent, it received clandestine support from Habyarimana's government and utilized transmitting equipment owned by Radio Rwanda, the official state-operated radio station. RTLM quickly became very popular, particularly among Hutu youths, who were drawn to the station by its popular music selections and other youth-oriented programming. Interspersed with that programming was destructive anti-Tutsi rhetoric and propaganda that demonized the minority group as "subhuman" and "cockroaches." The station was said to have had emboldened members of the Interahamwe, a rabid anti-Tutsi militia group that played a major role in the Rwandan Genocide.

RTLM worked closely with the anti-Tutsi newspaper known as *Kangura*. Hassan Ngeze, a journalist and head of *Kangura*, was also a major shareholder in RTLM. RTLM had a broad listenership that grew monthly. Although some members of the international community, including the United States, contemplated jamming RTLM's signals or destroying its transmitting towers, none took any action because it was feared that such action would be construed as abrogating free speech and expression. Meanwhile, anti-Tutsi hate speech and propaganda intensified, and after Habyarimana's assassination on April 6, 1994, RTLM took a central role in the ensuing genocide of Tutsis and murder of moderate Hutus by actively encouraging Hutus to kill their "enemies." The station also broadcast the location of Tutsis and sympathetic Hutus as the genocide unfolded.

On July 3, 1994, advancing RPF troops raided RTLM's Kigali studios, but the station continued to broadcast sporadically using mobile transmitters until the end of the month. In 2000, nearly six years after the genocide ended, RTLM's major players and supporters, including Ngeze, Jean Bosco Barayagwize, and Ferdinand Nahimana, were tried for war crimes, crimes against humanity, and genocide in conjunction with their work with RTLM and on anti-Tutsi propaganda campaigns. In December 2003, all three men were found guilty and eventually given lengthy prison sentences by the International Criminal Tribunal for Rwanda.

Paul G. Pierpaoli Jr.

See also: Akazu; Habyarimana, Juvénal; International Criminal Tribunal for Rwanda; *Kangura*; Media Trial in Rwanda; Nahimana, Ferdinand; Ngeze, Hassan; Ruggiu, Georges; Rwandan Patriotic Front

Further Reading

Eller, Jack David. *From Culture to Ethnicity to Conflict: An Anthropological Perspective on International Ethnic Conflict.* Ann Arbor, MI: University of Michigan Press, 1999.

Kressel, Neil Jeffrey. *Mass Hate: The Global Rise of Genocide and Terror.* New York: Plenum Press, 1996.

Valentino, Benjamin A. *Final Solutions: Mass Killing and Genocide in the Twentieth Century.* Ithaca, NY: Cornell University Press, 2004.

Waller, James. *Becoming Evil: How Ordinary People Commit Genocide and Mass Killing.* Oxford: Oxford University Press, 2002.

Rape

The history of the Rwandan Genocide requires an analysis of sexual violence. Rape was used as a weapon of genocide employed by the Hutu ethnic majority of Rwanda against the Tutsi ethnic minority. Although the exact number of victims will never be known, some observers estimate that every Tutsi female over the age of 12 who survived the genocide was sexually assaulted (Nowrojee 1996, 24). The pervasive use of rape during the genocide elucidates how perpetrators used sexual violence to dehumanize, humiliate, torture, and annihilate their victims. And rape has continued to have an impact on survivors long after the genocide.

Rape was widespread during the genocide. The United Nations (UN) estimates that the Interahamwe (a Hutu militia group), civilians, and the Rwandan Armed Forces (French: Forces Armées Rwandaises, FAR) systematically raped 250,000 to 500,000 Tutsi women and girls. Victims were often assaulted in a public or group setting and many were raped hundreds of times. Hutu women who resisted the genocide or were married to Tutsi men were also targeted, as were some men. Perpetrators commonly forced women and children to watch the torture of their family and afterwards were raped, raped and mutilated, or raped and murdered. More frequently, Tutsi women were not murdered outright, but held as sexual slaves and raped repeatedly by groups and/or individuals. In mid-May 1994, approximately five weeks after the start of the genocide, the government issued a centralized command to begin murdering Tutsi women in addition to the men, increasing the frequency of deaths among rape victims. The mostly Tutsi Rwandan Patriotic Army that that ended the genocide, also raped and enslaved women.

Hutu women participated in the mass murders, too. Pauline Nyiramasuhuko, head of family affairs and women's development minister prior to the genocide, is the most famous example of a woman's participation in inciting rape. Between April and June 1994, Nyiramasuhuko helped abduct hundreds of Tutsis in Butare, ordered their killings, and aided and abetted rapes.

Propaganda helped make the use of rape a common occurrence. Government propaganda and racist newspapers specifically targeted the sexuality of Tutsi women to enflame anti-Tutsi hatred and promote sexual violence.

Rape victims who survived the genocide suffered economic deprivation, extreme psychological trauma, physical mutilations, and permanent health problems, including an extremely high rate of HIV/AIDS. Their families and communities also often ostracized rape victims. Several thousand children were born as result of rape.

While the UN first acknowledged rape as an international crime in 1992 and a crime against humanity in 1993 (both prompted by the widespread rapes of women in the former Yugoslavia), the International Criminal Tribunal for Rwanda (ICTR) was the first international body to successfully prosecute rape as a tool of genocide. The UN Security Council created the ICTR on November 8, 1994. The international community legally recognized the use of rape as a form of genocide for the first time four years later. In a landmark case, on September 2, 1999 the ICTR convicted former mayor Jean-Paul Akayesu of ordering genocidal rape in the Taba Commune of Rwanda. In so doing, the court concluded that rape and sexual assault could—and did in the case of Akayesu—constitute acts of genocide.

Brian G. Smith

See also: Akayesu, Jean-Paul; International Criminal Tribunal for Rwanda; Nowrojee, Binaifer; Nyiramasuhuko, Pauline

Further Reading

Nowrojee, Binaifer. *Shattered Lives: Sexual Violence during the Rwandan Genocide and its Aftermath*. New York: Human Rights Watch, 1996.

United Nations, General Assembly, *Report of the International Criminal Tribunal for the Prosecution of Persons Responsible for Genocide and Other Serious Violations of International Humanitarian Law Committed in the Territory of Rwanda and Rwandan Citizens Responsible for Genocide and Other Such Violations Committed in the Territory of Neighbouring States between 1 January and 31 December 1994*, A/53/429 (23 September 1998), available from undocs .org/A/53/429.

Rawson, David

David Rawson served as the United States ambassador to Rwanda from 1993 to 1996. Some argue, among them current Rwandan president Paul Kagame, that Rawson's own biases influenced his country's failure to take action to first prevent and later to intervene in the genocide.

Although an American citizen, Rawson had the rare opportunity to spend his childhood in Burundi. His father was an American missionary and had gone to Burundi to set up a Quaker hospital. Rawson graduated with a Bachelor's degree from Malone College and earned his Masters and Doctorate from American University. In 1971 he joined the U.S. Foreign Service and over the course of his career held posts in Rwanda, Mali, Senegal, Madagascar, Somalia, as well as various positions throughout the United States.

At the age of 52, Rawson became the U.S. ambassador in Kigali, a position he held until 1996. He arrived in Rwanda at a time when support for the Arusha Peace Accords—the agreement signed between the Rwandan government and the Tutsi-led Rwandan Patriotic Front (RPF) that sought to end Rwanda's Civil War—was dissolving and the promise of violence was on the horizon.

Despite the mounting tensions within the Rwandan political arena between those who were willing to stick to the Arusha Accords (moderate Hutus and Tutsis) and those who wanted to abandon it completely (Hutu extremists), Rawson expressed hope that peace was just around the corner. Some contend that it was his wishful thinking combined with his refusal to view President Juvénal Habyarimana and his associates as in the process of planning a genocide that persuaded the United States to stay out of the slaughter once it began. Reflecting on his approach, Rawson described himself and his peers as "naïve policy optimists." He claimed he was so focused on establishing peace that he failed to see the warning signs. And once the killing began in earnest, he advocated for a ceasefire, which, in his own words, "wasn't really the issue" (Frontline 2004). As a result, the United States and UN pursued diplomatic action instead of military actions. In line with this view, U.S. and UN officials threatened to pull out peacekeepers.

In the wake of the Rwandan Genocide, human rights activists and genocide scholars have focused on creating warning systems for genocide so that future embassadors will not make Rawson's mistake of allowing uniformed optimism to forsake action. Professor Gregory H. Stanton and his nonprofit organization Genocide Watch, as well as the Simon-Skjodt Center for the Prevention of Genocide (a department of the United States Holocaust Memorial Museum in Washington, D.C.) have spearheaded the effort to identify countries at risk of genocide.

Alexis Herr

See also: Akazu; Arusha Accords; Bystanders; International Reactions; Moderate Hutus; Rwandan Civil War; Rwandan Patriotic Front

Further Reading

Bonner, Raymond, "Top Rwandan Criticizes U.S. Envoy," *New York Times* (November 8, 1994).

"Interview: David P. Rawson," Frontline (April 2004). http://www.pbs.org/wgbh/pages/frontline/shows/ghosts/interviews/rawson.html.

Power, Samantha. *"A Problem from Hell": America and the Age of Genocide.* New York: Harper Perennial, 2007.

Roman Catholic Church

The Roman Catholic Church influenced Rwandan society and politics for decades. Indeed, since the days of European colonization of Rwanda in the late nineteenth and early twentieth centuries, the colonial leaders afforded the Church preferential treatment. The Church's place in Rwandan society even outlived colonization. Although Rwanda achieved independence in 1962, the Church managed to remain behind even after the Belgian colonizers departed by supporting the Hutu-dominated government. Early on the Church had supported and elevated the status of Tutsis during the colonial period, however, starting with the Hutu Social Revolution (1959 to 1961), its support shifted to Hutus. The true nature of the Church's support of Hutus at the detriment of Tutsis was scrutinized after the genocide when a number of church leaders were tried for their involvement in the genocide.

For much of the 20th century, Catholic prelates and religious personnel played a

Main Religions in Rwanda, 2017

Roman Catholic	49.5%
Protestant	27.2%
Other Christian	4.5%
Muslim	1.8%
Animist	0.01%
Other	0.06%
None	3.6% (2001)
Unspecified	0.5% (2002)

Source: "Africa: Rwanda," Central Intelligence Agency, The World Factbook (August 01, 2017), accessed July 17, 2017, https://www.cia.gov/library/publications/the-world-factbook/geos/rw.html.

pivotal role in Rwandan society. Indeed, by mid-century, the majority of Rwandans—both Hutus and Tutsis—were Roman Catholic. The Church's support of the so-called Hamitic Hypothesis helped deepen the wedge between Hutus and Tutsis. The Church operated numerous schools, where teachers instilled in their students the faulty premise that the Tutsis and Hutus were racially separate, which encouraged racial segregation, mutual misunderstanding and mistrust, and even hatred. Similar messages emanated from many Catholic pulpits throughout Rwanda. In the colonial era, the Church supported the Tutsis, who dominated society even though they were the minority. When a Hutu-led government emerged after 1959, however, the Church switched allegiances and began to support the Hutus, even though many ruling Hutus even though some Hutu factions had advocated for ethnic cleansing.

This Church support came from archbishops and bishops within Rwanda, so it is hard to comprehend how leaders in the Vatican did not know about the Church's activities. Archbishop Vincent Nsengiyumva was a member of the Rwandan government's central committee for 15 years and publicly championed the iron-fisted rule of President Juvénal Habyarimana. In the 1950s, Archbishop André Perraudin helped establish the concept of "Hutu Power," a blatantly racist idea that called for the subjugation of the Tutsis. Even well after the genocide, Kigali's Catholic archbishop claimed that the Church had no power to stop the tragedy; he also denied that any clergy had been willing or active participants in the killings, despite considerable evidence to the contrary.

In the years since the genocide, physical evidence and eyewitness testimony have shown clearly that hundreds—perhaps thousands—of Rwandans died inside Catholic Churches or other alleged Catholic facilities, where some priests and nuns participated in the killings, encouraged them, or refused to intervene to stop them. Catholic churches at Nyange, Nyarubuye, Nyamata, Nyange, Ntarama, Saint Famille, and Cyahinda were all sites of various massacres in 1994. The International Criminal Tribunal for Rwanda convicted Father Athanese Seromba, the pastor at Nyange, in 2006 and sentenced Seromba to 15 years in prison. In April 1994, Seromba convinced some 2,000 men, women, and children to take refuge in his church. He then ordered local militiamen to set fire to the structure. To make sure that all the refugees were dead, and to hide his involvement, the priest then ordered the building bulldozed to the ground. In late 2006, the same court found a Rwandan nun Theophister Mukakibibi guilty of aiding genocide and sentenced her to 30 years in prison. She had participated in the mass killing of civilians who had been hiding in a hospital. Two other nuns were convicted for their roles in the genocide by a Belgian court in 2001. There are numerous other Catholic clergy wanted for crimes related to the genocide but who have not yet been apprehended.

Since 1994, there have been numerous reports that clergy involved in the genocide have sought and received refuge in Catholic churches in other parts of the world, including Europe. The Church's role in the genocide has resulted in a marked drop off in attendance at Catholic churches in Rwanda, and in fact there has been a major upswing in the number of Rwandans who have converted to Islam. During the genocide, many Muslims provided aid and refuge to the victims. Although Protestant churches in Rwanda also share responsibility for the tragedy, the power, size, and centrality of the Catholic Church in Rwanda means that it shares the lion's share of the blame.

While the stories of Church involvement in the massacres have received greater attention, it is worth noting that not all clergy and nuns behaved alike. Indeed, during the Rwandan Genocide we can also find examples of courageous and conscientious Catholic clergy, many of whom risked their own lives to aid the victims. For example, Sister Felicitas Niyitegeka, a nun in Gisenyi, smuggled hundreds of Tutsis to relative safety in Zaire (now known as the Democratic Republic of the Congo) before Rwandan government militiamen killed her.

A number of Catholic clergy—both nuns and priests—have more recently been successfully prosecuted for their roles in the 1994 Rwandan Genocide. These trials have occurred in Belgian courts as well as the International Criminal Tribunal in Rwanda. The Church recognizes that genocide took place in Rwanda, but officially it denies any direct responsibility for it, arguing that those clergy who were involved were acting on their own initiative and not on orders from the Vatican. Claiming that it had no advance knowledge of the activities of some of its personnel.

The Rwandan government has long pressured the Vatican to acknowledge the Church's role in the genocide. In March 2017, Pope Francis met with Rwandan president Paul Kagame and his wife, Jeannette Nyiramongi, at the Apostolic Palace in the Vatican, at which time he asked for forgiveness for the Church's role in the 1994 Genocide. Pope Francis acknowledged that some Catholic priests and nuns had participated in the genocide and in so doing committed sins and marred the ideals of Catholicism. He hoped that by acknowledging the failures of the Church he could help promote peace, purify memory of the atrocity, and a foster a renewed hope and trust between Rwandans and the Church.

Paul G. Pierpaoli Jr.

See also: Curic, Vjekoslav; de Saint-Exupéry, Patrick; Hamitic Hypothesis; International Criminal Tribunal for Rwanda; Monastery of Sovu; Mouvement Démocratique Républicain; Rwanda

Further Reading

Prunier, Gérard. *Africa's World War*. Oxford, UK: Oxford University Press, 2009.

Rittner, Carol, John K. Roth, and Wendy Whitworth, eds. *Genocide in Rwanda: Complicity of the Churches*. St. Paul, MN: Paragon House, 2004.

Sherwood, Harriet, "Pope Francis asks for forgiveness for church's role in Rwandan genocide," *The Guardian* (20 March 2017).

Straus, Scott. *The Order of Genocide: Race, Power, and War in Rwanda*. Ithaca, NY: Cornell University Press, 2008.

Ruggiu, Georges

Georges Ruggiu was a journalist and radio broadcaster instrumental in presenting anti-Tutsi programs prior to and during the Rwandan Genocide of 1994. He was born to a Belgian mother and an Italian father on October 12, 1957, in Verviers, Belgium. Ruggiu had previously worked as a state civil servant in Belgium's social security department, but in 1993, he moved to Rwanda, in part because of boredom in Belgium, and in part because of the prospect of work through an acquaintance, Ferdinand Nahimana, a founder of the private anti-Tutsi radio station Radio-Télévision Libre des Mille Collines

(RTLM). There were anomalies with Ruggiu, however. He was not Rwandan, neither Hutu nor Tutsi, and had no previous experience in journalism. He did not speak Kinyarwanda. Within the Rwandan Hutu Power hierarchy, he held no official position. When charged by the International Criminal Tribunal for Rwanda (ICTR) in 1997, he was the only non-Rwandan charged with involvement in the genocide.

With no previous experience in the media, Ruggiu began work as a journalist with RTLM on January 6, 1994. Between then and the following July, he was based in Kigali, writing, producing, and broadcasting programs that incited Hutus to attack and kill Tutsis and any Hutus who stood against them. His programs consistently encouraged his listeners to commit murder or serious attacks against the physical or mental well-being of Tutsis, moderate Hutus, and Belgians.

Ruggiu, as well as other RTLM announcers, used the radio waves to transmit aggressive misinformation about Tutsis before and during the genocide. The propaganda portrayed Tutsis as untrustworthy upsurpers, a message that was bolstered by a biased retelling of Rwandan history. On April 7, 1994—the day after Rwandan president Junvénal Habyarimana plane was shot down—Ruggiu went on air and read the official press release in French that the president had been killed. His broadcasts incited the public to attack Tutsis.

After the Rwandan Patriotic Front (RPF) defeated the radical Hutu regime in July 1994, Ruggiu fled the country—first to refugee camps in Zaire (now the Democratic Republic of the Congo), then to Tanzania, and finally to Kenya. There, he converted to Islam, adopted the name Omar, and joined a Somali Muslim community in Mombasa.

While on the run he was indicted by the ICTR, sitting in Arusha, Tanzania, on two counts of incitement to commit genocide and incitement to commit crimes against humanity. He was arrested in Mombasa on July 23, 1997, and transferred for trial to Arusha shortly thereafter. His indictment stated that Ruggiu played a key part in RTLM's campaign to spread extremist Hutu ideology. In October 1997, he pleaded not guilty, but changed his plea in May 2000, stating that he both affirmed that what happened in Rwanda was indeed genocide, and that he participated in it. On May 12, 2000, he pleaded guilty to the two charges in the indictment, admitting that he had incited murders of members of the Tutsi population with the intention of destroying, in whole or in part, the Tutsi ethnic group in Rwanda. He demonstrated remorse for his actions.

He was found guilty of incitement to commit genocide and to crimes against humanity (persecution), and on June 1, 2000, was sentenced to 12 years in prison on each of the charges, to be served concurrently. The Tribunal ruled that Ruggiu's time in custody since his arrest counted towards his 12-year imprisonment. The Rwandan government claimed that the sentence was insufficient, as the prosecutor had asked for a sentence of 20 years. Ruggiu did not appeal his sentence. In reaching its verdict, the Tribunal took note of a number of mitigating circumstances, namely, the fact that he pleaded guilty, his cooperation throughout the proceedings, the absence of any criminal record, his malleable character, his regrets and remorse, the fact that he had played a hand in saving a few Tutsi children, the fact that he neither belonged to the Rwandan ruling elite nor to the decision-making body of the RTLM, and finally that he had not participated directly in the massacres. His sentence was also influenced by his having agreed to testify against other members of the RTLM then awaiting or undergoing trial. Ruggiu was the third defendant to plead guilty at the ICTR, the first two being former prime minister Jean Kambanda and former militia leader Omar Serushago.

In February 2008 the ICTR decided to transfer Ruggiu to Italy, to serve out the remainder of his sentence. The move followed an agreement between the United Nations and the Italian government, after a Rome court had ruled that ICTR sentences could henceforth be enforced in that country. Then, on April 21, 2009, Ruggiu was granted an early release by the Italian authorities, a violation of Article 27 of the ICTR Statute, which states that only the president of the ICTR may decide on the early release of those convicted, no matter where the sentence is being served.

Georges Ruggiu remains the only non-Rwandan to be convicted by the ICTR for involvement in the genocide, and was the fourth person convicted by the ICTR to be released after serving out a sentence.

Paul R. Bartrop

See also: International Criminal Tribunal for Rwanda; Media Trial in Rwanda; Moderate Hutus; Nahimana, Ferdinand; Radio-Télévision Libre des Mille Collines

Further Reading

Cruvellier, Thierry, *Court of Remorse: Inside the International Criminal Tribunal for Rwanda* (Madison, WI: University of Wisconsin Press, 2010).

Kressel, Neil Jeffrey. *Mass Hate: The Global Rise of Genocide and Terror.* New York: Plenum Press, 1996.

Schabas, William A. *Genocide in International Law: The Crime of Crimes.* Cambridge, UK: Cambridge University Press, 2000.

Rusesabagina, Paul

Paul Rusesabagina is a much-honored former Rwandan, best known as a rescuer of Tutsis during the Rwandan Genocide between April and July 1994. He was born in Murama-Gitarama in the Central-South of Rwanda, about 50 miles from Kigali, on June 15, 1954. Of mixed Hutu-Tutsi background—his father was Hutu and his mother Tutsi—his parents and their nine children pursued the traditional vocation of many rural Hutus as farmers. Rusesabagina was educated at a local Seventh Day Adventist Missionary School in Gitwe, and spent three years as a theology student in Cameroon. He then studied in the Hotel Management Program at Utalii College in Nairobi, Kenya, and continued his studies in Switzerland. After graduating, he was hired as the assistant general manager of the Hôtel des Mille Collines in Kigali, a luxury property owned by the Sabena. He remained in this position from October 1984 until November 1992, when he was promoted to general manager of the nearby Hotel Diplomates, an equally prestigious property. On April 12, 1994—less than week after the genocide had begun—Rusesabagina returned to the Mille Collines as general manager.

In the 11 weeks that followed—he was managing both hotels. The Belgian owners of the Mille Collines had appointed him temporary manager because the previous manager had been evacuated along with all the other foreign nationals. Rusesabagina managed to shelter no fewer than 1,268 people, mostly Tutsis, from the Hutu militias bent on their destruction.

At first, troops from the United Nations Assistance Mission for Rwanda (UNAMIR), under the command of General Roméo Dallaire, provided protection for the hotel and those within, but this did not last indefinitely—nor could Dallaire's hard-pressed and tiny force have offered much resistance if it came to a showdown with the Interahamwe, Impuzamugambi militias, or the Rwandan Armed Forces. About halfway into the genocide, the protection detail of UNAMIR was largely withdrawn, and Rusesabagina was forced to rely on other means to protect the hotel and those he was sheltering inside, who included among their number both refugees and orphans.

Not only did the perpetrators continually threaten imminent death; they blockaded the hotel so that foodstuffs, water, electricity, and communication with the outside world were cut off. One phone/fax line, however, was missed and remained operative. Through this final linkage to the outside world the people at the Mille Collines were able to make desperate calls to international agencies to let the world know what was happening and to seek some form of intervention to save their lives. After the water supply was cut off, only the water in the hotel pool was available as a reservoir that could be tapped into for basic needs. Beyond this, all Rusesabagina had available to keep the militias at bay were a combination of diplomacy, flattery, and deception— and the hotel's well-supplied wine cellar, which was attractive to those besieging the hotel and its occupants.

At first he enjoyed a relatively favorable position, despite his mixed parentage and the fact that he had married a Tutsi woman. His business and personal connections with important Hutus, such as Georges Rutaganda and Colonel Augustin Bizimungu. led to a measure of protection, the more so after Rusesabagina found ways of paying them off with bribes funded through those the hotel was haboring.

Eventually, at the end of the genocide in July 1994, Rusesabagina and his family managed to escape to Tanzania, but soon afterwards he returned to Rwanda and to hotel management. He remained in Kigali running the Mille Collines for another two years, but his position became increasingly untenable owing to continued ethnic tensions and the controversy over his role during the genocide. He even faced death threats. In September 1996 he sought asylum in Belgium, and moved to Brussels. He found work as a taxi driver, but later developed a trucking company, which he now operates out of Zambia, shipping goods within Europe and Africa. He did not leave Rwanda behind him, however, and in 2005, he started the Hotel Rwanda Rusesabagina Foundation (HRRF), an organization that works to prevent future genocides and raise

Paul Rusesabagina was immortalized in the film *Hotel Rwanda* (2004), which portrayed Rusesabagina as the heroic manager of a hotel that provided shelter to over one thousand refugees during the genocide. (Drew Farrell/ Photoshot/Getty Images)

awareness of the need for a new truth and reconciliation process in Rwanda and Africa's Great Lakes region (Burundi, the Democratic Republic of Congo, Kenya, Rwanda, Tanzania, and Uganda).

For his efforts, Rusesabagina has since been referred to by some as "the Oskar Schindler of Rwanda," yet this is a title he plays down, preferring to offer the view that saving people from murder is nothing special, just the right thing to do. Others have not been so flattering. Many of those who remember the conditions at the Mille Collines during the genocide have recalled how Rusesabagina would charge for the water drawn from the pool; would only accept people who could pay cash to stay in the hotel; and would evict people who could no longer pay—their fate to be decided by the militias waiting outside. Criticism of Rusesabagina has become something of a cottage industry in Rwanda, with Rwandan president Paul Kagame suggesting that Rusesabagina has built his reputation on a falsehood, and that he is in fact not the hero that has been portrayed. In 2005, François Xavier Ngarambe, the president of Ibuka ("Remember"), an association of Rwandan Genocide survivors, challenged the claim that Rusesabagina was a hero, saying that he was more interested in making money out of the chaos in 1994 than in saving lives. The relationship between Rusesabagina and many in Rwanda, particularly the Kagame regime, continues to smolder. On June 23, 2011, Belgian police, on the advice of the Rwandan government, questioned Rusesabagina over his possible involvement with the Rwanda Democratic Forces for the Liberation of Rwanda (French: Forces démocratiques de libération du, or FDLR), a Hutu rebel group operating out of the Democratic Republic of the Congo. It includes several key perpetrators of the 1994 genocide who have so far evaded capture.

Rusesabagina's story has been told to high acclaim in the West, particularly the United States. In 2000, he was awarded the Immortal Chaplains Foundation Prize for Humanity in Minnesota. Early in 2005, he received a National Civil Rights Museum Freedom Award, and in October the same year was awarded the prestigious Wallenberg Medal from the University of Michigan in recognition of his rescue work during the genocide. Finally, on November 9, 2005, Rusesabagina received the U.S. Presidential Medal of Freedom from President George W. Bush.

In 2004, Rusesabagina and the story of the Hôtel Mille was the subject of the first major Hollywood motion picture on the genocide, *Hotel Rwanda* (director/writer/producer, Terry George, United Artists, 2004), an Academy Award–nominated movie starring Don Cheadle in the starring role. Rusesabagina told his own story in an autobiography, *An Ordinary Man*, published in April 2006.

Paul R. Bartrop

See also: Bizimungu, Augustin; Dallaire, Roméo; Hotel des Mille Collines; *Hotel Rwanda* (Film, 2004); Interahamwe; Rutaganda, Georges; United Nations Assistance Mission for Rwanda

Further Reading

Eltringham, Nigel. *Accounting for Horror: Post-Genocide Debates in Rwanda.* Londres: Pluto Press, 2004.

Rusesabagina, Paul. *An Ordinary Man: An Autobiography.* New York: Viking, 2006.

Rutaganda, Georges

Georges Rutaganda was the first defendant to be convicted of war crimes by the International Criminal Tribunal for Rwanda (ICTR). He was born on November 28, 1958, in Ngoma, Kibuye prefecture. A man of some wealth, Rutaganda was an agricultural engineer and businessman prior to the genocide of 1994. Rutaganda had been the second vice president of the Interahamwe Hutu militia since 1991 and was one of the most prominent leaders of the Interahamwe during the genocide.

Rutaganda was a member of the national and regional committees of the National Republican Movement for Development and Democracy (French: Mouvement Républicain National pour le Développement et la Démocratie, or MRNDD), the political arm of Rwandan president Juvénal Habyarimana's authoritarian regime. An anti-Tutsi militant, he was also a shareholder in the Hutu Power radio propaganda arm, Radio-Télévision Libre des Mille Collines (RTLM), and during the period of the genocide he spoke on RTLM in Kigali. In April 1994, Rutaganda was instrumental in directing, encouraging, and participating in the killing of vast numbers of Tutsis by the Interahamwe, as well as any Hutus who opposed the murders. It was alleged that he also participated in several killings of civilians, and led house-to-house searches during which Tutsis were captured and executed. His alleged crimes also included the distribution of guns and other weapons to the Interahamwe, and ordering and participating in the deaths of 18 Tutsis at a roadblock near his office. Some alleged that he had participated in the attack on the École Technique Officielle (Official Technical School) in Kicukiro commune after the withdrawal of United Nations (UN) forces, where unarmed people had found refuge. Rutaganda reportedly ordered and participated in the slaughter of men, women, and children at the school, and directed the forcible transfer of the survivors. It has been suggested that Rutaganda captured, raped, and tortured Tutsi

women in Interahamwe strongholds in Kigali. Throughout this time, it was said that Rutaganda's Interahamwe forces were supplied with weapons and other items stolen from the Rwandan military.

With the defeat of the Hutu Power government by the Tutsi-led Rwandan Patriotic Front, Rutaganda fled the country with tens of thousands of others in July 1994. He was tracked down and arrested in Lusaka, Zambia, on October 10, 1995, and indicted by the ICTR on February 13, 1996. The court charged him on eight counts including genocide, crimes against humanity, and violations of the Common Article 3 of the Geneva Conventions. In his defense, Rutaganda's attorneys argued that he had in fact attempted to save lives, and that he had no influence over the roadblocks where victims were stopped and singled out for immediate execution. He pleaded not guilty to all charges.

He was transferred to the custody of the ICTR in Arusha, Tanzania, on May 26, 1996, and, on December 6 the court found him guilty on three counts in his indictment: count one (genocide), count two (crimes against humanity: extermination) and count seven (crimes against humanity: murder). He was sentenced to life imprisonment.

Both Rutaganda and the ICTR prosecutor appealed the decision, respectively on January 5 and 6, 2000. The Appeals Chamber's decision was handed down on May 26, 2003. The five judges unanimously found Rutaganda guilty on four counts: genocide, crimes against humanity (extermination), and two counts of murder related to war crimes (violations of Common Article 3 to the Geneva Conventions). The Chamber confirmed the convictions relating to counts one and two, but acquitted Rutaganda of count seven due to a lack of coherence in statements from various witnesses. It further found Rutaganda guilty on two new counts of willful killing in violation of Common Article 3 of the Geneva Conventions, making this the first time a defendant before the ICTR had been convicted of war crimes. The Appeals Chamber considered that the revised verdict with respect to both the acquittal and the two new counts did not affect the validity of the facts on which the Trial Chamber's original decision had been based. Rutaganda's life sentence was thereby confirmed. He was the sixth Rwandan to be convicted of genocide by the ICTR, and the fourth to be sentenced to life in prison. On June 27, 2009, he was transferred to Cotonou, Benin, to serve out the remainder of his life sentence. On October 22, 2010, he died in jail following what was termed a "sudden complication" after a long illness.

In 2004, Rutaganda was controversially portrayed in an Academy Award–winning movie about the Rwandan Genocide, *Hotel Rwanda*, directed by Irish filmmaker Terry George. In the film, Nigerian-born British actor Hakeem Kae-Kazim played the part of Rutaganda. Rutaganda was represented in the movie as an unscrupulous anti-Tutsi fanatic and war profiteer, prepared to go to any lengths to kill Tutsis, elevate Hutus (and co-opt them into the genocidal project), and make as much money for himself as he could along the way. In the film, he had the most contact with the hero, Paul Rusesabagina, who was in reality an old friend of Rutaganda from the days before the genocide. The reasons behind the controversy came in the film's aftermath, as many who were witness to Rutaganda's actions during the genocide claimed that the movie misrepresented his efforts to lessen anti-Tutsi actions at roadblocks and elsewhere, in order to make the film's main characters— Rusesabagina and the UN commander,

Colonel Vincent (a mask for the real-life leader of the UN forces, General Roméo Dallaire)—look more benevolent. While the filmmakers took dramatic license for the sake of the plot, however, Rutaganda's indictment, trial, and verdict showed that any claim of his altruism was indeed false. During his trial in Arusha, the court did acknowledge that Rutaganda had saved some Tutsis (all of whom he knew personally), ultimately the court concluded that these acts paled in comparison to the gravity of his other crimes.

Paul R. Bartrop

See also: Habyarimana, Juvénal; *Hotel Rwanda* (Film, 2004); Interahamwe; International Criminal Tribunal for Rwanda; Radio-Télévision Libre des Mille Collines; Rwandan Patriotic Front; Rutaganda, Georges, Trial of

Further Reading

McGreal, Chris, "Life sentence for Rwandan genocide leader," *The Guardian* (December 7, 1999), accessed April 16, 2017: https://www.theguardian.com/world/1999/dec/07/chrismcgreal.

Melvern, Linda. *Conspiracy to Murder: The Rwandan Genocide.* London: Verso, 2006.

Prunier, Gérard. *The Rwanda Crisis, 1959–1994: History of a Genocide.* Kampala: Fountain Publishers, 1995.

Rutaganda, Georges, Trial of

Georges Rutaganda, the first vice president of the Interahamwe during the Rwandan Genocide, was arrested in Zambia in October 1995 and brought a month later to Arusha, Tanzania in anticipation of an International Criminal Tribunal for Rwanda (ICTR) indictment. The ICTR indicted Rutaganda on February 13, 1996 and charged him of having committed genocide, crimes against humanity, and violating Common Article 3 of the Geneva Conventions. The ICTR tried Georges Rutaganda between March 1997 and December 1999.

Rutaganda was from a well-known and politically influential family. He worked as a government agricultural engineer and later went into private business. His main concern was an import company that specialized in beer. He was also a shareholder in the Radio-Télévision Libre des Mille Collines, which later became known for broadcasting provocative anti-Tutsi propaganda. In 1991, he joined the National Revolutionary Movement for Development (French: Révolutionnaire National Pour le Développement, or MRND) and soon became a leader of its youth group, the Interahamwe.

The trial was held in Chamber 1, with Laity Kama from Senegal presiding along with Lennart Aspergen from Sweden and Navanethem Pillay from South Africa. James Stewart of Canada led the prosecution. Twenty-seven prosecution witnesses were called to support the allegations that Rutaganda was a key leader and was personally responsible for the killings. Tiphaine Dickson of Canada led the defense.

The specific charges against Rutaganda were based on a series of incidents in April 1994. Around April 10, Rutaganda reportedly organized the Interahamwe to establish roadblocks in Kigali. Those with Tutsi identification cards were separated out, interrogated by Rutaganda and later killed. On April 11, he reportedly led a massacre of hundreds who had taken refuge at the École Technique Officielle (ETO). Those who survived the ETO attack were forcibly moved to a gravel pit where the remaining Tutsi victims were killed. Rutaganda was also accused of leading house-to-house searches for Tutsis in Masango and then forcing those

captured into a river. Finally, Rutaganda reportedly pursued and killed with a machete a man who was fleeing another roadblock.

Throughout the trial, the prosecution and defense presented near opposite accounts of Rutaganda's life. The prosecution argued that, between 1991 and 1994, Rutaganda had risen in the party ranks and had become a party leader. As presented by the prosecution, the Interahamwe was a well-organized movement within the party of which Rutaganda was a key leader. Rutaganda argued that during this time he was an overworked businessman with little time for, or interest in, party affairs. He also claimed that the Interahamwe was never formally organized.

The prosecution and the defence also presented divergent narratives of Rutaganda's involvement in the crucial month of April 1994, when most of the killings of Tutsis occurred. The prosecution argued that the Interahamwe had transformed itself into a militia responsible for thousands of deaths. It claimed that Rutaganda, as a group leader, organized roadblocks separating out Tutsis, distributed weapons, and led several massacres in Kigali and the Masango commune. Rutaganda countered by saying that the Interahamwe had ceased to exist by the time of the April chaos. Furthermore, he portrayed himself as a man protecting his business interests, fearing for his own life, and helping many Tutsis flee.

The defense called witnesses who asserted that Rutaganda had not been at the locations in question. The defense also questioned the reliability of prosecution witnesses. The key to the defense, however, was Rutaganda's testimony. He sharply disputed the contention that the Interahamwe had become an organized militia. Instead, he portrayed the killings as a series of isolated events. He also described how he feared that his businesses would be looted or destroyed and that he feared for his own safety and that of his family should the shifting political landscape bring new people to power. Furthermore, he argued that rather than leading attacks on Tutsis, he made several efforts to shelter them or help people through the roadblocks. The prosecution argued that these comments in fact demonstrated that he did have influence over the Interahamwe, but Rutaganda denied this and concluded by arguing that he had been encouraged by the prospect of inquiries into the April events because he believed they would lead to his recognition as a humanitarian.

On December 6, 1999, the ICTR found Rutaganda guilty of genocide and two counts of crimes against humanity. The court sentenced Rutaganda to life in prison. He was found not guilty on two counts of crimes against humanity for murder, because the judges ruled that he was guilty of extermination in these same cases and should not be convicted twice for the same event. The court deemed him not guilty of violations of the Geneva Convention because the Interahamwe was not an organized combat force. The prosecution appealed in hopes of convicting him on more counts of crimes against humanity. The defense also appealed, claiming the Tribunal had been biased against Rutaganda and that his punishment was influenced by pressure from the Rwandan government after the Tribunal had released another defendant on technical grounds.

On May 26, 2003 the Appeals Chamber acquitted Rutaganda of murder and convicted him on two new counts of war crimes. Rutaganda was transferred to Benin on June 27, 2009 to serve the remainder of his sentence. Rutaganda died in prison in Benin on October 11, 2010.

John Dietrich

See also: Identity Cards, Rwanda; Interahamwe; International Criminal Tribunal for Rwanda; Mouvement Révolutionnaire National pour le Développement; Radio-Télévision Libre des Mille Collines; Rutaganda, Georges

Further Reading

Cruvellier, Thierry. *Court of Remorse: Inside the International Criminal Court for Rwanda*. Madison, WI: University of Wisconsin Press, 2010.

Des Forges, Alison, and Timothy Longman. "Legal Responses to Genocide in Rwanda." In *My Neighbor, My Enemy: Justice and Community in the Aftermath of Mass Atrocity*, edited by Eric Stover and Harvey M. Weinstein, 49–63. Cambridge: Cambridge University Press, 2004.

Rwanda

The first known inhabitants of Rwanda were the Twa, or Pygmies, but they were eventually displaced by the Hutu peoples, who migrated from the Congo River basin sometime between the seventh and tenth centuries. The Hutu agriculturists were well established by the time the Tutsi peoples arrived from the north in the 1600s. The Tutsis conquered the Hutus and ruled through an elaborate feudal system. Tutsi kings, or *mwamis,* governed with the Tutsi elite, who served as chiefs and subchiefs. The Hutu majority became serfs. The caste system was strictly enforced, with little intermarriage or mingling of cultures. The remaining Twa existed on the very bottom of the social hierarchy. By the late 18th century, a single Tutsi-ruled state dominated most of what is present-day Rwanda. The king had the ultimate power over his regional Tutsi vassals, who in turn ruled over the Hutu. The kingdom enjoyed its peak in the middle to late 19th century under the *mwami* Kigeri IV Rwabugiri, who had a standing army equipped with guns obtained from traders on the east African coast.

The first Europeans landed in Rwanda in 1858, and in the 1880s, German explorers arrived. In 1890, the *mwami* of Rwanda agreed—without a fight—to accept German rule and join German East Africa. However, in practice, the Germans had no real influence over the region and devoted few resources to the development of their new holding. Not until 1907 did Germany have an administrative center in Rwanda. After World War I, Belgian forces occupied the region, along with present-day Burundi, as the Territory of Ruanda-Urundi, as directed by the League of Nations. The Belgians held Rwanda as a United Nations (UN) trust territory after World War II.

Under Belgian rule, the traditional governing system remained intact. The Belgians forced the Tutsi aristocracy to phase out the unequal social caste system, but the Tutsis held on to their political power and the economic opportunities that came with it. That power emphasized class divisions and intensified the ethnic tensions that had been in place for centuries.

During the 1950s, the Hutus became increasingly vocal regarding their grievances about the inequalities of Rwanda's political and social systems. They published a manifesto calling for more Hutu influence in the region's affairs and demanded a change to the Tutsi-dominated feudal structure. When King Muratara III died and Kigeri V succeeded him in 1959, the Hutus rebelled and claimed that the new leader was inappropriately chosen. Fighting erupted, and the Hutus won the battle. Hundreds of thousands of Tutsis fled, including King Kigeri V, and the Hutus took political control. Elections were held in 1960, and Grégoire Kayibanda of the Hutu Emancipation Movement (French: Parti de l'émancipation du people Hutu, or Parmehutu) became prime minister. A year later, the government proclaimed Ruanda a republic and abolished the Tutsi monarchy. Under pressure from the UN, Belgium granted the country independence on July 1, 1962 with the Parmehutu Kayibanda as president. The country changed its name to Rwanda, while Parmehutu became the Democratic Republican Movement (French: Mouvment Démocratique Républicain, or MDR). Kayibanda was reelected in 1965 and 1969. For the first time in the region's history since the Tutsis arrived, the Hutus were in charge.

In 1964, the exiled Tutsis, who had fled when the Hutus revolted in 1959, returned to Rwanda as a rebel army and invaded from Burundi. The incursion was a failure and provoked a formidable retaliation by the Hutu army, which began a large-scale massacre of Tutsis. Although the two sides reached an agreement in 1965, the peace was uneasy, and sporadic ethnic violence continued. Just before the 1973 elections, Kayibanda was ousted in a bloodless military coup led by General Juvénal Habyarimana. Habyarimana dissolved the National Assembly and suspended the MDR, which by then had become the only legal party. He founded the National Revolutionary Movement for Development (French: Mouvement Révolutionnaire National pour le Développement, or MRND) as the new ruling party. A new constitution in 1978 officially reconfirmed the country as a single-party state, now with the MRND as the sole legal party. Habyarimana became president, and in 1983 and 1988, he was reelected unopposed. During the 1980s, an intense drought devastated agriculture, and an influx of thousands of Burundi refugees added pressure to the already-declining economy. International aid donors, weary of pouring money into a mismanaged economy, pressured the government to make political and economic reforms. Owing in large part to international pressure, opposition parties were legalized in 1990. In 1991, a new constitution provided for a multiparty government and other democratic reforms, and a new minister was appointed to head the MDR in order to break up Habyarimana's monopoly of power over the MDR and within government.

In the midst of the early reforms in the 1990s, Rwanda was waging a brutal civil war. The Rwandan Patriotic Front (RPF), made up primarily of Tutsis who had fled Rwanda to escape violence decades earlier, attacked Habyarimana's government in 1990. Belgium and southwestern African countries sent forces to help the government put down the rebellion. After sustaining a strong blow to its forces, the RPF changed its tactics to guerrilla warfare and launched violent attacks from Ugandan bases. The Hutus used that to justify large-scale exterminations of Tutsis within Rwanda. The Rwandan Civil War finally ended in a ceasefire following the Arusha Peace Accords signed between the RPF and the Rwandan government in Arusha, Tanzania on August 4, 1993. Unfortunately, the Arusha Accords failed to secure the peace.

In early April 1994, Habyarimana was killed in a suspicious plane crash. Hutu forces that credited Tutsi rebels with shooting down the president's aircraft began a series of large-scale massacres of Tutsis and Hutu moderates. It should be noted here that many analysts believe the plane was shot down by Hutu hard-liners opposed to Habyarimana's negotiations with Tutsi leaders in Arusha. Operating under a Chapter VI peacekeeping mandate, UNAMIR was not permitted to use force to stop the ethnic violence. Instead, they quickly became witnesses to hundreds of thousands of murders. When the genocide began the RPF stepped

in to try and stop the genocide. The RPF captured the capital in May 1994, and those in government fled. By July, RPF forces had established control over most of the country. By that time more than one million people—most of them Hutus fearful of Tutsi revenge for the massacres—fled from the victorious RPF troops. One-quarter of the pre-genocide population was either killed or fled the country during the conflict.

The RPF installed a new government led by Pasteur Bizimungu, a moderate Hutu. The National Revolutionary Movement for Development and Democracy (French: Mouvement Républicain National pour la Démocratie et le Développement, or MRNDD)—the MRND, formerly Habyarimana's party, had become the MRNDD in 1991—was forbidden to participate in the new administration. Meanwhile, hundreds of thousands of Hutu refugees in neighboring countries refused to return to Rwanda because they feared Tutsi retaliation. Toward the end of 1996, however, a rebellion launched by Tutsi rebels in Ziare (now known as the Democratic Republic of the Congo) and backed by Rwanda's Tutsi-dominated government led to the displacement of more than a million Rwandan Hutu refugees who had fled to Zaire in 1994. Hundreds of thousands of them returned home, although some fled west into Zaire's dense jungles. Many of the latter refugees died of disease and starvation during their trek across the country as the rebels swept to victory. The Zairian rebel forces, allegedly aided by Rwandan soldiers, were also accused of slaughtering tens of thousands of the Hutu refugees. Rebel leader Laurent Kabila, who became president of Zaire in May 1997 and renamed it the Democratic Republic of the Congo, has denied these allegations.

The UN had withdrawn its troops from Rwanda by early 1996 at the request of the

Rwandan government, which blamed the UN of failing to stop the 1994 genocide. An international war crimes tribunal for Rwanda was installed in Arusha, Tanzania in June 1995 and heard its first case in 1996. Justice, however, was slow coming and with more than 50,000 people still being held in overcrowded jails, the Rwandan government released 40,000 people in January 2003. Most played minor roles in the genocide and had already served more time than they would have received if convicted, but the government pledged that all would eventually be tried. In 2005, 36,000 prisoners were released, most of whom had confessed to involvement in the 1994 genocide. The slow pace of prosecution by the war crimes tribunal led the government to shift many cases to local *gacaca* courts, where suspects were tried by and in front of their local community.

Before the Zairian rebellion that led to the return of hundreds of thousands of refugees, remnants of the former Hutu government army and the Hutu militias that carried out most of the 1994 killings had already begun making incursions into Rwandan territory from their bases at the refugee camps in neighboring nations. The violence within Rwanda intensified after the return of the refugees, which included Hutu militants. Human rights groups have also accused Rwandan Army soldiers of carrying out indiscriminate killings of civilians as part of their conflict with the Hutu militants.

The attacks and violent clashes between ethnic groups continued through the late 1990s, but beginning in 1999, a series of government reform measures stabilized the country somewhat. In March 1999, local elections were held for the first time since the genocide, partly reestablishing precolonial systems of smaller, autonomous local governments. The government signed peace agreements with neighboring Uganda and the Democratic Republic of the Congo in 2001 and 2002, respectively, extracting its troops from spillover wars with those countries. In a decisive step toward overcoming ethnic rivalries, 93 percent of Rwandan voters approved a new constitution in May 2003. The constitution outlawed dominance by one party in the government and incitement of ethnic hatred; it also paved the way for national elections in August 2003, in which Kagame won in a landslide victory, getting 95 percent of the vote. Although he was accused by both opposition leaders and an international human rights group of suppressing opposition campaigning, including arresting at least 10 opposition leaders in the lead-up to the elections, international observers said they saw relatively few problems during polling. In 2004, the government allowed private radio stations to operate for the first time since the genocide.

The process of justice and reconciliation in Rwanda has been a long one. In the years that followed the genocide, more than 120,000 people were detained and accused of participating in the killings. Employing three court systems—Gacaca courts (community courts), the national court system in Rwanda, and the International Criminal Tribunal for Rwanda in Arusha, Tanzania—Rwandans have attempted to address the past and move forward. To further aid in this process, the government established the National Unity and Reconciliation Commission in 1999 to help promote healing, justice, human rights, good governance, and fight the genocide ideology that lead to the mass slaughter of some 800,000 Rwandans.

Paul R. Bartrop

See also: Arusha Accords; *Bahutu Manifesto*; Congo, Democratic Republic of the; Dallaire, Roméo; Forces Armées Rwandaises; *Gacaca*

Courts; Habyarimana, Juvénal; Interahamwe; International Criminal Tribunal for Rwanda; Kagame, Paul; Kayibanda, Grégoire; Media Trial in Rwanda; Mouvement Démocratique Républicain; Radio-Télévision Libre des Mille Collines; Rwandan Civil War; Rwandan Patriotic Front; United Nations Assistance Mission for Rwanda

Further Reading

Adelman, Howard, and Astri Suhrke, eds. *The Path of a Genocide: The Rwanda Crisis from Uganda to Zaire*. New Brunswick, NJ: Transaction Publishers, 1999.

Dorsey, Learthen. *Historical Dictionary of Rwanda*. Metuchen, NJ: Scarecrow Press, 1994.

Kamukama, Dixon. *Rwanda Conflict: Its Roots and Regional Implications*. 2nd ed. Kampala, Uganda: Fountain Publishers, 1998.

Prunier, Gérard. *The Rwanda Crisis, 1959–1994: History of a Genocide*. Kampala: Fountain Publishers, 1995.

Rwandan Civil War

The Rwandan Civil War took place between October 1, 1990, and August 4, 1993. The conflict pitted the Rwandan government under President Juvénal Habyarimana, which was dominated by the Hutus, against the armed component of the Rwandan Patriotic Front (RPF), which was a rebel group composed predominately of exiled Rwandan Tutsis. The Rwandan Civil War played a significant role in creating the conditions for the Rwandan Genocide of 1994, which began only months after a peace treaty was signed between the warring parties.

The Rwandan Civil War in had multiple causes in addition to the decades-old strife between the majority Hutus and minority Tutsis. The economy of Rwanda began to decline from 1989 to 1990, while inclement weather had produced low crop yields and food shortages. Meanwhile, a prodemocracy movement had been mounting in parts of Rwanda, which had received support from the French government. This led to increased political agitation toward President Habayrimana's regime. At the same time, thousands of Tutsis who had earlier fled Rwanda, many of them residing in appalling conditions in Uganda, had begun to coalesce around the RPF. That group was advocating a mass return to Rwanda, where it hoped to reclaim Tutsi land and sought political and social recognition. A number of Tutsis were also now serving in the Ugandan military. The Ugandan government, in the meantime, had forbidden non-Ugandans from owning land, which discriminated against Tutsi refugees living in Uganda. This made the Rwandan Tutsi exiles even more anxious to return home.

The Rwandan Patriotic Army, compromised of 4,000 to 6,000 rebels, launched an invasion into northern Rwanda from Uganda on October 1, 1990, setting off the three-year conflict. Many were dressed in Ugandan military uniforms and carried Ugandan weapons. The RPF rebels struck while both the Ugandan and Rwandan presidents were out of their countries attending a United Nations summit in New York. The RPF demanded an immediate end to ethnic segregation and discrimination in Rwanda and a more inclusive government. Within days, both Zaire (presently the Democratic Republic of the Congo) and France intervened by lending their supporting to the Rwandan government forces.

On the evening of October 4, 1990, Rwandan government forces launched an offensive in the capital of Kigali, chiefly to intimidate the city's residents and convince them to support the government. At least

10,000 Rwandans were also arrested for allegedly supporting the RPF rebels. By early 1991, the RPF decided to downplay the conventional aspects of their insurgency and instead focus on a guerilla-style war, principally in northern Rwanda. The guerilla war was a classic hit-and-run affair, which Rwandan troops found very difficult to defend against. Villages were often targeted, with many civilians killed or wounded.

Meanwhile, there were numerous attempts to broker a ceasefire, some by the international community. On June 12, 1992, truce talks finally commenced in Arusha, Tanzania, but those negotiations would drag on until August 4, 1993, when the Arusha Accords created a new power-sharing arrangement in Rwanda. A tenuous ceasefire had begun on July 31, 1992, although there was continued lower-level fighting for months thereafter. Within Rwanda, the civil war greatly increased the ethnic tensions already brewing between Hutus and Tutsis. Many Hutus were now bent on destroying the Tutsis, whom they feared would re-create the Rwanda of old, which was ruled by the Tutsi minority.

The results of the civil war helped create the conditions within which the Rwandan Genocide would occur. That bloody conflagration began in April 1994, just eight months after the conclusion of the Arusha Accords.

Paul G. Pierpaoli Jr.

See also: Arusha Accords; Forces Armées Rwandaises; Habyarimana, Juvénal; Hutu Social Revolution; Hutus; Kagame, Paul; Rwanda; Rwandan Genocide, Role of Propaganda in the; Rwandan Patriotic Army; Rwandan Patriotic Front; Tutsis; United Nations Assistance Mission for Rwanda

Further Reading
Ali, Taisier M., and Robert O. Matthews. *Civil Wars in Africa: Roots and Resolution.* Toronto: McGill-Queen's University Press, 1999.

Prunier, Gérard. *Africa's World War.* Oxford, UK: Oxford University Press, 2009.

Rwanda: Death, Despair and Defiance

Rwanda: Death, Despair and Defiance is a written report on the Rwandan Genocide first issued by the London-based human rights group African Rights in 1994. In 1995, a second edition was published and made available to the public for purchase. *Rwanda: Death, Despair and Defiance* was the first detailed account of the 1994 genocide in Rwanda. The report begins with a brief history of Rwanda and an analysis of how that history contributed to the mass bloodletting. Much of the work is based upon actual accounts of the events by survivors. The stories are unembellished and translated into English virtually verbatim. The report also examines the various institutions in Rwandan society and the role they played in the genocide. Thus, the genocide is examined at varying levels—from the personal, to the local, to the regional, to the national. The report also analyzes the ideology that underwrote Hutu extremism.

The survivors' accounts document the graphic and psychological horrors of the killing, and they also describe the betrayal of friends, neighbors, and even family during the ordeal. As well, the survivors describe flashes of brightness amid the dark terror, including the compassion and kindness of those who tried to help or shield them, as well as the resilience of the human spirit.

The report also details the Rwandan government's attempts to stifle and then liquidate Hutus who opposed the regime, as well as the propensity of genocide perpetrators to engage in violence against women and children. While the authors of the work reveal that a number of well-educated Hutus became willing participants in the genocide, they are not wholly successful in explaining why. Finally, the report examines world reaction to the events in Rwanda and how the international community failed to stop the carnage. Some critics of the report have asserted that the authors failed to assign adequate blame to the Rwandan Patriotic Front (RPF), arguing that its questionable activities went largely unexamined. Although the report has since been eclipsed by more recent studies, it remains a useful guide to understanding the Rwandan Genocide.

Paul G. Pierpaoli Jr.

See also: Rape; Rwanda; Rwandan Genocide, Role of Propaganda in the; Rwandan Patriotic Front

Further Reading

African Rights. *Rwanda: Death, Despair and Defiance.* 2nd rev. ed. London: African Rights, 1995.

Rwanda: The Preventable Genocide

Rwanda: The Preventable Genocide is a comprehensive report on the 1994 Rwandan Genocide sponsored by the Organization of African Unity and released in July 2000. An international panel of experts studied the issue and compiled the report. That panel included individuals from Africa, India, Canada, and Sweden. *Rwanda: The Preventable Genocide* consists of an introduction and 24 chapters, the last of which includes recommendations on how to avert future genocides. The report gives a summary of the causes, course, and results of the Rwandan Genocide, but its main focus is to assign blame to various players and bystanders who either helped create the conditions that allowed and encouraged the genocide to occur, or who did nothing to stop the killing once it began.

The report is highly critical of the United Nations (UN), particularly then Secretary-General Boutros Boutros-Ghali and the UN Security Council, for their failure to take sufficient action to prevent or limit the scope of the killings. The Security Council, the authors make clear, was slow to respond, and once it finally settled on the deployment of a peacekeeping mission, it hamstrung its efforts by forbidding UN forces from directly intervening in the genocide and by limiting the number of troops sent to Rwanda. The United States also shares responsibility in the disaster, so the report argues, because it did not exercise its clout within the UN and ultimately stalled the deployment of an adequate and effective peacekeeping force.

In addition to assessing U.S. and UN responsibility for the atrocities, the report also analyzes the actions and/or inactions of the French government, the Catholic Church, and other Western nations. The report scrutinizes France's policies in the region before, during and after the genocide and argues that France permitted thousands of genocide perpetrators to flee Rwanda for nearby Zaire. The Catholic Church is also faulted for its inaction during the genocide.

The report concludes that the genocide was entirely preventable, and goes so far as to claim that the genocide was possible only because of the international community's failure to intervene. The Rwandan Genocide was not, the report's authors argue, precipitated by poverty; rather, it was caused by long-standing racial hatred that had been stoked and even encouraged by colonial policies and the foreign policies of certain Western nations, including the United States, France, and Belgium. Finally, the report recommends the payment of reparations to the genocide survivors by those nations and institutions who stood by and did nothing to stop the bloodletting. That recommendation has, to date, not been realized.

Paul G. Pierpaoli Jr.

See also: Identity Cards, Rwanda; Roman Catholic Church; Rwanda; Rwandan Genocide, French Response to the; Rwandan Genocide, U.S. Response to the; United Nations Assistance Mission for Rwanda

Further Reading

Straus, Scott. *The Order of Genocide: Race, Power, and War in Rwanda*. Ithaca, NY: Cornell University Press, 2008.

Rwandan Genocide, French Response to the

France's long-standing involvement in Rwanda's affairs prior to, during, and after the Rwandan Genocide has led many to believe that the France was complicit in that catastrophe. As early as the early 1960s—when Rwanda was granted independence from Belgium—French leaders and policymakers sought to provide aid and support to the Rwandan government's Hutu leaders. This support increased substantially after François Mitterrand became the French president in 1981. He hoped to maintain the French language in Rwanda (French was the official language there until 2007) and expand French influence in Africa. He also cultivated an especially close relationship with Rwandan president Juvénal Habyarimana.

After the Tutsi-led Rwandan Patriotic Front (RPF) commenced open warfare with Habyarimana's regime on October 1, 1990—which in turn started sparked the 1990–1993 Rwandan Civil War—France stepped up its aid to Rwanda significantly. This aid, known as Opération Noroît, came in the form of military equipment and ammunition of all types as well as advice from French military advisers and other experts who were dispatched to Rwanda in great numbers. These advisers helped Habyarimana to expand his army from some 9,000 soldiers in late 1990 to more than 30,000 by 1991. French military personnel also helped train Rwandan army units, including Habyarimana's Presidential Guard. However, some of the French aid ended up going to anti-Tutsi militias, including the infamous Interahamwe, a Hutu paramilitary group, which played a key role in the Rwandan Genocide.

The genocide began after Habyarimana's presidential aircraft (which the French had loaned to him for his personal use) was shot down over Kigali on April 6, 1994. Habyarimana died in the attack. The Rwandan government blamed Tutsis and the RPF for the assassination, and almost immediately began to carry out its plans to annihilate Rwanda's minority Tutsi population, along with Hutus who tried to protect them. To this day, however, there is no conclusive evidence to indicate who was behind Habyarimana's death.

From April 8–14, 1994, as evidence of a mounting genocide was becoming clear, the French government implemented Opération Amaryllis, which evacuated some 1,500 individuals, most of them Europeans, from Rwanda. The operation also helped evacuate officials within the Habyramana government from the country. Later, the French were criticized for evacuating Europeans and government officials from Rwanda while they did nothing to evacuate Rwandans threatened by genocide. Indeed, the operation did not even extend to Rwandans who had been working for neither French military advisers nor technical experts. Meanwhile, a commander of the United Nations Assistance Mission for Rwanda (UNAMIR), which had been in

This image of French soldiers on patrol near Kayove, Rwanda, on June 26, 1994, highlights the contentious place France holds in the history of the Rwandan Genocide. Rwanda has accused the French government of having armed and trained the perpetrators of the genocide, a claim which France disputes. (Pascal Guyot/AFP/Getty Images)

Rwanda since the summer of 1993, reported that one of the French aircraft involved in the operation had unloaded some five tons of ammunition to be used by government forces. The French vehemently denied this claim.

Despite its checkered involvement in the genocide, during May and June 1994, while the international community fretted over—but did nothing—to stop the genocide, French officials at the United Nations (UN) supported a strengthened UNAMIR. French representatives to the UN also suggested another aid operation to Rwanda, Operation Turquoise. Under French leadership, the operation established a "safe haven" in southeastern Rwanda, where embattled Tutsis and moderate Hutus could seek refuge. The UN approved the operation, which

began on June 22 and lasted until August 22. Unfortunately, by then, the genocide had subsided and the operation occurred too late to save many lives. To make matters worse, many Hutu perpetrators sought refuge in the safe haven, which rendered them virtually immune to prosecution.

Since 1994, Franco-Rwandan relations have been on the tenuous, especially after Tutsi president Paul Kagame took power in 2000. His government has been highly critical of France's role in the genocide and believes that it must share the blame for it. The French government has engaged in several inquiries and commissions designed to gauge French complicity in the genocide, but none found any overt wrongdoing on the part of the French government.

In April 2004, Kagame publicly chastised the French for their failure to apologize for their complicity in the Rwandan Genocide. The French, in turn, accused Kagame of having orchestrated Habyarimana's death and therefore setting off the mass killings. Kagame categorically denies any such involvement. In August 2008, an independent Rwandan commission concluded that France had helped to train and equip Hutu militias. The commission's report went on to name 33 senior French government and military leaders who were responsible—directly or indirectly—for the genocide, including Mitterrand, as well as France's prime minister and foreign minister. The French government continues its official denials, although there are many Frenchmen, both civilians and government officials, who are suspect of the French government's position. In 2007, the Kagame regime made English the official language of his country and sought membership in the British Commonwealth, a sure sign that it is trying to purge Rwanda of its ties to France. In October 2016, France reopened an investigation into the shooting down of Habyarimana's plane, enraging Rwandan leaders in the process. In response, Rwanda launched its own investigation into the 20 French officials it claims were involved in the 1994 genocide. Not surprisingly, Franco-Rwandan relations remain very poor.

Paul G. Pierpaoli Jr.

See also: Habyarimana, Juvénal; Kagame, Paul; Rwanda; Rwandan Patriotic Front; Turquoise, Operation; United Nations Assistance Mission for Rwanda

Further Reading

Dallaire, Roméo. *Shake Hands with the Devil: The Failure of Humanity in Rwanda*. Toronto: Random House, Canada, 2004.

Melvern, Linda. *Conspiracy to Murder: The Rwandan Genocide*. London: Verso, 2006.

"Rwanda genocide: French officials face investigation," *BBC* (November 29, 2016), http://www.bbc.com/news/world-africa-38152791.

Rwandan Genocide, Role of Propaganda in the

Propaganda played a critical role in the implementation and execution of the 1994 Rwandan Genocide. Hutu extremists employed propaganda to weaponize ethnic tension within Rwanda and to mobilize Hutus to participate in the killing. In the weeks preceding the genocide and continuing throughout the massacre, propaganda that disparaged the Tutsi minority dominated Rwandan radio, television, newspaper, and all other forms of media. Galvanized by propagandic messaging, Hutus—including government officials, soldiers and police, political leaders, religious figures, and various militia members—killed 800,000 of their Tutsi family members, friends and neighbors, as well as moderate Hutus (ethnic Hutu who refused to participate in the massacres or spoke out against them), primarily using machetes, in just 100 days.

Propaganda served to cast Tutsis as the enemy, dehumanize the Tutsis, and to convince the Hutu population that killing Tutsis was the only option for survival. To achieve these ends, propaganda blamed Tutsis for historical inequities between Hutus and Tutsis, drawing heavily on stereotypes that had survived since the time when Hutu and Tutsi identities were first constructed by Belgian colonizers in the late 1800s and early 1900s. Messaging was strategically intended to make Hutus fearful for their lives and livelihoods. Radio broadcasts and newspapers claimed that the Tutsi Rwandan Patriotic Front (RPF) and Tutsi civilians were working to annihilate Hutus. Propaganda used imagery aimed at dehumanizing Tutsis by depicting them as *inyenzi* (cockroaches) that must be killed. Anti-Tutsi propaganda even specified the machete as the weapon of choice for killing. All propaganda from that time warned Hutus to kill or be killed. When the official call to action sounded after President Juvénal Habyarimana's death, many Hutus reasoned their survival depended on their participation in the genocide and thus picked up machetes and attacked their Tutsi neighbors.

The use of propaganda to incite acts of genocide in Rwanda was made criminal in a 2003 judgment by the International Criminal Tribunal for Rwanda (ICTR) in the so-called Media Case. The ICTR was established in 1994 by the United Nations Security Council for the prosecution of persons responsible for genocide and other serious violations of international humanitarian law in Rwanda between January 1, 1994, and December 31, 1994. The three defendants in the Media Case all held influential roles within the Rwandan media: one was the founder and editor-in-chief of the *Kangura* newspaper, another, a founding member of the Radio-Télévision Libre des Mille Collines, and the third the director of the Rwandan Office of Information. Based on their involvement in the anti-Tutsi propaganda campaign, ICTR judges found all three defendants guilty of conspiracy to commit genocide, genocide, and direct and public incitement to commit genocide. The landmark Media Case was the first to rule that the use of propaganda to incite and commit genocide entailed criminal responsibility, highlighting the significant role that propaganda played in the Rwandan Genocide.

Elinor O. Stevenson

See also: Hamitic Hypothesis; Identity Cards, Rwanda; *Kangura*; Nahimana, Ferdinand; *Radio-Télévision Libre des Mille Collines*; Rwandan Civil War

Further Reading

Des Forges, Alison, and Longman, Timothy. "Legal Responses to Genocide in Rwanda." In *My Neighbor, My Enemy: Justice and Community in the Aftermath of Mass Atrocity*, edited by Eric Stover and Harvey M. Weinstein, 49–63. Cambridge: Cambridge University Press, 2004.

Hatzfield, Jean. *Machete Season: The Killers in Rwanda Speak*. Translated by Linda Coverdale. New York: Farrar, Straus and Giroux, 2005.

International Criminal Tribunal for Rwanda, Prosecutor v. Ferdinand Nahimana, Jean-Bosco Barayagwiza, and Hassan Ngeze, Judgment and Sentence, Case No. ICTR-99-52-T (Trial Chamber 1, December 3, 2003).

Power, Samantha. *"A Problem from Hell": America and the Age of Genocide*. New York: Harper Perennial, 2007.

Rwandan Genocide, U.S. Response to the

Mirroring sentiments within the larger international community, the U.S. government chose not to intervene in the 1994 Rwandan Genocide, which resulted in the deaths of as many as one million Tutsis and moderate Hutus. After the carnage began on April 6, 1994, many of the world's leading powers refused to become involved in the genocide, terming it an internal Rwandan problem. France, China, and Russia all opposed intervention, and the United Nations (UN) was powerless to act, even though it had peacekeeping troops on the ground in Rwanda as part of the United Nations Assistance

Mission for Rwanda (UNAMIR). That mission had been dispatched in October 1993 to implement a peace arrangement between the Hutu-led Rwandan government and the Tutsi-dominated Rwandan Patriotic Front (RPF). Without a broad-based mandate to stop the killing, U.S. president Bill Clinton and his administration chose to not send in troops.

In order to understand Clinton's reluctance to send in troops to Rwanda, it is important to assess a botched intervention that occurred a few years earlier. The Clinton administration was hesitant to intervene in the Rwandan Genocide, in part, because of the disastrous 1992–1993 U.S. intervention in Somalia, an operation that Clinton had inherited from his predecessor, George H. W. Bush. After the humanitarian mission morphed into a program designed to disarm rival warlords in 1993, U.S. troops suffered a humiliating defeat in the October 3–4 Battle of Mogadishu. That engagement resulted in the deaths of 18 American soldiers and 73 others sustained injuries. As cameras rolled, one soldier's body was dragged through the streets by an angry mob. The incident was a deep embarrassment for the young, new president and drew much criticism from Republicans and Democrats alike. Clinton soon withdrew all troops from Somalia, convinced that unilateral military interventions were not worth the inherent risks involved with them.

As news of the Rwandan tragedy unfolded, Clinton came under increasing pressure to do something to stop the killing. But fearing another Somalia debacle, and unwilling to act without UN authority, the U.S. government chose a course of inaction. Furthermore, Clinton's main advisers and military commanders cautioned against an intervention in an unstable place, where the United States had few strategic interests.

The U.S. leaders' decision to not refer to the ongoing killings as genocide is highly political. Hoping to tamp down any public criticism, Clinton ordered his administration officials not to term the events in Rwanda as genocide, although documents released more recently indicate that in private administration officials were referring to the killings as genocide only two weeks after the cataclysm began. U.S. ambassador to the UN, Madeleine Albright also refused to term the conflict as genocide. Declassified documents released after Clinton left office reveal that the administration was weary to call the killings genocide because to do so who commit the United States to acting.

In addition, the United States refused to denounce the Rwandan government, did nothing to jam anti-Tutsi radio and television stations, and hesitated to send military supplies to the UNAMIR II mission, which was being mobilized in the final months of the genocide. Despite this great prevarication, documents show that the U.S. government was cognizant of the extent of the carnage in Rwanda only a week into the conflict, and that Clinton and his cabinet almost certainly knew that the Hutu Rwandan government was bent on annihilating the Tutsis within Rwanda.

Clinton's failure to respond to the Rwandan Genocide deeply troubled him. He later expressed much regret over his government's inaction and has stated that it was one of the low points of his eight-year presidency. He has visited Rwanda several times, and in 1998, while still president, he apologized for his "personal failure" to prevent the genocide. To help make amends, his Clinton Foundation has been heavily involved in reconstruction and humanitarian efforts in Rwanda. While the U.S. refusal to intervene in the Rwandan crisis was certainly a great humanitarian failure, it is important to remember that this failure is shared by the entire world.

Paul G. Pierpaoli Jr.

See also: Bushnell, Prudence; Hutus; Rwandan Patriotic Front; Support Hope, Operation; Tutsis; United Nations Assistance Mission for Rwanda; Wilkens, Carl

Further Reading

Gribbin, Robert E. *In the Aftermath of Genocide: The U.S. Role in Rwanda.* New York: iUniverse, 2005.

Power, Samantha. *"A Problem from Hell": America and the Age of Genocide.* New York: Harper Perennial, 2007.

Rwandan Patriotic Army

The Rwandan Patriotic Army (RPA) was the armed wing of the Rwandan Patriotic Front (RPF), a Tutsi rebel group established in 1987 by Tutsi refugees living in Uganda. For the most part, at least until 1994, when the RPA was absorbed into Rwanda's national defense establishment (now known as the Rwandan Defence Forces, or RDF) the RPA's history mirrored that of the RPF. By the late 1980s, the RPF was determined to destabilize Rwandan's Hutu-dominated government to oust it from power or force it into a power-sharing arrangement with the RPF. In so doing, the RPF hoped to create a governing power that would permit the 200,000-plus Hutu refugees living in Uganda to return to Rwanda. These refugees had been living in squalid conditions since the early 1960s and were routinely oppressed and harassed by the Ugandan government.

From 1989 to 1990, the RPA numbered only about 5,000 troops, and many had formerly served in the Ugandan military. Some of them were not well trained, and most did not have access to the latest weaponry. In 1990, the RPF, using the RPA, decided to commence a military campaign against the Rwandan government. This entailed engaging the Rwandan Armed Forces (French: Forces Armées Rwandaises, or FAR) as well as launching raids against civilian Hutus. The RPA's operations resulted in mounting deaths within Rwanda, which compelled the Rwandan government to seek military and financial help from France. The French government supplied the FAR with arms and ammunition, helped train its soldiers, and significantly enlarged the size of the army, which numbered between 40,000 to 50,000 men by 1994. The RPA's campaign resulted in the deaths of three of its original commanders—Fred Rwigyema, Peter Bayingana, and Chris Bunyenyezi—between 1990 and 1994.

By 1994, the command of the RPA had passed to Paul Kagame, who worked mightily to secure more and better weapons and to recruit soldiers. In the spring of 1994, when the Rwandan Genocide began, the RPA numbered 25,000 men. This, however, meant that the army was only half the size of the FAR. The chaos that resulted in the April 6, 1994 assassination of Habyarimana and the genocide that followed drove the RPA to overpower the FAR, and by August 1994, the RPA had secured most of the country and had stopped the killing. At that point, the RPF assumed control of the Rwandan government. Soon thereafter, the RPA was integrated into a new national military establishment, the RDF.

The RPA committed its own atrocities during and immediately after the 1994 genocide. RPA soldiers killed thousands of Hutus as they tried to flee Rwanda, and they killed many thousands more in refugee camps within Rwanda and in neighboring countries. It is estimated that as many as

200,000 Hutus died at the hands of the RPA. For this reason, the RPF, which now governed Rwanda, dissolved its army, and the RDF was constituted using soldiers from the RPA as well as some soldiers who had served in the extinct FAR. This arrangement was also part of the 1993 Arusha Accords. Today, the RDF is composed of the High Command Council, the General Staff, and the Rwandan Land Force. There are now four divisions divided by region; each division contains three brigades.

Paul G. Pierpaoli Jr.

See also: Arusha Accords; Forces Armées Rwandaises; Habyarimana, Juvénal; Hutu Social Revolution; Hutus; Kagame, Paul; Rwandan Patriotic Front; Tutsis

Further Reading

Ali, Taisier M., and Robert O. Matthews. *Civil Wars in Africa: Roots and Resolution.* Toronto: McGill-Queen's University Press, 1999.

Dallaire, Roméo. *Shake Hands with the Devil: The Failure of Humanity in Rwanda.* Toronto: Random House, Canada, 2004.

Rwandan Patriotic Front

The Rwandan Patriotic Front (RPF) was a Tutsi rebel refugee group established in Uganda in 1987, and which since 1994 has been the predominant political party in Rwanda. The RPF was created by exiled Tutsis who had begun to flee Rwanda in 1959, when the Hutus overthrew the Tutsi monarchy and systematically installed a Hutu-dominated regime there. Over time, the number of refugees ballooned, reaching some 200,000 in Uganda alone by 1990. Unfortunately, the Tutsi refugees in Uganda were treated abhorrently, especially after Uganda president Milton Obote's dictatorial government began enacting harsh and repressive anti-refugee legislation in the 1960s. Obote was ousted in 1985, with the help of disgruntled Tutsi refugees.

Ugandan politics remained quite unstable during the 1980s, and the Tutsis living there continued to be treated as third-class citizens. Some Tutis who had joined the Ugandan military opted out by the mid-1980s, now determined to regain their access to Rwanda, using military means if necessary. This proved to be the genesis of the RPF, which in most of its pre-governing years operated more of a militia than a political party.

The RPF had gained considerable traction by 1990, when it numbered roughly 5,000 armed militiamen, but it grew exponentially under the leadership of Paul Kagame. By 1994, the RPF numbered some 25,000 troops, which was known as the Rwandan Patriotic Army (RPA). At the same time, the RPF stepped up its efforts to destabilize Rwanda's Hutu-led government. Kagame's goal was to undermind Rwandan president Juvénal Habyarimana's regime to such an extent that he would be forced to accept a power-sharing arrangement with the RPF. Increasingly deadly raids carried out by the RPA accomplished that goal in June 1993, when the RPF and other rebel Tutsi groups compelled Habyarimana to reach a comprehensive peace settlement.

This shaky peace was shattered on April 6, 1994, when Habyarimana's plane was shot down over Kigali, resulting in the president's death. The Hutu government blamed the Tutsis for the assassination, while the Tutsis accused radical Hutus of having orchestrated the killing as a pretext for genocide against the Tutsis. This event triggered the Rwandan Genocide, in which as many as 800,000 to 1,000,000 Tutsis and moderate

The Rwandan Patriotic Front (RPF) has been the ruling political party in Rwanda since RPF troops, like those pictured here preparing to march into Kigali on May 26, 1994, overtook the capital and brought the genocide to an end. (Scott Peterson/Liaison/Getty Images)

Hutus were slaughtered. The RPF used the tragedy to oust the Hutus from power and end the genocide, and by August 1994 the RPF had taken form control of the country. Some have accused the RPF of having unleashed its own genocide against Rwandan Hutus fleeing the country during and after the genocide. Perhaps as many as 200,000 Hutu refugees died.

In March 2000, RPF leader and current Rwandan president Paul Kagame took office in Rwanda. Under his guidance, the RPF became a mainstream political organization and divested itself of the RPA, which was absorbed by the Rwandan Defence Forces (RDF). The RDF continues today as Rwanda's formal military establishment. Although Kagame and the RPF now rule in a coalition with other smaller parties, the RPF has held most seats in the Rwandan parliament for well over a decade. The Kagame government has attempted to move beyond the Rwandan Genocide by virtually outlawing the classification of Rwandans by race; all Rwandans are now simply Rwandans rather than Hutus, Tutsis, or Twas.

Paul G. Pierpaoli Jr.

See also: Arusha Accords; Forces Armées Rwandaises; Habyarimana, Juvénal; Hutus; Kagame, Paul; Rwandan Patriotic Army; Tutsis; Twas

Further Reading

Dallaire, Roméo. *Shake Hands with the Devil: The Failure of Humanity in Rwanda.* Toronto: Random House, Canada, 2004.

Des Forges, Alison. *Leave None to Tell the Story: Genocide in Rwanda.* New York: Human Rights Watch, 1999.

S

Sindikubwabo, Théodore

Théodore Sindikubwabo served as the interim president of Rwanda during the Rwandan Genocide. As the head of the Rwandan state from April 9 to July 19, 1994, he oversaw and instigated the annihilation of some 800,000 Tutsis and moderate Hutus.

Sindikubwabo had served the Rwandan government long before the genocide. He was born in Butare, Rwanda in 1928 and trained as a physician. In the years following the colonial period in Rwanda, Sindikubwabo served under Rwanda's first president, Grégoire Kayibanda, as the Minister of Health. Kayibanda was the leader of the Hutu Emancipation Movement (French: Parti l'émancipation du people Hutu, or Parmehutu), an anti-Tutsi political group. Following Juvénal Habyarimana's overthrow of Kayibanda on July 5, 1973, Sindikubwabo left the government and returned to practicing medicine. Later he adopted the political outlook of Habyarimana's political party, the National Revolutionary Movement for Development (French: Mouvement Révolutionnaire National pour le Développement, or MRND). His fever for the MRND later led him back to government work.

Sindikubwabo was serving under President Habyarimana on the day the President's plane was shot down on April 6, 1994. Following the assassination of Habyarimana, Colonel Théoneste Bagosora (minister of defence) and Colonel Pierre-Célestin Rwagafilita (the brother of Haybarimana's wife Agathe and a member of Akazu) assembled the Committee for Public Salvation (French: the Comité de Salut Public) to put in place a provisional government. They chose Sindikubwabo, the Speaker of the Assembly, to assume the vacancy left by Habyarimana. It has been suggested that Bagosora and Rwagafilita chose Sindikubwabo because they thought he would be easy to control and that he would not interfere with their plans to annihilate Rwanda's Tutsis. Indeed, they were right.

To say Sindikubwabo helped rally and incite violence during his presidency is an understatement. Perhaps the most famous example of his influence and outlook occurred on April 19, 1994 when he used a public speaking opportunity to encourage Hutus to murder Tutsis. Speaking at a ceremony to appoint a new governor of Butare (he had fired the previous governor who was subsequently killed), he incited his listeners to get to work and start murdering Tutsis. For the first 12 days of the genocide, Butare had remained calm, however, his speech helped change that. His hateful speech was broadcast countrywide on the national radio. After his speech, the government flew in members of the Presidential Guard and started bussing in members of the Interahamwe militia and weapons. Ten days later, he returned to Butare to oversee the killing of the area's Tutsis. Given his high office, Sindikubwabo's involvement in the genocide helped legitimize the killings and encourage Hutus to seek out and kill their neighbors without fear of punishment. Of the massacres that occurred during the genocide, those in Butare stand out. In less than three weeks, some 20,000

Tutsis were murdered in the Cyahinda parish and some 35,000 perished in the Karama parish.

Sindikubwabo must have feared for his own life when the Rwandan Patriotic Front (RPF)—the Tutsi-led militia group who liberated Rwanda—advanced on Rwanda's capital city of Kigali. Along with many other government leaders, Sindikubwabo fled Rwanda and sought refuge in neighboring Zaire (now known as the Democratic Republic of the Congo). Sindikubwabo took up residence in Bukavu.

In *We wish to inform you that tomorrow we will be killed with our families*, journalist Philip Gourevitch describes how he caught up with Sindikubwabo in 1995 in Bukavu. Gourevitch details the former president's elaborate home and possessions, which included two black Rwandan government Mercedes sedans in the driveway. In his mid-sixties at that time, Sindikubwabo appeared ill and gaunt. Gourevitch asked Sindikubwabo about the speech he had given in Butare in April 1994, but the former president refused to repeat what he had said in Butare. He insisted that his words had been misunderstood. While the two spoke, a picture of Sindikubwabo's predecessor, President Habyarimana, hung on the wall.

Despite his role in the genocide, the International Criminal Tribunal for Rwanda never brought charges against Sindikubwabo and he died in exile in the Democratic Republic of the Congo in the late 1990s, having never stood trial for his crimes.

Alexis Herr

See also: Akazu; Bagosora, Théoneste; Congo, Democratic Republic of; Habyarimana, Agathe; Habyarimana, Juvénal; Interahamwe; International Criminal Tribunal for Rwanda; Kayibanda, Grégoire; Rwandan Patriotic Front; *We wish to inform you that tomorrow we will be killed with our families*

Further Reading

Gourevitch, Philip. *We wish to inform you that tomorrow we will be killed with our families.* New York: Picador, 1999.

Prunier, Gérard. *The Rwanda Crisis, 1959–1994: History of a Genocide.* Kampala: Fountain Publishers, 1995.

Support Hope, Operation

The reverberations of the Rwandan Genocide in the Great Lakes region (Burundi, the Democratic Republic of the Congo, Kenya, Rwanda, Tanzania, and Uganda) continued after the genocidal killing concluded in July 1994. During the genocide—which began in April 1994 and resulted in the murder of 800,00 to one million Tutsis and moderate Hutus in 100 days—hundreds of thousands of Rwandans traversed Rwanda's borders and landed in refugee camps throughout the Great Lakes region. Approximately a million Rwandans escaped to Zaire (which changed its name to the Democratic Republic of the Congo in 1997) and in so doing overwhelmed United Nations (UN) agencies and humanitarian assistance groups. Flooded by the demands of so many in need, refugee camps struggled to provide food, medicine, shelter, and water and as a result many refugees succumbed to starvation and disease. In response to the humanitarian crisis and the UN plea for help, U.S. president Bill Clinton authorized Operation Support Hope (OSH) in July 1994.

OSH operated from July 24 to August 31, 1994. At its height, the United States had an estimated 3,600 troops stationed in the Great Lakes region, with its highest concentration of troops in Uganda and smaller units stationed in Goma and Kigali. The main objectives of the OSH mission were to provide humanitarian assistance to existing refuge agencies, set up water purification and distribution in Goma, manage and improve airfield facilities, and oversee and improve aid deliveries. Efforts by the OSH to improve water quality and make airplane deliveries were among its most successful endeavors. Working closely with the United Nations High Commission for Refugees (UNHCR), the United States operated more than half of all aid deliveries from an airbase in Entebbe, Uganda. These deliveries included desperately needed food, blankets, medical supplies, clothes, and water.

While the OSH certainly helped save lives, some have argued that it could have, and should have, done more to protect refugees. Camps set up in Zaire, for example, struggled to safegaurd refugees from the same Hutu perpetrators who were responsible for the genocide in the first place. Hutu extremists recruited in camps, killed those who opposed or resisted forced conscription into guerilla forces, and used the camps as a staging ground to launch new attacks against the reestablished Rwandan government. Tutsis who had fled the genocide were particularly vulnerable. While the UN pleaded with Zairean president Mobutu Sese Seko to supply troops to secure the camps, he refused their requests. Although the UN requested foreign governments like the United States (which already had troops on the ground) to help protect camps and separate Hutu perpetrators from other refugees, no such action was taken. Instead, the very aid and supplies sent to support legitimate refugees also fed, clothed, and helped fortify perpetrators of the genocide. In the years that followed the genocide, the Rwandan government launched successive attacks into Zaire to weed out perpetrators. The long-term consequences of these humanitarian failures and oversights resulted in two wars from 1996 to 2003, which involved eight countries surrounding the DRC, the deaths of more than five million people, and such extensive rape of Congolese women and children that some have called on the UN to revise its definition of genocide to add gender as a victimization category to those of ethnicity, race, and religion.

The failures and successes of Operation Support Hope illuminate the challenges that follow genocide. Much like the genocide, relief efforts afterward were complex and complicated.

Alexis Herr

See also: Congo, Democratic Republic of the; International Reactions; Rwandan Genocide, U.S. Response to the; Turquoise, Operation; Victims

Further Reading

DiPrizio, Robert C. *Armed Humanitarians: US Interventions from Northern Iraq to Kosovo.* Baltimore, Maryland: John Hopkins University Press, 2002.

Seybolt, Taylor B. *Humanitarian Military Intervention: The Conditions for Success and Failure.* New York: Oxford University Press, 2007.

Stearns, Jason. *Dancing in the Glory of Monsters: The Collapse of the Congo and the Great War of Africa.* New York: PublicAffairs, 2011.

Turquoise, Operation

Operation Turquoise was a French-led military operation to erect a safe haven for Tutsis and moderate Hutus in the southern quarter of Rwanda during the late stages of the 1994 Rwandan Genocide. In May 1994, as the genocide reached the zenith of its destruction, the United Nations Security Council (UNSC) enacted Resolution 918, which called for a larger and more potent force to augment the United Nations Assistance Mission for Rwanda (UNAMIR), which was already on the ground in Rwanda. The French government strongly supported this effort, and offered to deploy its own troops to Rwanda. UNSC Resolution 929 empowered the French to undertake that mission on June 22, and within days French forces had begun deploying to Rwanda. The mission concluded two months later.

The French dispatched 2,550 troops, who served with approximately 500 troops from neighboring African countries. This force established a safe zone (known as the "Turquoise Zone") in the southern part of Rwanda (comprising about one-fifth of the country), where embattled Tutsis and moderate Hutus could seek refuge, ostensibly free from danger. Operation Turquoise included a battery of 120 mm mortars, 10 armed helicopters, 4 French Jaguar fighter-bombers, 2 reconnaissance planes, and about 100 armored personnel vehicles.

Operation Turquoise proved highly problematic, however. First, the numerous roadblocks set up by the perpetrators outside the French zone meant that many Tutsis could not make their way to safety and consequently many died en route. Second, in July the operators of Radio-Télévision Libre des Mille Collines (RTLM), a radical Hutu media outlet that was exhorting Hutus to kill Tutsis, relocated their transmitters to the Turquoise Zone. The French made no immediate move to seize them or silence them. Third, most of the refugees who fled to the French safe zone were in fact Hutus rather than Tutsis; some of them had been involved in perpetrating the genocide, and they continued to kill Tutsis even within the safe zone. The French were unable to prevent many of these killings. Fourth, the French troops did a poor job of disarming those who sought refuge (especially Hutus), which ultimately endangered Tutsis within the French zone.

Other controversies also bedeviled the French operation. Some Tutsis in Rwanda and others in the international community accused the French of having undertaken the mission to prop up the Hutu regime responsible for starting the genocide. France had previously backed the Hutu government of President Juvénal Habyarimana and provided it with financial and military aid. Others alleged that the French were more interested in protecting Hutus from the Tutsi-dominated Rwandan Patriotic Army (RPA) instead of protecting Tutsis from the Hutus. Still others argued that by permitting so many Hutus into the Turquoise Zone, France permitted many genocide perpetrators to escape justice in Rwanda, or to flee the country entirely. That in turn enabled exiled Hutus to engage in warfare against the post-genocide Rwandan government from places like the Congo and Uganda. The French government has steadfastly denied these claims and allegations, insisting that it deployed troops to Rwanda in June 1994 based solely on humanitarian considerations.

Roméo Dallaire, the commander of UNAMIR, spoke out critically about Operation Turquoise in his memoir *Shake Hands with the Devil*. He argued that having two UN-mandated operations in the same country but with different missions was a recipe for confusion and ineffectiveness. The arrival of Operation Turquoise and a wave of French troops only intensified the Rwandan Patriotic Front's (RPF) mistrust of the UN and Dallaire found himself acting as an intermediary between Paul Kagame, leader of the RPF, and Operation Turquoise. Dallaire recalled that, "I told Kagame that . . . I would insist that the French not deploy in Kigali . . . For a moment Kagame just looked at me . . . [Kagame responded that] the French would not be entering Kigali. As to the reason why, his assessment was blunt: 'Tell France that Kigali can handle more body bags than Paris'" (Dallaire 2004: 434).

The last French troops were withdrawn on August 22, at which time UNAMIR II began its formal operations in Rwanda.

Paul G. Pierpaoli Jr.

See also: Dallaire, Roméo; de Saint-Exupéry, Patrick; Habyarimana, Juvénal; Hutus; Rwanda; Rwandan Genocide, French Response to the; Rwandan Patriotic Army; Rwandan Patriotic Front; Tutsis; United Nations Assistance Mission for Rwanda

Further Reading

Dallaire, Roméo. *Shake Hands with the Devil: The Failure of Humanity in Rwanda.* Toronto: Random House, Canada, 2004.

Melvern, Linda. *Conspiracy to Murder: The Rwandan Genocide.* London: Verso, 2006.

Tutsis

The Tutsis are a minority class of citizens that occupy the region of Rwanda-Burundi. Centuries of Tutsi rule in Rwanda ended in 1961. Tutsis in Rwanda were the victims of genocide at the hands of the Hutu majority in 1994.

The Hutu and Tutsi are descended from ancestors sharing a common language, Kinyarwanda, who settled the Rwanda-Burundi area of east central Africa more than a thousand years ago. Two forms of subsistence developed among these people. One group relied strictly on cultivation and farming. The other relied on raising cattle. Over time, the farmers came to be known as Hutus and the pastoralists as Tutsis. In this culture, cattle were a marker of wealth. With time, Hutu and Tutsi became class markers with the pastoral Tutsi as the wealthier members of the society.

By the time of the German conquest in the 1880s, Rwandan society had begun to polarize, with the majority Hutu occupying the peasant position and the Tutsi minority holding the tribal leadership roles. The German colonizers did little to interfere with the social makeup of the indigenous people. When Belgium assumed control over Rwanda at the close of World War I, the situation changed. The Belgians relied heavily on indigenous Tutsi leaders to govern the colony. This served to reinforce Tutsi control and provided an apparatus to repress the masses.

During the 1950s, Tutsi control over Rwanda began to erode as the United Nations supervised decolonization. Hutus were successful in exploiting the decolonization process to gain power throughout Rwanda. When Rwanda revolted against Belgium and secured its independence in 1961, the class roles were reversed, and the Hutus held the positions of power.

This photo of Tutsi refugees at the Nyarushishi Refugee Camp in Rwanda, on June 24, 1994, elucidates the refugee crisis that accompanied and then continued long after the genocide concluded. (Scott Peterson/Liaison/Getty Images)

Tutsi rebels challenged Hutu rule immediately. In response to cross-border rebel incursions, the Hutu government massacred some 20,000 Rwandan Tutsis and forced 300,000 to flee. In the aftermath, a military dictatorship solidified its power in Rwanda. Over the next two decades, the standard of living in Rwanda declined steadily. With the long-term economic downturn, the power base of the military leadership eroded. Rebel groups, most notably the Rwandan Patriotic Front, began to challenge the government from camps in neighboring states. As far as Rwanda's Hutu-led government was concerned, Tutsi participation with the rebels justified further repression of the Tutsis. The government began planning the genocide of the Tutsis.

The assassination of President Juvénal Habyarimana on April 6, 1994, initiated the action against the Tutsis. During the next 13 weeks, military forces compelled the Hutu population of Rwanda to massacre the Tutsis. More than 800,000 Tutsis were murdered.

Rob Coyle

See also: Habyarimana, Juvénal; Hutus; International Criminal Tribunal for Rwanda; Rwanda; Rwandan Patriotic Front

Further Reading

Adelman, Howard, and Astri Suhrke, eds. *The Path of a Genocide: The Rwanda Crisis from Uganda to Zaire.* New Brunswick, NJ: Transaction Publishers, 1999.

Webster, John B. *The Political Development of Rwanda and Burundi.* Syracuse, NY: Maxwell Graduate School of Citizenship and Public Affairs, Syracuse University, 1966.

Twas

The Twas, or Batwas, are pygmy peoples who live in the forests and savannah plains stretching from Uganda in the north down along the Lakes Region of Central Africa to Rwanda, Burundi, and the Democratic Republic of the Congo. In addition, there are Twa populations scattered in Botswana, Angola, Zambia, and Namibia, where they have adopted to living conditions in deserts and swamps as well as their more familiar forests. In 2000, Twas numbered around 80,000 in total and in some of these countries they represent significant minorities.

Like other pygmy peoples, the Twa have been dominated by their Bantu and Cushitic neighbors and speak their languages. Most Twas speak Kirundi and Kinyarwanda, the languages of the Hutus and Tutsis. In Rwanda and Burundi, the Twas make up 1 percent of the population in each country and, due to the heavy demands for farming and grazing lands, much of the natural forest habitat has been lost over the last several centuries. Like other pygmies, little of their own culture still exists.

The Twas are thought to be among the oldest living groups connected to the Tschitolian culture dating back some 25,000 years. They seem to have lived in a widespread area before the Bantu expansions starting in the second millennium BCE and lasting, with different waves and patterns, into the first centuries CE. The Twas, as hunters and gatherers, helped provide meat and honey to the Bantus in trade for iron goods and agricultural products. In some situations, the two were able to develop a symbiotic relationship, and the Kubas of Angola and southern Democratic Republic of the Congo have brought Twas into their mask societies. That is, among the masks made and worn at special occasions are those that represent Twas with a noticeably large head, large, bulging forehead, and wide nose. Called a *bwoon* mask, they are worn at funerals of important men who belonged to the initiation societies.

In the colonial period, Twa society began to unravel in a number of places. Their hunting and gathering skills were less and less needed and their natural habitat was quickly cut down. Twas began to gather on the outskirts of Bantu towns and villages and became a source of menial labor, in often very abusive terms. They were generally ignored in the postcolonial developments, and their communities still today suffer from the lack of schools, electricity, water, and medical treatment. Missions did not seek them out, and today it is estimated that only some 7 percent of Twas are Christians. The largest number of them adheres to syncretic apostolic forms that combine Christian belief with indigenous systems of belief or still follow indigenous (mainly Bantu) forms of belief. Twas have been able to preserve some of their specific cultural practices such as dances and songs during social gatherings. Hunting was banned in the 1970s, and though Twa men still know how to make bows and arrows, they have been persecuted and jailed for continued hunting.

In the fighting between the Hutus and Tutsis in Rwanda in 1994, the Twas suffered greatly and some 30 percent of the Twas in Rwanda died at the hands of the Hutu Interahamwe militias. According to the Unrepresented Nations and Peoples Organization (UNPO), some 10,000 Twas were killed in the Rwandan Genocide and another 8,000 to 10,000 fled to nearby countries.

Many Twa communities suffer from problems of alcoholism and are treated with contempt by their countrymen. In 2007, it was reported that with no source of income, over 40 percent of the Twas in Rwanda earned a living through begging. The majority are illiterate and many Twa children drop out of school due to harassment by other students. UNPO states that 91 percent of Twas have no formal education. Twa women are subject to harassment, including sexual harassment from Bantu men. A source of income and of cultural identity is pottery making; however, the swamp lands where the Twas have enjoyed joint land rights for centuries with Hutu farmers came into danger starting in 2005 with plans to develop rice plantations. In both Rwanda and Burundi, the Twas are not legally recognized, have no representation in government, and have no land rights. In 2009, Burundi began the process of bringing the Twas into the government in an attempt to finally deal with the situation. In addition, a number of different organizations have taken up the cause of not only the Twas, but also other pygmy peoples in Africa.

John A. Shoup

See also: Congo, Democratic Republic of the; Interahamwe

Further Reading

Adekunle, Julius O. *Culture and Customs of Rwanda*. Westport, CT: Greenwood Press, 2007.

Oyebade, Adebayo. *Culture and Customs of Angola*. Westport, CT: Greenwood, 2006.

Unrepresented Nations and People Organization. www.unpo.org/

U

United Nations Assistance Mission for Rwanda

The United Nations Assistance Mission for Rwanda (UNAMIR) was chiefly a humanitarian mission sent to Rwanda to help implement the August 1993 Arusha Accords, which intended to end the Rwandan Civil War. UNAMIR was officially established by United Nations (UN) Security Council Resolution 872 on October 5, 1993. It took almost five months for the mission to achieve its authorized strength of 2,500 personnel, however. Designed to encourage the peace process between the Rwandan government dominated by the Hutus and the Tutsi-led Rwandan Patriotic Front (RPF), the UN mission was also tasked with expanding the demilitarized zone, monitoring Rwanda's internal security situation, and providing humanitarian aid to refugees and others affected by the civil war. Unfortunately, UNAMIR was entirely unprepared for the outbreak of the Rwandan Genocide, which began in April 1994 and claimed the lives of 800,000–1,000,000 people.

The institution of a new, transitional government, as called for in the Arusha Accords, was significantly delayed, and when it was finally brought to fruition in January 1994, violence and political assassinations racked Kigali. On April 5, 1994, ironically one day before Rwandan president Juvénal Habyarimana's assassination, which triggered the genocide, the UN extended UNAMIR's mandate to July 29, 1994. The UN accompanied its extension with a statement expressing its "deep concern" with the worsening security situation in Rwanda.

When the mass killing began on April 6, UNAMIR was in no position to intervene. The mission was understaffed with poorly trained and equipped troops, was in a strictly defensive position, and was not authorized to employ arms to stop the genocide. Although it managed save the lives of several thousand Tutsis and moderate Hutus who fled to its base near Kigali, UNAMIR was largely a

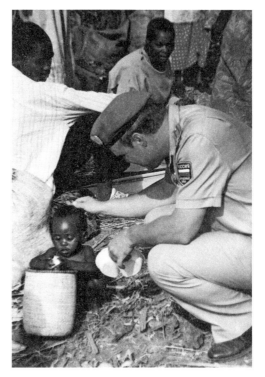

A Russian United Nations (UN) soldier visits with a baby in a Rwandan refugee camp. The UN had sent peace keepers to Rwanda in 1993 to help implement a peace agreement between the Hutu-led government and Tutsi rebels. (Corel)

passive bystander to the genocide. UNAMIR commander, Canadian general Roméo Dallaire, almost immediately asked for an additional 5,000 troops when the killings began, but the UN turned him down. Instead, on April 21, the UN Security Council passed Resolution 912, which dramatically reduced the size of UNAMIR, citing its concern for the mission's personnel. It also instructed Dallaire to help negotiate an immediate ceasefire. Dallaire was flabbergasted by this, and repeatedly asked for more troops, which the United Nations consistently denied.

Finally, on May 17, the United Nations passed Security Council Resolution 918, which would enlarge UNAMIR's presence to 5,500 troops and provide other badly needed military equipment. This, however, took almost six months to implement. Meanwhile, the genocide continued into the summer of 1994, as UNAMIR personnel watched in horror as hundreds of thousands of Rwandans died. Almost no additional UNAMIR troops entered Rwanda until after the Tutsi-led Rwandan Patriotic Army (RPA) had secured most of the country and overthrown the Hutu government. With the gradual insertion of these additional troops, UNAMIR became known as UNAMIR II, which helped administer post-genocide Rwanda. UN peacekeeping troops were also unable to prevent the murders of some 200,000 Hutus at the hands of the RPA.

Dallaire, citing extreme frustration and exhaustion, left his post as UNAMIR commander in August 1994, after the genocidal killing had stopped. Before departing, he lambasted the UN for not doing more to stop the carnage and for taking far too long to approve a troop surge, which he had requested within days of Habyarimana's assassination. UNAMIR II was tasked with stabilizing the Rwandan government, policing the fragile armistice, promoting long-term peace, and, most critically, tending to the monumental humanitarian crisis that followed the genocide. Indeed, by the fall of 1994, at least four million Rwandans were in refugee camps in Rwanda, Zaire (now know as the Democratic Republic of Congo), Tanzania, Uganda, and Burundi.

UNAMIR II operated until March 8, 1996, when the mission was withdrawn upon the request of the Rwandan government, which had by then begun to criticize the mission for its failure to prevent or stop the genocide. Between 1993 and 1996, 40 UN member states provided troops or civilian support personnel to UNAMIR. During that time, 22 soldiers, three military observers, one security officer, and one civilian staffer died while on duty.

Paul G. Pierpaoli Jr.

See also: Arusha Accords; Bystanders; Dallaire, Roméo; Habyarimana, Juvénal; Rwanda; Rwandan Civil War; Rwandan Patriotic Army; Rwandan Patriotic Front; Tutsis

Further Reading

Barnett, Michael. *Eyewitness to a Genocide: The United Nations and Rwanda*. Ithaca, NY: Cornell University Press, 2002.

Dallaire, Roméo. *Shake Hands with the Devil: The Failure of Humanity in Rwanda*. Toronto: Random House, Canada, 2004.

Uwilingiyimana, Agathe

Agathe Uwilingiyimana was Rwanda's first female prime minister and one of the earliest victims of the Rwandan Genocide of 1994. A Hutu, she was born on May 23, 1953, in the village of Nyaruhengeri, some 140 kilometers southeast of the Rwandan capital, Kigali. She was educated at Notre Dame des Citeaux High School, and at the age of 20 qualified as a teacher of humanities. In 1976 her qualifications were extended and she became a teacher of mathematics and chemistry. That same year she married Ignace Barahira, a fellow student from her village, and they settled down to a family life that would eventually produce five children.

In 1983 Uwilingiyimana became a teacher of chemistry at the National University of Rwanda, Butare. She received a bachelor's degree in science in 1985, and taught chemistry for four more years in the Butare area. During this time, she began her public life, first by helping establish a Savings and Credit Cooperative Society for the faculty at Butare, then, having attracted the notice of the central government, through her appointment in 1989 as a senior official in the Ministry of Commerce. In 1992 she joined the Republican and Democratic Movement (French: Mouvement Démocratique Républicain, or MDR), a moderate and multiethnic political party in opposition to President Juvénal Habyarimana's National Revolutionary Movement for Development (French: Mouvement Révolutionnaire National pour le Développement, or MRND). In that same year, Prime Minister Dr. Dismas Nsengiyaremye promoted her to minister of education.

In her capacity as minister of education, Uwilingiyimana abolished the system of ethnic quotas established by the Habyarimana regime, an antiquated measure that favored Hutu education and limited Tutsi schooling. Henceforth, attendance at public schools and scholarships were awarded in accordance with a merit principle and competitive examinations throughout the country. Politically, this was an unwise move. While her action was warranted, it alienated her from the government and Hutu nationalists. In their eyes, she was a Hutu willing to compromise on issues of ethnic supremacy and thus an adversary to be watched.

Following Prime Minister Nsengiyaremye's political downfall in July 1993, Uwilinigiyimana replaced him. At a meeting between Habyarimana and leaders of the other major political parties in the new pluralistic system she was discussed as the perfect "lame-duck" prime minister who could be easily controlled by both the president and the other political parties. She became prime minister at a critical juncture in Rwanda's history, when the Hutu-dominated government of Habyarimana and the Tutsi-dominated rebel force, the Rwandan Patriotic Front (RPF), were attempting a rapprochement. This was a period when it was hoped by many (though certainly not all) that the Arusha Accords—signed on August 4, 1993, between the government, its supporting parties and the RPF—that a multiparty democracy and a pluralistic political culture would be established.

Disgruntled by his removal, former prime minister Nsengiyareme suspended Uwilingiyimana's MDR membership. Habyarimana himself doubted his choice once he saw the discord the promotion had generated, and dismissed her as prime minister less than three weeks after her appointment. Faustin Twagiramungu was tasked with leading the MDR in the new arrangement. A new interim government was to have been set in place on March 25, 1994, at which time Uwilingiyimana would officially step down in favor of Twagiramungu. This was postponed, however, owing to the failure of the RPF to turn up to the swearing-in ceremony, and Uwilingiyimana remained in office in a temporary capacity until the handover ceremony could take place.

Following the shooting down of Habyarimana's plane on April 6, 1994, the genocide began. At this time, Uwilingiyimana became Rwanda's temporary head of state, and the commander of the United Nations forces in the country overseeing the Arusha agreement, General Roméo Dallaire, immediately dispatched Belgian and Ghanaian troops to her home in order to secure her safety and escort her to Radio Rwanda in order to enable her to make a broadcast to the Rwandan people and thus avoid a national crisis. Early the following morning, however, units of Rwanda's Presidential Guard—a corps that had been radicalized by Habyarimana's Hutu nationalists—forced the Belgian soldiers to stand aside and lay down their weapons. Led by Major Bernard Ntuyahaga, the Presidential Guard troops then slaughtered the Belgians and mutilated their bodies. These troops became the first UN casualties, ultimately leading the government of Belgium to abandon the Rwandan mission altogether.

In desperation, Uwilingiyimana and her family, still in their pajamas, fled their house, and sought refuge in the compound of the United Nations (UN) Development Programme. Presidential Guards reached the compound before reinforcements, who were held up by Hutu militia roadblocks, could arrive from Dallaire's headquarters. Uwilingiyimana and her husband, fearing for the lives of their five children, surrendered to the Presidential Guards, and were shot immediately at point-blank range. When Uwilingiyimana's body was found it had been horribly mutilated, left half naked, and with a beer bottle shoved in her vagina. Her five children remained in hiding, were smuggled by a Senegalese UN soldier, Captain Mbaye Diagne into the Hôtel des Mille Collines, and eventually took refuge in Switzerland. Captain Diagne was to lose his own life to RPF shelling several weeks later.

Agathe Uwilingiyimana was succeeded as prime minister of the interim government by an extremist Hutu hardliner, Jean Kambanda. During her prime ministership, she had advocated for an inclusive Rwanda free of ethnic exclusion and hatred. She set a standard to which other women in Africa could aspire, as one of only a very few women in the world to that stage (and the only one in Africa) to have attained the highest reaches of government office. Her life, as much as her death, marks her as a major figure in a troubled time.

Paul R. Bartrop

See also: Dallaire, Roméo; Diagne, Mbaye; Habyarimana, Juvénal; Kambanda, Jean; Mouvement Révolutionnaire National pour le Développement; Rwandan Civil War; Rwandan Patriotic Front; United Nations Assistance Mission for Rwanda

Further Reading

Dallaire, Roméo. *Shake Hands with the Devil: The Failure of Humanity in Rwanda.* Toronto: Random House, Canada, 2004.

Scherrer, P. Christian. *Genocide and Crisis in Central Africa: Conflict Roots, Mass Violence, and Regional War.* Westport, CT: Praeger, 2002.

Wallace, Gretchen Steidle

Gretchen Steidle Wallace is an American humanitarian campaigner dedicated to advancing women's rights and well-being in Rwanda and other countries affected by genocide. Born in 1974 as the daughter of a U.S. Navy admiral, she grew up in a variety of settings around the world. Living in the Philippines for a time as a child, she saw the effect that desperate poverty can have on a community, and has since worked to address the injustices and disparities that poverty can bring. She attended the University of Virginia from which she graduated with a BA in foreign affairs in 1996, and Tuck School of Business at Dartmouth College, where she obtained an MBA in 2001. Between 1996 and 1999, she worked in international project finance for PMD International, Inc., a boutique investment banking firm specializing in infrastructure development in poor countries.

In 2004, Wallace went to South Africa to help with the HIV/AIDS epidemic. Studying the AIDS initiatives of major multinational corporations, she learned of the financial consequences of AIDS with regard to health care costs and lost production. She also began to study the extent to which various companies developed and applied efficient solutions to these problems. She learned that many solutions were in fact flawed, due largely to a poor understanding of health care and the stigma attached to HIV/AIDS. It became apparent that many employees were reluctant to undergo AIDS testing or to seek assistance if they knew they were infected.

During her research, Wallace found that women faced distinct challenges when it came to preventing HIV/AIDs. Culturally, women were not empowered to insist on their partners using condoms. Wallace came to the realization that some form of social initiative was needed to promote the rights of women regarding sexual freedom and HIV/AIDS prevention. She knew that some South African women were already employing enterprising techniques at the grassroots level and that they were determined to address critical issues facing women and girls. She also found that these same organizations were struggling without the requisite training and resources necessary to ensure their success. Wallace decided to dedicate her work to supporting these emerging agents of change and their ideas.

As a result, later the same year Wallace established Global Grassroots, a nonprofit organization supporting conscious social change for women in post-conflict and developing countries, particularly in Africa. Through personal transformation work and social entrepreneurship training, Global Grassroots helps marginalized women and genocide survivors reclaim their lives and discover their value to society through the development of their own ideas for social change. Global Grassroots offers seed funding grants and 12 months of advisory support to launch those projects that advance the well-being and rights of women. Global Grassroots also engages in creative campaigns to raise awareness of critical women's issues globally.

With Global Grassroots established, Wallace saw an enormous amount of work awaiting her. Her first initiative, in 2005, connected her interests with those of her brother, Brian Steidle, who had already been doing significant work in raising awareness around the world about the ongoing genocide in Darfur, Sudan. Steidle and Wallace took their respective campaigns to the refugee camps of eastern Chad, where they worked on issues overlooked by aid organizations, such as establishing a human rights library and providing education about refugee rights, domestic and sexual violence, and female genital mutilation. Wallace also provided on-site training to try to ensure her projects would be sustained in the long term.

Returning to the United States, Wallace began to develop her new social entrepreneurship program but saw a great need to return to Africa in order to work with genocide survivors in Rwanda, where mass rape during the 1994 genocide had led to a huge spread of HIV/AIDS. In 2006, she trained 180 Rwandan women, many of them widows raising several children, and many of them rape victims, in the development of social projects in Kigali.

Dealing with the aftermath of rape is one of the issues for which Global Grassroots soon became best known. In Africa, as elsewhere, mass rape is a common problem, especially in situations of war and civil strife. The promotion of dialogue about rape is an important, although difficult, first step in raising awareness and addressing the issue. Again, knowledge of mass rape was brought home to Wallace through the observations of her brother Brian in Darfur, where the Janjaweed (a militia that operates in Sudan and Chad) raped female genocide survivors, often en masse.

Since 2006, Global Grassroots has trained 250 "change leaders," managing to fund several important locally designed projects serving thousands of vulnerable women and girls. These initiatives deal with issues relating to domestic violence, water access, child rape, prostitution, property rights, HIV/AIDS, discrimination, and illiteracy. Most of these are in post-genocide Rwanda, which has become the main field of operations for Global Grassroots, but projects among Darfur refugees in eastern Chad are also now underway. Global Grassroots is one of the major providers of assistance to female genocide survivors and focuses almost exclusively on the promotion of what Wallace calls "conscious social change" driven by and on behalf of marginalized women in post-conflict Africa.

In early 2007, Global Grassroots and Wallace were also heavily involved in producing an Emmy-nominated documentary film about the Darfur genocide, *The Devil Came on Horseback* (directed by Ricki Stern and Anne Sundberg). Based on Brian Steidle's memoir of the same title (which Wallace co-authored), *The Devil Came on Horseback* tells the story of Steidle's direct encounter with genocide in Darfur.

As a social entrepreneur, Wallace has always believed in inner-driven change, holding that decisions made with the greatest level of awareness will ensure the wisest response and most potent, effective results. This was one of the key motivators behind the establishment of Global Grassroots. Wallace's interests lay in looking for gaps in existing systems and fostering ideas of what to do about them. The greatest measure of success at Global Grassroots is the impact that locally chosen projects can have in transforming communities for the better. There is a focus on training and project design, and each project has built into it social impact goals and evaluation metrics. Monitoring of a project's progress, and the provision of high-engagement advisory support, takes place for a minimum of 12 months after it begins. Global Grassroots assists local project teams in developing their baseline study and working with their target population to assess the issue and their progress over time.

In recognition of her contribution to the betterment of the human condition through management and entrepreneurship strategies, in 2007 Wallace was honored by *World Business* magazine and Shell as one of the top International 35 Women under 35. By the end of the 21st century's first decade, the antigenocide enterprise created by one woman's vision had become an inspiration to communities throughout many parts of Africa, and a model for others to follow.

Paul R. Bartrop

See also: Allen, Susan; Nowrojee, Binaifer; Rape

Further Reading

Cheadle, Don, and John Prendergast. *Not on Our Watch: The Mission to End Genocide in Darfur and Beyond*. New York: Hyperion, 2007.

"Global Grassroots: Conscious Social Change for Women," http://www.globalgrassroots.org.

Steidle, Brian, and Gretchen Steidle Wallace. *The Devil Came on Horseback: Bearing Witness to the Genocide in Darfur*. New York: Public Affairs Books, 2008.

We wish to inform you that tomorrow we will be killed with our families

We wish to inform you that tomorrow we will be killed with our families: Stories from *Rwanda* was a book written by Philip Gourevitch and published by Farrar, Straus and Giroux in 1998 that details the Rwandan Genocide of 1994. Gourevitch is a respected journalist and writer who has long been affiliated with *The New Yorker* magazine and who once edited the *Paris Review*. Gourevitch based *We wish to inform you that tomorrow we will be killed with our families* on his extensive travels in Rwanda after the genocide, during which he interviewed scores of witnesses, survivors, perpetrators in prisons throughout Rwanda, talked to government officials, and gathered documentary materials for his book. Gourevitch's work focuses primarily on stories of the genocide and the aftereffects it has had on survivors and Rwandan society as a whole.

The book's title was taken from a letter, written in April 1994, by several Tutsi Seventh-day Adventist ministers who, during the genocide had taken refuge in an Adventist-run hospital in the Kibuye Prefecture, alongside other besieged Tutsis. In their letter to Adventist pastor Elizaphan Ntakirutimana, the ministers described their plight. The very next day, hundreds of refugees at the hospital were slain by Hutu rebels. In his research on the hospital massacre Gourevitch found that pastor Ntakirutimana had given away the refugees' position and had supported the perpetrators. Ntakirutimana was later convicted of war crimes by the International Criminal Tribunal for Rwanda, largely on the evidence produced in Gourevitch's book.

Gourevitch began writing his book in May 1995 and concluded his writing in April 1998. Over the past two decades, many of his original observations and conclusions have been expanded upon. While his book offers a brief history of events prior to 1994, it is not enough to explain fully how and why the genocide occurred. Readers will have to look elsewhere for that. Nevertheless, the book was awarded several prestigious awards in 1998 and set the stage for future scholarly analysis of the Rwandan Genocide.

Paul G. Pierpaoli Jr.

See also: International Criminal Tribunal for Rwanda; Ntakirutimana, Elizaphan; Rwanda

Further Reading

Gourevitch, Philip. *We wish to inform you that tomorrow we will be killed with our families: Stories from Rwanda.* New York: Picador, 1999.

Lemarchand, René. *The Dynamics of Violence in Central Africa.* Philadelphia: University of Pennsylvania Press, 2009.

Stewart, Rory. "Genocide in Rwanda: Philip Gourevitch's non-fiction classic," *The Guardian* (March 21, 2015). Accessed April 17, 2017: https://www.theguardian.com/books/2015/mar/21/genocide-rwanda-we-wish-to-inform-you-that-tomorrow-philip-gourevitch

Wilkens, Carl

Carl Wilkens is the former head of the Adventist Development and Relief Agency (ADRA) International in Rwanda, and, during the genocide in 1994 was the only American to remain in the country. Born in 1957, in 1978 he first went to Africa as part of a college volunteer program in Transkei, South Africa. He returned to the United States to complete his university undergraduate degree in industrial education, and then returned to Africa with his wife Theresa in 1981. The first settled in Zimbabwe and later moved to Zambia. Returning once more to the United States in 1987, Wilkens undertook an MBA course at the University of Baltimore. In 1990 he and Theresa and their three children moved to Rwanda, where Wilkens became country director of ADRA assisting in building schools and operating health centers around the country.

In the summer of 1993, the Wilkens family was on home leave in the United States, and they returned to Rwanda with high hopes for the country's future. The optimism continued through December 1993 and into January 1994, but things began to sour from then on. By February, there was fighting in Kigali, and Wilkens could feel the growing tension. All of a sudden, Adventist missionaries were being evacuated, and the question of whether to stay or leave began to circulate throughout the community.

At the U.S. embassy, there had previously been meetings with the expatriate community about evacuation in the event of a crisis, and how it would take place. Always in the back of Wilkens's mind, however, was the thought that even if an evacuation occurred, a core group who would stay behind and keep the embassy open. Immediately after the genocide began on April 6, 1994, Wilkens called the embassy, and found that they were already discussing establishing evacuation assembly points. The embassy's Laura Lane was at this time Wilkens's main contact person. When the embassy had the evacuation plans in place, Wilkens was told that the first group was going to be taken over the next few days, driving by road to Burundi. The Adventist American missionaries said they would wait until the Sunday of that first week before they left. Wilkens was in the thick of organizing the details of their evacuation, but he and his wife Theresa had already decided that he would himself stay. Conveying this information to Laura Lane, he invoked the right of a private citizen to choose his own path without the interference of the U.S. government. All Lane could do in the circumstances was to insist that Wilkens sign a statement to the effect that he had refused the help of the U.S. government to evacuate. Theresa and the children were eventually relocated to Nairobi, Kenya, where they managed to stay in touch with Wilkens by radio.

Wilkens chose to stay so as to be able to deliver aid to children in need despite the ongoing violence. His choice to remain would result in preventing the massacre of hundreds of children over the course of the genocide. For example, thanks to Wilkens's help the Gisimba Orphanage managed to secretly act as a safe haven for 400 people threatened by the genocide. When Wilkens arrived at Gisimba he saw up to 50 armed militiamen looking for an opportunity to close in and kill the orphans, but they appeared hesitant owing to Wilkens's presence as a witness. As a deterrent, Wilkens decided to sleep that night at the orphanage. He stayed there until there was some hope for a more prolonged protection for the orphans, and then drove out to try to find the local provincial governor and plead for their salvation. Amazingly, Wilkens made contact with the prime minister of Rwanda's interim extremist Hutu government, Jean Kambanda, and in a brazen act of nerve he simply asked him for his help in saving the orphans. Equally amazingly, Kambanda agreed to give assurances that the militias would be called off and those at the orphanage would be saved. Wilkens decided to move the orphans to a safer location, the Saint Michel Cathedral. Within a few days, he had organized two buses and a military escort to help them through the roadblocks, ensuring their security in this most insecure of situations. He was able to replicate this success in a number of other cases, and save hundreds of people as a result.

The complexity of living through the genocide and trying to be an effective agent of rescue found Wilkens often working at the fringes of compromise. Frequently, he found himself in situations that could have been interpreted as collaboration with the killers—just to save lives. Yet any ally in the process of human salvation was welcome, and sometimes Wilkens even found help among members of the Interahamwe. Personal contacts with the killers enabled him to obtain a free passage through the roadblocks, for example, providing him with the means to travel to places where he knew vulnerable people were hiding—people he managed in one way or another to smuggle to safety.

Not all of his contacts were with the killers. Before the onset of the genocide, Wilkens had known the Frenchman Philippe Gaillard of the International Committee of the Red Cross, and during the crisis the two met at every opportunity. For Wilkens, this connection served as an important emotional support, as here he found someone equally committed to staying in Rwanda and helping as many people as he could. Another avenue of support came from ADRA director David Syme, who actually went into Rwanda as the genocide was in progress, and spent several days with Wilkens in his home. Syme provided valuable items that enabled Wilkens to continue his work: hand-held radios, license plates bearing the ADRA mark that could be affixed to Wikens's vehicles, a UN flak jacket, and other supplies.

After the victory of the Rwandan Patriotic Front in July 1994, Wilkens remained in Rwanda to assist with the distribution of water, food, and equipment for the hardpressed inhabitants of Kigali. Reunited with his family, they returned to the United States for a period, but in 1995 they were back in Rwanda where they stayed for another 18 months, working for the Adventist Church in reconstruction activities.

Since 1996, the Wilkens family has been living in the United States. Carl Wilkens became an Adventist pastor in Oregon, and began speaking about his Rwanda experiences. As an initiative to confront the forces that can bring about a genocidal situation, and foster an appropriate response to genocide today, Wilkens has created *World outside My Shoes*, a nonprofit educational and professional development organization committed to inspiring and equipping people to enter the world of "The Other." He invites people to "Take a moment to try and put yourself in the shoes of the family members and friends who had loved ones taken from them," and to learn from Rwanda in order to equip and inspire oneself to enter the world of the "Other." The "Other," he shows, "may be under our own roof or on the other side of the globe." Through *World outside My Shoes*, Wilkens seeks to inspire and equip people to stand up against genocide, racism, and intolerance, through the promotion of values such as integrity, dignity, community, simplicity, and what he calls "respondability." The motto of *World outside My Shoes* is as straightforward as it is challenging: "One person really can ignite change when they discover the power of choice!"

Carl Wilkens's story, which he published as a short memoir (*I'm Not Leaving*) in 2011, is a constant reminder of the profound connection between history and the moral choices everyone faces each day. Staying in Rwanda even as others fled, Wilkens decided to remain at his post and help wherever he could. Today, he tours the United States to speak to students, teachers, parents, policymakers, and communities about his experience in Rwanda. When telling the story of how the genocide unfolded he prefers to focus on the courage and resilience he witnessed when people faced impossible choices relating to life and death, and what this can mean for everyone as they confront the challenges of the 21st century.

Paul R. Bartrop

See also: Gaillard, Philippe; Interahamwe; Kambanda, Jean; Lane, Laura; Rwandan Patriotic Front

Further Reading

Bodnarchuk, Kari. *Rwanda: A Country Torn Apart*. Minneapolis, MN: Lerner Publishing Group, 1998.

Wilkens, Carl. *I'm Not Leaving*. United States: C. Wilkens, 2011.

Primary Documents

I. Arusha Peace Accords

Representatives from the Rwandan Patriotic Front (RPF)—a rebel group composed largely of exiled Rwandan Tutsis residing in Uganda—and the government of Rwanda— led by President Juvénal Habyarimana and his Hutu-extremist party—met in Arusha, Tanzania on August 4, 1993, and signed the Arusha Peace Accords (also known as the Arusha Peace Agreement, or the Arusha negotiations). The Accords were the final product of a lengthy attempt by both parties involved, as well as the Organization of African Unity (a coalition of the African nations belonging to the United Nations), France, and the United States, to bring an end to the three-year-long Rwandan Civil War.

The Accords, cited here in part, contained 10 articles that called upon the Hutu-led Rwandan government to include Tutsis, create a transitional government, integrate the RPF and Rwandan state military, and resolve refugee resettlement issues. Ultimately, the Accords failed to secure peace in Rwanda and ultimately became fodder for Hutu-extremist propaganda during the genocide.

Peace Agreement Between the Government of the Republic of Rwanda and the Rwandese Patriotic Front

The Government of the Republic of Rwanda on the one hand, and the Rwandese Patriotic Front on the other;

Firmly resolved to find a political negotiated solution to the war situation confronting the Rwandese people since 1st October, 1990;

Considering and appreciating the efforts deployed by the countries of the Sub-region with a view to helping the Rwandese people to recover peace;

Referring to the numerous high-level meetings held . . . . aimed first and foremost at establishing a ceasefire so as to enable the two parties to look for a solution to the war through direct negotiations . . . .

Calling the International Community to witness;

Hereby agree on the following provisions.

Article 1

The war between the Government of the Republic of Rwanda and the Rwandese Patriotic Front is hereby brought to an end.

Article 2

The following documents are an integral part of the present Peace Agreement concluded between the Government of the Republic of Rwanda and the Rwandese Patriotic Front:

I. The N'SELE Ceasefire Agreement of 29th March, 1991, between the Government of the Republic of Rwanda and the Patriotic Front, as amended in GBADOLITE on 16th September, 1991 and at ARUSHA on 12th July, 1992;

II. The Protocol of Agreement between the Government of the Republic of Rwanda and the Rwandese Patriotic Front on the Rule of Law, signed at ARUSHA on 18th September, 1992;

III. The Protocols of Agreement between the Government of the Republic of Rwanda and the Rwandese Patriotic Front on Power-Sharing within the Framework of a Broad-Based Transitional Government, signed at ARUSHA respectively on 30th October, 1992 and on 9th January, 1993;

IV. The Protocols of Agreement between the Government of the Republic of Rwanda and the Rwandese Patriotic Front on the Repatriation of Refugees and the Resettlement of Displaced Persons, signed at Arusha on 9th June, 1993;

V. The Protocols of Agreement between the Government of the Republic of Rwanda and the Rwandese Patriotic Front on the integration of Armed Forces of the two parties, signed at ARUSHA on, 3rd August, 1993;

VI. The Protocols of Agreement between the Government of the Republic of Rwanda and the Rwandese Patriotic Front on Miscellaneous Issues and Final Provisions signed at Arusha on 3rd August, 1993 . . .

Article 3

The two parties also agree that the Constitution of nineteenth June, 1991 and the Arusha Peace Agreement shall constitute indissolubly the Fundamental Law that shall government the Country during the Transition period . . .

Article 4

In case of conflict between the provisions of the Fundamental Law and those of other Laws and Regulations, the provisions of the Fundamental Law shall prevail.

Article 5

The Government of the Republic of Rwanda and the Rwandese Patriotic Front undertake to make every possible effort to ensure that the present Peace Agreement is respected and implemented.

They further undertake to spare no effort to promote National Unity and Reconciliation.

Article 6

The two parties agree on the appointment of Mr. TWAGIRAMUNGU Faustin as Prime Minister of the Broad-Based Transitional Government, in accordance with Articles 6 and 51 of the Protocol of Agreement between the Government of the Republic of Rwanda and the Rwandese Patriotic Front on Power-Sharing within the framework of a Broad-Based Transitional Government.

Article 7

The Transitional Institutions shall be set up within thirty seven (37) days following the signing of the Peace Agreement.

Article 8

The current Government shall remain in Office until the Broad-Based Transitional

Government is established. The maintenance of that Government does not mean that it can encroach on the mandate of Broad-Based Transitional Government being established.

The current Government shall, in no case, take decisions which may detrimental to the implementation of the Broad-Based Transitional programme.

Article 9

The "Conseil National de Développement" (CND) shall remain in Office until the Transitional National Assembly is established. However, as from the date of signing the Peace Agreement, it shall not enact laws.

Article 10

The present Peace Agreement is signed by the President of the Republic of Rwanda and the Chairman of the Rwandese Patriotic Front . . .

Article 11

The present Peace Agreement shall come into force upon its signing by the parties.

Done at Arusha, on the 4th day of the month of August, 1993 both in French and English languages, the original text being in French.

Source: "Peace Agreement between the Government of the Republic of Rwanda and the Rwandese Patriotic Front," The United Nations (4 August 1993), accessed 26 July 2017, available from http://peacemaker.un.org/rwanda-peaceagreementrpf93.

2. Chapter VI and VII of United Nations Charter for Peace Keeping Operations

United Nations peacekeeping operations have been an important tool for the United Nations (UN) since the Security Council authorized the deployment of UN military observers to the Middle East in 1948. Since then, the UN has employed thousands of UN police and civilians from more than 120 countries in over 70 peacekeeping operations, most of which were deployed since 1988. Depending on the mandate, peacekeeping operations can serve many purposes such as, support and organization of elections, promotion of human rights, disarmament, protection of civilians, facilitate political processes, and help to restore the rule of law.

Peacekeeping operations in Rwanda took the form of the United Nations Assistance Mission for Rwanda (UNAMIR). The Security Council passed resolution 872 in October 1993 (six months prior to the genocide) and in so doing created UNAMIR to monitor the agreements (the Arusha Accords) made between the Hutu-led Rwandan government and Tutsi-led Rwandan Patriotic Front (RPF). UNAMIR troops were to operate under Chapter VI of the UN Charter for Peace Keeping Operations. As cited in full below, the Chapter VI mandate is based on the consensus of both parties in a dispute and can only use force for self-defense. While this mandate suited UNAMIR's operations prior to the genocide, following the onset of the killing in April 1994 the Chapter VI mandate prohibited UNAMIR forces from taking up arms against the génocidaires *to protect victims.*

While General Roméo Dallaire, the head of UNAMIR, would have preferred to operate under a Chapter VII mandate—which would have allowed his soldiers to fight the perpetrators—he was unable to persuade his UN counterparts in New York to act decisively. It was not until June 22, 1994 that the Security Council passed Resolution 929 which authorized a Chapter VII mandate.

Both Chapter VI and Chapter VII mandates reproduced here in full elucidate the complicated nature of UN peacekeeping operations and the legal processes by which troops are deployed. Depending on the charter passed, peacekeeping troops are directed to either use or not use force.

Chapter VI: Pacific Settlement of Disputes

Article 33

The parties to any dispute, the continuance of which is likely to endanger the maintenance of international peace and security, shall, first of all, seek a solution by negotiation, enquiry, mediation, conciliation, arbitration, judicial settlement, resort to regional agencies or arrangements, or other peaceful means of their own choice. The Security Council shall, when it deems necessary, call upon the parties to settle their dispute by such means.

Article 34

The Security Council may investigate any dispute, or any situation which might lead to international friction or give rise to a dispute, in order to determine whether the continuance of the dispute or situation is likely to endanger the maintenance of international peace and security.

Article 35

Any Member of the United Nations may bring any dispute, or any situation of the nature referred to in Article 34, to the attention of the Security Council or of the General Assembly.

A state which is not a Member of the United Nations may bring to the attention of the Security Council or of the General Assembly any dispute to which it is a party if it accepts in advance, for the purposes of the dispute, the obligations of pacific settlement provided in the present Charter.

The proceedings of the General Assembly in respect of matters brought to its attention under this Article will be subject to the provisions of Articles 11 and 12.

Article 36

The Security Council may, at any stage of a dispute of the nature referred to in Article 33 or of a situation of like nature, recommend appropriate procedures or methods of adjustment.

The Security Council should take into consideration any procedures for the settlement of the dispute which have already been adopted by the parties.

In making recommendations under this Article the Security Council should also take into consideration that legal disputes should as a general rule be referred by the parties to the International Court of Justice in accordance with the provisions of the Statute of the Court.

Article 37

Should the parties to a dispute of the nature referred to in Article 33 fail to settle it by the means indicated in that Article, they shall refer it to the Security Council.

If the Security Council deems that the continuance of the dispute is in fact likely to endanger the maintenance of international peace and security, it shall decide whether to take action under Article 36 or to recommend such terms of settlement as it may consider appropriate.

Article 38

Without prejudice to the provisions of Articles 33 to 37, the Security Council may, if all the parties to any dispute so request, make recommendations to the parties with a view to a pacific settlement of the dispute.

Chapter VII: Action with Respect to Threats to the Peace, Breaches of the Peace, and Acts of Aggression

Article 39

The Security Council shall determine the existence of any threat to the peace, breach of the peace, or act of aggression and shall make recommendations, or decide what measures shall be taken in accordance with Articles 41 and 42, to maintain or restore international peace and security.

Article 40

In order to prevent an aggravation of the situation, the Security Council may, before making the recommendations or deciding upon the measures provided for in Article 39, call upon the parties concerned to comply with such provisional measures as it deems necessary or desirable. Such provisional measures shall be without prejudice to the rights, claims, or position of the parties concerned. The Security Council shall duly take account of failure to comply with such provisional measures.

Article 41

The Security Council may decide what measures not involving the use of armed force are to be employed to give effect to its decisions, and it may call upon the Members of the United Nations to apply such measures. These may include complete or partial interruption of economic relations and of rail, sea, air, postal, telegraphic, radio, and other means of communication, and the severance of diplomatic relations.

Article 42

Should the Security Council consider that measures provided for in Article 41 would be inadequate or have proved to be inadequate, it may take such action by air, sea, or land forces as may be necessary to maintain or restore international peace and security. Such action may include demonstrations, blockade, and other operations by air, sea, or land forces of Members of the United Nations.

Article 43

1. All Members of the United Nations, in order to contribute to the maintenance of international peace and security, undertake to make available to the Security Council, on its call and in accordance with a special agreement or agreements, armed forces, assistance, and facilities, including rights of passage, necessary for the purpose of maintaining international peace and security.

2. Such agreement or agreements shall govern the numbers and types of forces, their degree of readiness and general location, and the nature of the facilities and assistance to be provided.

3. The agreement or agreements shall be negotiated as soon as possible on the initiative of the Security Council. They shall be concluded between the Security Council and Members or between the Security Council and groups of Members and shall be subject to ratification by the signatory states in accordance with their respective constitutional processes.

Article 44

When the Security Council has decided to use force it shall, before calling upon a Member not represented on it to provide armed forces in fulfillment of the obligations assumed under Article 43, invite that Member, if the Member so desires, to participate in the decisions of the Security Council concerning the employment of contingents of that Member's armed forces.

Article 45

In order to enable the United Nations to take urgent military measures, Members shall hold immediately available national air-force contingents for combined international enforcement action. The strength and degree of readiness of these contingents and plans for their combined action shall be determined within the limits laid down in the special agreement or agreements referred to in Article 43, by the Security Council with the assistance of the Military Staff Committee.

Article 46

Plans for the application of armed force shall be made by the Security Council with the assistance of the Military Staff Committee.

Article 47

1. There shall be established a Military Staff Committee to advise and assist the Security Council on all questions relating to the Security Council's military requirements for the maintenance of international peace and security, the employment and command of forces placed at its disposal, the regulation of armaments, and possible disarmament.
2. The Military Staff Committee shall consist of the Chiefs of Staff of the permanent members of the Security Council or their representatives. Any Member of the United Nations not permanently represented on the Committee shall be invited by the Committee to be associated with it when the efficient discharge of the Committee's responsibilities requires the participation of that Member in its work.
3. The Military Staff Committee shall be responsible under the Security Council for the strategic direction of any armed forces placed at the disposal of the Security Council. Questions relating to the command of such forces shall be worked out subsequently.
4. The Military Staff Committee, with the authorization of the Security Council and after consultation with appropriate regional agencies, may establish regional sub-committees.

Article 48

5. The action required to carry out the decisions of the Security Council for the maintenance of international peace and security shall be taken by all the Members of the United Nations or by some of them, as the Security Council may determine.
6. Such decisions shall be carried out by the Members of the United Nations directly and through their action in the appropriate international agencies of which they are members.

Article 49

The Members of the United Nations shall join in affording mutual assistance in carrying out the measures decided upon by the Security Council.

Article 50

If preventive or enforcement measures against any state are taken by the Security Council, any other state, whether a Member of the United Nations or not, which finds itself confronted with special economic problems arising from the carrying out of those measures shall have the right to consult the Security Council with regard to a solution of those problems.

Article 51

Nothing in the present Charter shall impair the inherent right of individual or collective self-defence if an armed attack occurs against a Member of the United Nations, until the Security Council has taken measures necessary to maintain international peace and security. Measures taken by Members in the exercise of this right of self-defence [ibid.] shall be immediately reported to the Security Council and shall not in any way affect the authority and responsibility of the Security Council under the present Charter to take at any time such action as it deems necessary in order to maintain or restore international peace and security.

Source: "Charter of the United Nations," United Nations (Accessed 15 May 2017), http://www.un.org/en/charter-united-nations/index.html.

3. Convention on the Prevention and Punishment of the Crime of Genocide

Having read of the slaughter of Armenians in the Ottoman Empire during World War I and narrowly escaping the mass murder of Jews and other groups in Europe during the Holocaust, Raphael Lemkin (a lawyer, Polish-Jew, and Holocaust survivor) coined the word "genocide." The term comes from the words "genos" (Greek for "family, tribe, or race") and "-cide" (Latin for "killing"). For years, he petitioned the United Nations to create the Genocide Convention to create the legal language necessary to prosecute perpetrators of genocide. The Convention on the Prevention and Punishment of the Crime

of Genocide was approved by the General Assembly of the United Nations on December 9, 1948. The Nuremberg Trials held in Germany after the Holocaust accused the Nazi perpetrators on trial of having committed genocide, however, the term genocide did not appear in the court's rulings. The first conviction for genocide occurred on September 2, 1998 when the ICTR judged Jean-Paul Akayesu guilty of having committed genocide in Rwanda. The passage of time between the 1948 Convention on the Prevention and Punishment of the Crime of Genocide and its application in the Akayesu trial 50 years later illustrates the progress the international community has made with regard to holding perpetrators of genocide responsible for their crimes.

The Contracting Parties,

Having considered the declaration made by the General Assembly of the United Nations in its resolution 96 (I) dated 11 December 1946 that genocide is a crime under international law, contrary to the spirit and aims of the United Nations and condemned by the civilized world,

Recognizing that at all periods of history genocide has inflicted great losses on humanity, and

Being convinced that, in order to liberate mankind from such an odious scourge, international co-operation is required,

Hereby agree as hereinafter provided:

Article I

The Contracting Parties confirm that genocide, whether committed in time of peace or in time of war, is a crime under international law which they undertake to prevent and to punish.

Article II

In the present Convention, genocide means any of the following acts committed with intent to destroy, in whole or in part, a national, ethnical, racial or religious group, as such:

(a) Killing members of the group;
(b) Causing serious bodily or mental harm to members of the group;
(c) Deliberately inflicting on the group conditions of life calculated to bring about its physical destruction in whole or in part;
(d) Imposing measures intended to prevent births within the group;
(e) Forcibly transferring children of the group to another group.

Article III

The following acts shall be punishable:

(a) Genocide;
(b) Conspiracy to commit genocide;
(c) Direct and public incitement to commit genocide;
(d) Attempt to commit genocide;
(e) Complicity in genocide.

Article IV

Persons committing genocide or any of the other acts enumerated in article III shall be punished, whether they are constitutionally responsible rulers, public officials or private individuals.

Article V

The Contracting Parties undertake to enact, in accordance with their respective Constitutions, the necessary legislation to give effect to the provisions of the present Convention, and, in particular, to provide effective penalties for persons guilty of genocide or any of the other acts enumerated in article III.

Article VI

Persons charged with genocide or any of the other acts enumerated in article III shall be tried by a competent tribunal of the State in the territory of which the act was committed, or by such international penal tribunal as may have jurisdiction with respect to those Contracting Parties which shall have accepted its jurisdiction.

Article VII

Genocide and the other acts enumerated in article III shall not be considered as political crimes for the purpose of extradition.

The Contracting Parties pledge themselves in such cases to grant extradition in accordance with their laws and treaties in force.

Article VIII

Any Contracting Party may call upon the competent organs of the United Nations to take such action under the Charter of the United Nations as they consider appropriate for the prevention and suppression of acts of genocide or any of the other acts enumerated in article III.

Article IX

Disputes between the Contracting Parties relating to the interpretation, application or fulfilment of the present Convention, including those relating to the responsibility of a State for genocide or for any of the other acts enumerated in article III, shall be submitted to the International Court of Justice at the request of any of the parties to the dispute.

Article X

The present Convention, of which the Chinese, English, French, Russian and Spanish texts are equally authentic, shall bear the date of 9 December 1948.

Article XI

The present Convention shall be open until 31 December 1949 for signature on behalf of any Member of the United Nations and of any non-member State to which an invitation to sign has been addressed by the General Assembly.

The present Convention shall be ratified, and the instruments of ratification shall be deposited with the Secretary-General of the United Nations.

After 1 January 1950, the present Convention may be acceded to on behalf of any Member of the United Nations and of any non-member State which has received an invitation as aforesaid.

Instruments of accession shall be deposited with the Secretary-General of the United Nations.

Article XII

Any Contracting Party may at any time, by notification addressed to the Secretary-General of the United Nations, extend the application of the present Convention to all or any of the territories for the conduct of whose foreign relations that Contracting Party is responsible.

Article XIII

On the day when the first twenty instruments of ratification or accession have been deposited, the Secretary-General shall draw up a procès-verbal and transmit a copy thereof to each Member of the United Nations and to each of the non-member States contemplated in article XI.

The present Convention shall come into force on the ninetieth day following the date of deposit of the twentieth instrument of ratification or accession.

Any ratification or accession effected subsequent to the latter date shall become effective on the ninetieth day following the deposit of the instrument of ratification or accession.

Article XIV

The present Convention shall remain in effect for a period of ten years as from the date of its coming into force.

It shall thereafter remain in force for successive periods of five years for such Contracting Parties as have not denounced it at least six months before the expiration of the current period.

Denunciation shall be effected by a written notification addressed to the Secretary-General of the United Nations.

Article XV

If, as a result of denunciations, the number of Parties to the present Convention should become less than sixteen, the Convention shall cease to be in force as from the date on which the last of these denunciations shall become effective.

Article XVI

A request for the revision of the present Convention may be made at any time by any Contracting Party by means of a notification in writing addressed to the Secretary-General.

The General Assembly shall decide upon the steps, if any, to be taken in respect of such request.

Article XVII

The Secretary-General of the United Nations shall notify all Members of the United Nations and the non-member States contemplated in article XI of the following:

(a) Signatures, ratifications and accessions received in accordance with article XI;

(f) Notifications received in accordance with article XII;
(g) The date upon which the present Convention comes into force in accordance with article XIII;
(h) Denunciations received in accordance with article XIV;
(i) The abrogation of the Convention in accordance with article XV;
(j) Notifications received in accordance with article XVI.

Article XVIII

The original of the present Convention shall be deposited in the archives of the United Nations.

A certified copy of the Convention shall be transmitted to each Member of the United Nations and to each of the non-member States contemplated in article XI.

Article XIX

The present Convention shall be registered by the Secretary-General of the United Nations on the date of its coming into force.

Source: United Nations Security Council, A/RES/260 (9 December 1948), available from http://www.un.org/ga/search/view_doc.asp?symbol=a/res/260%28III%29.

---

4. Death of Rwandan and Burundian Presidents in Plane Crash Outside Kigali

On the night of April 6, 1994, around 8 p.m. in Rwanda, unknown assailants shot down a plane carrying Rwandan president Juvénal Habyarimana and Burundian president Cyprien Ntaryamira as the leaders were returning to Rwanda from a meeting in Tanzania. Along with the plane's French aircrew and the presidents' senior aides, Habyarimana and Ntaryamira died in the crash. Widely acknowledged as the event that sparked the genocidal killing in Rwanda, the assassination of Habyarimana set in motion a chain of events calculated to destabilize the Rwandan government. In less than 24 hours, Presidential Guards had gone house-to-house and murdered prominent Rwandan leaders who had opposed Habyarimana, including the interim prime minister, Agathe Uwilingiyimana. The document that follows comes from a fax sent by Deputy Assistant Secretary Prudent Bushnell (the acting head of the U.S. State Department's Africa bureau) to Secretary of State Warren Christopher, informing him that the presidents had been killed and predicting that violence would soon follow. Bushnell also voices concern about the Rwandan government's refusal to allow United Nations troops access to the crash site.

April 6, 1994
To: The Secretary
Through: P—Mr. Tarnoff
From: AF—Prudence Bushnell
Subject: Death of Rwandan and Burundi Presidents in Place Crash Outside Kigali

Summary

A plane crash near Kigali has apparently resulted in the death of the Presidents of Rwanda and Burundi. There are unconfirmed reports that the plane was shot down by unknown attackers. The UN special representative in Rwanda has organized a meeting between the military and Western diplomats at the U.S. Ambassador's residence at 9:00 AM tomorrow to discuss the transition.

Discussion

According to reports from Kigali, the Rwandan military has reported that the private plane of Rwandan President Juvénal Habyarimana was shot down prior to landing at the Kigali airport sometime prior to 9:00 PM local time (3:00 PM Washington time) today. Military officials have reported that both President Habyarimana and Burundi President Cyprien Ntaryamira were killed in the subsequent crash. The two Presidents were returning from a one-day regional summit in Dar Es Salaam on the Burundi crisis; the Burundi President had reportedly asked to fly back via Kigali with President Habyarimana.

The UN peacekeeping operation, UNAMIR, travelled to the crash site, but the Rwandan military prevent the UN from inspecting the site. The Rwandan military also reportedly disarmed the UN (Belgian) peacekeepers stationed at the airport.

The Rwandan Ambassador to Washington confirmed President Habyarimana's death in a phone conversation with AF/C, but there has been no official announcement of the death over Rwandan radio as yet. In Burundi, the President of the National Assembly (next in line of presidential succession) appeared on television at 11:30 PM local time, along with the UN special envoy to Burundi Ahmedou Abdallah, the Minister of Defense and the Army Chief of Staff. The Assembly President confirmed that the Burundi President was travelling with the Rwandan President and that there had been some problem with the plan. There was no confirmation of any deaths.

The succession question will be difficult in Rwanda. The Arusha accords provide that the President of the Transition National Assembly assumes the presidency on an interim basis. However, the Assembly has not yet been installed. An armed forces delegation told UN special envoy Booh Booh that the military intended to take over power temporarily. Booh Booh encouraged the delegation to work with existing authorities and within the framework of the Arusha accords; however, the military was very resistant to working with the current (interim) Prime Minister, Agathe Uwilingiyamana. The delegation is to meet with Booh Booh and Western diplomats at the U.S. Ambassador's residence tomorrow morning at 9:00 AM. The military assured Booh Booh that forces will remain in the barracks.

Both our Embassies in Kigali and Bujumbura report that the cities are relatively calm, although an increase in sporadic gunfire and grenade explosions was noted in Kigali. Both posts have instructed the American community to stay at home until further notice. All Americans are believed safe. There are no Peace Corps volunteers in either country.

If, as it appears, both Presidents have been killed, there is a strong likelihood that widespread violence could break out in either or both countries, particularly if it is confirmed that the plane was shot down. Our strategy is to appeal for calm in both countries, both through public statements and in other ways. We are also in close contact with the French and Belgians. The White House has requested that we prepare a presidential statement expressing condolences and urging calm.

Source: National Security Archive, U.S. Department of State, Bureau of African Affairs, Memorandum from Deputy Assistant Secretary of State Prudence Bushnell to The Secretary through Under Secretary for Political Affairs Peter Tarnoff, "Death of Rwandan and Burundian Presidents in Plane Crash Outside Kigali", April 6, 1994, at http://nsarchive.gwu.edu/NSAEBB/NSAEBB53/rw040694.pdf

5. Excerpt from the Defense Attaché in Kigali, October 24, 1990

The Rwandan Civil War between the Hutu-led Rwandan government and the Rwandan Patriotic Front (RPF), a rebel group composed predominately of exiled Rwandan Tutsis, erupted when RPF forces attacked Rwanda on October 1, 1990. The following document demonstrates how the French government assessed and responded to the civil war.

On October 24, 1990, George Martres, French ambassador to Rwanda, and Colonel René Galinié, the French defense attaché, sent the following dispatch to the French Parliamentary Commission. On the same date this document was sent, France sent 314 French troops to Rwanda. According to France, the troops who arrived as part of Operation Noroit were dispatched to protect French civilians in Rwanda. This document helps elucidate the shape of violence that predated the 1994 Rwandan Genocide. According to this document, as early as the start of the civil war in 1990, French officials noted that a large-scale and targeted annihilation of Tutsis by Hutus was possible.

4.A.4. Assessment of the political situation

. . .

The situation is dominated by the combination of two destabilizing behaviors.

- The media and the diplomatic representatives of Rwanda's neighbors, have become, voluntarily or involuntarily, spokespeople for the invaders, or have even supported them openly.

  This has just been attested to by the way in which R.F.I. became aware this morning of the mission of the United Nations Commission on Human Rights, led by Mr. FEDER, a French national. In fact, while he obviously issued a certificate of good conduct to the Rwandan government, which strives to maintain the best conditions of treatment for suspects, this station retained only the negative items of his report.

- The Belgians continue to maintain confusion, brandishing the threat of a rapid pull-out of their citizens and their parachutists if President HABYARIMANA does not agree to exorbitant and unjustified capitulations.

These two behaviors are of a nature to discourage the governmental authorities ready to make important concessions. They cannot accept, in particular, abandoning some territory, in order to establish a cease-fire, to the profit of the Tutsi invaders eager to retake the power they lost in 1959. They can even less admit that these invaders, disregarding Rwandan reality, will probably reestablish the Honni regime of the first Tutsi kingdom, once installed in the northeast. This reestablishment, explicit or disguised, would result (in all likelihood) in the physical elimination of Tutsis in the interior of the country, 500,000 to 700,000 people, by the 7,000,000 Hutus.

The foreseeable intervention of the Zairian president will not necessarily solve the situation. Indeed, it is not impossible that Zaire, before the Belgian departure and in particular the hesitation of the O.A.U. [Organization of African Unity], sustained by MUSEVENI, could decide, for reasons of local prestige, to intervene once again, taking RWANDA under its supervision, without really having the means to do so. Current meetings within the C.E.P.G.L. (Economic

Community of the Countries of the Great Lakes: ZAIRE—BURUNDI—RWANDA) seem to demonstrate the probable manifestation of an intervention. It could materialize through the return of Zairian troops.

SIGNED: COL. GALINIE./.
G. MARTRES.

Source: The National Security Archive, 4.A.4 Excerpt from the defense attaché in Kigali's message, October 24, 1990, Assessment of the political situation (Accessed April 17, 2017) http://nsarchive.gwu.edu/NSAEBB/NSAEBB458/docs/DOCUMENT%201%20-%20ENGLISH.pdf

6. First Lady Hillary Rodham Clinton Radio Address to the People of Rwanda on March 25, 1997

On March 25, 1997, Mrs. Hillary Rodham Clinton, First Lady of the United States of America, visited the International Criminal Tribunal in Arusha, Tanzania. Mrs. Clinton, a lawyer by training, met with the prosecutor Justice Louise Arbour, president of the Tribunal Judge Laïty Kama, the new registrar of the Tribunal Mr. Agwu Ukiwe Okali, and the judge of the two Trial Chambers. While in Tanzania, she also attended a seminar organized by the Office of the Prosecutor that focused on acts of sexual violence in Rwanda and the former Yugoslavia. After addressing the seminar participants, Mrs. Clinton made a radio address to the people of Rwanda via Internews*, a broadcasting facility set up at the Tribunal in Tanzania. Her expression of support on behalf of the U.S. government expressed a level of commitment to humanitarian assistance in Rwanda that was absent during the genocide.*

Hello, my name is Hillary Rodham Clinton. My daughter Chelsea and I have come from America to visit many of the nations of Africa. I am sorry that we were not able to come to Rwanda, but I wanted to speak to you on behalf of the people of the United States and my husband, the President.

We know that you, the people of Rwanda, have endured suffering that is almost impossible to imagine. A terrible civil war. Unspeakable violence. Calculated attacks on women and children. Millions of families, pushed from their homes, forced into life as refugees.

We also know what you have accomplished in the last two years. Standing together, the people of Rwanda are turning back the forces of hatred and division. You are laying a strong foundation for peace in your country. By rebuilding your schools, your medical clinics, your roads, you are giving your people—especially your children—the opportunity to make the most of their God-given promise.

We in the United States are committed to lending a helping hand. One way we are doing that is through our support for the International War Crimes Tribunal in Arusha. In fact, that's where I am today. We all know that there have been problems with the Tribunal. But from what I have seen and heard this morning, let me assure you that the United Nations is making progress in reforming the Tribunal so that it does what it was supposed to do: Bring to justice the criminals who inflicted so much suffering on your country—particularly those who subjected women and children to sexual abuse and violence as a tactic of war.

We are also committed to supporting your efforts to strengthen democracy and expand the circle of economic opportunity in your country. Last year, the United States Agency for International Development helped millions of Rwandans return home from refugee camps around the region. This year, USAID is working with you to make that home more stable and secure. We are working with your lawyers and judges as they rebuild your courts and your legal system. We are helping to construct houses for those who lost theirs in the war. We are joining with communities to fight disease, like HIV and AIDS.

We will continue to stand with you in partnership as you do the hardest, most important work of all: healing your wounds, learning to live together, repairing your country.

In many ways, that is the lesson of this Holy Week, where we celebrate the passage from loss and despair to hope and redemption. May the lessons of Good Friday and Easter last you through the year and beyond, as old hatreds yield to the promise of new and peaceful beginnings.

Source: National Archives College Park, Records of the First Lady's Office (Clinton Administration), 1993–2001, HRC Speeches 12/96-3/97: [3/24 War Crimes Tribunal, Arusha, Tanzania], 40489386.

7. Gaspard Gahigi RTLM Broadcast of May 17–18, 1994

Gaspard Gahigi, the editor-in-chief of the extemist-Hutu Rwandan radio station Radio-Télévision Libre des Mille Collines (RTLM), used radio to spread anti-Tutsi propaganda, incite genocide, and justify mass murder. The following broadcast, quoted in part here, ran from May 17 to 18, 1994, approximately one month after the genocide began. This source exemplifies the violent messaging produced by the RTLM.

In this newscast, Gahigi uses a microphone to amplify his hatred and mistrust of Tutsis and to encourage Hutus to take up

arms against Tutsis and those who support them. Gahigi employs racial slurs, such as referring to Tutsis as Inyenzi *(a Kinyarwanda word meaning "cockroach") and a Banyarwanda myth on the origins of Hutus and Tutsis within the region in order to degrade the victims. Here he also debases the United Nations humanitarian mission to Rwanda led by the Canadian Roméo Dallaire, the Canadian government, and Caucasian leaders from the Europe and North America as an impediment to Hutus. He also blames the presidents of the United States (President Bill Clinton) and Uganda (President Yoweri Museveni) for colluding with Tutsis at the expense of Hutu lives.*

About a thousand persons cross the border daily, fleeing from the Inyenzi [a Kinyarwanda word meaning 'cockroach'], those Inyenzi who continue to target intellectuals, as well as those they accuse of being Interahamwe. They actually check identity cards and do not spare any Hutu. An estimated one thousand people flee daily across the border into Tanzania.

. . . Another item of information today is the announcement of the creation a United Nations Human Rights Commission which is due to meet in Geneva (Switzerland) on 24 and 25 May, that is next week. The aim is to choose a representative to investigate human rights violations in Rwanda, described as massacres.

The Commission of Inquiry was proposed by Canada, a country you know very well, since Dallaire is a national of that country . . . Canada wants to come and look into what is happening in Rwanda. We, shall no longer be conciliatory regarding what is happening in Rwanda; we shall fight relentlessly. Today, certain white people, especially Americans, Canadians and Belgians, believe that the villain in this country is the machete and cudgel-wielding Hutu, whereas the Hutu is only trying to ensure the Hutus are not annihilated by the descendants of Gatutsi.

For a long time, the white man has harbored the erroneous conception that the Tutsis are the good people. In the white man's view, the Tutsi is more handsome and more intelligent—even though the criteria for beauty have not been defined. Thus, as we were saying, it is the Tutsis, Museveni's group, that the Americans are assisting. Er . . . As I indicated earlier, the aid brought in by the Americans is for the Inkotanyi to go and study in their country, in places like Arkansas, Bill Clinton's home state. Such aid has now increased from $150,000 to $400,000 US dollars. Besides, they have disbursed $50,000, or rather $50,000,000 US dollars to Uganda to fund the demobilization of soldiers of Museveni's army. Nevertheless, there has been no reduction in the army strength, as most of the Ugandan troops concerned have been sent here. Part of the money was used to purchase arms, which is the reason we are living under the threat of annihilation.

And yet it is we, the Hutus, who are armed with machetes and cudgels in order to prevent our annihilation, who are considered wrong. We are the villains. Let them go ahead their enquiries, but not in our country, so long as they are not aimed at identifying the persons who assassinated His Excellency, the President of the Republic, those who caused us so much pain and plunged us into darkness. They will not catch us napping again. Even in Somalia they suffered defeat.

Moreover according to the media, this information comes from abroad; the number of murders in the United States has substantially risen since 1992, especially those committed with firearms, to such an extent that the United States now among high-risk countries, the countries considered dangerous.

Moreover, Parliament or similar institutions, that is to say the senate and congress met recently and voted an anti- corruption law. It is surprising to note that people accepted the bribe generation! The United States has a little known phenomenon called lobbying. This is donate money to leading candidates in return for favors once they are elected. This is a clever tactic. It is now used, for instance, by Museveni through certain wily individuals who defend his interest before American members of congress. Then the congressmen bring pressure to bear on the President of the United States. That is how this kind of decision is arrived at . . . Uganda uses American crooks and they tell the President to "kill the Hutus."

However, the American President will be astonished when he hears the truth about the Hutus in Rwanda and realizes that they represent 90 percent of the population, I believe he will be astonished. This is how we often fall victim to things we do not know. There is the story of a Hutu who went to serve a nobleman with Tutsi companions. One day he was asked blow on the fire during a vigil. But when he bent down to do so, the others exchanged signs as if to say: "Look at this fool who is blowing on the fire." Later, he spoke, but he realized that nobody was paying attention to what he had to say. Once he understood what had happened he said to himself: "I am in a tight spot." Therefore, we too must understand what we are victims of. The Tutsi groups have sold us with the assistance of American crooks. We do hope that when the President of the United States realizes that they want to exterminate the Hutus, he will stop listening to them.

I would like to conclude the news by congratulating all those we find on the roads we pass every morning returning from night duty at the roadblocks and patrols . . .

Source: Genocide Archive of Rwanda, RTLM 009, Translation of RTLM broadcast 17–18 May 1994 submitted to ICTR, accessed 11 July 2017, http://genocidearchiverwanda.org.rw/index.php?title=Unictr_Rtlm_0009_Eng&gsearch=.

8. The Genocide Fax and the United Nations' Reply

General Roméo Dallaire, the commander of the United Nations Assistance Mission for Rwanda (UNAMIR), sent a cable to the United Nations (UN) headquarters in New York dated January 11, 1994, to warn his superiors of the escalating violence and potential for genocide in Rwanda. In what has come to be known as the "genocide fax," Dallaire explained that he had been in contact with a senior official in the Interahamwe—the armed militia of the National Revolutionary Movement for Development (French: Mouvement Révolutionnaire National pour le Développement, or MRND)—from whom he learned of a plot to annihilate Tutsis. The MRND was the political party created by Rwandan president Juvénal Habyarimana. While Dallaire wanted to act on the information, as a condition of the Chapter VI mandate of the UN Charter for Peacekeeping Operations he was operating under, he was restricted from using force except for self-defense. Less than 100 days later, the Interahamwe led the mass murder of Tutsis and moderate Hutus in the Rwandan Genocide.

Documents released by the U.S. government, including evidence used during trials at the International Criminal Tribunal for Rwanda, have elucidated that the unnamed informant Dallaire spoke with was Jean-Pierre Turatsinze. He was responsible for distributing arms to the Interahamwe and had come under scrutiny from his superiors for allegedly selling some of the weapons to another rebel group in Burundi. He came from mixed Tutsi and Hutu heritage, which may explain why he contacted Dallaire and attempted to undercut the MRND, Interahamwe, and genocide to come.

The UN received Dallaire's January 11 fax and in it the intelligence shared by Turatsinze on the evening of January 10 owing to the seven-hour time difference between New York and Rwanda. The UN quickly drafted a reply that directed Dallaire not to raid the suspected arms caches and instead to consult with the Rwandan government. The response, cited in full here, was signed by Kofi Annan who at that time was Head of Peacekeeping Operations (Annan would become the seventh secretary-general of the United Nations in 1997) and drafted by his assistant Iqbal Riza.

The so-called Genocide Fax and the UN's reply have come to be viewed as the essential failure of the UN to make decisive and timely decisions to save Rwandan lives. In 2004, while testifying at the International Criminal Tribunal for Rwanda (the international court created by the United Nations Security Council in Resolution 955), Dallaire admitted that he did not have the intel needed at the time he sent the fax to confirm Turatsinze's statements. With that said, Dallaire was put in an impossible situation and lacked the resources and UN mandate to do his job the way he would have preferred. This statement is captured in the final line of his fax in which the Canadian national writes, "Peux ce que veux: Allons," meaning "Where there is a will, there is a way: Let's go."

Date: 11 January 1994
To: Baril\DPKO\UNations   New York
From: Dallaire\UNAMIR\Kigali

1. Force commander put in contact with informant by very very important government politician. Informant is a top level trainer in the cadre of Interhamwe-armed militia of MRND.

2. He informed us he was in charge of last Saturday's demonstrations which aims where to target deputies of opposition parties coming to ceremonies and Belgian soldiers. They hoped to provoke the RPF BN to engage (being fired upon) the demonstrators and provoke a civil war. Deputies were to be assassinated upon entry or exit from parliament. Belgian troops were to be provoked and if Belgians [ibid.] soldiers resorted to force a number of them were to be killed and thus guarantee Belgian withdrawal from Rwanda.

3. Informant confirmed 48 RGF Para CDO and a few members of the gendarmerie participated in demonstrations in plain clothes. Also at least one minister of the MRND and the sous-prefect of Kigali were in the demonstration. RGF and Interhamwe provided radio communications.

4. Informant is a former security member of the president. He also stated he is pad RF150,000 per month by the MRND party to train Interhamwe. Direct link is to chief of staff RGF and president of the MRND for financial and material support.

5. Interhamwe has trained 1700 men in RGF military camps outside the capital. The 1700 are scattered in groups of 40 throughout Kigali. Since UNAMIR deployed he has trained 300 personnel in three week training sessions at RGF camps. Training focus was discipline, weapons, explosives, close combat and tactics.

6. Principal aim of Interhamwe in the past was to protect Kigali from RPF. Since UNAMIR mandate he has been ordered to register all Tutsi in Kigali. He suspects it is for their extermination. Example he gave was that in 20 minutes his personnel could kill up to 1000 Tutsis.

7. Informant states he disagrees with anti-Tuti extermination. He supports opposition to RPF but cannot support killing of innocent persons. He also stated that he believes the president does not have full control over all elements of his old party\faction.

8. Informant is prepared to provide location of major weapons cache with at least 135 weapons. He already has distributed 110 weapons including 35 with ammunition and can give us details of their location. Types of weapons are G3 and AK47 provided by RGF. He was ready to go to the arms cache tonight—If we gave him the following guarantee: He requests that he and his family (his wife and four children) be placed under our protection.

9. It is our intention to take action within the next 36 hours with a possible H Hr of Wednesday at dawn (local). Informant states that hostilities may commence again if political deadlock ends. Violence could take place day of the ceremonies or the day after. Therefore Wednesday will give greatest chance of success and also be most timely to provide significant input to on-going political negotiations.

10. It is recommended that the informant be granted protection and evacuated out of

Rwanda. This HQ does not have previous UN experience in such matters and urgently requests guidance. No contact has as yet been made to any embassy in order to inquire if they are prepared to protect him for a period of time by granting diplomatic immunity in their embassy in Kigali before moving him and his family out of the country.

11. Force commander will be meeting with the very important political person tomorrow morning in order to ensure that this individual is conscious of all parameters of his involvement. Force commander does have certain reservations on the suddenness of the change of heart of the informant to come clean with this information. Recce [ibid.] of armed cache and detailed planning of radio to go on late tomorrow. Possibility of a trap not fully excluded, as this may be a set-up against the very very important political person. Force commander to inform SRSG first thing in morning to ensure his support.

12. Peux ce que veux: Allons-Y.

Source: The National Security Archive, The George Washington University, National Security Archive Electronic Briefing Book No. 452 (Posted January 9, 2014), nsarchive.gwu.edu/NSAEBB /NSAEBB53/rw011194.pdf

From: Annan, UNations, New York
Date: 11 January 1994
Subject: Contacts with Informant

1. We have carefully reviewed the situation in light of your MIR-79. We cannot agree to the operation contemplated in paragraph 7 of your cable, as it clearly goes beyond the mandate entrusted to UNAMIR under resolution 872 (1993).

2. However, on the assumption that you are convinced that the information provided by the informant is absolutely reliable, we request you to undertake the initiatives described in the following paragraphs.

3. SRSG and FC should request urgent meetings with [President Juvénal Habyarimana]. At that meeting you should inform the President that you have received apparently reliable information concerning the activities of the Interhamwe militia which represent a clear threat to the peace process. You should inform him that these activities include the training and deployment of subversive groups in Kigali as well as the storage and distribution of weapons to these groups.

4. You should inform him that these activities constitute a clear violation of the previsions of the Arusha peace agreement and of the Kigali weapons-secure area. You should assume that he is <u>not</u> aware of these activities, but insist that he must immediately look into the situation, take the necessary action to ensure that these subversive activities are immediately discontinued and inform you within 48 hours of the measures taken in this regard, including the recovery of the arms which have been distributed.

5. You should advise the President that, if any violence occurs in Kigali, you would have to immediately bring to the attention of the Security Council the information you have received on the activities of the militia, undertake investigations to determine who is responsible and make appropriate recommendations to the Security Council.

6. Before meeting with the President you should inform the Ambassadors of Belgium, France and the United States of your intentions and suggest to them that they may wish to consider making a similar demarche.

7. For security considerations, we leave it to your discretion to decide whether to inform the PM(D) of your plans before or after the meeting with the President. When you meet with the PM(D), you should explain to him the limits of your mandate. You should also assure him that, while the mandate of UNAMIR does not allow you to extend protection to the informant, his identity and your contacts with him will not be repeat [ibid.] not be revealed.

8. If you have major problems with the guidance provided above, you may consult us further. We wish to stress, however, that the overriding consideration is the need to avoid entering into a course of action that might lead to the use of force and unanticipated repercussions. Regards.

Source: The National Security Archive, The George Washington University, National Security Archive Electronic Briefing Book No. 452 (Posted January 9, 2014), https://www.documentcloud.org/documents/816324-19940111i-un-cable-from-annan.html.

---

9. Hutu Ten Commandments

In the sixth issue of Kangura *published in December 1990, the widely circulating extremist Hutu newspaper published the so-called Hutu 10 Commandments. Cited here, this list of directives lays out instructions for how Hutus can support each other by disenfranchising and discriminating against Tutsis. The document makes reference to the* Rwandan Civil War between the Hutu-led government and the Tutsi-led Rwandan Patriotic Front that began in October 1990, and the 1959 to 1961 Rwandan Revolution in which Hutus rebelled against the Tutsi-led government and colonists for greater autonomy in Rwandan society. In the post-genocide trial of Hassan Negeze, the chief editor of *Kangura, the prosecution team for the International Criminal Tribunal for Rwanda cited this essay, among others, as a key example of Negeze's role in inciting the Rwandan Genocide.*

---

1. Every Hutu male should know that Tutsi women, wherever they may be, are working in the pay of their Tutsi ethnic group. Consequently, shall be deemed a traitor:
   - Any Hutu male who marries a Tutsi woman;
   - Any Hutu male who keeps a Tutsi concubine;
   - Any Hutu male who makes a Tutsi woman his secretary or protégée.

2. Every Hutu male must know that our Hutu daughters are more dignified and conscientious in their role of woman, wife or mother. Are they not pretty, good secretaries and more honest!

3. Hutu women, be vigilant and bring your husbands, brothers and sons back to their senses.

4. Every Hutu male must know that all Tutsi are dishonest in their business dealings. They are only seeking their ethnic supremacy. "Time will tell." Shall be considered a traitor, any Hutu male:
   - who enters into a business partnership with Tutsis;
   - who invests his money or State money in a Tutsi company;

- who lends to, or borrows from, a Tutsi;
- who grants business favors to Tutsis (granting of important licenses, bank loans, building plots, public tenders . . .) is a traitor.

5. Strategic positions in the political, administrative, economic, military and security domain should, to a large extent, be entrusted to Hutus.

6. In the education sector (pupils, students, teachers) must be in the majority Hutu.

7. The Rwandan Armed Forces should be exclusively Hutu. That is the lesson we learned from the October 1990 war. No soldier must marry a Tutsi woman.

8. Hutus must cease having pity for the Tutsi.

9.
- The Hutu male, wherever he may be, must be united, in solidarity and be concerned about the fate of their Hutu brothers;
- The Hutu at home and abroad must constantly seek friends and allies for the Hutu Cause, beginning with our Bantu brothers;
- They must constantly counteract Tutsi propaganda;
- The Hutu must be firm and vigilant towards their common Tutsi enemy.

10. The 1959 social revolution, the 1961 referendum and the Hutu ideology must be taught to Hutus at all levels. Every Hutu must propagate the present ideology widely. Any Hutu who persecutes his Hutu brother for having read, disseminated and taught this ideology shall be deemed a traitor.

Source: *Kangura*, No. 6 (December 1990), page 8, accessed 13 June 2017, available from https:// repositories.lib.utexas.edu/bitstream/handle/2152 /9315/unictr_kangura_006a.pdf.

10. UN Report of the Independent Inquiry into the Actions of the United Nations During the 1994 Genocide in Rwanda

United Nations (UN) secretary-general Kofi A. Annan sent a letter to members of the UN Security Council on March 18, 1999 requesting that it set up an independent inquiry into the actions of the UN during the Rwandan Genocide in 1994. The Security Council confirmed Annan's request in a letter dated March 26, 1999 and the 82-page report was released on December 15, 1999. The independent inquiry committee began its work on June 17, 1999 and was mandated to report on the response of the UN to the genocide in Rwanda, covering the period October 1993 to July 1994. The Inquiry was also tasked with drawing relevant conclusions and identifying lessons to be learned from the tragedy.

The following excerpt from the "UN Report of the Independent Inquiry into the Actions of the United Nations During the 1994 Genocide in Rwanda" comes from the "Introduction" and openly acknowledges the UN's failure to prevent and stop the genocide.

"Approximately 800,000 people were killed during the 1994 genocide in Rwanda. The systematic slaughter of men, women and children which took place over the course of about 100 days between April and July of 1994 will forever be remembered as one of the most abhorrent events of the twentieth century. Rwandans killed Rwandans, brutally decimating the Tutsi population of the country, but also targeting [ibid.] moderate Hutus. Appalling atrocities were committed, by militia and the armed forces, but also by civilians against other civilians.

The international community did not prevent the genocide, nor did it stop the killing once the genocide had begun. This failure has left deep wounds within Rwandan society, and in the relationship between Rwanda and the international community, in particular the United Nations. These are wounds which need to be healed, for the sake of the people of Rwanda and for the sake of the United Nations. Establishing the truth is necessary for Rwanda, for the United Nations and also for all those, wherever they may live, who are at risk of becoming victims of genocide in the future.

In seeking to establish the truth about the role of the United Nations during the genocide, the Independent Inquiry hopes to contribute to building renewed trust between Rwanda and the United Nations, to help efforts of reconciliation among the people of Rwanda, and to contribute to preventing similar tragedies from occurring ever again. The Inquiry has analysed [ibid.] the role of the various actors and organs of the United Nations system. Each part of that system, in particular the Secretary-General, the Secretariat, the Security Council and the Member States of the organization [ibid.], must assume and acknowledge their respective parts of the responsibility for the failure of the international community in Rwanda. Acknowledgement of responsibility must also be accompanied by a will for change: a commitment to ensure that catastrophes such as the genocide in Rwanda never occur anywhere in the future.

The failure by the United Nations to prevent, and subsequently, to stop the genocide in Rwanda was a failure by the United Nations system as a whole. The fundamental failure was the lack of resources and political commitment devoted to developments in Rwanda and to the United Nations presence there. There was a persistent lack of political will by Member States to act, or to act with enough assertiveness. This lack of political will affected the response by the Secretariat and decision-making by the Security Council, but was also evident in the recurrent difficulties to get the necessary troops for the United Nations Assistance Mission for Rwanda (UNAMIR). Finally, although UNAMIR suffered from a chronic lack of resources and political priority, it must also be said that serious mistakes were made with those resources which were at the disposal of the United Nations."

Source: United Nations, Council on Foreign Relations, *UN Report of the Independent Inquiry into the Actions of the United Nations During the 1994 Genocide in Rwanda*, S/1999/1257 (15 December 1999), available from www.un.org/Docs /journal/asp/ws.asp?m=S/1999/1257.

II. Journalist Kantano Habimana, RTLM Broadcast of May 28, 1994

Kantano Habimana worked as a radio presenter on Radio-Télévision Libre des Mille Collines (RTLM), the radio station that spread propaganda, incited violence, and helped direct the Rwandan Genocide in 1994. In the broadcast cited in part here, Habimana uses racial slurs and deception to justify and encourage the mass slaughter of Tutsis and Hutus who did not support the killings. He often uses the word "Inkotanyi," which is the nickname given to the Rwandan Patriotic Front (RPF), the force that fought against the génocidaire. *By demonizing the resistance, Habimana attempts to enrage ordinary Hutus and provoke them to join in the killing.*

Listeners of R.T.L.M. continue standing firm against Inkotanyi, in this war based on terrorism, self- admiration, malice and lies. To fight in this war is to stand firm and if someone wants to use malice to you, tell him that his intention is clearer than a day.

If they throw a bomb say that no one must be afraid of a thunder while he is under the sky. Then Inkotanyi will get disappointed, sit down and accept negotiations . . .

I don't understand whether those grand-children, our Tutsi brothers who fled in the 1950s want to show us that where they lived they learnt only to destroy and not to construct. It is like saying that if one fails to take something, one destroys. This reminds me of a similar case of a woman who, in the bible, told the King Salmon to share the child into two parts.

R.P.F. seems to say that since it can't take Kigali, better destroy it and then return to where it was. If then these Tutsi brothers want to show us that they only know how to destroy, there are not our brothers. They should stay where they went because they are good for nothing. We must fight against these destroyers, dare-devils. Then when time comes, we will capture and ask them why they have destroyed our town and made it look like Kampala. They throw bombs anywhere, they have destroyed houses no matter whom they belong to. Actually no one can know the intention of Inkotanyi.

The interesting news is that on Mont Kigali, normally the route for people fleeing from the town, I haven't seen a lot of fugitive people. It is not good to flee. Stay in your town, our soldiers are vigilant. They are everywhere with guns and enough bullets. Stand firm on barriers; imitate our army and control Inkotanyi to know where they come from and their destination.

. . . Let's fight without fear because we are sure of the victory. You people of Kigali let's fight together against R.P.F., don't flee. Let's fight against Inkotanyi no matter how many

years the war can take provided we kill them all.

. . . . If you are a cockroach you must be killed, you cannot change anything, if you are Inkotanyi you cannot change anything. No one can say that he has captured a cock-roach and the latter gave him money, as a price for his life, this is cannot be accepted. If someone has a false identity card, if he is Inkotanyi, a known accomplice of R.P.F. don't accept anything in exchange, he must be killed. People who oblige you to write that you have a loan of 150000 for them and that it should be given back today, this is cheating. It is a pity . . .

Inkotanyi are brave and we too have to be like them. They can give a machine to a crip-ple, put him somewhere and tell him to stay there promising to bring him food. They ask him to continue shooting to disturb us. We have no choice; We have to stand firm as Inkotanyi do. It is not understandable to see that a crippling Inkotanyi or the one suffer-ing from AIDS can spend one month on a machine gun and we fail to stop them.

Yesterday I have tried to look at them through the binoculars. Some were running at RWANTEXICO with their heavy weap-ons. I was at Kimisagara. They too had bin-oculars I didn't know that they were looking at me. They tried to shoot at me but I ran and escaped. I don't see why those sons of bitches, can continue being there. Why should they continue being there while we see them? People were puzzled to see that people of Nyamirambo, Gikondo have fled to Gisenyi where they are doing nothing while we who live at Muhima, Nyaru-genge, Karambo see, insult and fight against Inkotanyi. Why should we flee from Inkot-anyi? What are they? They have guns; we too have got them; they have machetes and we have them, they have small hoes and we have them; they bleed and we bleed.

They are human beings. You have seen all those dirty young men who were at C.N.D. (The house of the National Counsel for Development).

We have strength and arms, why then should these people chase us from our country? We must fight against them. If they insult us we have to respond; if they shoot at us, we must shoot at them and if they beat us we must beat them until we show them that we are angry, that they can't defeat us and make them understand that they made a mistake. They are dull, Arusha had given them a lot of things but they will not get any. We can no longer call them brothers. This is how things are . . . [*inaudible*] We have to fight until we defeat them. Those who are fleeing will regret. It is said that you refuse to die for your country and die like a dog. We must combat those dare-devils, who use doping; who spend their time running, crying and thinking that that is the way they can take the power, the country, by inspiring fear to ignorant coward Hutus.

This is not possible, we have to refuse this image of an ignorant coward Hutu who runs away without any reason. We have to stop these things because they dishonor us. To see someone coming with a Kalashnikov with five bullets and who runs away after when bullets are over. We have to stop this . . .

But meanwhile, they have diffused the dreams of Kanyarengwe and Kagame alias Kagome (Nickname he give him to mean 'wicked') that they have taken the half of the country and they need people to live there. This is also like a dream. To say that you have taken the half of the country and that you want people to live there. The people you chased from their properties; people you ill-treated, I don't know whom they want to talk about. In addition Kagame and Kanyarengwe, the latter who wants to be president of Rwanda, ignore that Rwanda is one country;

the one accepted by the International Community. We don't have the Rwanda for Kanyarengwe and Kagome and the Rwanda for Théodore Sindikubwabo and Kambanda Jean. So, it is clear that this is like a dream of Inkotanyi. Actually Kigali the capital is in the hands of its people: the Rwandan army and all Rwandans who love their country, no other people. The cockroaches are running there in our cassava plantation, where they are digging out bananas, eat and make beer from bananas they didn't plant, there far at Gatsata, where they use heavy guns on Bumbogo hill in Gikomero commune and there far at Kanombe but there they can't enter the military camp where they are set a trap for so that they can die all.

They are also at the airport. But Unamir soldiers are asking them what they are doing there since the Rwandan government has given the airport to Unamir, U.N. and there are no Rwandan soldiers. Due to their self-admiration, they continue running on the airport. Let them do. But the town of Kigali, in its entirety, belongs to its people.

In a short time we will have a turn at Kacyiru, Kanombe, Gatenga, I am from Kimisagara, Cyahafi. You will hear voices of people who are on barriers and don't pay attention to the propagators of rumors that Hutus have fled appealing to Tutsis to come and rule. This has been diffused by journalists of Radio France Internationale, who serve as Inkotanyi 's tools. The wish of these white men is that the preferred race, by God, must rule Rwanda. It is like saying that the race of God has won in Kigali town. They tell lies to the international community so that it can continue assisting them. But I think that people will get used and don't pay attention to such a policy or to the war which leans on lie without power.

In fact, we are reassuring our listeners. We tell them that the town of Kigali is in the hands of its owners that is the Rwandan army. In all corners, we don't see any Inkotanyi and it is understandable, Normally to take the town is to come and open the banks, go to the office of the president, to invite people to march in the center town. It is to show truly that you have taken the town; you take the post office, all important places and important things in town are known; all the places are under the Rwandan army's control. I don't from where French people get the idea that Inkotanyi will take the town. They will die before they realize their dreams.

Source: Genocide Archive of Rwanda, RTLM 0011, Translation of RTLM broadcast from 28/5/1994 submitted to ICTR, accessed 9 July 2017, http://genocidearchiverwanda.org.rw/index.php ?title=Unictr_Rtlm_0011_Eng&gsearch=.

12. Judgement of Judge Mohamed Shahabuddeen on Ferdinand Nahimana, Jean-Bosco Barayagwiza, and Hassan Ngeze in the Appeals Chamber of the International Criminal Tribunal for Rwanda, 28 November 2007

The following excerpt comes from The International Criminal Tribunal for Rwanda (ICTR) Appeal Chamber judgment (November 28, 2007) concerning Ferdinand Nahimana, Jean-Bosco Barayagwiza, and Hassan Ngeze in the so-called Media Case. The United Nations established the ICTR after the Rwandan Genocide to try the leaders of the Rwandan Genocide. In the Media Trial, the court examined the activities of Nahimana and Barayagwiza with regards to the Radio-Télévision Libre des Mille Collines (RTLM)—the radio station that broadcast propaganda, incited mass violence, and helped direct the killings during the

genocide—as well as Ngeze's responsibility for the genocide as the editor-in-chief of the Kangura newspaper. The court found all three guilty of conspiracy to commit genocide, genocide, and crimes against humanity.

The accused appealed their sentences and convictions. Ultimately the Judge Mohamed Shahabuddeen of the ICTR reduced their sentences: Nahimana's life sentence was replaced with 30 years imprisonment; the court reduced Barayagwiza's 35-year imprisonment to 32 years; and Ngeze's sentence was changed from life imprisonment to a sentence of 35 years. The document that follows comes from the summary conclusion of Judge Shahabuddeen and elucidates the complicated nature of trying the perpetrators of the Rwandan genocide.

73. The case is apt to be portrayed as a titanic struggle between the right to freedom of expression and abuse of that right. That can be said, but only subject to this: No margin of delicate appreciation is involved. The case is one of simple criminality. The appellants knew what they were doing and why they were doing it. They were consciously, deliberately and determinedly using the media to perpetrate direct and public incitement to commit genocide. The concept of guilt by association is a useful analytical tool, but, with respect, it can also be a battering ram; in my opinion, there is no room for its employment here. It was the acts of the appellants which led to the deeds which were done: a casual nexus between the two was manifest. The appellants were among the originators and architects of the genocide: that they worked patiently towards that end does not reduce their responsibility. The evidence reasonably supported the finding by the Trial Chamber that—

Kangura and RTLM explicitly and repeatedly, in fact relentlessly, targeted the Tutsi population for destruction. Demonizing the Tutsi as having inherently evil qualities, equating the ethnic group with 'the enemy' and portraying its women as seductive enemy agents, the media called from the *extermination* of the Tutsi ethnic group as a response to the political threat that they associated with Tutsi ethnicity.

74. In light of that and other similar findings, the Trial Chamber correctly noted that the 'present case squarely addresses the role of the media in the genocide that took place in Rwanda in 199d'. In its view, the 'case raises important principles concerning the role of the media, which have not been addressed at the level of international criminal justice since Nuremberg. The power of the media to create and destroy fundamental human values comes with great responsibility. Those who control such media are accountable for its consequences'. I agree.

75. For the foregoing reasons, I would maintain the judgement of the Trial Chamber save on three points. First, I agree with the Appeals Chamber in reversing the convictions of Mr. Ngeze as far as they relate to his acts in Gisenyi; this is due to the findings of the Appeals Chamber as to the credibility of a prosecution witness, there being in particular a question as to whether he recanted his testimony after the trial. Second, I agree with the Appeals Chamber that Mr. Barayagwiza cannot be held liable for all the acts committed by any CDR members, and accordingly support the reversal of his convictions pursuant to article 6(3) insofar as they relate to his superior responsibility over CDR militias and *Impuzamugambi*. Third, I agree with the Appeals Chamber in reversing a conviction in case where two

convictions for the same conduct have been made under both paragraphs 1 and 3 of article 6 of the Statue, only a conviction under one paragraph being allowed.

76. These variations do not disable me from recognizing that the case was a long and complicated one. The Trial Judgement has been the subject of many comments—all useful and interesting, if occasionally unsparing. For myself, I am mindful of the danger of thinking differently from respected fellow-members of the bench. I am sensible to the force of the opposing arguments, and appreciate the wisdom of being wary of a 'doctrinal disposition to come out differently'. These weighty considerations oblige me to regret that, on the record, I see no course open to me but to dissent in part.

[Signed]

Mohamed Shahabuddeen
Judge

Signed 22 November 2007 at The Hague, the Netherlands and rendered 28 November 2007 at Arusha, Tanzania.

Source: International Criminal Tribunal for Rwanda, Ferdinand Nahimana, Jean-Bosco Barayagwiza, and Hassan Ngeze (appellants) v. The Prosecutor (respondent), Case No. ICTR-99-52-A, Judgement of 28 November 2007, available from http://www.un.org/en/preventgenocide/rwanda/pdf/NAHIMANA%20ET%20AL%20-%20APPEALS%20JUDGEMENT.pdf.

---

13. Pre-Meeting Briefing Notes for President Clinton in Anticipation of a Meeting with Rwandan vice president Paul Kagame in 1996

The following meeting notes, created by a White House staffer prior to President Bill

Clinton's encounter with then Vice President Paul Kagame of Rwanda in 1996, demonstrate the challenges facing post-genocide Rwanda and the eagerness of the United States to funnel money into the rebuilding of Rwanda.

The relationship between President Clinton and Rwanda is one fraught with controversy. When the genocide began in April 1994, Clinton failed to lead the United States to take actions to stop the genocide. It was not until hundreds of thousands of victims had been annihilated that he even referred to the ongoing slaughter as genocide. While the United States, as well as the international community at large, abandoned Rwandan, Kagame led the Rwandan Patriotic Front that ultimately defeated the génocidaires. Years later when reflecting upon U.S. policy during the genocide, both to the press and in his memoir, he called his failure to intervene in Rwanda one of the biggest regrets of his presidency.

Since the genocide, Clinton and Kagame have formed a close friendship and the U.S. government, as well as the former U.S. president's organization, the Clinton Foundation, have funneled millions of dollars into Rwanda. As a result, the Clinton Foundation has been criticized by some as funding Paul Kagame's government despite his allegedly despotic policies. Others celebrate the substantial foreign aid from governments like the United States and nonprofit organizations like the Clinton Foundation, and view it has having played an essential role in creating the necessary infrastructure (such as schools, hospitals, etc.) to rebuild after the genocide.

MEETING WITH RWANDAN VICE PRESIDENT PAUL KAGAME

CONTEXT OF MEETING

Vice President, Minister of Defense and pre-eminent Rwanda politician Paul Kagame, a Tutsi and member of the (mainly Tutsi) RPF has been in office since the then guerrilla RPA took Kigali in July, 1994. Kagame is one of the "59ers" who grew up as a refugee in Uganda and served in Museveni's army. He led the RPA to victory, but ceded the top spot to President Pasteur Bizimungu, a moderate Hutu.

Kagame can be expected to seek further development aid and diplomatic/political support from the USG. He has indicated an interest in obtaining non-lethal military equipment from DOD stocks. Vice President Kagame will have met with Undersecretary of State Tim Wirth and Assistant Secretary of State George Moose on August 6, and Defense Secretary Perry on August 7.

The RPF-led coalition government has brought a large measure of stability to the country, while also encountering several formidable problems since taking power. The judicial system and administrative state were decimated in 1994. There are over 75,000 prisoners in Rwandan jails 'in horrific conditions, most arrested since Kagame took office. Members of Congress, NGOs and the international community are concerned about this problem, and the GOR' s apparent lack of: response to it. There are delays in putting a new law in place to handle this huge case load. There are 1.7 million Rwandan refugees, most of them in eastern Zaire and some of them armed. Most of the refugees receive international assistance and are under the control of the government and militia responsible for the genocide. Armed attacks back into Rwanda from this population have increased. Rwandan troops have committed atrocities since Kagame took office. There is a sense that guerrillas linked to the former genocidist regime now launch attacks in western Rwanda, as well as assassinations throughout the country, at will. This fuels the RPF's feeling of insecurity, which in turn makes it unwilling to release prisoners.

The USG has supported the current I government. We have given over $750 million in emergency and humanitarian aid to the subregion (much more than development aid for Rwanda, a sore point with Kagame); AID has given substantial sums in development aid, DOD has provided humanitarian assistance and IMET training; various agencies have contributed money and personnel to efforts to ready the International Tribunal and Rwandan court system to try those suspected of crimes against humanity, including genocide. We have also supported the Rwandan government at the UN, including support for lifting the arms embargo against Rwanda. European governments believe that the USG is especially credible with the GOR.

OBJECTIVES
o To assure Vice President Kagame that the USG supports the Government of Rwanda and its goals of repatriation, reconciliation, reconstruction and bringing those guilty of genocide to justice.
o To reaffirm to the President that we are very interested in seeing a successful voluntary repatriation of Rwanda refugees, and note that a key step towards this goal would be reducing the prison population so that refugees feel less of a threat of arrest and imprisonment. The genocide bill currently before Rwanda's Parliament is a good first step.
o To impress upon the Vice President the US interest in working with Rwanda to end arms flows to Burundi and press,

with the regional leadership, for talks between the Burundi government and Hutu insurgents.

TALKING POINTS
o We wish to reaffirm our support for. your government's objectives. The situation in Rwanda has not been easy. Despite the very difficult problems! you have had to face, you have brought a measure of stability to your country, and we wish to continue to work with you.
o We feel that the only long-term solution for Rwanda will be a power-sharing arrangement in which all non-genocidist elements of Rwanda can participate. It must be up to Rwandans to develop this arrangement, since no amount of outside assistance can replace consensus among the Rwandan people. This may be your government's biggest challenge.
o The continued presence of 1.7 million Rwandan refugees in Zaire and Tanzania is destabilizing and untenable. It is neither the Rwandan government's nor the international community's interest to continue with the status quo. It is critical that there be an expeditious and successful voluntary repatriation of Rwandan refugees in Zaire. The USG is discussing with the international community relocation of camps away from the border and resulting closure of those that have been most problematic, and taking steps to encourage voluntary repatriation. Rwanda - would have serious responsibilities if such a strategy is adopted, including being prepared to receive large numbers of returnees and moving the Petit Barriere camp deeper into Rwanda.
o At the same time, we are deeply concerned by the actions taken several weeks ago by Burundi authorities in

expelling thousands of Rwandans from refugee camps against their will. We were equally disturbed by reports that this action, which contavenes [ibid.] Burundi's obligations under the Refugee Convention and established international practice, may have enjoyed the support of your government.

o In order to encourage voluntary repatriation, it is essential that conditions be created inside Rwanda which will encourage refugees to return. There has been progress, but it is particularly important that the prison population be reduced significantly, that there be security for those who repatriate to their homes, and that abuses at the hands of security forces be minimized. This is of grave concern to us all.

o The large numbers of prisoners in Rwanda, and their conditions, are being used by the extremist Hutus to make refugees fear for their safety upon return. The same is true of reports of killings of military-age Hutu men and other civilians.

o We share your concern that the Rwanda Tribunal has not moved as quickly as we all would like. We hope your government will cooperate to the fullest extent with the Tribunal, including by providing access to witnesses and documents. It is in all of our interest to see perpetrators brought to justice.

o We were pleased that your government ceased its participation in the recent forced participation of Rwandan refugees from Burundi. Ignoring internationally accepted humanitarian principles not only leads to further regional instability, but also undermines the credibility of the GOR's policy of welcoming refugees home in safety and dignity.

Your visit comes in the wake of the Buyoya coup and the Arusha II summit of regional leaders, including Rwanda, that called for extensive sanctions as a "shock therapy" for the Bujumbura regime. We would be very interested in your views. As sanctions come into force, we will count very much on your government's key role in enforcing them.

If Asked:

o Military Equipment: We will consider requests for acquisition of non-lethal US military equipment by Rwanda on a case-by-case basis. However, we note that our concern about prisons, especially on Capitol Hill, could limit our ability to act.

Source: National Archives, "Meeting with Rwandan Vice President Paul Kagame, ca. August 1996, available from https://www.archives.gov/files/declassification/iscap/pdf/2013-040-doc20.pdf

14. President Juvénal Habyarimana to Visit France, 1990

The French government's connection with Rwanda's Hutu-led government leading up to and during the genocide has been the focus of much scrutiny by journalists and genocide scholars and openly criticized by Rwanda's current president, Paul Kagame. During the Rwandan Civil War—a three-year period of intense fighting from 1990 to 1993 between the Rwandan state and the Rwandan Patriotic Front—French troops bolstered Rwandan president Juvénal Habyarimana's military by providing weapons and training Rwandan soldiers. Ultimately, French involvement during the Rwandan Civil War meant arming and training men who would later become the key perpetrators of the Rwandan Genocide. The telegram below sent on March 12, 1990, from Georges Martes, French ambassador to Rwanda, to the French Foreign Ministry describes the political situation in Rwanda and predicts what Habyarimana will likely ask of France when the president visits in the near future.

TD KIGALI 111 MARCH 12 1990
RECORDED 3/13/90 AT 2:37 PM
STRICTLY LIMITED DISTRIBUTION
SUBJECT: OFFICIAL VISIT OF PRESI-
DENT HABYARIMANA TO PARIS
(APRIL 2nd, 3rd, and 4th 1990)
KEY WORDS: RWANDA, HABYARI-
MANA, OFFICIAL VISIT
IN RESPONSE TO TELEGRAM #110.

The increasingly bitter and discouraged population, which the single party seeks to revitalize, feels the economic and food crisis harshly. The southern Hutus, who had power during Grégoire Kayibanda's first republic, criticize social inequality, which now benefits the northern Hutu clans, who currently hold the political power.

This opposition manifests itself in foreign-edited pamphlets, but does not seem to be sufficiently organized within the country to mobilize students and urban workers on the same scale as in other African capitals, or to provoke unrest likely to put the government into difficulties. Also, the emigrant Tutsi opposition would constitute a genuine danger only if it were able to generate an armed expedition supported from abroad.

The president could be in danger from his own clan, from that of his wife, or from that of his "friends" from Ruhengeri. He has put some distance between himself and his brothers-in-law, even though one of them

controls foreign trade more and more by running "The Central" corporation, which benefits from a privileged position. The president has also neatly divided the direction of the army among several rival military chiefs, none of whom seems to be able to worry him. The most powerful of the colonels is Major Sagatwa, his private secretary, who belongs to the "clan of the first lady." Even if she were very attached to her family's interests, one doesn't see why these interests would push her to promote the eviction of her husband. It is hard to imagine, behind the soft and simple appearance of Agathe Habyarimana, the cruel Tutsi queen-mother Kangojera, to whom she is compared by the Rwandan opposition in exile.

President Habyarimana will seize the opportunity of his official visit to Paris to bolster his image and that of his country, to be sure from the President of the French Republic of French support in negotiations that Rwanda will not be able to avoid in 1990 with the World Bank and the IMF, and to attempt to eventually obtain a promise of financial support from our country, specially allocated for structural adjustment. He will strive to take advantage of the trip to make Rwanda better known in France and to attract future French investors, despite an administrative and legal environment—as in the rest of Africa—not conducive to expatriate entrepreneurs.

Military affairs, however, will be at the center of President Habyarimana's preoccupations. He currently appears very preoccupied with the threat that Tutsi emigrants and their Bahima brothers from southern Uganda pose for him. He will therefore speak not only about replacing his caravel with a more modern plane but also about his concern to assure the security of the Kigali airport, as well as that of the adjoining military camp and the presidential residence. He will therefore ask for effective radar surveillance and adequate anti-aerial artillery to be put in place. This point will be the subject of a separate communiqué. 130815./.

MARTRES

15. Resolution 925 Adopted by the United Nations Security Council

The United Nations Security Council (UNSC) passed Resolution 925 on June 8, 1994 at its 3,388th meeting. Resolution 925, cited in full here, came on the heels of a report published on May 31, 1994 by the secretary general in which he concluded that the killings in Rwanda met the UN definition of genocide.

After failing to acknowledge that the events unfolding in Rwanda since the assassination of Rwandan president Juvénal Habyarimana on April 6, 1994 constituted genocide, the UNSC finally verbalized that the atrocities were indeed genocide in Resolution 925, two months after the bloodshed had begun. By the time Resolution 925 was passed in early June, the genocide had already claimed the lives of hundreds of thousands. By the time the genocidal killings came to an end in July, some 800,000 Tutsis and moderate Hutus had died. This document elucidates the failure of the UN to take decisive and timely action to upend the killing. It also demonstrates that time is of the essence when it comes with dealing with atrocity.

The Security Council,

Reaffirming all its previous resolutions on the situation in Rwanda, in particular its resolutions 912 (1994) of 21 April 1994 and 918 (1994) of 17 May 1994, which set out the mandate of the United Nations Assistance Mission for Rwanda (UNAMIR),

Having considered the report of the Secretary-General dated 31 May 1994 (S/1994/640),

Bearing in mind the statement made by the President of the Council on 3 May 1994 (S/PRST/1994/22),

Reaffirming its resolution 868 (1993) of 29 September 1993 on the security of United Nations operations,

Noting with concern that, to date, the parties have not ceased hostilities, agreed to a cease-fire, or brought an end to the violence and carnage affecting civilians,

Noting with the gravest concern the reports indicating that acts of genocide have occurred in Rwanda and recalling in this context that genocide constitutes a crime punishable under international law,

Reiterating its strong condemnation of the ongoing violence in Rwanda and,

in particular, the systematic killing of thousands of civilians,

Expressing its outrage that the perpetrators of these killings have been able to operate and continue operating within Rwanda with impunity,

Noting that UNAMIR is not to have the role of a buffer force between the two parties,

Noting also that UNAMIR's expanded military component will continue only as long as and to the extent that it is needed to contribute to the security and protection of displaced persons, refugees and civilians at risk in Rwanda and to provide security, as required, to humanitarian relief operations,

Underscoring that the internal displacement of some 1.5 million Rwandans facing starvation and disease and the massive exodus of refugees to neighbouring countries constitute a humanitarian crisis of enormous proportions,

Reiterating the importance of the Arusha Peace Agreement as the basis for the peaceful resolution of the conflict in Rwanda,

Commending the countries which have provided humanitarian assistance to Rwandan refugees, as well as emergency aid to alleviate the sufferings of the Rwandan people, and those countries which have contributed troops and logistical support to UNAMIR, and reiterating the urgent need for coordinated international action in this respect,

Welcoming the cooperation between the United Nations and the Organization of African Unity (OAU) and the contributions of the countries of the region, especially that of the facilitator of the Arusha peace process, and encouraging them to continue their efforts,

Welcoming the visit to Rwanda and to the region by the United Nations High Commissioner for Human Rights,

Noting the appointment, pursuant to resolution S-3/1 of 25 May 1994 adopted by the United Nations Commission on Human Rights, of a Special Rapporteur for Rwanda, Reaffirming its commitment to the unity and territorial integrity of Rwanda,

1. Welcomes the Secretary-General's report of 31 May 1994 (S/1994/640);
2. Endorses the Secretary-General's proposals contained therein for the deployment of the expanded UNAMIR, in particular:
   (a) The immediate initiation of the deployment of the two additional battalions in phase 2 in close synchronization with phase 1;
   (b) The continuation of urgent preparations for the deployment of the two battalions envisaged for phase 3; and
   (c) Flexible implementation of all three phases to ensure effective use of available resources to accomplish the tasks listed in paragraphs 4 (a) and (b) below;
3. Decides to extend the mandate of UNAMIR, expiring on 29 July 1994, until 9 December 1994;
4. Reaffirms that UNAMIR, in addition to continuing to act as an intermediary between the parties in an attempt to secure their agreement to a cease-fire, will:
   (a) Contribute to the security and protection of displaced persons, refugees and civilians at risk in Rwanda, including through the establishment and maintenance, where feasible, of secure humanitarian areas; and
   (b) Provide security and support for the distribution of relief supplies and humanitarian relief operations;
5. Recognizes that UNAMIR may be required to take action in self-defence against persons or groups who threaten protected sites and populations, United Nations and other humanitarian personnel or the means of delivery and distribution of humanitarian relief;
6. Demands that all parties to the conflict cease hostilities, agree to a cease-fire and immediately take steps to bring an end to systematic killings in areas under their control;
7. Welcomes the assurances of both parties to cooperate with UNAMIR in carrying out its mandate, recognizes that such cooperation will be essential to the effective implementation of the mandate, and demands that both parties adhere to those assurances;

8. Demands further that all parties cease forthwith any incitement, especially through the mass media, to violence or ethnic hatred;

9. Urges Member States to respond promptly to the Secretary-General's request for resources, including logistical support capability for rapid deployment of additional UNAMIR forces;

10. Requests the Secretary-General to ensure that UNAMIR extend the close cooperation it has with the Department of Humanitarian Affairs and the United Nations Rwanda Emergency Office also to the Special Rapporteur for Rwanda appointed by the United Nations Commission on Human Rights;

11. Demands that all parties in Rwanda strictly respect the persons and premises of the United Nations and other organizations serving in Rwanda, and refrain from any acts of intimidation or violence against personnel engaged in humanitarian and peace-keeping work;

12. Emphasizes the necessity that, inter alia:

   (a) All appropriate steps be taken to ensure the security and safety of the operation and personnel engaged in the operation; and

   (b) The security and safety arrangements undertaken extend to all persons engaged in the operation;

13. Commends the efforts of States, United Nations agencies, international organizations and non-governmental organizations which have provided humanitarian and other assistance, encourages them to continue and increase such assistance, and urges others to provide such assistance;

14. Welcomes the intention of the Secretary-General to establish a special trust fund for Rwanda and invites the international community to contribute generously to it;

15. Commends the tireless efforts of the UNAMIR Force Commander to prevent more innocent lives from being lost, and to bring about a cease-fire between the parties;

16. Commends also the efforts of the Secretary-General and his Special Representative to achieve a political settlement in Rwanda within the framework of the Arusha Peace Agreement, invites them, in coordination with the OAU and countries in the region, to continue their efforts, and demands that the parties undertake serious efforts to bring about political reconciliation;

17. Decides to keep the situation in Rwanda and the role played by UNAMIR under constant review and, to that end, requests the Secretary-General to report to the Council as appropriate, and in any case no later than 9 August 1994 and 9 October 1994, on progress made by UNAMIR in the discharge of its mandate, the safety of populations at risk, the humanitarian situation and progress towards a cease-fire and political reconciliation;

18. Decides to remain actively seized of the matter.

———

Source: United Nations Security Council, S/RES/925 (1994), available from http://www.un.org/en/ga/search/view_doc.asp?symbol=S/RES/925(1994).

16. Statement by Alison Des Forges Before Congress, 1998

Alison Des Forges, a historian and human rights researcher, was the leading American advocate for U.S. action during the Rwandan

Genocide and is counted among the first for-eigners in April 1994 to refer the violence as genocide. Des Forges presented the follow-ing statement on May 5, 1998 before Interna-tional Operations and Human Rights, a subcommittee of the Committee on Interna-tional Relations, U.S. House of Representa-tives. Here she questions and analyzes the failure of the United States to make decisive actions to help save lives during the Rwan-dan Genocide and criticizes what motivated the lack of U.S. response to the atrocity.

_____

. . . I would like to deal more specifically now with some other aspects of U.S. respon-sibility. If we can go back just a little bit— actually quite a bit before the start of the genocide and look at the question of U.S. aid. In the late 1980's and early 1990's, Rwanda was for a long time considered the model of economic development, and here is a lesson which is very important for the current situ-ation in Rwanda. Are we prepared to sacri-fice human rights considerations for economic progress and so-called political stability? That was the choice that we made at the end of the 1980's and early 1990's when we turned our eyes away from the massacres of Tutsis and other abuses in order to continue this hope of economic progress with a regime that we thought was stable.

In that situation in 1991, when the United States was beginning to put money into democratization projects in Rwanda, a team of consultants looked at the whole political situation there, and their first recommenda-tion to the U.S. Government, and, in fact, to all of the donor communities, because the U.S. Ambassador called together the ambas-sadors of the other embassies to hear their report, and the first recommendation was any further economic assistance to this government must require them to give up the

use of ethnic classification on the identity cards. That was in July 1991, and no one responded to that suggestion, including the U.S. Government. Had that suggestion been implemented at that time, identity cards would not have borne the mark "Hutu" or "Tutsi" when the genocide began.

When you come to the question of the establishment of the UNAMIR [United Nations Assistance Mission in Rwanda], of the U.S. peacekeeping force, it is important to look at the influence of the United States in shaping the size and the mandate of that force. Because of financial considerations, because of the desire to economize, partly prompted by pressures within the Congress, the Administration had in its mind the idea that this peacekeeping force must be cheap. It must not cost a lot. Therefore, when mili-tary experts from the United Nations said to be effective this force must have at least 5,000 soldiers and should have 8,000 sol-diers, the United States countered by saying 500. Now, the figure that was finally settled on was slightly less than 3,000, but it was clear that this was the U.S. pressure in part that forced the limiting of the size of the first U.N. force and consequently the limiting of its mandate.

The mandate spelled out in the Arusha Accords was quite a serious mandate that tasked the soldiers with protecting citizens throughout the country during the transition period. By the time the force was actually negotiated at the Security Council, what emerged was a force which had the task of supervising—not guaranteeing, supervising security not within the entire country, but in the capital of Kigali, so a vast shrinking of its area of responsibility.

On the question of what was known throughout this period, there is a great deal of evidence from many sources about warn-ings that went on throughout this period.

There was on December 3 a letter by high-ranking military officers to General [Roméo] Dallaire, and I quote, "They told him that massacres are being prepared and are supposed to spread throughout the country beginning with the regions that have a great concentration of Tutsis." That was a month before the famous telegram.

After January, Dallaire submitted no fewer than six requests in that period to have more troops and an extended mandate, so he clearly knew—and the telegram that [Senator Alain] Destexhe quoted from, February 3, made that point again, that we are being backed into a corner. We are not going to be able to do our job here unless you give us something more to work with.

The question of what the United States knew, something which hasn't been mentioned today is the CIA study which was called for within the U.S. Government, produced at the end of January, a look at possible scenarios in Rwanda in the coming months, and the worst-case scenario at the end of January predicted renewed conflict with half a million people to be killed. This was our own CIA study. It was produced by an analyst whose work was otherwise highly valued in the Intelligence Community, but in this case they disregarded his conclusions.

At the end of March when the mandate was once more being considered at the Security Council, Boutros-Ghali brought forth the information on the training of militia and the distribution of arms, for the first time formally presented that to the Council, although it was true that there were informal briefings before that time, but instead of requesting an extended mandate and more soldiers and better arms as Dallaire had been asking for, he said instead what should happen is an additional 45 policemen should be sent; the reason for 45 policeman rather than many more troops and a better mandate, because it fell within the cost parameters which were being set by major players on the scene, namely the United States.

In terms of when the violence began—sorry, let me go back 1 minute.

When Senator Destexhe was talking about Habyarimana he probably figured that if they did nothing about the information from the January 11 telegram, that meant that it would be OK to go ahead with the genocide and no one would intervene, that wasn't a deduction that had to be made, that was the specific message that was delivered by Boutros-Ghali in a phone call to Habyarimana. He said to him, if you keep up with this kind of stuff, we are going to pull out. So it was already clearly specified from January on that the United Kingdom did not intend to play a serious role if there was a renewal of conflict.

At the time, the first weekend, it was already clear that this was going to be a campaign of ethnic cleansing and of terror. It is true that there was confusion in the minds of many people between civil war and genocide. It is true that many of the press accounts were inaccurate, but the *New York Times* on April 11 published a story saying that civilians were seeking refuge in U.N. posts because they were, "terrified by the ruthless campaign of ethnic cleansing and terror."

As I mentioned, the April 8 telegram which came into the U.N. headquarters from Dallaire and [Jacques-Roger] Booh Booh, Dallaire also specified in [it] that ethnic cleansing was going on in a systematic fashion throughout the city.

Let me refresh your memories. That weekend there were more than a thousand elite Belgian and French troops sent in. The Italians followed soon after, and the U.S. Marines were on standby 20 minutes away in Bujumbura [the main port of Burundi], all for the purpose of evacuating foreigners.

Let me quote the opinion of the Commander of the Belgian troops in the U.N. peacekeeping force at the time. He said, in a confidential assessment after the fact, speaking of that weekend, the responsible attitude would have been to join the efforts of the Belgian, French and Italian troops with those of UNAMIR and to have restored order in the country. There were enough troops to do it, or at least to have tried. When people rightly point the finger at certain persons presumed responsible for the genocide, I wonder after all if there is not another category of those responsible because of their failure to act.

On the question of troop withdrawal, it is clear that the Belgians were very embarrassed by pulling out their troops, and the United States, wanting to help out a friendly country, participated in that effort to decide to pull out the entire force.

I would like to make a point here that seems to me of extremely great importance, and that is the extent to which international actions had their impact within Rwanda and helped to shape the course of this genocide.

In those first hours moderate military officers made contact with the United States, with France, and with Belgium and asked for support in opposing the genocide. They received no encouragement, so they did not ever come together in a cohesive enough force to oppose the genocide.

The RPF [Rwandan Patriotic Front] on April 9 proposed a joint military operation between RPF troops, moderate military of the government, and UNAMIR troops to put down the massacres, to stop the killing, but because the United Nations was circumscribed by its mandate, there was no response from that quarter, and that effort failed.

Within the country there was a constant awareness on the part of the extremists about what was happening in the rest of the world

and a serious attempt to maintain contact with foreigners. There were delegations sent abroad to try to publicize the Rwandan Government position, including to the United Nations itself, and there one of the most disgraceful scenes in the United Nations was at the Security Council table when the representatives of the genocidal government were allowed to present a justification of their point of view and where virtually none of the delegates at that table had the guts to confront the representatives of this government about what it was doing back home.

I believe that there were very few—I know that the Czechs spoke up and the New Zealanders spoke up, but many others did not. They simply sat there and listened to this. And of course they never challenged the right of this government to continue to sit on the Security Council.

On April 15, there was a confidential session of the Security Council to discuss the withdrawal of the U.N. troops. Of course, the member from Rwanda was present, and he heard this discussion. At that session the United States took the position that the entire force should be pulled out. Now, they later changed this position, but at that point that was at the close of business on that day, that was what the Security Council was leaning toward was a complete withdrawal. It was the next morning that the Rwandan Council of Ministers met and decided to extend the genocide into the central and southern parts of the country, which had until then been relatively untouched.

I think that it is certainly a reasonable conclusion that the information that the international community was planning to get itself out of there facilitated those extremists who wanted to push for the extension of the genocide into other parts of the country.

The protests of the United States when they finally were made were heard not just in the councils of government, but all of the way down to the level of the local communities out on the hills. The responsiveness to international criticism was such that it transcended down that administrative hierarchy to the prefecture of Kibuye in the western part of the country, and communications networks may have been disrupted, but they were working well enough for signals from Washington, faint as they were, to reach down to those hills so that the local government official told people, you've got to stop killing because Washington is making that a precondition for dealing with our government.

Now, did they really mean it? Of course, this was so late, many people were already dead by then. Or did they mean simply remove the killing from public view, because they went on to say, remember there are satellites overhead that are monitoring what we are doing.

That was the level of consciousness, not appropriate, not accurate, but there was a sense that we need to be careful because of what people are thinking about us.

And the other prime example of that is when Rwandan military went to Paris and asked for support and for arms, the French response was, we cannot help you as long as you continue doing these horrible things so publicly. And the message went out 2 days later over Radio Rwanda or Radio RTLM, I have forgotten which one, saying to people, please, no more cadavers on the road. Get them out of the way.

So you can see the extent to which international opinion could have its influence within this system, how it could have influenced moderates and given them courage to resist, how it could have influenced extremists to control their behavior. But none of that happened because we didn't act.

The lessons from all of this we will be talking about for a long time to come, but the superficial lesson is the easy lesson. We all know don't let a genocide happen again; if you see the signs, do something about it.

But what I would like to say is that there is another lesson underneath that lesson, because we are not likely to see this same situation again. Why not? Because although the international tribunal is not doing a great job, it is working. There has been a condemnation. Ambassador Khan apparently wasn't aware of that. There has been one guilty verdict handed down already, and people in that region are now knowing enough not to go out and put it on the radio that our intention is genocide or to publicly organize militias to go out and kill. Instead it is becoming more difficult to know exactly what is happening.

The next time around we will have the problem not just of mobilizing the political will when we have a situation that we clearly know the realities, we will also have the problem of knowing the realities, and in that connection I want to draw your attention to a whole series of problems that we are now encountering in knowing what is going on in the Congo with the lack of cooperation from the Kabila Government, with the end of the effective post of special rapporteur for Rwanda, with the banning of the special rapporteur from the Congo, with the suppression of the results of international investigations as was done with the Gersony report in the Rwanda context, with the whitewash of the Kibeho massacre, and now with the effort on the part of the Rwanda Government to end the monitoring function for the U.N. human rights field operation.

We must find accurate sources of information. We must know, or the next time we will end up compounding the error of the Rwanda genocide because not only will we not act, we will not know that we should be acting.

Source: U.S. House of Representatives. Subcommittee on International Operations and Human Rights. *Rwanda: Genocide and the Continuing Cycle of Violence.* 105th Congress, 2nd Session, May 5, 1998 (Accessed September 18, 2017), http://commdocs.house.gov/committees/intlrel/hfa49306.000/hfa49306_0f.htm.

17. Statement by President Barack Obama on the Twentieth Commemoration of the Genocide in Rwanda, April 6, 2014

The following document, stated in full, comes from U.S. president Barack Obama's statement issued on April 6, 2014, to mark the twentieth anniversary of the start of the Rwandan Genocide.

We join with the people of Rwanda in marking twenty years since the beginning of the genocide that took the lives of so many innocents and which shook the conscience of the world. We honor the memory of the more than 800,000 men, women and children who were senselessly slaughtered simply because of who they were or what they believed. We stand in awe of their families, who have summoned the courage to carry on, and the survivors, who have worked through their wounds to rebuild their lives. And we salute the determination of the Rwandans who have made important progress toward healing old wounds, unleashing the economic growth that lifts people from poverty, and contributing to peacekeeping missions around the world to spare others the pain they have known.

At this moment of reflection, we also remember that the Rwandan genocide was neither an accident nor unavoidable. It was a deliberate and systematic effort by human beings to destroy other human beings. The horrific events of those 100 days—when friend turned against friend, and neighbor against neighbor—compel us to resist our worst instincts, just as the courage of those who risked their lives to save others reminds us of our obligations to our fellow man. The genocide we remember today—and the world's failure to respond more quickly— reminds us that we always have a choice. In the face of hatred, we must remember the humanity we share. In the face of cruelty, we must choose compassion. In the face of intolerance and suffering, we must never be indifferent. Embracing this spirit, as nations and as individuals, is how we can honor all those who were lost two decades ago and build a future worthy of their lives.

Source: "Statement by the President on the 20th Commemoration of the Genocide in Rwanda," The White House (April 06, 2014), Office of the Press Secretary, accessed 15 July 2017, available from https://obamawhitehouse.archives.gov/the-press-office/2014/04/06/statement-president-20th-commemoration-genocide-rwanda.

18. United Nations Security Council Resolution 918 (1994): Operation Turquoise

The United Nations (UN) Security Council adopted Resolution 918, cited in part here, on June 22, 1994 and consequently the French-led Operation Turquoise was launched the following day. The UN deployed Operation Turquoise to Rwanda nearly a year after the United Nations had sent in the United Nations Assistance Mission for Rwanda

(UNAMIR) on October 5, 1993 under UN Security Council Resolution 872. Unlike UNAMIR, Operation Turquoise was given a Chapter VII mandate, which allowed it to use force, if needed, to ensure the protection and security of those at risk. Operation Turquoise was intended to augment UNAMIR, which was already on the ground, however, Roméo Dallaire, the head of the UNAMIR in Rwanda, has since criticized the UN's decision to send in an additional force instead of expanding his operations and changing the UNAMIR mandate from a Chapter VI mandate (essentially observers) to a Chapter VII mandate. By the time the UN deployed Operation Turquoise, the genocide had already reached its zenith, which has led many to criticize the UN for not acting sooner.

RESOLUTION 918 (1994)
Adopted by the Security Council at its
3377th meeting, on 17 May 1994

The Security Council,

Reaffirming all its previous resolutions on the situation in Rwanda, in particular its resolution 872 (1993) of 5 October 1993 by which it established the United Nations Assistance Mission for Rwanda (UNAMIR), its resolution 909 (1994) of 5 April 1994 which extended the mandate of UNAMIR until 29 July 1994, and its resolution 912 (1994) of 21 April 1994 by which it adjusted the mandate of UNAMIR,

Recalling the statements made by the President of the Council on 7 April 1994 (S/PRST/1994/16) and 30 April 1994 (S/PRST/1994/21),

Having considered the report of the Secretary-General dated 13 May 1994 (S/1994/565),

Reaffirming its resolution 868 (1993) of 29 September 1993 on the security of United Nations operations,

Strongly condemning the ongoing violence in Rwanda and particularly condemning the very numerous killings of civilians which have taken place in Rwanda and the impunity with which armed individuals have been able to operate and continue operating therein,

Stressing the importance of the Arusha Peace Agreement to the peaceful resolution of the conflict in Rwanda and the necessity for all parties to recommit themselves to its full implementation,

Commending the efforts of the Organization of African Unity (OAU) and its organs, as well as the efforts of the Tanzanian Facilitator, in providing diplomatic, political, and humanitarian support for the implementation of the relevant resolutions of the Council,

Deeply concerned that the situation in Rwanda, which has resulted in the death of many thousands of innocent civilians, including women and children, the internal displacement of a significant percentage of the Rwandan population, and the massive exodus of refugees to neighbouring countries, constitutes a humanitarian crisis of enormous proportions,

Expressing once again its alarm at continuing reports of systematic, widespread and flagrant violations of international humanitarian law in Rwanda, as well as other violations of the rights to life and property,

Recalling in this context that the killing of members of an ethnic group with the intention of destroying such a group, in whole or in part, constitutes a crime punishable under international law,

Strongly urging all parties to cease forthwith any incitement, especially through the mass media, to violence or ethnic hatred,

Recalling also its request to the Secretary-General to collect information on the responsibility for the tragic incident that resulted in the death of the Presidents of Rwanda and Burundi,

Recalling further that it had requested the Secretary-General to make proposals for the investigation of reports of serious violations of international humanitarian law during the conflict,

Underlining the urgent need for coordinated international action to alleviate the suffering of the Rwandan people and to help restore peace in Rwanda, and in this connection *welcoming* cooperation between the United Nations and the OAU as well as with countries of the region, especially the facilitator of the Arusha peace process,

Desiring in this context to expand the mandate of UNAMIR for humanitarian purposes, and *stressing* the importance it attaches to the support and cooperation of the parties for the successful implementation of all aspects of that mandate,

Reaffirming its commitment to the unity and territorial integrity of Rwanda,

Recognizing that the people of Rwanda bear ultimate responsibility for national reconciliation and reconstruction of their country,

Deeply disturbed by the magnitude of the human suffering caused by the conflict and

concerned that the continuation of the situation in Rwanda constitutes a threat to peace and security in the region,

A

1. *Demands* that all parties to the conflict immediately cease hostilities, agree to a cease-fire, and bring an end to the mindless violence and carnage engulfing Rwanda;
2. *Welcomes* the report of the Secretary-General dated 13 May 1994 (S/1994/565);
3. *Decides* to expand UNAMIR's mandate under resolution 912 (1994) to include the following additional responsibilities within the limits of the resources available to it:
   (a) To contribute to the security and protection of displaced persons, refugees and civilians at risk in Rwanda, including through the establishment and maintenance, where feasible, of secure humanitarian areas;
   (b) To provide security and support for the distribution of relief supplies and humanitarian relief operations;
4. *Recognizes* that UNAMIR may be required to take action in self-defence against persons or groups who threaten protected sites and populations, United Nations and other humanitarian personnel or the means of delivery and distribution of humanitarian relief;
5. *Authorizes* in this context an expansion of the UNAMIR force level up to 5,500 troops;
6. *Requests* the Secretary-General, as recommended in his report, and as a first phase, immediately to redeploy to Rwanda the UNAMIR military observers currently in Nairobi and to bring up to full strength the elements of the mechanized infantry battalion currently in Rwanda;

7. <u>Further requests</u> the Secretary-General to report as soon as possible on the next phase of UNAMIR's deployment including, <u>inter alia</u>, on the cooperation of the parties, progress towards a cease-fire, availability of resources and the proposed duration of the mandate for further review and action, as required, by the Council;

8. <u>Encourages</u> the Secretary-General to accelerate his efforts, in conjunction with the Secretary-General of the OAU, to obtain from Member States the necessary personnel to enable deployment of the expanded UNAMIR to proceed urgently;

9. <u>Invites</u> Member States to respond promptly to the Secretary-General's request for the resources required, including logistical support capability for rapid deployment of the UNAMIR expanded force level and its support in the field;

10. <u>Strongly urges</u> all parties in Rwanda to cooperate fully with UNAMIR in the implementation of its mandate and in particular in ensuring its freedom of movement and the unimpeded delivery of humanitarian assistance, and <u>further calls upon</u> them to treat Kigali airport as a neutral zone under the control of UNAMIR;

11. <u>Demands</u> that all parties in Rwanda strictly respect the persons and premises of the United Nations and other organizations serving in Rwanda, and refrain from any acts of intimidation or violence against personnel engaged in humanitarian and peace-keeping work;

12. <u>Commends</u> the efforts of States, United Nations agencies and non-governmental organizations which have provided humanitarian and other assistance, <u>encourages</u> them to continue and increase such assistance, and urges others to provide such assistance;

B

<u>Determining</u> that the situation in Rwanda constitutes a threat to peace and security in the region,

<u>Acting</u> under Chapter VII of the Charter of the United Nations,

13. <u>Decides</u> that all States shall prevent the sale or supply to Rwanda by their nationals or from their territories or using their flag vessels or aircraft of arms and related <u>matériel</u> of all types, including weapons and ammunition, military vehicles and equipment, paramilitary police equipment and spare parts;

14. <u>Decides also</u> to establish, in accordance with rule 28 of the provisional rules of procedure of the Security Council, a Committee of the Security Council consisting of all the members of the Council, to undertake the following tasks and to report on its work to the Council with its observations and recommendations:

(a) To seek from all States information regarding the action taken by them concerning the effective implementation of the embargo imposed by paragraph 13 above;

(b) To consider any information brought to its attention by States concerning violations of the embargo, and in that context to make recommendations to the Council on ways of increasing the effectiveness of the embargo;

(c) To recommend appropriate measures in response to violations of the embargo imposed by paragraph 13 above and provide information on a regular basis to the Secretary-General for general distribution to Member States;

15. Calls upon all States, including States not Members of the United Nations, and international organizations to act strictly in accordance with the provisions of the present resolution, notwithstanding the existence of any rights or obligations conferred or imposed by any international agreement or any contract entered into or any license or permit granted prior to the date of the adoption of this resolution;

16. Decides that the provisions set forth in paragraphs 13 and 15 above do not apply to activities related to UNAMIR and UNOMUR;

17. Requests the Secretary-General to provide all necessary assistance to the Committee and to make the necessary arrangements in the Secretariat for this purpose;

C

18. Requests the Secretary-General to present a report as soon as possible on the investigation of serious violations of international humanitarian law committed in Rwanda during the conflict;

19. Invites the Secretary-General and his Special Representative, in coordination with the OAU and countries in the region, to continue their efforts to achieve a political settlement in Rwanda within the framework of the Arusha Peace Agreement;

20. Decides to keep the situation in Rwanda under constant review and requests the Secretary-General to report further, including on the humanitarian situation, within five weeks of the adoption of this resolution and again in good time before the expiration of the current mandate of UNAMIR;

21. Decides to remain actively seized of the matter.

Source: United Nations Security Council, S/RES/918 (17 May 1994), available from https://documents-dds-ny.un.org/doc/UNDOC/GEN/N94/218/36/PDF/N9421836.pdf?OpenElement.

19. U.S. Ambassador to Rwanda Warns of Outbreak of Violence, April 1, 1994

David Rawson served as the U.S. ambassador to Rwanda from 1993 to 1996 and began his term in Kigali when the Arusha Peace Accords—the agreement signed between the Rwandan government and the Tutsi-led Rwandan Patriotic Front (RPF) that sought to end Rwanda's civil war—was floundering. From 1993 to the start of the genocide on April 6, 1994, Ambassador Rawson reported on the state of Rwandan political affairs and the challenges the government was having implementing the Arusha Peace Accords. In the telegram cited here, Ambassador Rawson sends his analysis of political affairs in Rwanda to George Moose, U.S. assistant secretary of state for African Affairs, and Johnnie Carson, U.S. ambassador to Uganda. In his telegram dated April 1, 1994—five days before the genocide began—Ambassador Rawson warns Moose, who was at the time meeting with Ugandan president Yoweri Museveni, that Rwanda was headed towards an outburst of violence. As we now know, his prediction noted in the fifth point of this telegram was accurate as less than a week after he sent his missive, the genocide began and on April 10, the U.S. State Department ordered Ambassador Rawson to evacuate the embassy. His analysis of the political situation on the ground just days before genocide began elucidates the mounting tensions within the Rwandan government provoked, in part, by the Rwandan government's reluctance to implement the Arusha Peace Accords. Interestingly, he highlights the Coalition pour la Défense de la République (CDR), a Hutu-extremist political party formed in February 1992 that frequently reproached Rwandan president Juvénal Habyarimana for negotiating with the RPF and signing the Arusha Peace Accords. When the genocide began following the assassination of Habyarimana on April 6, the CDR collaborated with the hastily created interim government that led the genocide.

FM Amembassy [ibid.] Kigali
TO Amembassy [ibid.] Kampala Immediate
Info Secstate WashDC Priority 6124

Kampala for Assistant Secretary Moose
And Ambassador Carson from Ambassador

. . .

2. In view of your 4/4 [April 4th] meeting with Museveni, I wanted to get you the latest from here on the state of negotiations toward establishment of transition institutions. A round of good Friday calls to observers, the UN and key players suggests that the sides are inching towards each other, but afraid to make the final offer. Many observers believe installation of institutions will have to await the Arusha summit on Burundi . . .

The CDR Issue
3. Internal opposition parties told me [on May 31] that if the President were to make a clear cut declaration that admission of the CDR to the national assembly was the last issue inhibiting installation of the institutions, they would lobby for CDR. RPF told Ambassador Tambwe [Saleh Tambwe was the Tanzania representative and facilitator to Arusha] the same day that, if they got formal

assurances from the President that CDR was the last issue at stake, they would take a look at their position. As of now, their position is that the CDR must wait a month or two before the national assembly acts on its application to join. Meanwhile, in spite of the assassination of one of its youth leaders, CDR continues to urge its partisans to be patient. Kigali has remained relatively quiet with daily traffic at usual levels. The night of 3/31 did, however, offer up several grenade explosions and some gunshots. There is one reported fatality amongst youth who were reportedly taunting guards at the presidency late at night and drew their fire.

Is the CDR the last issue?
4. Over the last three days, I have concentrated my diplomatic efforts on presidential counselors. I reminded them that our support for equity to all parties, including the CDR, derives from our support for the Arusha Peace Accord. All other current disputes are interparty questions that should be resolved after the institutions have been put in place. Presidential cabinet director [Enoch] Ruhigira said that the CDR was the last outstanding substantive issue for the president. He noted, however, that the president did not control party sentiment. Presidential counselor Runyinya elaborated the links between election of the national assembly president and a possible revolt by PL Mugenzi over installation of ministers. According to Runyinya, if Mugenzi's candidate, former minister of Justice Mbonampeka, wins either the presidency or the vice presidency of the national assembly, Mugenzi will be satisfied. If Mbonampeka loses both offices, Mugenzi will not feel adequately rewarded FB having given up the justice ministry to his party opponent, Minister Ndasingwa. Mugenzi would then probably call for a suspension of the installation ceremony for government.

Minister of transport and communications (the president's recent envoy to western capitals and the United Nations) said all would be well with the national assembly once the CDR were admitted, but outstanding questions might still trouble the formation of government. I made it clear to all the above that the international community considered the installation ceremony to be one and indivisible. The president and the political parties should go to that ceremony prepared to complete it without further delay or raising any new issues.

5. We believe that the CDR issue is the one remaining real impediment to putting the institutions in place. If the president gets satisfaction on that, he will carry through with the installation, but the presidency is waiting for RPF to budge. Each party is afraid to make final commitment for fear of losing advantage. Both Tanzanian ambassador and German ambassador (current president of the Europeans) believe that the institutions will not be established until President Habyarimana gets back from the Arusha summit on Burundi. Our major fear is that the relative calm which has characterized Kigali the last couple of weeks will not hold until then. I have urged all my interlocutors to use every influence at their disposal to encourage calm as we approach this last turn on the course.

Source: National Archives, The US and the Genocide in Rwanda 1994, "Document 2 Kigali 01458, 1 Apr 94," available from http://nsarchive.gwu.edu/NSAEBB/NSAEBB117/Rw02.pdf.

20. USAID Input into Operation Support Hope Transition

The document that follows is the U.S. State Department's and the U.S. Agency for International Development's recommendations

for what more the U.S. military should do to aid Operation Support Hope (OSH) before the program concluded. U.S. president Bill Clinton authorized OSH in July 1994 in response to the United Nations' (UN) inability to service the millions of Rwanda refugees displaced during the Rwandan Genocide. OSH operated from July 24 to August 31, 1994 and during its tenure sent thousands of troops to the Great Lakes region (primarily Uganda) along with military and humanitarian supplies to assistance in the refugee crisis that followed the genocide. This document reveals the sustained crisis that the Rwandan Genocide created in Rwanda and the Great Lakes region even after the killings ended. This document addresses the significant humanitarian needs, the logistics involved in transporting materials, and the need to rebuild key infrastructures such as roads.

We are now five months into the Rwandan emergency. The unprecedented, large-scale, rapid population movements that characterized the earlier months have largely ceased though hundreds are still reported to be fleeing Rwanda on a daily basis. The goal of massive refugee repatriation is still elusive though many of the 1960-era Rwandan refugees are reported to be moving back to Rwanda. The regional Rwandan and Burundi refugee, returnee and internally displaced persons caseload is over five million. The refugee population of some three million can be expected to remain at that level for at least another six months.

The U.S. military aspect—known as Operation Support Hope (OSH)—of the USG [Under-Secretary-General] relief effort provided a critical and massive boost in the emergency relief response. DOD [Department of Defense] has done an outstanding job under difficult circumstances. With the principal initial taskings to OSH either completed or well in hand, our goal is to achieve a seamless, mutually satisfactory handover from the U.S. military to the more traditional humanitarian assistance agencies, particularly the UNHCR [United Nations High Commission for Refugees] which has the lead on refugee relief.

DOD's assistance in arranging and financing humanitarian airlift under its regular humanitarian assistance authorities (Section 2551, Title II of the DOD Appropriations Act, 1994 (PL103-139) and Title 10) should be considered separately from the issue on OSH's continued life and should be maintained as this provides critical assistance to international and non-governmental organizations attempting to move urgently needed equipment and supplies to the region.

With respect to ongoing U.S. military assistance under the OSH rubric, UNHCR has just (9/7) forwarded its requests (attached) for additional relief capacity that it currently judges can only be covered by military assets. UNHCR requests center around critically needed logistics capacity for air delivery of relief, a service that UNHCR would like extended for another six months. Although the situation in the region is still very fragile, this is much longer than we want or need to commit U.S. military assets absent significant renewed violence and population displacements. State and USAID recommend addressing some, not all, of UNHCR's requests. Depending on the response, the U.S. military's presence may be required beyond September 30, but for less than six months. The Ad Hoc meeting on Rwanda should review the policy implications of this.

In summary, additional requirements may be grouped as

I. AIR OPERATIONS

1. The U.S. military should inform UNHCR (and other UN agencies and NGOs) of the remaining time under OSH that it will airlift humanitarian assistance supplies from Europe to the region and within the region so relief agencies can plan their delivery schedules. Included in these deliveries should be the airlift of four satellite terminals from Patrick APB; two pickup Toyotas, two water tankers, and two trucks from Frankfurt; and twenty trucks and fifteen water tanker trucks from Germany and Mombasa already requested by UNHCR. (N.B. Humanitarian airlift for UNHCR and NGOs on a case by case request should continue under DOD's regular humanitarian assistance authorities as noted above.)

2. UNHCR is specifically requesting that the U.S. military handling and cargo handling based in Kigali and continue12-hour airfield support services at Kigali airfield. Since the JTF [Joint Task Force] reports that substitute civilian assets are already or will soon be in place, this request should be the subject of further detailed technical discussions between UNHCR and the USG. Agreeing to the request would, of course, require U.S. military presence beyond September 30 and would require that a new timeline be established.

3. Ground control of landing aircraft in Kigali is currently are slowly [ibid.] coming back on the job and were receiving training from the USAF [United States Air Force]. U.S. military should complete training before departing Kigali.

4. The British Overseas Development Administration (ODA) in Kigali is currently offloading civilian humanitarian

aircraft. USAF material handling equipment is essential to supplement the ODA equipment for certain requirements. ODA relies on the U.S. military K-loaders to offload the wide-bodied high aircraft. The departure of the two K-Loaders, currently scheduled for Sept. 11, will put a damper on the operations and significantly increase operational costs.

5. UNHCR requested on 8/30 and reiterated on 9/7 that OSH transfer the following equipment for continued operations at the Kigali airport: 2-25K loaders; 1-40K loader, 4-10K forklifts; 3 generators; 1 high mobility vehicle; and 1 airfield lighting system. State and USAID reiterate their recommendation for providing this critical equipment as Section 506(a)2 authority would permit. A fully cleared interagency position on a response to UNHCR should precede any withdrawal of equipment from Kigali.

6. In Goma, CARE manages offloading operations at the airport utilizing three U.S. military forklifts which remain at the airport despite U.S. troop departure. Per the DART, turnover to UNHCR of at least two of these forklifts is needed for continuation of offloading operations.

7. The U.S. military should expedite the airlift from Scotland the trucks, bulldozers and other heavy equipment funded by BHR/OFDA [Bureau of Humanitarian Response/Office of US Foreign Disaster Assistance] in the Action A.I.D./Assist UK grant for urgent refugee site preparation activities specifically in Goma. This is important as site preparation equipment is integrally linked to enhanced security in the camps.

8. Although the U.S. military does not fly into Bukavu, the USAF forklift positioned in Bukavu to offload the Saffair and New Zealand flights has been essential to the relief operation there. Should the USAF pull out the forklift, air operations to Bukavu would stop. UNHCR specifically requested a second forklift. It is essential that the U.S. military leave at least one forklift in place in Bukavu. Two are recommended as long as the Bukavu airport is operating. It may be closed for some runway repairs.

9. UNHCR has requested that USAF C-130s fly to Goma and Kigali (or other locations) from Dar Es Salaam, Entebbe, Kigoma and Mombasa. The Ad Hoc Rwanda Group should review the possibility of making those air assets available for an additional period beyond OSH compared to the possibilities of civilian contract.

10. UNHCR has requested that Geneva aircell participation in monitoring and technical assistance for the Rwanda emergency be extended for six months. Six U.S. military officers have already been recalled, with only three officers remaining. The Rwanda Ad Hoc Group should review this requirement separately.

11. UNHCR has requested that DOD turnover to it Entebbe aircraft loading equipment with the option of redeployment to other airports in the region. This request should be reviewed by the ad hoc group.

II. WATER OPERATIONS

1. Until its departure on August 26, the U.S. military supported water distribution operations in Goma refugee camps. The U.S. military transferred the operation and $2.8 million worth of selected equipment to the U.N. that contribute to

water distriubution [ibid.] as well as site preparation.

2. As formally requested by UNHCR, the U.S. military should provide to UNHCR the tools and spare parts kits for the donated equipment to allow for continued operation (list attached). (NB: This request also applies to the road/site preparation heavy equipment which is related to the security issue vis-à-vis preparation of smaller, more manageable camps.)

III. ROADS

o UNHCR has requested that the U.S. military repair the road from Kisoro-Bunagana-Rutshuru and Sake to Bukavu, particularly between Kalebe Airport and Bukavu.

o This would be a new task for DOD and would require the reintroduction of troops, therefore DOS/USAID recommend that UNHCR be encouraged to contract privately or seek other donor support for this item.

Source: "DOS/USAID Input into Operation Support Hope Transition," US Dept. of State and US Agency for International Development (USAID), PD-ACS-422, available from http://pdf.usaid.gov /pdf_docs/PDAC422.pdf.

Historical Dilemmas

The Historical Dilemma section introduces students and researchers to debates and controversies in the study of certain genocides and atrocities. It presents a historical question with different perspectives on the issue, showing users not only how scholars utilize evidence to present their respective arguments, but how certain topics in genocide studies continue to be debated.

Could the United Nations have done more to stop the genocide in Rwanda?

Introduction

In 1994, over the course of 100 days, an estimated 800,000 Rwandans were killed in a genocide that pitted the majority Hutu against the minority Tutsi population. The genocide came at the end of a short civil war between a small band of Tutsi refugees, the Rwanda Patriotic Front (RPF), and the Rwandan government's Hutu military. The conflict drew the attention of the international community, and both the Organization of African Unity, in 1992, and the United Nations (UN), in 1993, sent observation and peacekeeping missions to the region to help implement a ceasefire and power-sharing agreement signed in Arusha, Tanzania. Despite these efforts, tension within the small nation remained high, with Hutu militias determined to maintain power

by spreading a violent anti-Tutsi message throughout the country.

On April 6, 1994, a missile shot down a plane carrying Juvénal Habyarimana, the Rwandan Hutu president, as it approached the Rwandan capital. Who was responsible for the plane crash is still debated, but the event triggered an immediate outbreak in violence that became the Rwandan Genocide. Over the 100 days that followed, Hutus throughout the country, civilian and military, murdered ethnic Tutsis. Moderate Hutus were also targeted, and the RPF continued to wage its war in hopes of capturing the capital. An estimated 800,000 people—and according to some claims as many as 1.1 million people—were brutally killed in just over three months. When the genocide began, the UN already had a small peacekeeping force in place in Rwanda, but these troops were not given the support, funding, or mandate to effectively stop the violence. More than 16 years later, the UN and the international community are still trying to learn from this mistake in order to find a way to truly prevent genocide and other crimes against humanity. Could the UN have done more to stop the genocide in Rwanda?

In early 1994, a small group of UN peacekeeping forces tasked with monitoring the implementation of the Arusha Accords between Rwanda's Hutu government and a

Tutsi rebel group stood by helplessly as evidence of an impending humanitarian disaster mounted in front of them—which they communicated to the UN. Since the genocide ended in the summer of 1994, the failure of the UN to take stronger action to prevent or stop the massacre has been the subject of analysis and debate.

This debate continues in the following essays. In the first essay, international studies scholar Isabelle Lagarde argues that the UN was hampered by a lack of will among the international community to act more forcefully. The United States in particular was instrumental in preventing UN involvement, she argues, and U.S. leaders and citizens were not enthusiastic about spending money or putting lives in danger to intervene in little-known countries. Alanna Pardee, also an international studies expert, argues in the second essay that UN authorities could and should have responded much more quickly and forcefully to the situation by strengthening the terms of the mandate and more effectively communicating with commanders on the ground in Rwanda. She argues that those failures played a major role in eroding international support for forceful intervention.

Pro/Con 1: The UN Could Not Have Stopped the Genocide

In 1994, the international community stood back and watched as the Rwandan Genocide claimed almost one million lives. Despite specific information and intelligence from sources on the ground, both leading up to and during the genocide, the United Nations failed to send a substantial peacekeeping force that could have worked to stop the mass violence. Indeed, when the killings were under way, the United Nations (UN) Security Council voted to abandon their mission rather than reinforce it. The UN was created

to maintain peace and to prevent exactly this kind of horrendous event, but it failed to stop the genocide in Rwanda. The UN could not have stopped the genocide because it lacked support from the international community.

The United Nations was established after World War II as an international organization designed to preserve peace and security, promote social development, and foster friendly relations among states. Currently, there are 192 member states, each weighted equally in the General Assembly. However, the victors of the World War II reserved a special leadership role for themselves in the form of the five permanent seats (P5) on the Security Council. The Security Council is one of the six main branches of the UN and is charged with maintaining peace and security around the world. The P5 countries are the United States, United Kingdom, China, Russia, and France, and these countries alone have the power to veto any resolution that comes through the Security Council. They also boast a great deal of influence due to their status and their large financial contributions to the organization.

The United States, in its position as a world superpower, holds a great deal of sway over the Security Council, and was instrumental in preventing the UN from getting involved in the Rwandan conflict. U.S. involvement in the UN is highly influenced by domestic politics, and foreign aid and intervention is often a low priority for Americans, so involvement in unknown countries with no direct ties to U.S. interests can be unpopular among the American population.

In 1992, the Security Council sent a peacekeeping mission to the East African nation of Somalia, with the support of the United States, in order to oversee a ceasefire and help deliver humanitarian aid. In 1993, during the Battle of Mogadishu, Somali militia killed 18 U.S. soldiers, and a nineteenth was killed shortly after. These events shocked the American population and severely diminished support for international humanitarian involvement. One year later the Security Council began to discuss a peacekeeping mission to Rwanda, and accordingly U.S. support for and commitment to such a mission was negligible. President Bill Clinton, not wishing to become involved in another ethnic conflict, presented the violence as an internal civil war and refused to let Americans, or the UN, become involved in any significant way.

Before the genocide began, several countries did provide troops to the original UN Assistance Mission to Rwanda (UNAMIR) in 1993, among them Rwanda's former colonial power, Belgium. These troops were on the ground at the start of the genocide, but were quickly targeted by the Hutu militias. During the first few days of the genocide, 10 Belgian peacekeepers were tortured and murdered, putting the UN on high alert and prompting the Security Council to reconvene. With international support dwindling, and many seeing a repeat of the debacle on Somalia, the UN Security Council unanimously voted to reduce the UN peacekeeping mission to a skeleton force of barely 200 soldiers. Cables from the U.S. State Department to the U.S. mission to the UN show how American policy was set against intervention, and pushed the UN to withdraw troops and prevent a stronger mandate. It is also important to note that at this time Rwanda held one of the 10 rotating seats on the Security Council, and the Hutu government's representative did his part to discourage action and diminish fears of a genocide.

In international law, language is extremely important, and the international community's failure to apply the term "genocide" to Rwanda shows a clear decision to ignore the events happening on the ground to remain uninvolved. The term genocide was defined in 1948 in the UN's Convention on the Prevention and Punishment of the Crime of Genocide. This document also recognized genocide as a crime under international law and obligated its signatories to prevent and punish genocide anywhere in the world. Presently there are 147 states that have ratified or acceded to the convention, including each of the P5, which are therefore legally required to act when genocide is determined to be taking place. In August 1993, the UN human rights investigator in Rwanda first raised the possibility of genocide, and in January 1994, Lieutenant General Roméo Dallaire, head of UNAMIR, sent a letter warning of the risk of genocide. Once the violence erupted, Clinton and the members of the Security Council had access to irrefutable evidence of genocide through embassy staff, nongovernmental organization staff, Dallaire, and journalists on the ground. Despite these warnings and information, the UN Security Council failed to use the term genocide to describe the conflict until late June, a few weeks shy of the end of the conflict, thereby shielding themselves from any obligation to intervene.

The UN is only as strong as its members make it, especially the P5 members. International law lacks real enforcement measures, and one powerful member state can decide how or if the UN becomes involved in an international incident. The UN and the international community have since recognized their negligence and abandonment of Rwanda in 1994, and after a damning report, the UN even admitted to failing to prevent the genocide. The combination of the peacekeeping failure in Somalia and a lack of strategic or political interests in Rwanda made members of the international community, especially the United States, unwilling to become involved. This atmosphere of fear and denial led to a failure to acknowledge the atrocities being committed as genocide. In the end, the collective lack of will, and the pressure from the United States, prevented the UN from intervening in Rwanda until it was already too late.

Isabelle Lagarde

Pro/Con 2: The UN Could Have Stopped the Genocide with a Stronger Mandate

The United Nations (UN) was created in 1945 to promote the universal values of international peace, security, and human rights—concepts that are believed to be supranational ideals. Although these are admirable goals, many argue that the UN lacks the power to resolve pressing international conflicts because it lacks sufficient support from its member states. However, in the case of the Rwandan Genocide, the UN, although admittedly poorly supported, could have done more to stop the genocide. In not issuing a stronger peacekeeping mandate, the UN allowed the mass killings to continue for 100 days, and nearly one million Rwandans perished.

The first mistake in Rwanda was that the UN did not give a strong enough mandate to the United Nations Assistance Mission for Rwanda (UNAMIR), which was deployed to Rwanda to aid in carrying out the Arusha Accords, a peace agreement signed by the Rwandan government and the Rwandan Patriotic Front (RPF) in Arusha, Tanzania, in August 1993. Under the UN Security Council Resolution 872, UNAMIR was initially given 2,548 troops and a Chapter VI Mandate, which extended into April 1994 when the atrocities began. Under the UN Charter, a Chapter VI mandate does not allow UN peacekeepers to use force or implement the will of the UN; they can facilitate and oversee but not engage.

The Chapter VI Mandate advised UNAMIR that their mission was strictly to monitor the Arusha Accords and ease the transition to a new power-sharing government that incorporated the RPF. The UN personnel were present to ensure security in Kigali, the capital, and monitor the armistice: this was a mission with limited troops, and almost no legal power to protect the Rwandan people. As the violence began to unfold, UNAMIR continued to follow and was legally bound to their Chapter VI mandate. UNAMIR was so restricted by the mandate that the troops literally had to stand and watch as the massacre of Tutsis continued.

The lowest point for UNAMIR came early in April 1994 when the Rwandan army killed 10 Belgian commandos. Under the Chapter VI monitoring mandate, the UN troops were unsure of whether or not they could use force to defend themselves or Rwandan civilians. After handing over their weapons to government soldiers, as advised by their commander, they were killed with their own weapons. Belgium, knowing that the mission would now be unpopular with its citizens at home, immediately withdrew its other troops in reaction to the deaths. Three weeks into the genocide other countries also horrified by the attacks began to withdraw their troops, and UNAMIR's peacekeepers dwindled to only 270 military personnel. If the United Nations had clearly outlined the details of the mandate and communicated better with their troops and commanders, the course of the genocide in Rwanda could have been drastically different.

UNAMIR's weak and unclear Chapter VI Mandate led to the failure of the UN in Rwanda and lost important international support for the mission. Furthermore, it allowed the genocide to proceed at a rapidly destructive pace. As the violence escalated and it became clear that the Arusha Peace Agreement was no longer a viable mission in Rwanda, the UN should have acted quickly to change UNAMIR's mandate to a Chapter VII mandate, which allows for the possibility of enforcement. A Chapter VII mandate would have allowed the UN Security Council to establish the threat to peace and security and take military or nonmilitary action to deter any potential threats. Although this eventually did happen, it took months for it to be approved and even longer for countries to commit troops to the mission. This was not consistent with UNAMIR commander Roméo Dallaire's request for 5,000 troops to arrive immediately. The mission was still unclear on whether they could use force to stop the mass killings, even with the Chapter VII mandate. By the time increased troops arrived, the genocide was basically over. Had UNAMIR been more strongly supported by the UN, and General Dallaire's request for more troops been filled, UNAMIR would not have been considered a failure.

The UN could have done more in Rwanda if it had acted swiftly and had established mechanisms in place to deal with international conflicts. The UN, like many other international organizations, is only as strong as its member countries allow it to be. The UN depends on the financial and political support of its members. For these reasons, UN actions are rarely consistent and are subject to the fluctuations of member-state politics, which are often in disagreement. For example, in 1994, the idea of resolving conflicts in faraway places, and risking troops in the process, was not popular in the United States. The country had just been involved in a failed mission in Somalia, which both humiliated and infuriated the American populace. For this reason, the United States was hesitant to give full support to the mission in Rwanda. As a result, other countries were hesitant to commit troops and necessary military equipment to the mission. The UN needs to be especially aware of how the results of other political and humanitarian missions affect each other, to ensure that a proper mandate is given. The UN should be faulted for not realizing how the mission in Somalia would affect UNAMIR and for not changing strategies when they realized the failures of the Somalian peacekeeping force.

Even though its members limit its power, there are certain aspects of the UN within the organization's control that must be properly established in order to both increase the efficacy of UN peacekeeping missions and ensure international security. Troops must be properly informed of their mission and their right to take military and/or nonmilitary action. Missions, especially failed ones like in Somalia, should be thoroughly reviewed and used to inform future missions. The bureaucracy and lack of speed with which the UN responded to the Rwandan genocide was unacceptable. The UN's identity crisis, whether it is solely a peacekeeping or intervening organization, also prolonged the genocide in Rwanda.

Alanna Pardee

Was French involvement in Rwanda a major factor in the 1994 Rwandan Genocide?

Introduction

French involvement in Rwandan political, economic, and military affairs in the years leading up to, during, and after the Rwandan Genocide raise many troubling questions about France's relationship with Rwanda and its connection to the genocide. From early on, Rwanda (although not a French colony) was unduly influenced by French economic ambitions in the region. After being granted independence in 1962, Rwanda was drawn into the economic orbit of French investments in the region. As a result, Rwanda developed close ties with France which lasted for decades. The relationship between France and Rwanda's Juvénal Habyarimana government (which extended from 1973 to 1994) soon became the subject of debate after the genocide. Given France's close relationship with Habyarimana, the question quickly arose, Was French involvement in Rwanda a major factor in the 1994 Rwandan Genocide?

In the essays that follow, Sarah E. Brown and Alexis Herr, both genocide scholars, analyze French involvement in Rwanda and discuss whether it was a major factor in the 1994 atrocity. Brown's analysis condemns France's complicity in the genocide and elucidates the ways in which France has impeded justice after the genocide. Herr highlights France's dubious actions leading up to, during, and after the atrocity as illustrative of the failure of the international community at large to upend the genocide.

French Complicity in the Rwandan Genocide

French military, diplomatic, and economic support was elemental to the planning, organization, and perpetration of the 1994 Rwandan Genocide. Even today, France continues to thwart justice mechanisms by hosting and protecting dozens of suspected genocide perpetrators on its soil. France's complicity in the Rwandan Genocide, extensively documented by academics, politicians, and experts in the Great Lakes region of Central Africa, is still subject to debate in France. Despite overwhelming evidence of its involvement, France, a once-staunch ally of Rwanda's genocidal government, has yet to formally apologize for its role in the genocide.

From 1973 until his assassination in 1994, Rwanda was controlled by Juvénal Habyarimana, a former military officer who assumed power following a bloodless coup d'etat. Habyarimana quickly forged political and personal ties with France who, in an effort to supplant Rwanda's former colonial ruler, Belgium, and maintain influence in francophone Africa, assumed a patron-client relationship with Rwanda. During Habyarimana's 21-year reign, Rwanda's Tutsi minority suffered discrimination, marginalization, and occasional bouts of violence that escalated in the 1990s. In October 1990, after decades of exile in Uganda and abroad, a group of armed Tutsi rebels known as the Rwandan Patriotic Front (RPF) invaded Rwanda and demanded, among other things, the right to return home and a role in Rwanda's government. Their initial advance was swift and alarmed Habyarimana. In response to his plea for assistance, France deployed forces in Rwanda and drove back the RPF, resulting in the stalemate that catalyzed peace negotiations and an agreement known as the Arusha Accords (1993).

During this period of peace negotiations, France assisted Habyarimana's government in training and expanding their military forces and participated in operations meant to control the civilian population. Rwanda's military, known as the Rwandan Armed Forces (French: Forces Armées Rwandaises, or FAR), was assisted by the French as they carried out operations against Hutu political moderates who posed a challenge to the increasingly extremist government and Tutsis. France even went so far as to circumvent the Arusha Accords and arm the military; in January of 1994, United Nations (UN) peacekeeping forces intercepted a French shipment of arms meant for the FAR. This was but one of 36 known shipments of weapons sent to Rwanda from France, worth an estimated $11 million, between 1990 and 1994. While that shipment was confiscated by UN peacekeepers, France delivered untold amounts of weapons into the hands of the perpetrators who would murder up to one million Tutsis and moderate Hutus during the genocide.

When the genocide began, France continued to support the genocidal government. As a permanent member of the UN Security Council, France's role at the UN in support of the extremists controlling Rwanda further ensured the policy of non-intervention in Rwanda, a policy supported by other permanent members. On April 21, 1994, France voted to reduce the number of the United Nations Assistance Mission for Rwanda (UNAMIR) peacekeeping force size to just 270. In addition, France (along with other permanent members of the UN Security Council) safeguarded Rwanda's rotating seat on the Security Council; a seat Rwanda held during the genocide. Thanks to French support and international inaction, the genocidal government was able to utilize the UN platform to perpetuate a narrative of civil war and tribal strife in Rwanda and make certain that the genocide continued unabated.

Eventually, in light of the overwhelming evidence that genocide was indeed being perpetrated in Rwanda, the international community decided to take action and authorized a second peacekeeping mission, UNAMIR II. In the interim period before the reinforcements and equipment arrived in Rwanda, France volunteered to intervene and establish a "safe zone." On June 23, 1994, French troops entered southwestern Rwanda as part of Operation TURQUOISE, a French mission to establish a "humanitarian corridor" and provide support until more international peacekeepers could arrive. While France claims it saved countless lives during Operation TURQUOISE, and indeed,

lives were saved, its role in perpetuating killings in the area and support for the genocidal government that had fled into the French-protected region is brushed aside.

Gérard Prunier, a French academic who advised the French government on Operation Turquoise, provided critical firsthand accounts that cast doubt on the humanitarian nature of France's participation. Claims that France's military assisted the Interahamwe in rounding up and massacring Tutsis were further fueled by the massacres in Bisesero; the French drew out Tutsis in hiding who were later massacred by the Interahamwe. Despite claims that the perpetrators unknowingly manipulated them, French military cooperation was construed as genocidal by many survivors. This assessment was further buttressed by France's refusal to arrest suspected perpetrators of the genocide, including high level members of the genocidal government, who had fled to the French-controlled safe zone. As a result, many were free to seek refuge throughout Africa, in Belgium, and also in France.

Today, France continues to host several dozen wanted perpetrators of the Rwandan Genocide. One of the most famous suspected perpetrators is Habyarimana's own wife, Agathe, a personal friend of former French president François Mitterrand. She was flown to Paris just days after the genocide began and given a gift of $40,000 from the government marked as "urgent assistance to Rwandan refugees." Today, Agathe Habyarimana remains in France despite the government twice rejecting her request for asylum. France continues to disregard numerous calls from the Rwandan government and the UN International Criminal Tribunal for Rwanda to hand over suspected *génocidaires* living in France so that they may face prosecution. More recently, Pascal Simbikangwa, a known architect of the Rwandan Genocide living in France, was tried by a French court and found guilty of complicity in genocide and sentenced to 25 years in prison. While this landmark trial signaled a shift in policy, it is unclear if France will try all of the suspects on its soil.

While the silence and inaction of the international community contributed to the horrors of the Rwandan Genocide, France's active complicity stands out as especially heinous. Despite conclusive evidence of its military, diplomatic, and economic support for the genocidal government that mass murdered nearly one million Tutsis and moderate Hutus, France refuses to formally apologize. Those responsible for the Rwandan Genocide relied on French support throughout the genocidal process, from inception to perpetration to absconding responsibility. Without French support, the genocide's scope and scale would have been greatly reduced or may never have occurred.

Sara E. Brown

Colonialism, France, and the Rwandan Genocide

In the weeks leading up to the 20th anniversary of the Rwandan Genocide in April 2014, tensions flared between Rwandan president Paul Kagame and the French government. Kagame had led the resistance movement that eventually silenced the genocide in 1994 and has since called attention to what he views as France's failure to stop the genocide. Furthermore, he has accused the French government of having supported the Hutu militia that cut down 800,000 minority Tutsis with machetes in a 100-day period. Kagame's accusations may contain a kernel of truth, but France's actions alone did not spur or incite genocide. Indeed, the twisted road to the Rwandan Genocide had started decades earlier and many foreign nations,

France included, share responsibility for the disastrous outcome.

German (1894–1918) and then Belgian (1918–1962) colonial rule codified ethnic diversity in Rwanda into rigid "racial" classes. Prior to European rule, Hutus (85 percent), Tutsis (14 percent), and Twa (less than 1 percent) lived peacefully side-by-side. Distinctions between Hutus and Tutsis prior to colonization were primarily tied to social class, not "race." The European settlers imported racial ideology to Africa, and soon Rwandans internalized the racial strata thrust upon them. In so doing, deep divisions within society emerged. The Germans placed the Tutsis in positions of power and provided them with greater access to education. Following Germany's loss of its colony in Rwanda in the wake of World War I, Belgium took over. The Belgians introduced ethnic identity cards in 1926 that all Rwandans had to carry. The identification cards (which in appearance look like passports) marked the transformation of the mobile social strata of Hutus and Tutsis into immobile racial identities.

The Hutu majority came to resent the colonizers' favoritism and rallied to overthrow the Tutsi-led government. They formed Parmehutu (Party for the Emancipation of the Hutus) in 1957 and two years later led a successful rebellion against Belgian colonizers and the Tutsi elite. When the Belgians withdrew from Rwanda from 1961 to 1962, they left Hutus in power. A wave of Hutu violence targeting Tutsis ensued. With the colonizers gone, no one came to rescue the vulnerable Tutsis. Over the span of 68 years, Rwandans had gone from communal neighbors to identifying themselves as "racial" enemies.

The international community stood idly by as the Hutu leadership oppressed Tutsis, forcing thousands to flee to neighboring countries, including Uganda, Zaire (presently the Democratic Republic of the Congo), and Burundi. Life had become so unbearable that half of all Rwandan Tutsis had fled their homeland by the mid-1960s. In Uganda, the Rwandan exiles formed the Rwandan Patriotic Front (RPF) in 1986 and positioned themselves to invade Rwanda to reclaim their home and gain influence in the Rwandan government.

While Rwanda's early history is tied to Germany and Belgium, the question of France's role in the genocide is primarily rooted in its interactions with Hutus starting in the early 1990s. The Hutu government called upon French and Zairian forces to defend Rwanda's Hutu-led government in October 1990 when RPF fighters mounted an attack from Uganda and crossed into Rwanda. Thanks in large part to French troops, the RPF failed to overthrow the government and had to contend itself with isolated attacks on Hutus in the border regions. From 1990 to 1993, ethnic tension during the Rwandan Civil War mounted and Hutus often attacked their Tutsis neighbors, accusing them of supporting the RPF.

Three years later, the Organization of African Unity (OAU)—a United Nations (UN) Committee of African nations—France, and the United States negotiated a peace accord and Rwandan president Juvénal Habyarimana and leaders of the RPF signed it in August 1993. The Arusha Accords (so named after Arusha, Tanzania, where the accord was signed) called for a multiparty government and granted Tutsis access to leadership roles in exchange for international economic support. In support of the Accords, the UN deployed 2,500 peacekeeping troops to the Rwandan capital of Kigali to ensure Habyarimana followed through, which he was slow to do.

Habyarimana's personal relationship with the late French president François Mitterrand

(the 21st president of France, 1981–1995) in the early 1990s is rich with speculation. The two appear to have enjoyed a close relationship, and Habyarimana used to dine with Mitterrand. Furthermore, following the assassination of Habyarimana on April 6, 1994—the event that sparked the genocide—French soldiers evacuated his widow Agathe Kanziga Habyarimana to France. She moved to Africa in 1995, but returned to France in 1997 fearing retribution from the RPF. Despite the Rwandan government's repeated requests to extradite Agathe to Rwanda to stand trial for allegedly helping plan the genocide, France has refused to do so.

On the tenth anniversary of the genocide, former RPF leader and current president of Rwanda Paul Kagame accused France of helping train Hutu troops in the days leading up to the 1994 genocide. As Habyarimana stalled the implementation of an equal-access Hutu-Tutsi government, he ramped up the training of his civilian militia known as Interahamwe, which in Kinyarwanda (the national language of Rwanda) translates to "those who stand together." During the genocide, the Interahamwe were the key perpetrators. Kagame has blamed Mitterrand's government for supplying arms to the Hutus in preparation for the genocide.

France's murky place in the history of the genocide becomes even cloudier when we consider Operation Turquoise. The French government wanted to establish safe zones in southwest Rwanda and on June 20, 1994, sent a draft resolution to the UN Security Council seeking authorization. Two days later, the UN issued Resolution 929 known as Operation Turquoise, which granted French soldiers jurisdiction to set up protected zones. The safe area, which became known as the "Turquoise Zone," comprised 20 percent of the country and was intended to act as a buffer between Rwanda and Zaire. Tutsis were fleeing Rwanda into Zaire at alarming numbers and the Turquoise Zone was also an attempt to slow the Tutsi exodus.

While the protected zones were supposed to provide a safe haven to Tutsis running for their lives, many contend that the French soldiers allowed Hutu extremists to enter the Tutsi camps and continue their killing. Some even claim that the French soldiers let in Hutus and allowed them to cross into Zaire in order to save them from the advancing RPF soldiers.

Questions surrounding France's involvement in the years leading up to and during the Rwandan Genocide illuminate the complicated nature of understanding how and why genocide occurs. The import of a European racial theory and the international community's failure—France included—to prevent and stop the killings are key factors in this history. France's contributions to the genocidal outcomes of 1994 are just one component in a multidimensional, complicated, and contested past.

Alexis Herr

Does the film *Hotel Rwanda* accurately depict the Rwandan Genocide?

The 2004 film *Hotel Rwanda* presents the story of Paul Rusesabagina, a hotel manager who saved the lives of more than 1,000 refugees during the Rwandan Genocide. Since its release, the film has become a popular way for educators to teach students about the 1994 genocide in Rwanda and introduce the concept of an upstander (a person who acts in support of an individual or cause, particularly someone who intervenes on behalf of a person being attacked). Despite the positive message behind the film, critics allege that it emphasizes only one side of the story and exaggerates Rusesabagina's efforts to shelter Tutsis. And while *Hotel Rwanda* has

undoubtedly become the most recognizable film about the Rwandan Genocide, questions about its accuracy remain.

In the essays that follow, Sarah E. Brown and Alexis Herr, both genocide scholars, weigh the historical accuracy of *Hotel Rwanda* and analyze Paul Rusesabagina's role in rescuing Rwandans targeted for annihilation. Brown contends that the film did bring much needed attention to the Rwandan Genocide, however, she argues that Rusesabagina is the not the hero he claims to be. In conclusion, Brown argues that the revisionist narrative the film presents has done more damage than good. While Herr agrees that the film does not offer an accurate portrayal of Rusesabagina or what occurred in Hotel des Milles Collines, she argues that it is not worth writing off completely.

Historical Revisionism and Paul Rusesabagina

Hotel Rwanda, a 2004 Hollywood film that catapulted the Rwandan Genocide into mainstream media just 10 years after its occurrence, was a cinematic success that brought to light the horrors of the 1994 genocide. Unfortunately, the movie, based upon the falsified accounts of Paul Rusesabagina, a hotel manager during the genocide, promulgated a false version of events and ultimately did more harm than good. In the end, the success of *Hotel Rwanda* perpetuated a fictional version of history and enabled Rusesabagina to orchestrate and fund a vitriolic campaign against Rwanda, survivors of the Rwandan Genocide, and stability in the Great Lakes region of Central Africa.

Hotel Rwanda disseminates historical revisionism according to one man, Paul Rusesabagina, who offered a fabricated account of his actions during the 1994 Rwandan genocide in a nefarious effort to lionize himself and cover up his misdeeds. In the film, Don Cheadle plays Rusesabagina, the manager of the Hotel des Milles Collines in Kigali, Rwanda, and savior of over a thousand individuals targeted for mass murder. Cheadle portrays Rusesabagina as soft spoken, humble, and compassionate, a man who goes to great personal lengths to save the refugees in his hotel. Survivors of the Hotel des Milles Collines offer a starkly different depiction of Rusesabagina as an extortionist, opportunist, bully, and friend of the genocidal government orchestrating the genocide. While Rusesabagina fiercely denies claims that he demanded payment for rooms and food at the hotel, Edouard Kayihura, survivor of the genocide and former refugee at the hotel, describes in detail how Rusesabagina took over management of the hotel and changed the tenor of the hotel just a week into the genocide. Disobeying direct orders from Sabena, the parent company in charge of the hotel, and ignoring a letter from the International Committee of the Red Cross, he charged refugees for room and board, including donated food. In addition, Rusesabagina denied entrance to those who could not pay, thereby effectively ensuring their death, threatened those inside who could not afford his rates, and attempted to remove the United Nations Assistance for Rwanda (UNAMIR) peacekeepers protecting the Hotel des Milles Collines. While Paul Rusesabagina did assist in the survival of over a 1,000 people housed in the hotel, he is certainly not the hero he claims to be.

By falsely portraying historical events during the 1994 Rwandan Genocide without thought to the long-term consequences, *Hotel Rwanda* has perpetuated a host of historical inaccuracies that blatantly disregard the survivors of the Hotel des Milles Collines and silence the outcry of survivor organizations in Rwanda such as IBUKA

("remember" in Kinyarwanda). Survivors of the genocide tell a different story about their time at the hotel and of their antagonists and rescuers, the true heroes of the story. As a result of *Hotel Rwanda's* aggrandizing of Rusesabagina, an opportunity to recognize and emulate the true heroes of the Hotel des Mille Collines, the very same who were downplayed in Rusesabagina's narrative, was missed. Rusesabagina all but ignored the critical role that UNAMIR peacekeepers and a handful of United Nations (UN) military observers played; individuals who, a great personal risk, stood between the Interahamwe stationed just outside the white walls that surrounded the hotel's perimeter and the people hidden inside. Additionally, it was a number of influential diplomats and leaders who were refugees in the hotel, not Rusesabagina, who used their international contacts to ensure that their plight was known outside of Rwanda, thereby holding the genocidal government in check and preventing an attack. Individuals such as Captain Mbaye Diagne, overlooked by Rusesabagina and by Hollywood, rejected the bystander culture and risked their lives to save others. Relying on the fictionalized version of events results in a missed opportunity for discussion of how to proactively develop a new generation of, to use the former U.S. ambassador to the United Nations, Samantha Power's term, "upstanders," people willing to speak out and take a stand against human rights abuses, mass atrocities, and genocide.

Nevertheless, despite overwhelming evidence of Rusesabagina's actual deeds and public outcry within and beyond Rwanda, he manipulated the platform provided by *Hotel Rwanda* for personal profit and political influence. Commanding high fees for speaking engagements, the controversial recipient of the Lantos Foundation for Human Rights and Justice Award and veteran of the West's talk-show circuit took every opportunity to profit from his newfound fame. In an effort to leverage his ill-gained popularity for political clout, he launched a public relations offensive against the current Rwandan government that relied heavily on ethnic rhetoric that pitted Hutus against Tutsis and began to fundraise for his own electoral campaign in Rwanda. His political hopes were temporarily dashed after evidence tying him to the Democratic Forces for the Liberation of Rwanda (French: Forces démocratiques de liberation du Rwanda, or FDLR), a murderous rebel group embedded in the Democratic Republic of the Congo (DRC) comprised of veteran perpetrators of the Rwandan Genocide and responsible for massacres, genocidal rape, and destruction in eastern DRC for decades, came to light and resulted in his investigation in Rwanda. Even today, Rusesabagina continues to attack the government in Rwanda, deny any wrongdoing during the genocide, and collect accolades for courageous acts he did not commit.

While Don Cheadle's masterful performance makes it easy to admire Hollywood's version of Paul Rusesabagina, *Hotel Rwanda* has erroneously taken the place of historical fact for many who rely upon the film to provide an accurate rendering of events during the 1994 Rwandan Genocide. Survivors of the Rwandan Genocide remember Rusesabagina as an insidious businessman who used the genocide for personal profit. Today, he is reviled as a supporter of genocidal groups operating in the DRC and abroad. Celebrating a man for acts of rescue he did not commit and perpetuating a false narrative with far reaching implications for survivors of genocide, Rwanda, and the region, *Hotel Rwanda* continues to harm Rwanda even today.

Sara E. Brown

Hotel Rwanda and Memory

The 2004 film *Hotel Rwanda* offers a Hollywood-styled retelling of the Rwandan Genocide. While certain elements of the story surrounding Paul Rusesabagina's efforts to shelter Tutsis in Hotel des Mille Collines from the Hutu militia were stylized for cinematic effect, for all its flaws *Hotel Rwanda* has succeeded in bringing the Rwandan Genocide to the attention of a much broader and international audience. While it provides an easily approachable narrative to people unfamiliar with the Rwandan Genocide, it also distorts the actual story and the role of Rusesabagina in saving potential victims, thus raising the question of the cost of oversimplifying a complicated event.

Hotel Rwanda tells the story of Paul Rusesabagina, a hotel manager at Hotel des Mille Collines in Rwanda. Despite being a Hutu (the nationality of a majority of the perpetrators), Rusesabagina put his and his family's lives at risk when he decided to turn the hotel into a refugee sanctuary for over a 1,000 Tutsis (many of whom were targeted by the Hutu militia for annihilation). Actors Don Cheadle and Sophie Okonedo were both nominated for Academy Awards for their brilliant portrayals of Paul Rusesabagina and his wife Tatiana. Cheadle's portrayal as Rusesabagina in particular, as well as his prominent status as a human rights activist, brought prominence to the film as the standard Hollywood narrative of the Rwandan Genocide.

Despite the film receiving high acclaim from many movie critics, others have rejected the positive portrayal of Rusesabagina as nothing more than a Hollywood perversion of a greedy man. For example, Roméo Dallaire, the Canadian who led the United Nation (UN) troops on the ground during the genocide has spoken out against the film. In an interview with the Huffington Post in 2011, Dallaire referred to the film as nothing more than Hollywood junk. Other Rwandan groups have also attacked the film, claiming it is a revisionist history and fails to show how Rusesabagina profited from the refugees he is shown to have saved. Some critics have also scrutinized what they view as the film's failure to show the widespread violence of the Hutu militia in favor of a narrative narrowed in on Rusesabagina.

Films created for mass consumption like *Hotel Rwanda*—as opposed to historical documentaries or classroom shorts—often cut corners in order to craft a compelling, dynamic, and relatable story. Released in 2005, *Hotel Rwanda* paints a vivid picture of the 1994 Rwandan Genocide in broad strokes. The role that colonization played in solidifying the arbitrary ethnic categories of Hutus (approximately 85 percent of the population) and Tutsis (approximately 14 percent of the population) into contentious "racial" classes is mentioned, however, only in a few sentences in the first 20 minutes of the film. While the Rwandan Patriotic Front (RPF) is presented as ending the genocide, little to no background on the establishment of this organization and its post-genocide legacy are shown. Some reference is made to mass rape, but the film fails to elucidate the scale of sexual assault that took place. As a result, the film takes a very narrow approach to an otherwise vast event that encompassed an entire country.

The film also struggles to illuminate the important timeline of the genocide, starting with the Arusha Accords (a peace treaty signed by the Rwandan government and the RPF) that took place in August 1993. A viewer with limited knowledge of the genocide might fail to grasp that the Arusha Accords took place half a year before the genocide. And while *Hotel Rwanda* does play the infamous radio interview of Madeleine Albright (the U.S. ambassador to the UN during the genocide) in which she fails to call the atrocity genocide, the film never identifies the speaker or the significance of Albright's elusive language. By not referring to the mass slaughter of Tutsis as genocide, the United States and the UN were not legally obliged to act.

Despite its historical flaws, this film does offer something important: an accessible go-to film on the Rwandan Genocide. While the Holocaust is the subject of countless popular films such as *Schindler's List*, *Boy in the Striped Pajamas*, *Life is Beautiful* (all of which have come under fire for failure to offer a historically accurate portrayal of that genocide), *Hotel Rwanda* is the first movie on the Rwandan Genocide to receive popular acclaim. Yes, the film is not a perfect representation of the Rwandan Genocide. Yes, Rusesabagina was not the hero he is made out to be. Yes, a viewer will not gain a solid understanding of the historical precedents that created the genocide. And despite all its flaws, this film is an entry point into an important history.

Alexis Herr

Chronology

1884

During negotiations between the European powers gathered at the Conference of Berlin, Germany is awarded the territory of Rwanda.

1899

Rwanda is incorporated into German East Africa.

1911

Tutsi chiefs assist German troops (*Schütztruppe*) to crush a popular uprising in northern Rwanda. This event will be used by Hutu extremists in the years leading up to the genocide to demonize Tutsis.

1913

Coffee is introduced as cash crop.

1916

During World War I, Belgian troops occupy Rwanda (then called Ruanda-Urundi).

1923

Following Germany's defeat in World War I, the Treaty of Versailles designates Rwanda a protectorate of the League of Nations to be governed by Belgium.

1931

The Belgians depose *Mwami* (King) Yuhi V Musinga and replace him with his son Charles Rudahigwa Mutara.

1933–1934

The Belgian administration in Rwanda conducts an official census which ascribes an ethnic identity to each Rwandan as Hutu, Tutsi, or Twa. Identity cards that include the ethnic classification of each citizen are disturbed to all Rwandans.

1944

Raphael Lemkin, a Polish-Jewish lawyer, coins the word "genocide" from the *genos* (Greek: nation or tribe) and suffix—cide (Latin: to kill).

1945

October 24: The international community replaces the ineffective League of Nations with the United Nations.

1948

December 9: The United Nations General Assembly adopts the Convention on the Prevention and Punishment of the Crime of Genocide (UNCG).
The first UN Trusteeship Council mission visits Ruanda-Urundi.

1952

January 12: UNCG comes into force as international law.

1957

March 24: The Bahutu Manifesto, a document criticizing Hutu exclusion from power, is published.

June: Hutu Emancipation Movement (French: Parti de l'émancipation du people Hutu, or Parmehutu) is formed.

September: The Rwandan National Union Party (French: Union Nationale Rwandaise, or UNAR)—a political party calling for Belgian forces to leave Rwanda in the hands of a hereditary Tutsi monarchy—is formed.

1959

July: While in Bujumbura, Burundi, Rwandan King Rudahigwa mysteriously dies (July 25) while under the care of a Belgian physician. He is succeeded (July 28) by his brother Kigeli Ndahindurwa.

November: Hutus lead a rebellion against the Belgian colonialists and the Tutsis ruling elite, causing some 150,000 Tutsis to flee to Burundi. Several hundred people died before the Belgians restored order. This marks the start of the so-called Peasant Revolution or Hutu Revolution that will last until 1962.

1960

December 14: The United Nations General Assembly adopts the Declaration on the Granting of Independence to Colonial Countries and Peoples to help speed up the process of decolonization. It states that all people have the right to self-determination. In Rwanda's first municipal elections, the Parmehutu dominate.

1961

September: 80 percent of Rwandans vote in a referendum to end monarchy rule and the first Rwandan republic is declared. More Tutsis flee the country as Hutus take control of key leadership positions.

1962

July: Rwanda and Burundi gain independence from Belgium. Grégoire Kayibanda, leader of the Parmehutu party, becomes first president of independent Rwanda.

Tutsi refugees in Tanzania and Zaire (now known as the Democratic Republic of the Congo) stage attacks on Hutu leaders.

1963

Tutsi exiles launch more attacks against Hutus in Rwanda, which escalates the violence between Tutsis and Hutus and causes Rwandan Tutsis to seek refuge in neighboring Uganda, Tanzania, Burundi, and Zaire.

November—December: an estimated 1,000 Tutsis are killed by Hutus in retaliation for Tutsi attacks from across the borders.

1967

Tutsi exiles attack and Hutus retaliate. Between 1962 and 1967, 10 such attacks occur and each time the retaliatory killings of Tutsis creates a new wave of Tutsi refugees.

1972

Mass killing of Hutus by the Tutsi-dominated army in Burundi. During this genocide, some 100,000 to 200,000 Hutu, as well as Tutsis who tried to stop the killings, are murdered.

1973

Coup d'état by Major Juvénal Habyarimana. He founds the National Revolutionary Movement for Development (French: Mouvement Révolutionnaire National pour le Développement, or MRND). The government begins a process of suppressing Tutsi rights. Tutsis are restricted to 9 percent of available jobs in public service and are expelled from universities.

1975

July: Habyarimana's political party, the MRND, becomes the sole political party allowed in Rwanda.

France and Rwanda sign military agreement.

1978

December: The Habyarimana government approves a new constitution in a referendum. He is elected to a five-year term as president and was the only candidate in the election. Hutus are favored in government.

1983

Habyarimana is reelected president with 99.98 percent of the vote.

1988

The Rwandan Patriotic Front (RPF) is founded in Kampala, Uganda, with the goal of securing repatriation of Rwandan exiles and reforming a more inclusive Rwandan government. Habyarimana is reelected president.

1990

May: The inaugural issue of *Kangura*—a Hutu extremist newspaper—is published.

July: Habyarimana concedes to international pressure to create a multi-party democracy.

September—October: Roman Catholic Pope John Paul II visits Rwanda.

October: the RPF invades Rwanda, thus starting the Rwandan Civil War.

December: *Kangura* publishes "the Ten Commandments," a list of discriminatory directives against Tutsis.

The Interahamwe—the paramilitary organization of the MRND—forms.

1991

June: Rwanda adopts a new constitution that allows for a multi-party government.

1992

June 12: Peace talks between the RPF and Habyarimana government begin in Arusha, Tanzania.

Pauline Nyiramasuhuko is made the Minister of Family Welfare and Women's Affairs.

The Coalition for the Defense of the Republic (French: Coalition pour la Défense de la République, or CDR) is founded.

The Impuzamugambi—a Hutu militia group—forms.

1993

July 8: Radio-Télévision Libre des Mille Collines begins broadcasting.

August 4: The Rwandan government and the RPF sign the Arusha Peace Accords.

October 3: 24 UN peacekeepers and 18 U.S. soldiers are killed in Somalia.

October 5: The United Nations creates the United Nations Assistance Mission for Rwanda (UNAMIR).

October 21: President Melchior Ndadye of Burundi is assassinated. During the chaos that follows, 10,000 are murdered, and approximately 375,000 flee to Rwanda.

October 22: UNAMIR Force Commander Roméo Dallaire arrives in Kigali.

November: Jacques-Roger Booh-Booh becomes head of UNAMIR.

1994

January 11: Dallaire writes to the United Nations headquarters and requests protection for an Interahamwe military informant providing information on weapons caches and planned attacks on RPF and Belgian soldiers.

February 21: Political leaders Félicien Gatabazi and Martin Bucyana are assassinated.

March: Businessman Félicien Kabuga reportedly imports 50,000 machetes from Kenya, which will become the weapons wielded by the perpetrators during the genocide.

April 6: Rwandan president Habyarimana and Burundian president Cyprien Ntaryamira are killed when their plane is shot down.

April 7: Rwandan prime minister Agathe Uwilingiyimana and her husband are murdered. UN military observer Captain Mbaye Diagne rescues her five children from a nearby compound. Minister for Labor and Social Affairs Landoald Ndasingwa, and his family, are killed by members of the Presidential Guard. Ten Belgian UN officers are killed. Tutsis seeking shelter at the parish of Musubi are killed. The Interahamwe set up roadblocks and begin killing Tutsis and moderate Hutus.

April 8: The evacuation of foreigners in Rwanda begins. The interim government is established. The RPF launches a major effort to rescue some 600 of its soldiers—placed there prior to the genocide in accordance with the Arusha Accords—surrounded in Kigali.

April 9: Agathe Habyarimana, widow of former president Habyarimana, is evacuated to France. Interahamwe forces attack a church at Gikondo, in Kigali. Approximately 100 die. The RPF proposes a joint force with UNAMIR and the Rwandan army to end the slaughter of civilians. It is rejected. RPF begin assassinating individuals connected to the Rwandan government, army, or hostile political groups, such as Sylvestre Bariyanga (a former prefect of Ruhengeri) and his family.

April 11: Ex-patriates and Belgian soldiers are evacuated from the Ecole Technique Officielle (ETO), in a suburb of Kigali. Civilians at ETO under UNAMIR protection are massacred following its departure.

April 12: The Nyange parish is surrounded by Hutu soldiers and Interahamwe militiamen. Attacks on the parish last until

April 16, when the church is bulldozed and all survivors are killed.

April 14: Just one week after 10 Belgian soldiers are murdered, Belgium withdraws its soldiers from UNAMIR.

April 15: The Adventist compound of Mugonero is surrounded by Hutu extremists. Three thousand die following the attack begun the next morning. RPF forces arrive at Ntarama, ending the killing of 5,000 Tutsis in the area. Patients being carried by a Red Cross Ambulance are killed at a roadblock.

April 16: Augustin Bizimungu is promoted to major general, and made head of the Rwandan army.

April 17: Over 100 Tutsis are killed by soldiers and militiamen in Nyanza.

April 18: Following a meeting with Rwanda's interim government, mayor Jean-Paul Akayesu stops protecting Tutsis in Taba and promotes citizens to participate in the killings. The Mabirizi Roman Catholic Church is attacked by local militiamen armed with grenades and machine guns. Of the 2,000 seeking refuge there, only an estimated 200 survive.

April 21: The UN Security Council (UNSC) reduces its forces in Rwanda from 2,500 to 250. A number of UN personnel remain against Security Council orders. Sister Felicitas Niyitegeka is executed.

April 23: Government troops attack Butare hospital, killing nearly 170 patients.

April 25: Kabuga heads the newly created National Defense Funds Acting Committee (French: Comité Provisoire du Fonds de Défense Nationale, or FDN). Militias attack Tutsis who were misled into believing Red Cross aid was being provided at the Butare football stadium. The RPF begins evacuating civilians to Byumba and Rutare.

April 28: Five hundred Tutsis are killed while trying to escape from a stadium in Cyangugu.

April 30: The UNSC passes a resolution condemning the violence in Rwanda, but fails to call the atrocity genocide.

May 17: A United Nations Security Council resolution states that "acts of genocide may have been committed," however, bickering over who will fund a larger troop deployment delays action.

Mid-May: The International Red Cross estimates half a million Rwandans have been killed since the genocide began in April.

May 31: UN Captain Mbaye Diagne is killed in an RPF attack on a Hutu extremist checkpoint.

June 2: Some 40 people are killed by RPF forces near Runda.

June 5: Archbishop Vincent Nsengiyumva and other clergymen are killed in Kabgayi, allegedly by advancing RPF soldiers.

June 13: UN forces successfully evacuate 300 from the Saint-Famille church complex.

June 14: Forty Tutsi boys are taken from the Saint-Famille church complex and killed.

June 19: RPF soldiers fire on crowds gathered in Mukingi, killing over 100 individuals.

June 22: The UNSC passes Resolution 929, which sets in motion Operation Turquoise, a French led and UN supported military operation in Rwanda. Operation Turquoise soldiers create a "safe area" in a government controlled territory in Rwanda, however, the killing of Tutsis continues in that zone.

June 27: The Bisesero Hill massacre occurs.

July 1: Shahryar Khan replaces Booh-Booh as the head of UNAMIR.

July 3: RPF forces shutdown Radio-Télévision Libre des Milles Collines.

July 4: RPF forces capture Kigali.

July 14: RPF forces capture Rehengeri.

Mid-July: The Hutu government flees the country, most of whom head to Zaire.

July 17: Goma, Zaire, is bombed. The UN Emergency Rwandan Aid Office in Goma reports that more than one million Rwandans sought refuge in Zaire. RPF forces capture Gisenyi, a city in the Rubavu district in Rwanda's Western Province.

July 18: The RPF gains control over Rwanda. A ceasefire is declared. It is estimated that 800,000 have been killed prior to the ceasefire.

July 19: Pasteur Bizimungu is sworn in as president.

July 22: Operation Support Hope—a U.S. military effort to provide relief and support for Rwandans—begins.

July 31: Operation Turquoise troops withdraw.

August: UNAMIR II begins its formal operations in Rwanda. The newly established Rwandan government agrees to the creation of an international tribunal established by the UNSC to try high-level *génocidaires*.

September 20: UN soldiers find 8,000 bodies in Gafunzi.

November 8: The United Nations establishes the International Criminal Tribunal for Rwanda (ICTR) to locate and prosecute those responsible for the 1994 Rwandan Genocide.

1995

December 12: The ICTR releases its first indictments against eight perpetrators and charges them with genocide and crimes against humanity.

1996

February 13: Prominent Interahamwe militia leader Georges Rutaganda is arrested.

March 9: Colonel Théoneste Bagosora, former defence minister, is arrested.

Fall 1996: The African Crisis Response Initiative, later renamed the African Contingency Operations Training and Assistance Program, is founded.

1997

July 18: With the help of Kenya, seven suspects (including the former prime minister of the Rwandan government during the genocide), are arrested in Nairobi, Kenya.

1998

March 25: In a speech in Kigali, U.S. president Bill Clinton apologizes the victims of the genocide for not acting "quickly enough after the killing began."

May 1: Jean Kambanda, the former interim government prime minister during the genocide, makes history when he becomes the first person accused of genocide to admit responsibility for it.

May 7: UN secretary-general travels to Kigali, Rwanda and apologizes to the Rwandan parliament for failing the people of Rwanda during the genocide.

September 4: The ICTR accepts Kambanda's guilty plea and in so doing becomes the first international tribunal since the Nuremberg trials that followed the Holocaust to issue a judgment against a former head of state.

September 9: The ICTR finds Akayesu guilty of genocide and in so doing his case becomes the first international tribunal to enter a judgment for genocide according to the definition of genocide set forth in the 1948 Geneva Conventions.

Philip Gourevitch publishes *We Wish to Inform You that Tomorrow We Will be Killed with Our Families.*

1999

December 15: The UN "Report of Independent Inquiry into the Actions of the United Nations During the 1994 Genocide in Rwanda," also known as the Carlsson Report, is released.

Alison Des Forges publishes *Leave None to Tell the Story: Genocide in Rwanda.*

2000

April 7: Belgian prime minister Guy Verhofstadt issues an apology for Belgian withdrawal during the Rwandan Genocide.

October 23: The Media Trial, with defendants Jean-Bosco Barayagwiza, Ferdinand Nahimana, and Hassan Ngeze, begins. All were found guilty and sentenced to jail time.

2001

March: Rwanda adopts *gacaca* law.

2002

February 14: A Rwandan census reveals that approximately one seventh of the population had been murdered, and 94 percent of victims were Tutsis.

2003

September 12: Paul Kagame is sworn in as president.

2004

September: The trial of Augustin Bizimungu and his co-accused, known as "Military Trial 2," opens.

December 22: Film *Hotel Rwanda* is first released in the United States.

Patrick de Saint-Exupéry publishes *L'inavouable: La France au Rwanda.*

2006

April: *An Ordinary Man*, an autobiography by Paul Rusesabagina, is published.

October 2: The trial of singer Simon Bikindi begins. He is later sentenced to seven years in prison and his music is banned from national radio stations.

November: Rwanda ends diplomatic relations with France.

2007

January 4: Political asylum is denied to Agathe Hayarimana in France.

Rwanda abolishes the death penalty.

2008

December 18: Bagosora, Ntabakuze, and Nsengiyumva are found guilty of war crimes, genocide, and crimes against humanity.

2010

Dallaire publishes *They Fight Like Soldiers, They Die Like Children*.

March 2: Agathe Habyarimana is arrested.

June 24: Presidential candidate Bernard Ntaganda is arrested on charges of divisionism.

August 9: Kagame is reelected as president.

2011

June 24: History is made when the ICTR convicts Pauline Nyiramasuhuko for rape as a crime against humanity. She is the first woman to be convicted of genocide, conspiracy to commit genocide, and rape as a crime against humanity.

2012

February 2: The high-ranking members of the MRND are held responsible for crimes by their youth wing, the Interahamwe, by the ICTR in the trial of Edouard Karemera and Matthieu Ngirumpaste.

June 18: After trying some two million genocide subjects, Rwanda's *gacaca* courts are closed.

December 20: The ICTR delivers its Final Trial Judgment in the trial of Augustin Ngirabatware.

2015

Rwandans vote in favor of a constitution referendum that would allow President Kagame to extend his tenure to govern till 2034.

2017

March: Pope Francis asked Rwandan president Paul Kagame for forgiveness for the failures and sins of the Catholic Church during the genocide.

August: Rwandans reelect Paul Kagame for a third presidential term.

Abbreviations

ACOTA
African Contingency Operations Training and Assistance Program

ACRI
African Crisis Response Initiative

ADLF
Democratic Alliance for the Liberation of the Congo (French: Alliance des Forces Démocratiques pour la Libération du Congo-Zaïre)

ADRA
Adventist Development and Relief Agency

CDR
Coalition for the Defence of the Republic (French: Coalition pour la Défense de la République)

CNDP
National Congress for the Defense of the People (French: Conseil National pour la Défense du Peuple)

DPKO
United Nations Department of Peacekeeping Operations

DRC
Democratic Republic of the Congo

FAR
Rwandan Armed Forces (French: Forces Armées Rwandaises)

FDD
Forces for the Defense of Democracy (French: Forces pour la Défense de la Démocratie)

FDLR
(French: Forces Démocratiques pour la Libération du Rwanda)

FDN
National Defense Funds Acting Committee (French: Comité Provisoire du Fonds de Défense Nationale)

FNL
National Liberation Forces (French: Forces Nationales de Libération)

HRW
Human Rights Watch

ICC
International Criminal Court

ICRC
International Committee of the Red Cross

ICTR
International Criminal Tribunal for Rwanda

IDPs
Internally displaced persons

JRR
Rwagasore Youth Revolutionists (French: Jeunesses Révolutionnaires Rwagasore)

KGM
Kigali Genocide Memorial

MDR
The Democratic Republican Movement (French: Mouvement Démocratique Républicain)

MILOB
Military observer

MONUC
United Nations Mission in the Democratic Republic of the Congo (French: Mission des Nations unies en République démocratique du Congo)

MRND
National Revolutionary Movement for Development (French: Révolutionnaire National Pour le Développement)

MRNDD
National Republican Movement for Development and Democracy (French: Mouvement Républicain National pour le Développement et la Démocratie)

NGO
Nonprofit governmental organization

OAU
Organization of African Unity

ODA
Official Development Assistance

ORINFOR
Rwandan National Information Office (French: Office Rwandais d'Information)

OSH
Operation Support Hope

Parmehutu
Party for Hutu Emancipation (French: Parti de l'émancipation du peuple Hutu)

PL
Liberal Party (French: Parti Liberal)

PSD
Social Democratic Party (French: Parti Social Democrate)

RDF
Rwandan Defense Forces (French: Forces Rwandaises de Défense)

RPA
Rwandan Patriotic Army

RPF
Rwandan Patriotic Front (French: Front patriotique rwandais)

RTLM
Free Radio and Television of the Thousand Hills (French: Radio-Télévision Libre des Mille Collines)

SRSG
Special Representative of the Secretary-General of the United Nations

UN
United Nations

UNAMIR
United Nations Assistance Mission for Rwanda

Unar
Rwandese National Union (French: Union Nationale Rwandaise)

UNHCR
United Nations High Commission for Refugees

UPC
Union of Congolese Patriots (French: Union des Patriotes)

UPRONA
Union for National Progress (French: Union pour le Progrès National)

UNSC
United Nations Security Council

Bibliography

Adekunle, Julius O. *Culture and Customs of Rwanda*. Westport, CT: Greenwood Press, 2007.

Adelman, Howard, and Astri Suhrke, eds. *The Path of a Genocide: The Rwanda Crisis from Uganda to Zaire*. New Brunswick, NJ: Transaction Publishers, 1999.

African Rights. *Rwanda: Death, Despair and Defiance*. 2nd rev. ed. London: African Rights, 1995.

Africa South of the Sahara 1994. London: Europa Publications Limited, 1994.

"Agnes Ntamabyariro," Trial International (13 June 2016), accessed 12 July 2017. https://trialinternational.org/latest-post/agnes-ntamabyariro/.

Akyeampong, Emmanuel K. and Henry Louis Gates, Jr., eds. *African Biography*. Oxford, UK: Oxford University Press, 2012.

Ali, Taisier M., and Robert O. Matthews. *Civil Wars in Africa: Roots and Resolution*. Toronto: McGill-Queen's University Press, 1999.

Anyidoho, Henry Kwami. *Guns Over Kigali: The Rwandese Civil War, 1994. A Personal Account*. Accra: Woeli Publishing Services, 1997.

"Augustin Ndindiliyimana," Trial International (10 June 2016), accessed 17 July 2017. https://trialinternational.org/latest-post/augustin-ndindiliyimana/.

Barnett, Michael. *Eyewitness to a Genocide: The United Nations and Rwanda*. Ithaca, NY: Cornell University Press, 2002.

Barnett, Victoria J. *Bystanders: Conscience and Complicity During the Holocaust*. Westport, CT: Greenwood Press, 1999.

Beigbeder, Yves. *Judging War Criminals: The Politics of International Justice*. New York: St. Martin's Press, 1999.

Bodnarchuk, Kari. *Rwanda: A Country Torn Apart*. Minneapolis, MN: Lerner Publishing Group, 1998.

Booh-Booh, Jacques-Roger. *Le Patron de Dallaire Parle: Révélations sur les dérives d'un général de l'ONU au Rwanda*. Paris: Duboiris, 2005.

Boot, Machteld. *Genocide, Crimes Against Humanity, War Crimes: Nullum Crimen Sine Lege and the Subject Matter Jurisdiction of the International Criminal Court*. Antwerp: Intersentia, 2002.

Bornkamm, Paul Christopher. *Rwanda's Gacaca Courts: Between Retribution and Reparation*. Oxford: Oxford University Press, 2012.

Brown, Michael, Gary Freeman and Kay Miller. *Passing-By: The United States and Genocide in Burundi, 1972*. New York: The Carnegie Endowment for International Peace, 1973.

Cameron, Hazel. *Britain's Hidden Role in the Rwandan Genocide: the Cat's Paw*. New York: Routledge, 2013.

Chakravarty, Anuradha. *Investigating in Authoritarian Rule: Punishment and Patronage in Rwanda's Gacaca Courts for Genocide Crimes*. Cambridge: Cambridge University Press, 2015.

Cheadle, Don, and John Prendergast. *Not on Our Watch: The Mission to End Genocide in Darfur and Beyond*. New York: Hyperion, 2007.

Chrétien, Jean-Pierre. *The Great Lakes of Africa: Two Thousand Years of History*. Translated by Scott Strauss, New York: Zone Books, 2003.

Clark, Philip. *The Gacaca Courts, Post-Genocide Justice and Reconciliation in Rwanda: Justice Without Lawyers*. Cambridge: Cambridge University Press, 2011.

Cohen, Stanley. *States of Denial: Knowing About Atrocities and Suffering*. Cambridge: Polity Press, 2001.

Cruvellier, Thierry. *Court of Remorse: Inside the International Criminal Court for Rwanda*. Madison, WI: University of Wisconsin Press, 2010.

Dallaire, Roméo. *Shake Hands with the Devil: The Failure of Humanity in Rwanda*. Toronto: Random House, Canada, 2004.

Davies, Lizzy and Chris McGreal, "Widow of assassinated Rwandan president arrested," *The Guardian* (2 March 2010), accessed 17 July 2017. https://www .theguardian.com/world/2010/mar/02 /widow-assassinated-rwandan-president -arrrested.

Des Forges, Alison. *Leave None to Tell the Story: Genocide in Rwanda*. New York: Human Rights Watch, 1999.

Des Forges, Alison, and Timothy Longman. "Legal Responses to Genocide in Rwanda." In *My Neighbor, My Enemy: Justice and Community in the Aftermath of Mass Atrocity*, edited by Eric Stover and Harvey M. Weinstein, 49–63. Cambridge: Cambridge University Press, 2004.

DiPrizio, Robert C. *Armed Humanitarians: US Interventions from Northern Iraq to Kosovo*. Baltimore, Maryland: John Hopkins University Press, 2002.

Dorsey, Learthen. *Historical Dictionary of Rwanda*. Metuchen, NJ: Scarecrow Press, 1994.

Eller, Jack David. *From Culture to Ethnicity to Conflict: An Anthropological Perspective on International Ethnic Conflict*. Ann Arbor: University of Michigan Press, 1999.

Eltringham, Nigel. *Accounting for Horror: Post-Genocide Debates in Rwanda*. Londres: Pluto Press, 2004.

Evans, Glynne. *Responding to Crises in the African Great Lakes*. Oxford: Oxford University Press, 1997.

Friedrichs, David O., ed. *State Crime*. Brookfield, VT: Ashgate/Dartmouth, 1998.

George, Terry, "Smearing a Hero," *Washington Post* (May 10, 2006).

Gourevitch, Philip. "The Arrest of Madame Agathe," *The New Yorker* (2 March 2010), http://www.newyorker.com/news/news -desk/the-arrest-of-madame-agathe.

Gourevitch, Philip. *We wish to inform you that tomorrow we will be killed with our ramilies: Stories from Rwanda*. New York: Picador, 1999.

Gribbin, Robert E. *In the Aftermath of Genocide: The US Role in Rwanda*. New York: I Universe, 2005.

Grünfeld, Fred and Anke Huijboom. *The Failure to Prevent Genocide in Rwanda: The Role of Bystanders*. Boston: Martinus Nijhoff, 2007.

Hatzfield, Jean. *Machete Season: The Killers in Rwanda Speak*. Translated by Linda Coverdale. New York: Farrar, Straus and Giroux, 2005.

Herr, Alexis. *The Holocaust and Compensated Compliance in Italy: Fossoli di Carpi, 1942–1952*. New York: Palgrave Macmillan, 2016.

Hilberg, Raul. *Perpetrator Victims Bystanders: The Jewish Catastrophe, 1933–1945*. New York: Aaron Asher Brooks, 1992.

Hoeksema, Suzanne, "Re-educating the Perpetrators in the Aftermath of the Rwandan Genocide," in *Genocide: New Perspectives on its Causes, Courses, and Consequences*, ed. Ugur Ümit Üngör. Amsterdam: Amsterdam University Press, 2016: 195–215.

"The ICTR in Brief," United Nations Mechanism for International Criminal Tribunals (February 2017), http://unictr.unmict.org /en/tribunal/.

International Criminal Tribunal for Rwanda, Prosecutor v. Ferdinand Nahimana, Jean-Bosco Barayagwiza, and Hassan Ngeze, Judgment and Sentence, Case No. ICTR-99-52-T (Trial Chamber1, December 3, 2003).

"Interview: Major Brent Beardsley," Frontline (1 April 2004). http://www.pbs.org/wgbh/pages/frontline/shows/ghosts/interviews/beardsley.html.

Jennings, Christian. *Across the Red River: Rwanda, Burundi and the Heart of Darkness*. Londres: Phoenix, 2000.

Jokic, Aleksandar, ed. *War Crimes and Collective Wrongdoing: A Reader*. Malden, MA: Blackwell Publishers, 2001.

Jones, Adam. *Genocide: A Comprehensive Introduction*. London and New York: Routledge, 2011.

Kagan, Sophia, "The 'Media case' before the Rwanda Tribunal: The Nahimana et al. Appeal Judgement," The Hague Justice Portal (24 April 2008), http://www.haguejusticeportal.net/index.php?id=9166.

Kamukama, Dixon. *Rwanda Conflict: Its Roots and Regional Implications*. 2nd ed. Kampala, Uganda: Fountain Publishers, 1998.

Katongole, Emmanuel. *Resurrecting Faith after Genocide in Rwanda*. Grand Rapids, MI: Zondervan, 2009.

Klinghoffer, Arthur Jay. *The International Dimension of Genocide in Rwanda*. New York: New York University Press, 1998.

Khor, Lena. *Human Rights Discourse in a Global Network: Books beyond Borders*. New York: Routledge, 2013.

Kressel, Neil Jeffrey. *Mass Hate: The Global Rise of Genocide and Terror*. New York: Plenum Press, 1996.

Kuperman, Alan. *The Limits of Humanitarian Intervention: Genocide in Rwanda*. New York: Brookings Institution Press, 2001.

Leatherman, Janie L. *Sexual Violence and Armed Conflict*. Malden, MA: Polity Press, 2011.

"Leon Mugesera," Trial International (1 June 2016), accessed 17 July 2017, https://trialinternational.org/latest-post/leon-mugesera/.

Lemarchand, René. *Burundi: Ethnic Conflict and Genocide*. New York: Cambridge University Press, 1997.

Lemarchand, René, ed. *Forgotten Genocides: Oblivion, Denial and Memory*. Philadelphia: University of Pennsylvania Press, 2011.

Lemarchand, René. *The Dynamics of Violence in Central Africa*. Philadelphia: University of Pennsylvania Press, 2009.

Mageza-Barthel, Rirhandu. *Mobilizing Transnational Gender Politics in Post-Genocide Rwanda*. New York: Routledge, 2015.

McGreal, Chris, "Life sentence for Rwandan genocide leader," *The Guardian* (December 7, 1999), accessed April 16, 2017: https://www.theguardian.com/world/1999/dec/07/chrismcgreal.

Melvern, Linda. *Conspiracy to Murder: The Rwanda Genocide*. Rev. ed. London: Verso, 2006.

Melvern, Linda. *A People Betrayed: The Role of the West in Rwanda's Genocide*. New York: Zed Books, 2000.

Meredith, Martin. *The Fate of Africa: A History of the Continent Since Independence*. New York: PublicAffairs, 2011.

Midlarsky, Manus I. *The Killing Trap: Genocide in the Twentieth Century*. Cambridge, MA: Cambridge University Press, 2005.

Newbury, David. *The Land Beyond the Mists: Essays on Identity and Authority in Precolonial Congo and Rwanda*. Athens: Ohio University Press, 2011.

Ndahiro, Tom. "Genocide-Laundering: Historical Revisionism, Genocide Denial and the Rassemblement Républicain pour la Démocratie au Rwanda," in Clark, Phil, and Kaufman, Zachary, eds., *After Genocide: Transitional Justice, Post-Conflict Reconstruction and Reconciliation in Rwanda and Beyond*. London: Hurst Publishers, 2008.

Neier, Aryeh. *War Crimes: Brutality, Genocide, Terror, and the Struggle for Justice*. New York: Times Books, 1998.

Newbury, Catherine. *The Cohesion of Oppression: Clientship and Ethnicity in Rwanda, 1860–1960*. New York: Columbia University Press, 1988.

Nowrojee, Binaifer. *Shattered Lives: Sexual Violence during the Rwandan Genocide and its Aftermath*. New York: Human Rights Watch, 1996.

Off, Carol. *The Lion, The Fox and The Eagle: A Story of Generals and Justice in Rwanda and Yugoslavia*. Toronto: Random House Canada, 2000.

Oyebade, Adebayo. *Culture and Customs of Angola*. Westport, CT: Greenwood, 2006.

Power, Samantha. *"A Problem from Hell": America and the Age of Genocide*. New York: Harper Perennial, 2007.

Prunier, Gérard. *Africa's World War: Congo, the Rwandan Genocide, and the Making of a Continental Catastrophe*. New York: Oxford University Press, 2010.

Prunier, Gérard. *The Rwanda Crisis, 1959–1994: History of a Genocide*. Kampala: Fountain Publishers, 1995.

"Rebel Leader in the Congo is Flown to The Hague," *The New York Times*, March 22, 2013.

Rittner, Carol, John K. Roth, and Wendy Whitworth, eds. *Genocide in Rwanda: Complicity of the Churches*. St. Paul, MN: Paragon House, 2004.

Ronayne, Peter. *Never Again? The United States and the Prevention and Punishment of Genocide since the Holocaust*. Lanham, MD: Rowman & Littlefield Publishers, 2001.

Rusesabagina, Paul. *An Ordinary Man: An Autobiography*. New York: Viking, 2006.

Schabas, William A. *Genocide in International Law: The Crime of Crimes*. Cambridge, UK: Cambridge University Press, 2000.

Scherrer, P. Christian. *Genocide and Crisis in Central Africa: Conflict Roots, Mass Violence, and Regional War*. Westport, CT: Praeger, 2002.

Seybolt, Taylor B. *Humanitarian Military Intervention: The Conditions for Success and Failure*. New York: Oxford University Press, 2007.

Shaw, Martin. *War and Genocide: Organized Killing in Modern Society*. Cambridge, UK: Polity, 2003.

Shaw, Martin. *What Is Genocide?* Cambridge: Polity Press, 2007.

Sherwood, Harriet, "Pope Francis asks for forgiveness for church's role in Rwandan genocide," *The Guardian* (20 March 2017).

Sjoberg, Laura. *Women as Wartime Rapists: Beyond Sensation and Stereotyping*. New York: New York University Press, 2016.

Smith, M. James, ed. *A Time to Remember. Rwanda: Ten Years after Genocide*. Retford, UK: The Aegis Institute, 2004.

Stearns, Jason. *Dancing in the Glory of Monsters: The Collapse of the Congo and the Great War of Africa*. New York: PublicAffairs, 2011.

Stewart, Rory. "Genocide in Rwanda: Philip Gourevitch's non-fiction classic," *The Guardian* (March 21, 2015). Accessed April 17, 2017: https://www.theguardian.com/books/2015/mar/21/genocide-rwanda-we-wish-to-inform-you-that-tomorrow-philip-gourevitch.

Straus, Scott. *The Order of Genocide: Race, Power, and War in Rwanda*. Ithaca, NY: Cornell University Press, 2008.

Straus, Scott and Lars Waldorf, eds. *Remaking Rwanda: State Building and Human Rights after Mass Violence*. Madison, WI: University of Wisconsin Press, 2011.

Strozier, Charles B. and Michael Flynn, eds. *Genocide, War, and Human Survival*. Lanham, MD: Rowman & Littlefield Publishers, 1996.

Thompson, Allan ed. *The Media and the Rwanda Genocide*. Ann Arbor, MI: Pluto Books, 2007.

Thomson, Susan, "Reeducation for Reconciliation: Participant Observations on Ingando," in *Remaking Rwanda: State Building and Human Rights after Mass Violence*, eds. Scott Straus and Lars Waldorf. Madison, WI: University of Wisconsin Press, 2011: 331–339.

Totten, Samuel and Paul R. Bartrop, eds. *The Genocide Studies Reader.* New York: Taylor & Francis, 2009.

Totten, Samuel and Paul R. Bartrop, *Dictionary of Genocide*, Volume II (Westport, CT: Greenwood Press, 2008).

Totten, Samuel, William S. Parsons, and Israel W. Charny, eds. *Century of Genocide: Eyewitness Accounts and Critical Views.* New York: Garland Publishing, 1997.

Williams, Paul. *Memorial Museums: The Global Rush to Commemorate Atrocities.* New York: Berg, 2007.

United Nations, General Assembly, *Report of the International Criminal Tribunal for the Prosecution of Persons Responsible for Genocide and Other Serious Violations of International Humanitarian Law Committed in the Territory of Rwanda and Rwandan Citizens Responsible for Genocide and Other Such Violations Committed in the Territory of Neighbouring States between 1 January and 31 December 1994*, A/53/429 (23 September 1998), available from undocs.org/A/53/429.

United Nations General Assembly Resolution 58/234, *International Day of Reflection on the 1994 Genocide in Rwanda* (23 February 2004), available from undocs.org/A/RES/58/234.

United States v. Munyenyezi, No. 13-1950 (United States Court of Appeals, First Circuit, 2015.

Valentino, Benjamin A. *Final Solutions: Mass Killing and Genocide in the Twentieth Century.* Ithaca, NY: Cornell University Press, 2004.

Waller, James. *Becoming Evil: How Ordinary People Commit Genocide and Mass Killing.* Oxford: Oxford University Press, 2002.

"Wanted: Félicien Kabuga," U.S. Department of State (June 2002), accessed 17 July 2017. https://www.state.gov/j/gcj/wcrp/206033.htm.

Webster, John B. *The Political Development of Rwanda and Burundi.* Syracuse, NY: Maxwell Graduate School of Citizenship and Public Affairs, Syracuse University, 1966.

"Why did Infamous War Criminal Bosco Ntaganda Just Surrender at a US Embassy?," *Washington Post*, March 18, 2013.

Wilkens, Carl. *I'm Not Leaving.* United States: C. Wilkens, 2011.

Editor and Contributor List

VOLUME EDITOR

Alexis Herr, PhD

Postdoctoral Fellow

Saul Kagan Claims Conference

Associate Director

Jewish Family and Children Services,
Holocaust Center

CONTRIBUTORS

Dr. Paul R. Bartrop

Professor of History

Director of the Center for Judaic,
Holocaust, and Genocide Studies

Florida Gulf Coast University

Amy Hackney Blackwell

Independent Scholar

Dr. Sara E. Brown

Lecturer

San Diego State University

Rob Coyle

Independent Scholar

Dr. John Dietrich

Associate Professor of Political Science

Bryant University

Lynn Jurgensen

Independent Scholar

Isabelle Lagarde

Independent Scholar

Dr. René Lemarchand

Emeritus Professor of Political
Science

University of Florida

Alanna Pardee

Independent Scholar

Dr. Paul G. Pierpaoli Jr.

Fellow

Military History, ABC-CLIO, Inc.

Dr. John A. Shoup

Professor of Anthropology

Al Akhawayn University,
Morocco

Dr. Brian G. Smith

Associate Professor of Political Science

Georgia Southwestern State University

Elinor O. Stevenson

Attorney

Public International Law and
Policy Group

Index

Page numbers in **boldface** indicate main entries in the book; (doc.) indicates the entry is a document.

About the Editor

Dr. Alexis Herr earned a doctorate in Holocaust History from the Strassler Center for Holocaust and Genocide Studies at Clark University in 2014. She has held teaching positions at Northeastern University and Keene State College and is the author of *Compensated Compliance and the Holocaust in Italy: Fossoli di Carpi, 1942–1952* (2016). Dr. Herr is the Associate Director of the San Francisco Jewish Family and Children Services Holocaust Center.